For Kenny
in friendship &
admiration

Gail Pellett
2015

FORBIDDEN FRUIT

禁
果

1980 BEIJING – A MEMOIR

GAIL PELLETT

VanDam Publishing Inc.
121 West 27th St
New York, NY 10001

Please address queries to: info@vandam.com

VanDam books may be purchased for educational, business or sales promotional use. For information please e-mail the Sales Department at info@vandam.com

Parts of this book previously appeared in articles:
"Who's Out There," The Quill, March, 1982; "Is There Art After Liberation? Mao's Scorched Flowers Go West," Village Voice, 1986; "Ai Wei Wei, New York Photographs 1983-93, Photo exhibit and book," Trans-Asia Photography Review, 4th Quarter 2011; "Facing the Truth in China," Moyers Media, Truthout and Common Dreams, January 18, 2014.

Lyrics for "Guilty" written by Randy Newman, courtesy of Randy Newman Music and WB Music Corp © 1973, 75.
Lyrics for "A Song for You" written by Leon Russell, courtesy of Irving Music Inc. © 1970; Universal Publishing Group and Skyhill Publishing Co.

Art Direction by Rudy
Book and cover designed by Eamonn Fitzmaurice
Chapter head calligraphy by Wang Mansheng

Library of Congress Cataloging-in-Publication Data is pending.

ISBN: 1-934395-59-5

Printed on recycled paper

For Stephan

This work is based on memory, letter-writing, journal keeping and journalism.
Some names have been changed.

Contents

The self-absorption that seems to be the impetus and embarrassment of autobiography turns into (or perhaps always was) a hunger for the world. Actually, it begins as hunger for a world, one gone or lost, effaced by time or a more sudden brutality. But in the act of remembering, the personal environment expands, resonates beyond itself, beyond its subject, into the endless and tragic recollection that is history.

Patricia Hampl, *A Romantic Education* (1981)

Prologue
序

Tears froze on my cheeks as Gobi Desert winds hurled a mix of grit and coal dust, like tiny shards of glass, into my eyes. A cotton face mask prevented me from gulping in the mix. I could barely feel my feet pumping on my one-speed Shanghai Phoenix. Few bicyclists were on the streets at this hour. An occasional Soviet-era Volga passed as I pedaled from pool to pool of street light. It was a strain to push on in my bundle of clothing—blue jeans underneath my baggy People's Liberation Army pants, then three layers of sweaters under my black cotton padded jacket with the stand-up collar. "That's what old men wear," the comrades told me at the office. I found the long PLA padded coats too cumbersome for bicycling. In this numbing, life-sucking, bitter wind, I conceded to the padded Army hat with the ear flaps. Only my eyes would reveal the truth. That I was a *waiguoren*—a foreigner, outsider. In the dark on this withering night, I doubted whether anyone could see my Western boots. Or my starved libido.

The excitement of a forbidden invitation to a local guy's apartment was pulsing adrenalin through my veins and resurrecting my torpid mojo, despite the plunging temperatures and seven kilometers to his building.

Whether from the exertion of bicycling in all this padding or the anticipation of going to an illicit rendezvous, I could feel the moisture forming between my breasts. I visualized steam underneath my sweaters and pants.

Ming had instructed me to wear the local uniform. I had been hanging onto my New York wardrobe to bolster my identity crisis here, but this time I did not resist the pressure to conform. And although he had looked doubtful about my navigational skills when he pointed out his street corner on my Beijing map, it was along one of my regular bike routes and was by now a deeply grooved mental map directing my legs to overcome isolation, loneliness and despair.

I had been in Beijing for four months and had already learned sad and frustrating lessons about the bizarre policy that separated foreigners from the Chinese. And the surveillance and fear that made it work. There could be serious consequences for fraternizing with a native. The Chinese could lose the most. Jobs, housing and worse. If they were suspected of discussing state secrets—who knew what *they* were—they could go to jail.

And even though I had been invited to work as a "foreign expert" at Central Broadcasting precisely for my broadcast journalism skills, the fact that I was a journalist had sent out huge warning flares to all the Chinese around me. It was as if I had a tattoo in psychedelic paint spelling "SPY" across my forehead. I felt as if I were radioactive. I could be arrested and deported if the government intelligence gatherers—who were everywhere—discovered I was meeting secretly with a Chinese man. Already other Chinese acquaintances had been warned away from me.

I had met Ming in unusual circumstances, far away from the Party informants among my comrades at Radio Beijing and the spying eyes and ears at the building where I lived. When he invited me to visit his apartment, I was stunned. First, because it meant defying a potent government policy, but also, because of the housing crisis, I was puzzled how a young single man—a student—could procure an apartment for himself. Throughout the city several generations were crammed into one and two rooms with shared kitchens and bathrooms. Even young married couples sometimes had to live separately— with parents or in singles' dorms. How did Ming pull off his own apartment? He had to be part of that maligned category that the comrades referred to while frowning—the spoiled sons of high cadres. That, too, aroused me.

I knew my attraction to him was superficial. Since we didn't share a language, we acted out all of our conversations in childish charades and furious dictionary consultations. But his kinetic humor broke through the dirty screen doors of the language barrier. He also had a seductive face, round with full lips and mischievous eyes. Even if he were ten years younger, how could I resist this opportunity? I was ecstatic. At the corner, hunched against the wind, buried in layers of army garb, he was waiting.

Ming seemed both nervous and pleased that I was decked out in Chinese drag. Not a stray long, curly red hair leaked from underneath my hat. Surely I could get away with passing a neighbor or two at the entrance to his building. But then, while biting his lip, he motioned me to the *back* of his building. We were plunged into darkness. Looking in all directions, he then checked to see if the fire escape was clear and motioned me ahead.

Was I making a horrible mistake? Would he rob me? Imprison me? Or worse? I tamped down those thoughts. We crept up the unlit stairway, a hazardous course, since tenants had tied their bicycles to the railings and stored stuff on the landings. When we reached the fourth floor, he waved his arms "no" in front of the entrance, later explaining that he shared a kitchen in the hall with another family. He then beckoned me to follow him—through the window off the stairwell.

Was I crazy? At the age of thirty-seven, I was sneaking into the apartment of a much younger guy in Beijing *through the window*? Was this a blinking neon sign of how far I had regressed here?

"*Zou ba!*" Let's go! he said. An avalanche of fear flooded my serpent brain. Was he going to turn out to be a rapist or ax murderer? Would I disappear? My body parts found years later? That panic fused with the thrill of attempting something profoundly illegal.

Bicycling to Ming's apartment in this brutal weather, padded in PLA layers, sneaking up the fire escape, crawling through a fourth floor window, I felt like I was about to score some drugs. Contraband.

And then, yes, *then*, it felt quite natural. Of course. How else could we do this? An older Western woman visiting a much younger Chinese guy. How else but through a window?

As I plunged headfirst through that window, I realized I would have to exit through that window, too. Only later would I understand this wickedly naughty act as a search for transcendence of all that was denied here. Free association. Critical thoughts. Lascivious thoughts. The sensual. Desire. Passion.

Pitching through that window became a metaphor for my belief that it might be possible to make a deep connection with the forbidden, with the radical Other. We might find we had something in common. Lust? Was that finally what enlightenment about the Other meant? Was that too personal, too selfish a need? Was I evading the more profound question of whether we could truly understand another culture? Another history? Perhaps, too, I was simply determined to be free. After all, the personal *is* political.

Beijing, 1980

Chapter One

Somewhere Else
天各一方

I'm on a jet nose-diving into Beijing. It's freezing. But I take my pants off. My underpants. Sometimes I have no other clothing on. Nathan, a Chinese-American friend, is talking to me while strangers dance wildly around us. Suddenly I am mortified by my nudity. I jam my legs into pants while scrambling away. I try to climb a wall that morphs into a sheer cliff. I fall and catch myself. Repeatedly. Miraculously, I have hooks for hands. I clamber up again.

Surfacing from this foreboding dream, I noticed that 200 or so pairs of Chinese eyes were fastened on a grainy screening of Buck Rogers in the twenty-fifth century. I was the only non-Asian in the economy section of this crowded 747 halfway between Paris and Beijing. It was the first day of August, 1980. As I left New York, the Kennedy and Carter camps were still squabbling over upcoming rules for the Democratic Convention. Already the importance of that universe waned.

I was more interested in the intensity with which this planeload of Chinese Communists were watching the celluloid dream of Buck Rogers. And that momentarily distracted me from the transparent message of my dream. Taking my pants down, then shamed by the exposure, wanting to flee: it was a hackneyed scenario about vulnerability and fear. My usual strident self-confidence and pluck washed out by self-doubt. More like panic. And the only exit was straight up; an otherwise impossible situation if I did not have hooks for hands. As I watched Buck Rogers solve problems in space with cowboy determination, I promised to remember those hooks.

"You will polish scripts and teach classes in broadcast journalism and other subjects" was the job description in the polite but terse letter from China's equivalent to Voice of America. I had been invited by the Central Broadcasting Bureau of China to work for two years as a "foreign expert" in the English language department of Radio Beijing. Miles above the Gobi Desert, I was thrilled and terrified.

Looking at the mass of China's countryside out of the plane window and laboring for a sense of a billion people, mostly peasants, I recalled the hardscrabble stories my mother told me about growing up on the raw Canadian prairie. Stories about breaking the land and being broken by it; tales of trickster heroes who lived at the mercy of sun, rain, frost, credit and falling grain prices. The trick was survival. Those stories left me with compassion for those who work the land.

My grandparents had emigrated from a bucolic English village after WWI to a remote corner of Saskatchewan. Being British, my grandfather had fancied himself a gentleman farmer, not a peasant. Only his talents had run more toward the circus and inventing playful gimmicks—like the twirling Christmas tree on a turntable. He had been a failure in Saskatchewan. The Depression had hollowed out his motivation for the land. By the end of WWII, my grandparents and most of their family followed the exhausted but hopeful pilgrimage of prairie people to the end of the railway line on the West Coast. Grandpa bought a dilapidated rooming house in Vancouver. My mother and I were their first tenants.

No, the peasant had no real part in our psychological history, despite those years and stories of cruel hardships on the unforgiving rocky soil north of Saskatoon. On my first trip to a peasant country—Haiti—I had realized how difficult it was for those of us from urban, industrialized, high-tech societies to understand a peasant mind.

Now here I was, cruising over a land of millions of peasants who had upended their feudal social system with an agrarian revolution. As I watched my fellow travelers on this 747, I wondered whether I would ever understand that revolution the way they did and whether they understood it the way peasants did. Would anyone in this crowd have peasant roots?

Growing up in Canada I was spared the intensity of the anti-Communist terror that had swept the United States during the 1950s. Yet it was just a matter of degree. In twelve years of public schools, mostly during the 1950s, China had never once been discussed. Funny. Because Chinese objects and *Chinamen*—an old racist term we used in those days—were everywhere. Victoria and Vancouver, where I lived, both had visible Chinese communities—

Chinatowns where neon characters flashed and windows offered miraculous cures with dried rhinoceros testicles, where antique stores smelling of cedar and sandalwood were crowded with Ming vases, ornately carved tables and ivory fans. Yet I associated the Chinese more with laundries, restaurant kitchens and trucks that brought fresh vegetables to our neighborhood streets. *Chinamen.* Separate. Insular. Was their absence from official Canadian history anti-communism or raging racism? Or both?

China, if it was ever referred to during the 1950s and 1960s, was first Red China, then Communist China. Never without that qualifier. I did not "discover" China until the late 1960s when the news of the Great Proletarian Cultural Revolution inspired a generation of radicals in the West. By this time, I had migrated to San Francisco, where everyone—from anti-war activists to feminists, from radical psychiatrists to guerrilla theater groups—was integrating the language and methods from Mao's *Little Red Book*: "Dare to struggle, Dare to win!" and "Bombard the Headquarters!" motivated the Anti-War Movement. "Speak bitterness," "*Fanshen* (Stand up)" and "Women hold up half the sky" were transforming concepts to feminists. Within the Movement, "criticism/self-criticism" and "struggle, struggle, struggle" were exhausting exercises.

Like the Cultural Revolution ideology that had inspired us—at least how I understood it then—our ideas were anti-authoritarian, egalitarian, revolutionary. And no other group had embraced that Cultural Revolution ideology more passionately than had the Black Panthers. I had occupied a front row seat at the explosion of this controversial and provocative new Movement, and at a fundraiser for the Panthers in Oakland, I met a man who would inspire my next move.

In 1969, I followed Carl, a New Left radical, to St. Louis, where he began teaching in the political science department of Washington University. There, after eight years of dropping in and out of universities in Victoria, Vancouver and Berkeley, I finished a master's degree. My thesis described the family revolution in China.

Then somehow, during the 1970s, my interest in China waned. For more than two decades, China had closed itself off from much of the West. In the US, news from China had been scanty. Lin Biao's fatal airplane accident had baffled China followers. Nixon's ping-pong diplomacy with Mao was suspect. Chinese foreign policy, like its support for Pinochet in Chile, was horrifying. And, after Mao's death in 1976, all the talk of the Gang of Four belonged to musical comedy rather than Realpolitik. Meanwhile, American Maoists had become intolerant, sectarian and insufferable.

It was perplexing enough to analyze the demise of the American New Left in the '70s from an inside position, but from the Western hemisphere, to understand what had gone wrong with the Cultural Revolution was impossible.

China entered my consciousness again in 1979 when I reconnected with my best friend from high school days. Wendy had been developing cutting-edge methodology for China's newly minted English language teachers. Canada had normalized relations with China in 1970, whereas the US would not establish diplomatic relations for another eight years. A few of my New York lefty friends had visited China in the mid-'70s on highly curated tours. Their reports had been puzzling and confused. Now, my old friend Wendy was getting ready to return to a college in Guangzhou (formerly Canton) for a second stint.

"There is something hopeful about New China," she insisted. "You should bring your documentaries to China. My students would love to hear them. And perhaps you could make radio and video documentaries there to broadcast here."

It seemed far-fetched.

By the late 1970s I had spent a decade honing radio and video documentary skills, including two years in Boston working with a feminist radio collective producing a prime-time women's show for a progressive rock 'n' roll station. That work had led to WBAI in New York City, where I was news and public affairs director, producing documentaries and interviews. When National Public Radio geared up, I fashioned features for their new program, "All Things Considered," while freelancing on TV documentaries at the local NBC station.

In the fall of 1979, after completing a dozen short videos on the art and religion of Haiti for a local museum and a series of radio programs about storytelling for WNYC—New York's public radio station—I decided to take a tenure-track position at Rutgers University to teach media studies and broadcast journalism—an acknowledgement of the brutality of the freelance life. I wanted a predictable income and medical coverage. But when I took off during the Christmas break for a solo trek through Mexico, my all-male department howled. I had not deciphered the unwritten code that as the junior member of the department—and its only woman—I was supposed to stay at the school during the holidays and fix the broken equipment. Then, when I landed several assignments from a new magazine show at NBC, they grumbled again. When I met James Aronson in the spring of 1980, I knew I would be leaving.

Aronson was a professor at Hunter College, where I had lectured, and had been a founder—in the late '40s—of a highly respected Leftist newspaper, the *Guardian*. Just back from a speaking tour in China, he explained that the Chinese wanted training in Western-style journalism and were eager to communicate with the West. On the trip he had made contacts at Radio Beijing, their international broadcast service.

"They would be very interested in your experience," he said. "They hire 'foreign experts' for their different language departments. In the past, it was sufficient that they were native speakers and politically left. You would be the first experienced broadcast journalist they have hired in their forty-year history. But it means going for two years."

Going to China had not been a burning desire—simply a vague interest. But the possibility of living and working with the Chinese rearranged my priorities.

Only five months after meeting Aronson, I was cruising over the Gobi Desert. I did not speak or read Mandarin. I knew very little about China. From the little I did know, I harbored a deep gut feeling that everything about me was antithetical to being Chinese. It was like walking into the ocean on a moonless night. Part sensation, part guts, part raw fear.

It was Camus who pronounced that the only real meaning of travel was based on fear. My earliest memory is a travel memory drenched in terror. I was with my mother on a Canadian National Railroad train somewhere in the middle of the Rocky Mountains of British Columbia.

My nose pressed to the window, I was first delighted then distraught because I was looking into a deep abyss. The train was on a creaky trestle bridge suspended over what seemed a fathomless ravine.

I was three years old, wailing, clinging to my mother's warm neck. I would come to understand the context and layers of meaning of this trek in later years. My mother had just left my father behind in a stifling Saskatchewan town.

Unaware of my mother's courage and trepidations in making this journey in 1946, I was simply traumatized by the craggy depth of that ravine. Fear of falling is etched into my bone marrow. Still, it is a demonic, seductive fear. A compulsion for the edge. The abyss.

THERE WAS no city skyline visible on the descent into Beijing's airport. No neat rows of suburban houses. No shopping malls or parking lots. No network of freeways. Only rice fields. Serene, emerald rice fields.

On the ground at the capital city airport of the world's most populous country, there seemed to be less technology than at the Provincetown airport on Cape Cod. A dozen workers in grey, baggy overalls squatted in the shade of a sleeping jet, bicycles parked nearby. Chopsticks flew between mouths and metal boxes. The ground crew that flagged in our gigantic aircraft made frenetic arm movements, then stood with their fingers in their ears.

It was mid-afternoon when we disembarked. The air was hot and dense. And the airport looked empty. I was in the legendary People's Republic and I had stomach cramps.

I scanned the arrivals room for signs of New China, and they were immediately apparent—immigration officials wearing People's Liberation Army uniforms. Angular faces, determined jaws, proud bodies, tiny waists cinched tight with leather belts. Framed by plain wooden cubicles, their psychedelic pea-green uniforms looked more eerie and awesome than their portrayal in those revolutionary posters so popular during the late 1960s. The star on the cap and the detail at the collar popped out with a more perfect vermilion than any poster ink.

I remembered the intensity of those posters that presented the PLA soldiers out in front with their fists held high, the fierce expressions, the deep furrowed brows and the fire in their eyes. Caricatures. Comical. Here, these immigration officials looked serious. Human, after all. Yet something from that visual memory of the posters imbued these guys with magical power.

For me, revolution was a fantasy. A faded dream. For the Chinese, it was real, part of recent history, a living memory. I had harbored my egalitarian and feminist utopian hopes until the early 1970s. By August of 1980, that dream had withered. What remained were ideas from books, melancholy memories of ideals and values, the sacrificing of a lucrative career path for "meaningful work." And there I was, turning my back on a tenure-track teaching position and heading for the unknown in a Communist country in the mysterious East.

A propaganda image of revolution that had been so significant to me in the late '60s was stamping my passport. All these thoughts jostled in my brain while I watched giant boxes wobble over the edge of the conveyor belt. Boxes marked SONY, BLACK & DECKER, RCA, IBM. TVs, washing machines, cassette recorders, sewing machines and typewriters. My Chinese traveling companions pushed and puffed their way to the customs room with their loot. No porters. No carts or buggies.

"Is this your first trip to China?" A tall, dapper-looking man stood next to me. I guessed his age at sixty.

"Yes, I've come to work at Radio Beijing." I thought perhaps he was an American-Chinese—he spoke excellent English—but he didn't look completely comfortable in his three-piece suit. "Is this your hometown?"

"Yes. I've been lecturing in the United States. I'm a geologist. I received my PhD from Harvard in the '40s. This was my first trip back in thirty years."

"What do you think? Lots of changes?"

"Nothing has changed," he laughed. "It's just more expensive."

With that, he spotted his bag and handed me his business card. "Call me. It would be interesting to hear what you think of China."

Another voice intervened.

"Are you Miss P...Pel...Pellett?"

I turned to a woman wearing a pleated beige polyester skirt, a white cotton blouse and pearly plastic slingback sandals. Her black hair was pulled back into a low ponytail. Perhaps thirty. Slender, erect, smiling and in command all at once.

"I'm Chung Way from the English department at Radio Beijing." (In a week's time I would learn to spell her name: Zhang Wei.) Her smile revealed perfect teeth. "I recognized you from the photograph." She hesitated and adjusted her large square glasses with brown plastic rims. This time, her smile implied amusement.

"Your hair, do you call it 'golden'?"

"Red." I laughed nervously, groping for some more appropriate first words for the Middle Kingdom. For New China. "I'm so excited to be here!"

I was humiliated that my wilted state prevented me from mouthing something more significant or restrained. My stomach cramps were getting worse.

Zhang Wei beamed and introduced me to a round-faced, chubby man— "Lee-oo" was what the name sounded like. I didn't get the other name. What will I do about the names?

"Lee-oo" was the official representative from the foreign experts' office at Radio Beijing. He spoke no English but was full of smiles. He clutched a black plastic zippered case and was blushing.

By then conscious of how strange I must look in this crowd with my wrinkled cotton shirtwaist dress—black with tiny white flowers—Mexican silver bracelets, earrings and long, curly red hair, I wondered if "Lee-oo" was embarrassed to see who he had hired.

"That man...is he a friend of yours?"

At first I wasn't sure I had heard her correctly. To whom was she referring? My reflexes were disoriented.

"Oh, him! I just met him. Very friendly. He's been visiting the States. He gave me his card and suggested that I contact him."

A frown descended on Zhang Wei's face. Something was wrong. I was trying to give the impression that I was social and eager to be friendly with the Chinese. Suddenly, I was in unfamiliar territory. But the signals had first appeared at the Paris airport.

DRIFTING FILAMENTS of cigarette smoke pearlized the air in the waiting room at the Charles de Gaulle Airport. Radio Beijing was paying my way to China and offered two choices: from San Francisco or Paris. Each city scheduled once-a-week flights to Beijing. In the waiting room, dozens of mostly middle-aged Chinese men and a few women occupied every available chair. I stood to the side to study them. Crew cuts. 1950s glasses. Uneven dental work. Several men had pushed up their pant legs to scratch their calves. They looked like officials. A sense of controlled excitement permeated their low-volume chatter. They were going home.

I was taken aback by their style and postures. What did I think they would look like? The impeccable tailoring of their suits—some in Western styles, others in what I would learn to call a Sun Yat-sen cut that Zhou Enlai had made famous—surprised me. Startled by the range of bone structure and skin tone, I searched for physical clues to answer questions that had been stacking up in my brain. What did it mean to be a socialist man or woman? What were the psychological effects on this generation of so much change in one lifetime? How could people who had questioned so many aspects of their society remain conservative in their appearance and manner and puritanical in their sexual lives, or had they?

I remembered a Fox Butterfield piece about ultra-conservative sexual mores. Butterfield had set up his *New York Times* office in Beijing in 1979, not long after Jimmy Carter had normalized relations with the Chinese. And just a year before I had arrived. It was the first time since Liberation that China was allowing American reporters into the country.

In the airport lounge more questions surfaced. Were these some of the victims of the Cultural Revolution who had now returned to power? Again my reference was a Fox Butterfield article that reported on some of the criticisms developing about the Cultural Revolution. On the plane from New York I had been reading Orville Schell's *In the People's Republic*. He had joined the first group of Leftist American scholars to visit China in the mid-'70s. His take felt as if it was filtered through the official Cultural Revolution lens. Since the Chinese had just opened to the West, this group in the Paris airport must have been some of the first to be stationed abroad. If so, what was it like for them to journey to the decadent West for the first time? Were capitalism and democracy better or worse than they had expected?

Some of this crowd were old enough to have fought in the anti-Japanese and Civil War with Chiang Kai-shek's forces in the '40s. What was it like to have those memories? And since a big part of the propaganda about China had been about the liberation and equality of women, why were there so few women in this group? And why, given how bizarre I must have looked to them, would not one acknowledge my presence in this crowded room?

"Are you American?"

I jumped at the voice from a tall slender guy in a Sun Yat Sen suit.

"No, I'm Canadian. But I've lived in the US for a long time."

"I like Canadians. I work for the *People's Daily*." (The *People's Daily* is China's version of the *Washington Post* or *New York Times*—except that it is edited and published by the Chinese Communist Party, which is the state.) "I've been traveling around the US and Canada and have had lots of good conversations with the people."

This reporter seemed eager to talk to me, but he was also very nervous. He kept looking over his shoulder, scanning the room. For what? For whom?

"Are you nervous to be seen talking to a foreigner?" I asked boldly.

"No." He giggled nervously and then walked away into the smoky, congested room. Was I too direct?

Once on board the plane, despite the full seating, I was in a row by myself. A woman was originally sitting next to me and explained she worked for the Foreign Trade Bureau. Just as I was considering the enlightening prospect of conversation with her, a stewardess made a commotion and moved her to another seat. I was left totally alone. Quarantine or privilege? The vitriolic comments of Simon Leys echoed through my brain.

For several months I had been clipping articles to stuff into a file folder marked "China." Pieces with headlines like "China's Passion for the Movies," "Arthur Miller in Beijing." I had pulled dusty China books from my shelves, including *Fanshen* and *Red Star Over China*, all leftovers from my student days. In lucid moments between grading papers and producing short features for NBC's new magazine show, I had scoured Manhattan bookstores for more on China: politics, history, short stories, poetry. All would have to be read there. Except for one.

I don't know why I chose to read the most critical book I could find before leaving—Simon Leys' *Chinese Shadows*. Perhaps I wanted to get to the worst fast. After all, I was going to be working for the Chinese government, for one of their propaganda operations. I needed a balancing perspective. And if I allowed myself to meditate on China in the twentieth century, the image that emerged was awe-inspiring and mystifying. I needed some grounding.

Leys' story was so disturbing that I kept searching for the fatal flaw in his history or character that would explain his vehemence. He was a scholar of classical Chinese culture which might account for his anti-communism. But you did not have to be anti-Communist to grieve the persecution of intellectuals and the destruction of classical architecture during the Cultural Revolution. The real power of the book for me, however, was in his description of Chinese foreign relations. If what Leys said was true, it was impossible to have open relationships with Chinese people. He quoted one of China's most famous writers, Lu Xun, who died in 1936: "Throughout the ages, the Chinese have only two ways of looking at foreigners: up to them as superior beings or down on them as wild animals. They have never been able to treat them as friends, to consider them as people like themselves."

It was not encouraging.

But I noted that Leys had written his book in 1972, in the middle of the Cultural Revolution. Surely now—eight years later—a lot had changed. But the frown that transformed Zhang Wei's face after I told her about my encounter with the pleasant Harvard-trained geologist in the baggage room indicated otherwise.

Moments after Zhang Wei's scowl, we were speeding past a stately row of poplars on the road to Beijing. The driver was a roundish man so short that his rubber sandals barely reached the gas pedal. Knee-length pants buttoned over a sleeveless white singlet or undershirt, called a "wife-beater" in some ethnic circles. I was getting punchy. The driver in the wife-beater was also wearing short white cotton gloves. Grasping the wheel with both hands, he drove fast, alternately laughing and honking. Buses, army jeeps, horse-drawn carts, bicyclists and pedestrians moved aside reluctantly.

The sun was already reclining behind those enormous poplars, their silver leaves shimmering like sequins, reflecting sparks of the orange sunset. An ochre haze obscured the details of faces. It was later than I thought. But I could still identify peasants on the back of a truck or on a bicycle.

Through the car window the land looked flat, the air hung heavy and moist like St. Louis in August. I was excited, exhausted and sweating profusely. The knot in my belly tightened with each question or comment. I learned that

Zhang Wei was thirty-four, married and had a three-year-old daughter. She had studied in England for two years and had never adapted to the weather or food. She translated for "Lee-oo" and the driver, who kept laughing.

"Where will I live?" I tried to make it a casual question.

"At the foreign experts' dormitory at Radio Beijing." Zhang Wei straightened her back.

At the word "dormitory" my intestines twisted and squeezed. Karol Kovanda—a friend of a friend who had worked as a "foreign expert" in Beijing—had advised me to stay at the Friendship Hotel.

I attempted a tone of disinterest. "I thought I would be staying at the Friendship Hotel?"

"No." Zhang Wei adjusted her glasses and smiled an official smile. "The building at Central Broadcasting is much more convenient to your work. It's close by." Her face morphed into earnest concern. "And it's much quieter."

On the word "quieter" my gut clenched. I knew that the Friendship Hotel was where most foreigners working for the Chinese lived. There were tennis courts, a swimming pool, a gym, a movie theater. Kovanda had explained it was a ghetto. "But you'll need that ghetto," his remark echoed in my brain.

I wondered what Zhang Wei meant by "quieter." A life of work and sleep? All the stories of Chinese puritanism clamored between my temples, and the pain in my belly was turning this conversation and this car ride into a torture chamber.

Normally I explored unknown turf, met strangers and entered novel situations with humor and ease. I had always loved the challenge of new worlds and fresh ideas, along with alternative ways of thinking and dreaming. It partly explained why I was a documentary producer. I enjoyed hearing the way people described or reasoned through their world.

I had interviewed prisoners and judges, prostitutes and johns, illegal immigrants and lawyers, African guerrilla leaders, American tycoons, voodou priests, famous artists and lesser-known poets. What was so difficult about meeting an articulate, English-speaking Chinese woman in China? As an interviewer I had learned to listen. But I was having difficulty hearing Zhang Wei.

Was it fear? As a reporter I had traveled at all hours into neighborhoods where perhaps I did not belong. In Haiti I had packed portable video equipment on my head through a turbulent river after dark. I had trekked by foot and bus around Mexico alone. During the Anti-War Movement I had been gassed and had stared down cops with dogs and FBI agents at my door. I had read the graffiti on the inside of a jail cell after enduring a vaginal exam by a guard with long, broken and red-chipped fingernails. Yet as our car approached Beijing, the contortion of pain in my abdomen was becoming all-consuming.

Was it because I was in a socialist country for the first time? And what did that mean? Principles, beliefs and values at stake? Was I suppressing doubts about how much I would be able to support China this close up? Would I find the Chinese too authoritarian, too bureaucratic, too conservative, too judgmental of an individualist from the capitalist West?

Before leaving for China, I met Sidney Rittenberg and his wife, Mei Ling. Recently featured in a *New York Times* article, Rittenberg was an American and a long-term China resident and member of the Chinese Communist Party who had been jailed twice, including one stint for ten years during the Cultural Revolution. He had been "rehabilitated" and was now with the newly created Social Sciences Institute in Beijing. He was in New York to write a book about his experiences. I was introduced through an artist friend.

We met for breakfast in their friend's Village penthouse. While munching toast at a glass table in a sumptuous sun-drenched room surrounded by patio gardens, I sensed that I was not the only one who felt the focus of our interest was strangely out of sync with our surroundings. Yet Sydney and Mei Ling were gracious and gentle. They looked at ease with themselves if not with the furniture.

They had both worked in the very English language department at Radio Beijing where I would be, so I wanted to know what advice they could give me about working there. They were encouraging and dealt with my questions seriously without saying much. Diplomacy and cautious avoidance, a social strategy that wouldn't become meaningful until I reflected back upon it a few months into my Radio Beijing adventure.

"Since news is sketchy from China, I have some ideas about the kind of radio programs I would like to hear. What possibilities will there be to produce at Radio Beijing?"

"If you have an idea for something, if you want to do something new," Sydney suggested, "talk to the staff first, get their support, then go as a group to the leaders." It was highly political advice. Contrary to the way I usually worked as a freelancer, whereby I was an ideas generator constantly pitching stories or assigned projects by an editor or executive.

If I had known then what I came to know about Sydney, I would have asked him a completely different set of questions. Such is hindsight. Our conversation must have been pleasant and superficial because I remembered so little, except a gesture that signified more after my time in China. While I sat on one of the velvet couches, basking in the early morning sun, Mei Ling came and sat beside me. She put her arms around me and squeezed. The timing of that hug implied reassurance. From her gesture I felt support and warmth. I was surprised then by her embrace. Even more as I reflected back on it months later.

MEANWHILE, I was in the backseat of a Soviet-era Volga approaching Beijing with a vise in my gut. Was it about commitment? I had agreed to work for two years at Radio Beijing, longer than I had committed myself to anything. Ever. Well, that was not exactly true. I had a two-year tenure-track contract at Rutgers University that I was deserting after one year to go to China. My Rutgers colleagues—all men—had been incredulous. My willingness to give up a tenure-track position was outside of their paradigm.

"China is backward. She is very poor." Zhang Wei's screwed-up face looked just as it did when she was describing English food. "Beijing is crowded. There is not enough housing." Her tone was apologetic as she readjusted her glasses.

The city plan looked jumbled on the low horizon. Buildings seemed arbitrary, dilapidated, shabby, forlorn. In all directions cranes stood in the dusk.

"There is a lot of construction going on." I tried to sound upbeat.

"We are building new high rises because the old traditional housing is too poor, too crowded."

"And how do people like moving into the high rises?" I was struggling for conversation.

"They like the old housing because the elevators sometimes don't work in the new buildings."

In rapid, staccato Mandarin, Zhang Wei talked to "Lee-oo" (a name I would soon learn to spell "Liu" in Pinyin, the new romanization of Chinese characters). The traffic was denser. People were trudging, leaning, squatting. Distinctions blurred in the dust. A chorus of bicycle bells saturated the warm air. At every stoplight, our driver turned off the car engine. As the light flashed green, he twisted the key to start again. To my incredulous query Zhang Wei explained, "To save gas."

It was almost dark, and none of the cars were using headlights.

"It's a law," Zhang Wei emphasized. "Cars do not use headlights at night."

"Isn't that dangerous?"

"We have good streetlights. And, besides, the car lights can cause problems for bicyclists."

By the time we reached the foreign experts' dormitory, I was in a daze of cramps, jet lag and heat meltdown. They directed me to a furnished two-room apartment filled with late-day dusk. Nobody turned on a light. Zhang Wei introduced me to the "leading comrade" of the building, a large-framed lady with an enormous face and a mixing-bowl haircut. She smiled without lifting her chin from her neck. Watching her open six bottles of warm orange soda and deliver them to each of us—a group that now included an important official from Radio Beijing—she seemed capable of complete authority as well as total subservience. Or was I dreaming?

Liu began describing procedures, regulations and schedules to Zhang Wei, who translated for me. I remembered nothing, not even their leaving.

August 2, 1980, Journal:
It's 2 a.m. The air is still, crushing and silent. Only darkness greets the window. The fan doesn't work. My cramps are gone and I fumble for a cigarette.

LANDING IN Beijing, I was alone, again. Leaving one world for another, again. Pulling up, saying goodbye, looking into that abyss, again. Since the age of two, I had been hopping from city to city. Eight cities in the US and Canada. In 1964—at age twenty-one—I stumbled, bleary-eyed, off a Greyhound bus in San Francisco with a tambourine in one of my bags. No contacts, no job, no money. Just wanderlust. Eventually, after six years of working as a secretary interwoven with semesters at UC Berkeley; after love-ins, acid, the Fillmore Auditorium, mescaline, the Monterey Pop and Jazz Festivals as well as peace marches, I followed Carl to St. Louis.

In St. Louis I finished an MA, spoke at anti-war rallies, taught the first feminist courses, participated in women's groups and worked at a community radio station. After waitressing on weekends, I distributed leaflets about our poisoned rivers and wrote for an underground paper. In the summers I returned to Berkeley to produce the first women's news show at KPFA. After all that, I left Carl and moved to Boston. Two years later, I moved to New York.

This peripatetic life was in my DNA. My grandfather, after serving in the British army during WWI—driving a truck from what he called Mesopotamia through Afghanistan's Khyber Pass to India—had returned to his little village in southern England, packed up his wife and six children and sailed off to Canada. Ties of generations to place and family shattered. My mother's flight from North Battleford, Saskatchewan, to Vancouver and Victoria meant we were nomads of the twentieth century. I counted that with my mother I had already lived in eight homes and four cities by the time I was nineteen. Since leaving my mother's house, I had changed apartments more than twenty-five times, living in cities scattered across the continent.

With each of these moves had come the truth of aloneness. Impermanence. Essential loneliness. Deep lessons from being an only child of a single, divorced and working mum, of immigrants and wanderers. A latchkey kid.

Arriving in Beijing, I was alone again—a condition I abhorred and desired.

Going somewhere else is never simply about the allure of new landscapes, but can also be motivated by the desire to leave past choices behind. My decision to go to China was aided by a deep, private voice that had been giving me signals about New York.

I had spent five full years—tough years—in a place whose values fought with those I had been raised on—humility, self-effacing humor and cooperation. I hadn't been fully prepared for the hubris, self-promotion, currying after power and connections, and the ruthless competition at the heart of the Big Apple. Yet I hardly lacked ambition. And I was far from timid or quiet. In fact, I loved New York for its decibel levels, its energy and the imagination and talent it attracted.

When I finally succumbed to a stable paycheck as a university professor, I found myself craving the creative and intellectual thrills of my former freelance production life. In the midst of this conflict, I convinced myself I was ready to consider other schemes and leave behind the egocentrism of New York, of the United States. I was ready to transport my Canadian soul—and ass—elsewhere. But there were secretive impulses, too. An illicit affair with an older married man had reached its frustrating limits. I could not see a romantic future.

Once again I was hitting the road with opposing voices ricocheting off of each other. One pushing me toward adventure, the other pulling me back. One wanted to expand and take risks; the other wanted to contract and perfect. One argued for roots, community and continuity; the other wanted new challenges and continual change. One said *you are a seeker, bold and courageous*; the other said *you are a heartbroken coward. You're running away.*

Embarking on this incredible journey, with my wispy threads of knowledge, I wanted to discover new stories. I didn't know it then, but the major story I would be spinning out was *my* own.

August 2, 1980. Journal
It's 3 a.m. in my new Beijing digs, I have begun unpacking my two-year supply of batteries and eye makeup, a shortwave radio and henna, music cassettes and Tampax...things I was told would be difficult to come by north of Hong Kong.

View from my apartment window into grounds of Radio Beijing, 1980

Women working in the alley everyday at Radio Beijing, 1980

Chapter Two

The View From My Window
我的窗外景色

On my first conscious evening at my new home, I met my next-door neighbors, Punam and Joshi, from what we called then Bombay, who seemed erotically woven together with their new baby around the smells of breast milk and incense, curry and baby poop. They edited the Hindi language scripts at Radio Beijing.

Our plain four-story brick apartment building housed a dozen or more "foreign experts" and their families from Niger to France and Malaysia to Chile, all laboring to make Radio Beijing's broadcasts palatable to folks back home. Bahdra, my diminutive neighbor across the hall, edited scripts in the Sinhalese language. A veteran of the international peace movement, she was attracted to China by its egalitarian revolutionary ideals and socialist scheme. She admitted to profound disappointment with Deng Xiaoping's new focus on dismantling communes while promoting consumer goods production and consumption. Although Bahdra was friendly, I sensed that my presence represented some part of her disenchantment. I realized by then that I was a Deng Xiaoping hire. My expertise was considered vital to Deng's modernization plan. Bahdra tilted her head to the side and looked at me as if my clothing was impregnated with selfish, individualist, Western, capitalist ways bent on polluting and undermining the Communist model.

I had bigger concerns: rearranging furniture in my new home. My one-bedroom apartment—minus kitchen and dining room—was functional and spacious by New York City standards. Furnishings included a bulky sepia-stained wooden closet, a desk and drawers along with dark brown plastic-covered arm chairs. Zhang Wei had emphasized that the wooden floors, big bathroom and hot water were luxurious compared to Chinese living standards. I acknowledged that it was comfortable except for the straw mattress with the mountain ridge down the middle. This housing was part of my package deal.

Another perk was a dining room downstairs. While I had to pay for the food, having someone to cook for me felt opulent after years of gulping chicken salad sandwiches during late-night editing sessions or wolfing carrot sticks and cheese while standing at the refrigerator after a long teaching day and commute. And, being single, I welcomed company with my meals, although I had yet to see anybody actually eat in the dining room. My neighbors ordered food and then carried it back to their apartments, where everyone seemed to have a hot plate. It would be weeks before I understood their desire to eat with their mates or families was an essential need for privacy and intimacy in a political culture that worked against both. After several lonely meals listening to my chopsticks and cutlery clink as the only sound in the room—like the final scene in Kubrick's *2001*—I started carrying food back to my flat, too. Better to be alone there, where I could listen to my cassettes. I had brought a suitcaseful from New York.

August 4, 1980, Journal:
Tonight I'm listening to a compilation of classical piano by Chopin, Liszt, Mozart and Schubert. I've discovered I cannot eat to Thelonious Monk, Art Tatum, Glenn Gould's Goldberg Variations *or the Talking Heads.*

I feel particularly wistful listening to a piece by Chopin that I once played for my Toronto Conservatory exams in Victoria. National examinations held by judges who spread out across the vast Canadian landscape, setting up their somber desks in dowdy recital rooms in each major city to evaluate nervous new students. We played scales, chords, difficult exercises and both memorized and sight-read pieces. I progressed as far as Grade Nine in that system before forsaking it all to play jazz and the American Songbook. *Giving up my piano with my itinerant lifestyle was perhaps the greatest sacrifice I ever made. No dwelling on that now. Enough tears have been shed over that history. Instead, I will play Miles Davis's* 'Round About Midnight, *reminding me of a culture I just left behind.*

IN THE mornings, a giant, colorful thermos of boiling water appeared at my door and a woman arrived to sweep the floor. I could not ask her name or say "thank you" without tripping over the strangeness of the sounds. *Xie, xie.*

Pronounced something like "shay, shay."

The only telephone was attached to the wall at the end of the long hall. Too far for me to hear, and using it required asking the operator for the number in Mandarin. So, of course, I was struggling to learn the numbers...*Y, er, san, tse, wu*...I had to completely relearn how to work my mouth, jaw and tongue.

Zhang Wei's forehead wrinkled earnestly as she adjusted her glasses and told me that they would move me as soon as possible to the south side of the building. Apparently, she was not only to be my interpreter but also the reference on all things and go-to *responsible member*.

"In winter, you will need the warmth," she insisted.

Since the apartment now offered a respite from the heat and humidity of August, worrying about the lack of central heating and needing southern sun seemed far off.

There was really only one problem—the view from my window.

From my third-story rooms, I looked down upon a yard heaped with the remains of a number of construction projects. Hunks of broken concrete and mounds of sisal were scattered around an old shell of a boiler. A contraption for pulleying tar to a roof leaned up against sheets of corrugated metal, rusted pipes and bricks. Along one side of the yard stood a low shed housing something that consumed a glacier of coal—presumably a functioning boiler. The black rocks flowed out into the yard. I had to remind myself this was Central Broadcasting in Beijing.

Beyond this garden of industrial debris stood rows of four-story Socialist Realist brick buildings—the color of baked clay. This was where workers at Central Broadcasting lived behind sad windows. Was it Goethe who said architecture was frozen music? I pondered what music the designers of this form of mass housing had in mind.

Lying on my new straw bed, staring at the blue wallpaper with the white flowers, I contemplated other apartments and houses I had lived in. How many days—weeks—would it take before this one resembled the patina of those places? Walls covered with my own amateurish artwork, photographs, intriguing found objects from the streets, particular articles of clothing or jewelry that I found so irresistible that I hung them on the wall for their visual enjoyment. In my Mott Street tenement, I had covered the old crumbling walls with all of my '40s dresses and secondhand costumes, feather boas and wide-brimmed hats along with Haitian masks and iron sculptures. They had kept company with drawings and paintings by artist friends and a collection of men's ties that I had found in a dumpster. Most of that bohemian stockpile got left behind, so things would necessarily be more restrained here.

In one of my first Beijing dreams I was wandering through my grandparents' Carolina Street rooming house in Vancouver—my home for several years. Grandpa had earned a little money painting benches in famous Stanley Park and would bring home "extra" cans of orange, red or forest green paint. Every odd wooden chair and sometimes the old floors upstairs were painted in those colors. He would set rhinestones into the clawed hands of padded armchairs he had picked up "for a song" at the local secondhand store. He also grew geraniums, marigolds and nasturtiums in cracked pots on the porch and rhododendrons in the front garden—the deep vermilions, blasting oranges and seductive pinks a legacy of his years in India during the First World War although never acknowledged as such. His enthusiastic embrace of passionate colors and secondhand detritus had entered my bloodstream. I could not remember how that dream resolved itself. But I sensed that the dream about color and texture signaled trouble ahead.

MY FIRST two mornings in Beijing were spent in a "company" car—one of those ubiquitous 1950s Volgas—with Zhang Wei chaperoning to get my photo taken for an ID and to find toilet paper. And just maybe a cup of coffee at the Beijing Hotel. On the third day she arrived at 8 a.m. to introduce me to my new workplace.

Walking past the tiny front yard of our foreign experts' apartment building, I admired the carefully planted grass, flowering shrubs and poplar trees. But their simple beauty was eclipsed by what came into view as we turned into the alley leading to the grounds of Radio Beijing. As I practiced my new expressions for Zhang Wei—"*Ni Hao, ma?*" (Hello! How are you?) and "*Zaijian, zaijian*" (Goodbye/See you again)—we passed mounds of sand, piles of bricks, heaps of gravel and lime that bordered the ten-foot wall surrounding the Central Broadcasting complex.

After showing our IDs to rifle-carrying guards at the gate, the massive building housing Radio Beijing stretched up and out like a wedding cake on steroids. But first came the potent sensation that I was stumbling into Dickens' Coketown. Mountains of finely ground coal covered an area the size of a hockey rink. Green army trucks unloaded the black gravel while tractors pushed it into jagged peaks. Slender boys in sooty overalls shoveled the ebony dust into a giant furnace housed in a barn.

We gingerly picked our way past a variety of construction scenarios—men and women in smeared overalls making bricks here, stacking them there and loading them beyond. In a continuing industrial tableau, another cluster of slender waifs were melting tar, stirring lime and sifting sand. Dusty young men pedaled three-wheeled platform bikes hauling buckets overflowing with lime and stacks of red brick. The whole panorama gave meaning to the title of China's weekly "news" magazine for foreigners, *China Reconstructs*. Zhang Wei explained proudly that the object of all this activity was an extension to the TV studios in the back. Sprawling before us was a gigantic shallow pool filled with green water.

"It is the cooling system for the new TV studios," she said.

TV was the new mass media in China. TV in Coketown.

Dickens' grubby, industrial England banged up against Fritz Lang's *Metropolis*, that nightmare of the twentieth century, as a steady stream of hundreds of workers—dressed in identical marine blue, pea green or dusky grey pajama-like suits—trudged in the fine dirt mixed with coal dust past the TV building, the workers' bathhouse and sheds where vehicles were repaired.

Following Zhang Wei into the mud-colored fortress, I felt like I was on a journey into gloom. Halfway up a flight of stairs, a woman worked a pail and mop, but the stairs she had washed look no cleaner than the dust-ground ones she was about to tackle.

Zhang Wei led me to the second floor opening to an ominously dark hallway. One small bulb dangled from the high ceiling, along with several clocks, each indicating a different time. None worked.

"This is the English department," she announced.

In a sequence of large offices, Zhang Wei introduced me to staffers with a bewildering variety of names—Ma Riuliu, Li Dan, Mai Xiaomei, Fan Fuquang, Zhou Hong, Dam Ping. Last names first. Many shared the same last names.

"The hundred old names," one staffer laughed. I couldn't get the humor of the chaos of new sounds. "It means 'common people,'" he added. I couldn't hear the commonality. I was drowning in a phonic sea.

Again, I was struck by the range of features and skin tones of these Northern Chinese. So different from the bone structure of the Cantonese or Southerners that I was familiar with in Vancouver, San Francisco and New York.

Some bold, others shy, they posed a passel of questions.

"What are your impressions of Beijing?"

"You must be very tired?"

"How do you like Chinese food?"

"Do you like your apartment?"

It seemed rehearsed. Of course, I wasn't really expected to answer with anything but exuberance. But while they were asking, I observed them.

At first glance, my new colleagues seemed to share some physical commonalities. Bodies disappeared into their loose-fitting clothing. Although fashions and hairstyles appeared uniform and simple, how different was this from a nation of blue-jeans-and-sneaker wearers that I had just left behind? Men and women wore similar baggy pants, but my eyes dropped to their ankles. They all revealed the same beige silk ankle socks, whether in sandals or canvas shoes. Even the few younger women in skirts sported those dainty ankle socks. The women modeled an identical sober blouse buttoned to the chin. There was no trace of makeup or jewelry. The men all sported 1950s brush cuts while many of the women had short hair pulled back into two ponytails.

Although it was a realization that came to me slowly, I was experiencing a group of people whose self-image wasn't constructed by mass media, by advertising or by media celebrities. Their loose-fitting costumes had a de-eroticizing effect. Even their body movements were different. My new colleagues shuffled rather than walked. No wiggling or sashaying. No lopes or strides. And nobody commented on my full lavender skirt and red sandals.

Zhang Wei led me through the offices of the English department—rooms crammed with stolid, worn wooden furniture. Desks, chairs, file cabinets and shelves all pressed against each other, stacked with yellowing papers, tape boxes, occasional large 1940s-style radios and manual typewriters with Swedish, Italian, Russian and Chinese brand names. The dark hallways, dense clutter of cumbersome furniture, manila walls and lethargic pace generated an overcast feeling I associated with municipal offices and police stations in New York City.

The sunless room where I would work six days a week faced the courtyard. Zhang Wei assured me it was much cooler than the other offices on the sunny side of the building. No one mentioned the wintertime effect. Doors and windows yawned open. Clearly there was no central air-conditioning here from the green pool outdoors.

I shared this small office with four others. Their names immediately dispersed into an opera of Mandarin notes and chords cascading in my brain. Then Zhang Wei directed me to my desk. The centerpiece was a 1960s-era manual Underwood typewriter. A gooseneck lamp stood next to a small tin holding straight pins. No paper clips. There was a pencil and a small knife to sharpen it. And an electric fan.

"Only foreign experts get electric fans," Zhang Wei stressed.

"We can share it in this office," I offered.

The other real object of privilege was my gold-and-red ballpoint pen. My coworkers, I noticed, all used ballpoint refills wrapped tightly with paper. A basin of water rested on the floor in one corner "to wash your hands." Squatting muscles required.

Passing by other offices, I saw scrawny men in short pants, sleeveless undershirts and rubber sandals hunched over weathered wooden desks, breezing themselves by hand with round bamboo fans. Cigarette smoke clouded the rooms. Nobody hurried. Everyone drank hot water from glass jars.

"Tea is too expensive," Zhang Wei claimed.

I was learning so much with every breath and gaze that my skull was cracking.

It appeared that Zhang Wei would be my "shadow," in Simon Leys' terminology—the person designated by the Party to not only take care of my needs but—I also suspected—to report on me. My need for her as a mediator and interpreter had already become a little irritating. She tried to be very efficient and voiced concern for my comfort, but on the first day, as she shepherded me around, she also asked me point-blank, "Do you hate children?"

I was flummoxed. This was neither the moment nor the place to talk about why I didn't have children, which was what I imagined her invasive question was really about. So I tried gracefully to sidestep. It would be the first of many hints that my status as a single thirty-seven-year-old woman was suspect and peculiar here. How would I explain my generation of feminist friends and the absence of children in some of our lives? I had a difficult enough time rationalizing it to myself. Some days.

On my first day at the office, Zhang Wei seemed overly determined to inform me of the special privileges of the "foreign expert."

"Only foreign experts get a lamp on their desks."

"Only foreign experts get a fan."

"Only foreign experts get a special pen."

My office mate, Li Shutian, translated "foreign expert" to "*zhuanjia*" in Pinyin, the new alphabetization system that had been replacing the old Wade–Giles. That's what I was: a *zhuanjia*. I would never be comfortable with this job title. And I was already picking up signals of resentment from the very person assigned to take care of my needs.

The most distinctive sound amid the clatter of typewriters, Mandarin whispers and the hush of soft-soled shoes was the long, deep, guttural hawking or clearing of the throat, which preceded spitting. Spittoons sat in the hallways and just inside the door of each office.

Bathrooms at the end of the hall could be traced by their unsavory fumes. Toilets were the squat variety. My neighbor, Bahdra, said a debate raged over whether they originated in Japan or China. Once inside the bathroom, the stench rendered the debate meaningless. Unlike the restrooms in the Beijing Hotel that were sweetly pungent with coils of burning incense, in the English department no effort was made to ease the olfactory attack. The toilets were filthy and without toilet paper. Four thousand years of culture.

North Americans are fussy—perhaps overly so—about toilet facilities. It's cultural. My British grandmother had still used a chamber pot in the rooming house where we lived in Vancouver in the 1940s. Even though a toilet was available, it was ingrained. The groove—or comfort—of habit. And I was conscious that poverty dictated different standards. My mother always told stories about the outhouse across the yard from their one-room prairie home. The dread and trauma of the night-time dash in sub-zero weather. They had never seen toilet paper like city slickers knew it. But there had always been an old Sears catalogue hanging on a string to be scavenged for usable pages. At Radio Beijing, part of Central Broadcasting that dances to the tune of the Propaganda Committee of the Central Committee of the People's Republic of China, you brought your own. By the third day I gave up on the toilets. If I had a need, I ran back to my apartment. It was the first advantage I could see of living so close to the office.

Despite the anarchy of the hallway clocks, the workday began punctually at 8 a.m. and was rigidly routinized. When I arrived in the morning, Liu Hui (pronounced "Lew Hway")—a female comrade—would be sweeping the office floor; another comrade would be washing off the considerable night accumulation of soot from the windowsill while several others carried giant thermoses out to the boiler shed to keep a supply of boiled drinking water in each office.

"Should I share in these tasks?" I asked Leader Zhang Qingnian—yes, another female Zhang, the closest one yet that I could figure was actually my boss.

"No, we need you to catch up polishing scripts. We have been waiting for you!"

And indeed there was a tall stack on my desk to be questioned, re-thought, edited, rewritten. I will never understand the concept of "polishing."

Leader Zhang—no relation to Shadow Zhang—may have been in her mid-fifties. She spoke a soft, fluent American English without an accent. In a low voice, almost conspiratorial, I learned that she and her husband had studied in the United States and had returned to help build New China just after Liberation. Apparently, there were many others who had followed that same path. But short stories and films were beginning to emerge revealing that Mao's policies had been tough on intellectuals.

As I studied Leader Zhang's refined hands and listened to her placating voice, I wondered if I would ever learn how she felt about the choice she and her husband made thirty years before.

Was she what they called a "cadre"...a Party official? It didn't feel appropriate to ask her, but somehow I sensed that she wouldn't be in charge without being a member of the Communist Party. I had yet to learn the real significance of Party membership.

When I arrived in the morning, I could hear the blaring, stilted syllables of Voice of America's *News in Special English* and traced it to one of the rooms down the hall, where a group of comrades sat attentively around a Sanyo shortwave radio buzzing and hissing out this annoying version of the English language—simple vocabulary, slowly and deliberately enunciated. Li Shutian, whose desk bordered mine, preferred to read the *People's Daily*, the Party's official paper with the largest circulation of any newspaper in China. Perhaps Comrade Li had been assigned to set that example for me—to illustrate a golden rule that news should come from the Party, not from the mistrusted West. I took his photograph reading the *People's Daily*.

At half past eleven the office symphony ceased abruptly and the building spilled out its captives for lunch. A stampede of 2,000 workers rushed to the canteen across the street. Flashes of *Metropolis* again. Inside the canteen it looked and sounded as if a riot had broken out. The most animated scene of the day played out in a brick airplane hangar-like shed with concrete floors as comrades lunged for enamel bowls, tin boxes and chopsticks stored in slats on the back wall. The decibel level of laughing and shouting rose to a deafening din as lines zigzagged halfway across the length of the building. At the front of each line, plump workers in white jackets ladled food from enormous basins. You could mix cement in those things.

"On the right, cold, cooked vegetables. Tomatoes, cucumbers, green peppers," Yan Aizhen, an office mate, instructed me on my first day. "At those counters they serve hot dishes. Today, eggplant stew. Over there, rice and buns."

Comrade Yan was searching for the right coupons from my wallet overflowing with indistinguishable tags of soiled paper—ration coupons for cotton, flour and rice products along with half a dozen different shapes and colors for buying food in the workers' dining hall. Since I could not read the characters printed on them, how would I ever figure it out?

Some workers were leaving the building and hopping on bikes with tins stacked with rice, vegetables and buns. Others maneuvered bum room on one of hundreds of rough benches while elbowing space at a table with a dozen others, frantically gobbling down food—tins held up to the mouth for speedy shoveling. Bones were spat onto the table or floor. After gulping their lunch, everyone dove for the sink to rinse their bowls and push them back into slots. All at breathtaking speed. Lively and loud. I decided after my second day to forgo this experience. Too fast, too loud and way too many people.

I wanted to use my lunchtime writing, studying Chinese, exploring and photographing—not getting indigestion. Besides, there would be no opportunity to talk to coworkers in this madhouse scene.

Why the rush, I wondered, *since they had two hours?* I learned that first day that the long lunch hour wasn't about meeting with the girls or clothes shopping or running a million errands, or even eating at your desk while catching up with work but rather...sleep. The comrades were heading back to the office to snooze. *Xuxi*, pronounced "shoo-she." Napping.

In one room, a middle-aged comrade lay on a straw mat spread across two desk tops. A washcloth covered his eyes. In my little office, two young women staffers pulled armchairs together to make a bed, sleeping spoon style. I didn't yet suspect that those few who bicycled home for lunch may have had another agenda. Given crowded housing conditions with generations living together, the fact that other family members might be out of the apartment for the working day meant a couple might have enough privacy to rendezvous for sex.

Two hours later, the office came lethargically to life again, continuing its somnolent pace until 5 p.m. This schedule repeated itself six days a week. Rooted in the rhythms of the countryside, this was the schedule of peasants.

When I queried Leader Zhang about the long lunch hour for city workers, she didn't answer directly but instead spoke about the years of the "Great Leap Forward" twenty years earlier—when Mao's disastrous economic experiment (my words, not hers) led to more than 20 million starving to death (at least, that was the figure available in 1980—since then scholars have raised the estimated deaths to as much as 42 million). Leader Zhang also didn't mention the deaths. I knew from my night-time reading that Mao's Great Leap Forward policy was a reaction to China's split with the Soviets. Aimed at self-reliance, Mao encouraged everyone—peasants and city dwellers—to melt down their pots and tools to make iron in their backyards or at their work units. Combined with simultaneous forced collectivization and terrible drought, harvests diminished. Starvation ensued.

"Offices throughout Beijing allowed workers to sleep half the day," said Leader Zhang. "Here at Radio Beijing, sometimes the comrades only worked every other day."

"Not enough protein or calories," my neighbor Joshi told me that night.

I sensed the enormity of what I would be learning in the weeks and months ahead. I would also learn that the Great Leap Forward—the starvation part and the deaths—was a taboo topic at Radio Beijing. Like Tibet.

"CHINA IS poor and very backward."

I had been in Beijing only a few days and already I had heard this statement from every Chinese person who could speak to me in English. This time it came from Ma Riuliu, the leader of the news section in the English department. Short and in his mid-forties, Ma led me through a maze of hallways, up and down stairways, to show me the recording studios. Beethoven's *Violin Concerto in D* mingled with Chinese traditional music and the squealing of tape at high speed.

Peter, a Chinese-American friend from New York who had just arrived to work in Beijing, told me that China's conservatories had been closed during the Cultural Revolution. Western classical music had been banned. Accomplished Soviet-trained musicians and composers had been persecuted and sent to remote regions to do manual labor. Red Guards had smashed instruments. The presence of sheet music or recordings in your home could have led to severe consequences. Only Chinese traditional instruments had been allowed, and any compositions had to be modeled after eight revolutionary operas that had been approved by Mao's wife, Jiang Qing.

"When did Western classical music reappear?" I asked Leader Ma.

He shrugged and blushed. "Two years ago—1978. The Central Conservatory of Beijing reopened."

I calculated that meant Western classical music hadn't been performed or heard for at least twelve years. As a Canadian, I was sensitive to cultural imperialism. There were quotas for Canadian radio stations as to how much American music could be played in a broadcast hour. I was also conscious that

Asian tonal scales and instrumentation were seldom studied or appreciated in the West. But then, music of all cultural sources tended to leak and spill over borders despite efforts to prohibit it. What I was learning about the censorship of musical expression, curiosity and knowledge in China was deeply troubling. One of my neighbors told me that blues, jazz and rock 'n' roll were still considered decadent, evil, polluting and taboo.

Dark circles were growing under my arms. Was it the heat and humidity or my thoughts about cultural policing? Was I anxious about the choice I had made to live in this censorious system? I ripped at a tissue to mop my wet forehead.

Through a window in the wall we could see a woman sitting in a closet-sized recording booth. She was sweating profusely while reading a script in Polish. We could hear her in the outer room. She faltered, stopped and spoke Mandarin to a woman in the studio, who rewound a tape deck, then signaled the script reader, who proceeded. I had compassion for the announcer trapped in a tiny, closed recording booth in this suffocating heat without AC.

"Does every language department have their own engineers?" I asked, wiping my face, searching for something nonpolitical to ask.

Ma Riuliu—who didn't seem to be sweating—hesitated. His brow bunched up. "No. For a long time we did not have *any* engineers. During the Cultural Revolution, we could not have them. Everyone was supposed to be able to engineer. So things broke down. It was not very good. Now we are beginning to have engineers again. But they are not too good. All the departments have to share a few engineers."

So much for avoiding a political question!

As I listened to Ma's carefully constructed sentences without contractions or the repetitive connective tissue of colloquial speech, I realized that *what* he was saying was familiar to me. Beginning in the late 1960s and into the '70s, when I had first started producing radio, I was part of several women's radio collectives—in St. Louis, Berkeley and Boston. We, too, had rejected the hierarchies and division of labor that came with specialized skills. That impulse had been accompanied by a technological revolution whereby new, more miniaturized audio and video equipment helped to democratize those media. Previously, radio, television and filmmaking had been mostly an exclusive club—male and white. I had been part of the movement to change that—creating fresh programming for community radio stations and taking advantage of the new port-a-pac video technology, then advocating for public access channels as cable connected the country.

In those years, I had learned to do all parts of radio and video production:

interviewing, writing, recording, shooting, editing and engineering or mixing the finished program and narrating—all shared with other women. For some of us, ideas about this kind of self-reliance and collective, nonhierarchical work came from books about China's Great Proletarian Cultural Revolution. When I told Ma this, he looked shocked and then chortled—a laughter of disbelief, much like when I told several of the comrades that I had studied Marxism in university and participated in various movements comprising something called the New Left. It was a mocking laughter erasing the possibility of Marxism or left ideas outside of a Communist country. Outside of China. And the conversation ended with their looks of amusement.

From my reading, I learned that this problem of the entrenched power of technocrats and engineers was one reason Mao had challenged the Soviets and they had pulled out—taking all their expertise and tools with them. He had then launched the Cultural Revolution as another way to get at the problem of bureaucratic hierarchies.

It was the "Red vs. Expert" issue. Was it better to have good politics or good technical skills with the division of labor that comes with that? I wondered if my being hired had divided the English department along those lines.

Ma smiled sympathetically, then shrugged his shoulders. I suspected that the issue was still not resolved at Radio Beijing. As I mused on this curious parallel in our experience, I noticed there was not a scrap of audiotape on the floor or even in the wastebaskets in any of the studios. No razor blades, no splicing blocks.

"We do not cut tape," Ma explained. "We have never done that. It is too expensive. When Leader Zhang visited Voice of America in the US last year, she noticed piles of tape on the floor. We cannot afford that. We use our tape, over and over again."

Memories flooded back to me of hours spent sitting at an editing machine in windowless cubbyholes late into the night. I would be listening, relistening, squealing tape, back and forth, splicing, reconnecting, pasting segments of various lengths of tape onto the walls with labels of phrases, arguments, comments from interviews that I had been interweaving to make—with music and sound effects—a compelling story or documentary. Miles of rejected verbiage on tape had billowed at my feet.

But here, in 1980, at Radio Beijing, the thought of no splicing blocks, no air-conditioned studios, no copy machines, no electric typewriters, no paper clips—no toilet paper—meant I was going to have to rethink some things.

34

Beijing, 1980

Chapter Three

My Shanghai Phoenix
我的上海凤凰

August 5, 1980, Journal:

I feel dead. Besides the nausea, I have severe headaches that I suspect are caused by the coal pollution. You can smell it and see it. Sometimes breathing is painful. Coal, God. Memories of Grandpa's basement coal bin in the 1940s! Was that before or after the sawdust furnaces?

"In the winter, it will get worse," Bahdra says. "Fierce winds from the Gobi Desert and Inner Mongolia fling tons of grit and sand mixed with coal dust across Beijing daily."

She tells me that the topsoil of Beijing blew away decades ago. "During the Cultural Revolution they dug up the little patches of grass. It was considered bourgeois." She sighs. "Now they are planting trees and grass again." In a horrible flashback to the late 1960s, I remembered accusing my working-class mother of being bourgeois because she kept a manicured lawn. I sounded like a sectarian Puritan. Or a Maoist.

"YOU SHOULD bring earth and water from your old home to your new home and then you will not get sick."

Li Shutian, whose desk joined mine, was sharing some ancient Chinese wisdom in an effort to ease my suffering from nausea and diarrhea during my first week. While one voice agreed that my body was reacting normally to new food and water—and pollution—another, deeper voice suggested my physical disturbances were a response to the sensual and architectural environment of

Beijing. According to Ernest Dimnet, French literary priest and author of *The Art of Thinking*, "architecture, of all the arts, is the one which acts the most slowly, but the most surely, on the soul."

August 6, 1980, Journal:

Beijing is ugly. Flat. Grim. Trees grace the broad avenues, but there is still no sign of Bahdra's grass. Buildings and grounds are the color of dry mud. Clay boulevards border the main streets. Narrower roads are lined by eight-foot walls of plaster, stone, brick and mortar in an infinite range of greys.

DURING MY first excursions in the official Radio Beijing car, peeking out the curtained windows as we honked our way along Chang'an—the Avenue of Heavenly Peace running east and west—I recoiled at the imposing examples of Soviet-influenced architecture. Soviet Brutalism. Built in the 1950s, the Great Hall of the People, the Museum of Revolutionary History, the telegraph office and Central Broadcasting were authoritarian in their superhuman scale. Not phallic like New York architecture, but massive and severe. Mies van der Rohe, the god of modern architecture, said architecture "is the will of an epoch translated into space." If so, the implications of Beijing's architectural behemoths were disturbing.

Just as I had experienced my own insignificance looking up at Manhattan's glass and steel monuments, oppressed by the sheer weight of those colossal altars to corporate wealth, I was also dwarfed and alienated by the austere gigantism of these post-Liberation monstrosities at the heart of Beijing. Where was the egalitarian spirit of socialism in these dominating structures? They left me with a taste of...totalitarianism.

Standing in Tiananmen Square—itself the size of dozens of football fields—outside the imposing gates leading to the Forbidden City, I felt lost. It took an act of defiance to enter those gates, perhaps because of the surreal combination of huge images of Mao, Marx, Lenin and Stalin adorning the front façade, with millions of bicyclists like a wave of minnows undulating in the foreground. Powerful. Diminishing the individual spirit. I was shocked to see Stalin's image at such a scale in China. Here I was, contemplating the central address of the most populated and mysterious country on earth, and I felt suspicious.

The architectural plan and details of the Forbidden City have inspired acres of print in the West as the epitome of all that is wondrous and unique about Asian design, including thoughts by the father of a New York friend. Ed Bacon had become one of the foremost urban planners in the US. His portrait had been on the cover of *Time* magazine back in the 1960s when he was re-shaping and re-vitalizing the city of Philadelphia. His seminal book, *The Design of Cities*, was required reading for every university urban planning and architecture course. Visiting Beijing in the 1930s and witnessing the Forbidden City had had a huge impact on Bacon's thinking: "It taught me that city planning is about movement through space, an architectural sequence of sensors and stimuli up and down, light and dark, color and rhythm."

Bacon had studied the relationship between sectors of the Forbidden City and the surrounding Imperial City. For him this plan was unique in the world because it duplicated itself at any scale. He had also praised this icon of Chinese design for its harmony with nature. These observations might have held for the city that Bacon witnessed in the '30s, but Beijing had sprawled since then. Many of the walls and their gates had been removed in the 1960s to make way for a road to circle the city.

Inside the Forbidden City, close up, I appreciated the density of beauty and skillful craftsmanship in the glazed tile work, the trademark upturned roof corners, creating convex lines that Bacon had argued implied a modesty of man. The intricacy of carved wooden details under the eaves and especially the boldness of vermilion, blue and gold paint were stunning. But on that first visit, I found myself more drawn to the faces of peasants who were wandering in clusters throughout the palace. I wondered what they saw in this icon to the power and wealth of past dynasties—a once-forbidden territory for their class.

In fact, scholars have revealed that the plan of the Forbidden City and the urban spaces outside were designed to ensure social order and political control. Surrounded by its wide moat and high walls, the Forbidden City was itself encircled by the Imperial City and its walls. Outside of those walls was the Inner City and the Outer City, ensuring a perfect hierarchy of order.

An early pictograph of the character *yi*, for the concept of "city," implied a man kneeling beneath an enclosure. It represented the submission of the people to the moral authority of the state. Even though the Forbidden City was by 1980 a museum, those giant images of Mao, Marx, Lenin and Stalin stuck in bold on the front façade made the original message of ideological authority clear.

I couldn't help recalling my journey eight months earlier through Mexico's major cities, famous for their Spanish Colonial architecture. Querétaro, Guanajuato, Oaxaca, San Cristobal de las Casas and Mexico City had stunning examples of Moorish-baroque, primarily in churches, monasteries and government palaces. Work had begun on them a century after the construction on the Forbidden City and continued for several centuries.

Later details in baroque and rococo—or an ultra-baroque style called Churrigueresque—meant many details, from columns to altars, played out in the most extravagant, fantastical designs. The Spaniards had to create an architecture that would impress the Indians, whom they had physically conquered and who then had to be spiritually converted and convinced. And they had often built their dazzling churches on top of Mayan or Zapotec spiritual sites.

I was inspired to think about that dazzling power factor while contemplating the epicenter of 1980 Beijing.

In contrast to the blood-red exteriors of the Forbidden City buildings, the Soviet-era fortresses outside resembled the color of chicken broth. And like the exclusive power that had once resided in the Forbidden City, these Communist counterparts surrounding Tiananmen Square also commanded distance with an unyielding supremacy.

Architecture is politics. But nobody could see the real structures of power in Beijing—Zhongnanhai, where the top leadership were all squirreled away behind high walls wrapped around an artificial lake next door to the Forbidden City. They lived and worked there, and, just as in imperial times, the public was excluded.

Clustered throughout Beijing were dreary rows of four-story apartments. Dusty, grey, lifeless testimonials to a 1950s architectural vision of mass housing. I pondered why—from New York to London—such a meanness of aesthetic spirit infused "worker's housing." It was a testament to architectural and government failure of imagination or, more likely, an absence of respect. In Beijing, even the new thirteen-story prefab high rises going up along the main arteries were stamped out of two or three basic designs, their façades a mixture of oyster and beige—the color of new concrete. There was no chaos or color that might have indicated a human presence.

On first glance driving around the city, there also seemed to be no public places, except the space for a million in Tiananmen Square. In the urban core, little plazas, promenades, restaurants, cafes and teahouses were either hidden from view or nonexistent. There was no place to sit. I couldn't see a bench. Throughout the city, men and women squatted on their haunches along the edge of curbs or up against the fronts of buildings to seek the shade. I was having difficulty recognizing Beijing as urban in the Western sense, meaning a complexity of diverse activity. Commerce, government, culture, entertainment. The expressive and playful city. But I was blinded by my illiteracy. I couldn't read a single sign. What was I thinking? That there would be English names? Other than Chinese characters, there was no other signage—graphic imagery—to offer a hint as to the activity behind a door or window.

August 7, 1980, Journal:
I am already in crisis. I am a journalist. And I cannot read the city.
The city is numbing. Mono-tonal. Mono-rhythmic. Bicycle and walking pace meld into a singular languid motion. Not lazy, rather deliberate, phlegmatic, as if in defiance of something.

MY FIRST Sunday in Beijing, I bought a Shanghai Phoenix. My nausea subsided and my depression lifted as I pedaled the eight kilometers home from the Friendship Store, that marketplace for foreigners and Chinese with connections. Like all bikes in Beijing, my Shanghai Phoenix was only one speed, perfectly adequate for the mostly flat terrain. From that moment, it became my main means of transportation.

August 11, 1980, Journal:
After work, I maneuver into position on Chang'an, which, like all the wide avenues dissecting the city, has entire traffic lanes blocked off on both sides of the street for cyclists. At rush hour, the density of bikes is like a slow-moving pilgrimage to Mecca. Some cyclists move along in pairs, chatting as they maintain identical rhythm. A young couple holds hands while bicycling side by side. Bikes carry everything—bags of eggplants, lumber, TVs, double beds!

At all hours, it was a war between bikes and motor vehicles. But the bicycles were losing. *Newsweek*—sold only at the Beijing Hotel—reported that Beijing had one of the highest traffic death tolls in the world.

Cyclists represented a potent resistance movement. They simply did not want to yield to cars. I liked to think of it as a risky feud with technology and privilege. Private car ownership was forbidden. Each work unit had a few cars available for officials or emergencies; consequently, those who had access to cars, including the drivers, had special status.

Watching the war on the streets could be breathtaking. Everywhere, teenage rebels broke pace—pulling out, speeding ahead, weaving their bikes around cars and trucks or playing "chicken" with an oncoming taxi or bus. Pumping frenetically, they left behind a miffed and lethargic ocean of pedal-pushers.

Amid the uninterrupted tinkling of bicycle bells, these kids who accelerated played out a forceful and deliberate uptempo beat, working syncopated sounds from their bells, creating complex rhythms as their legs flew. Against a background of evenness, where life seemed to move like sludge, this is where the thrills were.

Their baggy, army green pants were cinched tight at the waist. The wind made their shirts balloon in the back. I wanted to follow their energy, see where they headed. Already I felt the exhilaration of cycling fast. I caught the kids' magic. Millions of chiming bells crashed past my ears.

I had a hunch that my Shanghai Phoenix would become my ticket to freedom—perhaps that was too grandiose—but it at least offered a sense of unstructured time and space, a way to escape the deadening routine at Radio Beijing, where clock time ruled, even if the clocks were all broken.

I BEGAN riding every day after work to explore and photograph. On my second evening out, I could feel my pedal mechanism beginning to slip. Within another block, it fell apart. Unless I could find help, it would be a long walk back, and it was getting dark. Within a few minutes several cyclists stopped, and with gestures I indicated the broken pedal. I had never felt so illiterate. Like an infant.

All the guys who stopped carried tool kits on their bikes. After some brief dialogue with each other, one of them did what he could to fix it. And one drew an image of the part I needed and then drew a diagram of the streets, directing me to a shop where I could buy it. All this within a matter of minutes.

By the time I got to the central shopping streets where their diagram directed me, the sun was setting. The bike broke down again, and I showed the scribblings to a young man on the street, then gestured to my bike. He directed me personally to the corner where I needed to turn. When I found the repair shop, all I had to do was point to the pedal, and a young man in a sleeveless t-shirt took the bike and gave it a complete overhaul, tightening all the screws and adjusting the spokes. A clean machine. Unable to comprehend the cost, I simply opened my fist of money and he took a few coins. It seemed ridiculously inexpensive. But I had navigated my first crisis through the language barrier.

The next day, Comrade Li told me that this was the first privately owned bicycle repair shop in Beijing. Open at all hours for a city of millions of cyclists.

The experience had taught me something important about the Chinese, their willingness to help and their self-reliance—qualities in people I had so admired when traveling alone through the countryside in Haiti. Hardly a socialist country. If I had a flat tire or ran into a rural ditch, suddenly a dozen peasants appeared out of the fields and would physically lift my car out of the ditch or help change a tire or repair it at a friend's place close by. Granted, they wanted some money for the service. But it was a spirit of eagerness and ingenuity to solve a problem. It was humbling, and here in Beijing, I had encountered something of this same spirit. Bicycling home, I felt a rush of motivation to hit my Mandarin language books. I now suspected my bike would become the conduit to discovery and enlightenment.

August 14, 1980, Journal:

I cause a sensation everywhere. With so few foreigners here—especially Westerners—a redheaded Caucasian woman wearing purple pants and a lime-colored t-shirt must be a freak show. Everywhere I bicycle, people stop, jaws drop. If I hesitate to look at something, a crowd of at least twenty surround me and stare. They push in close, look me over, carefully. My shoes are always the real object of curiosity. Today my Keds sneakers were being thoroughly examined. Claustrophobic. Unnerving. I, the only child, who loves being the center of attention, wanted to flee.

My clothes already feel ridiculous, but I'm hanging on for a few weeks yet. I am ruminating about my New York City wardrobe hauled to Beijing. What was I imagining? An expat life in 1930s Shanghai? Where will I wear all my 1940s vintage dresses and jackets? My high heels?

Between my hair and bright colors, I have already caused accidents—men bicycle into the backs of trucks while staring at me. That's why I started bicycling at night.

"You must be very careful and never ride at night," Comrade Li, my office mate, warned.

This bit of advice would not have been so curious if seven of my coworkers had not already said the same thing. Of course, I defied their warnings.

On my first after-dark excursion, I discovered the ancient part of Beijing. The part my comrades never spoke about and, of course, never took me to see on the first sightseeing excursions. This old part of the city—away from the gigantic modern avenues—felt more human scale, less ordered and regimented, a labyrinth of life force. Traditional family courtyard houses were visible slightly through open gates. The dominant posture was squatting—a group of men perched on their haunches to play cards or checkers on the clay sidewalk, and old men smoked two-foot-long pipes. Messy street markets oozed with teenage boys selling t-shirts with Hong Kong logos out of a box on the back of a bike.

I got a glimpse of a more relaxed, unofficial life that wasn't evident in daylight. A certain quality of hanging out. Something was happening that felt dissident to the official China that I was surrounded by at work.

However, a script I had translated revealed the "youth problem." The average age in China was twenty-six—all born since Liberation. They were now products of the Cultural Revolution, which meant they hadn't received much formal education, as the schools had been closed for six years. Many of them were returning from the countryside, where they had been sent for years of manual labor. Their return was contributing to high unemployment. Combined with a recent opening to the West and the import—whether legal or not—of Western media, from TV to music, it seemed to signal trouble. The script equated an over emphasis on Western clothing with juvenile delinquency. Apparently, in order to obtain these clothes, you would need to steal, since the average salary was below $40 US a month.

When I returned to my apartment building after a night-time ride, the young People's Army soldier who stood with his fixed bayonet at the guard hut was often watching a black-and-white TV with other building staff. Every lunch hour I observed boxes of TVs being carried out by workers. Apparently, they had all been helped by Radio Beijing to purchase a black-and-white set. In the evenings, when I bicycled around the city, I could see the blue glow of light emanating from windows.

August 15, 1980, Journal:
Before returning to the building tonight, I stopped at the Beijing Hotel bar—one of the only places for foreigners to congregate or get a drink—and found fat German tourists, Canadian teachers and men from all developing nations looking very horny. The consul of Yemen said he was shipping his family home for a holiday and would be having some big parties and I should DEFINITELY come. I wondered how lonely I would have to be to go to one of his parties. Although we both complained about the lack of street life, cafes and bars, I was eager to get back into the streets to figure out if I could ever penetrate the life that is there.

"Professor"/Comrade Li Shutian, Radio Beijing, 1980

English Department Features Leader Zhang Qingnian

Chapter Four

Who's Out There?
何许人也？

"How many of you *ever* listen to the broadcast?"

A chair squeaked.

It was my first class on broadcast journalism for the English department staff, and I wanted to know how often they listened to the final program. The reply was a room full of puzzled faces.

"But if *you* don't listen, how do you expect somebody thousands of miles from here to listen?"

Leader Zhang cleared her throat. "The comrades decided a long time ago that the broadcast was boring."

It was my first indication that there was little that I would have to say about Radio Beijing's airwaves that my coworkers did not already know.

August 19, 1980, Journal:

I feel like I have hit quicksand at eighty miles an hour. Nothing in the ambiance here feels familiar to me as radio. There is none of the electricity or nervous energy that characterizes news and features departments in the US. There is none of the excitement of reporters racing in to check out stories, locate sources, chase down interviews, argue with editors or fight for access to editing booths.

(This was pre-digital anything! Before cell phones. Before computers. It was pre-CDs and Walkmans. The boom box had just landed before I left for Beijing. In US radio, we used cassette decks the size of a Midwestern city telephone book with large punch buttons to play and rewind. We would plug in a handheld microphone the size of a cucumber to record interviews in the field. To edit we

used a reel-to-reel machine with a splicing block, razor blades and sticky tape to reconnect. To mix we used a studio with multiple reel-to-reel consoles, turntables, cassette decks, microphones and mixing board).

In the offices of the English department, I never sensed the thrill of a reporter who had just captured the essence of a story in the cadence of a human voice as it articulated an old idea in a fresh way, or a new idea with startling power, or disentangled a complicated issue. Of course, interviews that had to be translated lost some of their poetry and power, but that was simply another art, to massage the magic.

Also missing was the anxious marathon against the second hand of the clock. There was none of the fear of failure as the minutes raced and you faced miles of tape, seemingly disconnected arguments and a mass of details that had to be written into an intelligible two-minute report or complex feature. It was more like rip 'n' read and a dogged sense of clock time that portioned the day into routines of fetching hot water, cleaning the office, reading the *People's Daily*, exercising during morning and afternoon breaks, and dreaming through long lunch hours. The only tinge of anarchy came from the actual clocks suspended from the dark corridor ceilings. Each worked for only a few minutes a day. Each pointed to a different time. And it wasn't about regional time zones.

Perhaps it was unfair to compare Radio Beijing with the broadcast environments I had experienced. During the 1970s, I had worked in passionate and eclectic radio stations, whether community supported or commercial—KDNA in St. Louis, KPFA in Berkeley, WBCN in Boston and WBAI in New York. I had produced radio plays, documentaries, dramatic readings of novels and public affairs shows, including an all-day teach-in on the politics of Southern Africa. When NPR had opened their New York bureau, I began producing elaborate feature stories for *All Things Considered*. Of course, these had been exceptional entities, even in the American broadcasting landscape, but they had been *my* experience, my frame of reference in China.

At Radio Beijing I was confronting a propaganda agency. In 1980, *The East Is Red* was still its theme song. This song and opera, produced in the mid-1960s on the cusp of the Cultural Revolution, had glorified Mao and the Party. Yet when I tuned in my new shortwave radio to Voice of America's daily news magazine with its smooth vision of American pluralism, I realized that I would have been frustrated working there, too. Compared to domestic American radio, VOA's programming was less hectic and diverse, and more cautious while putting more emphasis on the virtues of "the American way." It promoted American music, like jazz, as a model of free expression. Of American freedom. If Radio Beijing's goal was to create splendid and seductive propaganda through glossy stories of the People's Republic of China, it was a laughably dismal effort.

BORN IN revolution, Radio Beijing had begun on a transmitter supplied by Moscow to the Chinese Communist Party. Veterans of the Long March had started broadcasting from the caves of Yan'an in 1940 during the anti-Japanese war that at its heart was also a conflict between Mao's Communist peasant movement and Chiang Kai-shek's Nationalist forces. Sidney Rittenberg had begun translating scripts into English for this cave-based station in the mid-'40s. He had been a US Army translator posted to China during the Allied effort to help the Chinese resist the Japanese invasion. But when WWII ended and civil war broke out between the Communists and the Nationalist Party, the Americans supported Chiang Kai-shek, and Rittenberg chose to join Mao's Communist Party. He married the first English announcer for Radio Beijing, Wei Lin. Divorced for many years, she was still in the department when I arrived.

By 1980, Radio Beijing's programs were beamed at the rest of the world in four dozen languages. Each language department hired at least one "foreign expert," a native speaker who edited scripts and sometimes announced. Among the foreign experts that I had met so far—an unscientific survey—it appeared that none were trained as journalists. Their credentials were more often political. It was the first indication that I was working for a propaganda institution rather than a journalistic agency. Initially I rationalized the mission of Radio Beijing as necessary, just as Voice of America rationalized its enterprise. Every country wanted to control the big story it had to tell.

By the time I arrived, Radio Beijing's largest departments were English and Japanese—unsurprising, given Deng Xiaoping's new emphasis on modernization and openness to the West. A staff of forty in the English department produced a one-hour daily program of news (twenty minutes) and features (forty minutes)that was rebroadcast nineteen times a day. "The news" at Radio Beijing in 1980 was updated every eight hours.

The single source of information for Radio Beijing's twenty-minute newscast was Xinhua, the New China news agency, which by 1980 had reporters stationed in most world capitals.

Not long after I arrived, Ma Riuliu, the leader of the news section, sat in the brown plastic-covered armchair next to my desk.

"We're thinking about getting more newswire services," he began, "like AP, UPI and Reuters. What do you think?"

Leader Ma was referred to by staffers as Lao Ma, which meant "old horse." He was short and spoke English with the accent of Guangzhou (Canton), his family home. He had a big nose for a Chinese man, and his hair was cropped close. His eyes, circled by 1950s-style clear plastic-rimmed glasses, were fixed eagerly on mine.

"It would provide more variety of news," I assured him. "But you know it's expensive to subscribe to those services."

I was already painfully aware of the economic realities. Despite the heavy heat of Beijing's summer, there was no AC, not even fans. Halls were dark. Not one good microphone was available for interviews in the field. The one copy machine in the building was for exclusive use by top leaders in Central Broadcasting, the super-agency that ran both domestic and overseas radio and TV. There was also the foreign currency problem.

"I understand it is expensive," Leader Ma said. Nervous and shy, he twisted in his chair and repeatedly looked away as he spoke. "We could tap off the machines at Xinhua."

"I think that might be illegal." I immediately realized how irrelevant my comment was in the People's Republic.

"Oh, I did not think of that." Ma chortled awkwardly, his mouth twisting mischievously to the side of his face as he smiled. Suddenly, he was serious again. "If we got the machines, could you teach us how to use them? Would we be able to learn how to use them?" His tone was tentative, but he was searching my face.

"Sure, that's easy. It only takes a few minutes to learn to operate them. Look, since you have only one wire service now, it would certainly provide a broader range of news if you had others, particularly American and European. The real problem is that those machines produce huge volumes of information. Who is going to read all that information quickly? And more important, who's going to make the decision about how to use that news?"

Even though I had only been there a few weeks, I already understood something about the torpor of the working style and system. There were already hints at taboo subjects and perspectives.

"I never see anyone in the department reading much English. In my classes, the comrades seem unwilling or unable to read a short article in a week. Those machines require a lot of quick scanning. If it's for the education of staff, how will they manage all of that information?"

"I did not think of that," Leader Ma giggled again, completely unselfconsciously. "You are right."

It was an improbable conversation anywhere, perhaps, but especially in China, where technology and science hovered as a new cosmology over a land where the majority of people still did almost everything with their hands, where a billion hearts and minds had been enlightened by the politics of self-reliance and communal strength, not by the philosophers of industrial progress, and where the question of who made decisions produced paralysis because those bodies and souls had been damaged by the cruel changes of ideological winds. I had already learned this much by the end of my first month in Beijing.

I, who had come from the city of frantic speed, from a culture of risk taking, from a profession of instantaneous history and Jurassic egos, at first thought the decision-making sludge at Radio Beijing was a result of 2,000 years of bureaucratic practice. "You must be patient," my coworkers told me time and again. Soon I would understand the overlay of thirty years of tacking between two lines. One line, usually associated with Mao, called for more political participation, retribution for lack of ideological purity and social revolution combined with slower industrial development. The other line, associated with Deng Xiaoping, argued for faster industrialization and more centralized control. My understanding of this tacking would become more complex in the years ahead.

Meanwhile, Ma and I shared a shrug and a smile together. I never heard anything more about the wire services.

Roughly forty minutes of the broadcast hour was devoted to long features under snappy program titles like *China in Construction*, *Culture in China* and *Travel Talk*. Every morning I faced a stack of freshly translated scripts on "friendship" and "modernization," two major themes of the broadcasts. Reports of scientific and cultural exchanges underscored China's policy of friendship with mostly Western countries. Proof that Deng Xiaoping's new Four Modernizations policy was in full swing was provided by reports on the improvement in kumquat production in Hubei, the increasing numbers of hydroelectric power stations, the use of lasers in medical operations and the greater availability of TV sets and sewing machines.

"Friendship" was also the hidden agenda behind *Travel Talk*, a regular program enticing "foreign friends" to tour China's "scenic" and "historic" spots to look at "relics" and "breathtaking sites."

A third theme dominated the news stories: anti-Soviet hegemonism. One common genre of news story—I called it "banquet news"—combined both friendship and anti-Soviet hegemonism. At these endless banquets, Chinese government officials gave speeches to visiting envoys of foreign governments about the threat to security posed by the Soviet Union and the importance of friendship between the two assembled parties.

Of greater interest to me were the rare reports on social issues, like improvements in education. One script revealed that TV university had become popular. Giant halls filled with TV monitors broadcast classes for millions of young people—now in their twenties and thirties—who had missed out on high school and university during the Cultural Revolution, when many schools had been closed, or taught only Mao's *Little Red Book*.

In the course of Radio Beijing's broadcast hour, peasants were rarely mentioned. In 1980, eighty percent of the Chinese were peasants.

During my first class on broadcast journalism, I discovered that most of the staff had never written anything original in English and they had no reportorial skills. Some who had worked in the department for more than twenty years had never conducted an interview. None of the staff had chosen to be broadcast journalists. Instead, they had been assigned to this job after graduating from language schools in Guangzhou, Shanghai or Beijing. There was little job choice or mobility. Upon graduating from middle school or university, people were assigned to a work unit, usually for life.

Since the staff were mostly translators, I kept asking, who wrote these atrocious scripts? Responses were vague.

For my classes, I began taking notes on the finished programs. Most scripts contained all the classic pitfalls of radio journalism: long, complicated sentences, unnecessary use of the past tense and passive voice, too many statistics and lists. The formal language and print style ensured lifeless delivery. The overall effect was like listening to magazine articles read aloud. In fact, program segments usually began with "This is an article about..."—a formula that I soon traced to its source.

Foreigners working in China were all advised to bring shortwave radios to accompany our new life. What a novelty it was for me, fiddling with dials to bring in buzzing stations flung around the globe. There was a certain thrill in listening to the idealistic vision put forth by nations that I only knew as colors on a map. And there I found the origin of reading magazine articles on the air—Radio Moscow. Of course. They would have trained the Chinese during their era of influence in the early 1950s. At least, that's how I imagined it. Deadly. Just like their influence on the architecture.

Some feature scripts were copied directly from Chinese publications printed in English, like *Women in China* or *Sports in China*. There was no concept of plagiarism and no copyright laws. The author of the original article would not be credited unless he or she was "a responsible member," as my coworkers were fond of saying. At this naïve stage of my time at Radio Beijing, I could only imagine who these "responsible members" were. Meanwhile, no effort was made to check the accuracy of the original article.

Scripts, whether from magazine articles or the mysterious anonymous elsewhere, were consistently dreadful. They were often simplistic to the point of cant. Occasionally so many questions were left unanswered that I suspected the script might have the opposite of the effect intended.

Since none of the comrades had ever written a script from scratch, I gave an assignment in the first class. All were to write a couple of pages about their Sundays.

Two out of twenty-five handed in a finished assignment. One made hers up.

It was through the trauma that this assignment created that I began to understand something about the private lives or lack of them for my coworkers. They worked a six-day week. While I had Saturday afternoons off, they were required to stay on for political education lectures. Sunday, their one down day, was spent washing clothes by hand, cleaning a cramped apartment, purchasing food and preparing the one special meal of the week. Even in the cities, many residents still carried water from a central faucet in the courtyard. Washing was all done by hand. Few people owned refrigerators, so food needed to be purchased regularly. The lines at the markets were long.

Leader Zhang explained, "The comrades didn't want to write about their Sundays because they fear that you will think they are dull."

The two who did write described idyllic days spent bumping into old friends in the park. One wrote how good it was to go to the park so "life won't be so boring." "Boring" was used regularly in my dealings with the comrades.

Meanwhile, I was left to wonder about the interests of the staff. While they listened to Voice of America every morning, either in Mandarin or in "special English," few of them seemed to have any real interest in radio, in the potential of the medium to educate or inform.

Was their resistance to the writing assignment also a reflection of the gaps in their education, since the younger ones had missed so much academic work during the Cultural Revolution? Or was it a reflection of the Chinese approach to education that was more about rote memorization than creative or critical thinking? Was it the lack of encouragement for individual expression? Was it groupthink? The group over the individual? My interior dialogue led me to ponder how radically different our histories, cultures and consciousness were. I, who came from Canada, had lived and worked for years in the United States—both countries of "can do" immigrants, entrepreneurs, individualists and strivers. Even if Canada produced a kinder social system—social democracy—or valued communal values more, we had still been taught to think critically in school. I was butting up against the diametric opposite of all of that in the English department. How would my skill set work here?

In that first class, I also noticed how exhausted, wary, fearful and self-protective the comrades seemed.

The announcers, too, were puzzling. Some had pleasant enough voices, but there was little indication that they cared about what they were saying. There was no anchor to connect pieces of the program or speak directly to the listener. For years announcers had been nameless, but a few months after I arrived, this changed, to the delight of some longtime listeners. Their general alienation from the material, however, was a reflection of something much deeper that I had yet to grasp.

Some days I wondered about Li Shutian, whose desk bordered mine. I already adored him. His nervous laughter after every statement. His mischievous, corny, old-fashioned sense of humor. He seemed to have little power or status in the department and reported that although he had applied twice for the Party over the past fifteen years, he had not been admitted. Yet Li was designing and writing the scripts and the accompanying textbook for the *Learn to Speak Chinese* program. Some days, as he bent over his desk with a crushed cigarette between his nicotine-stained fingers, I could hear his mind working. I started to call him "Professor Li." He had that kind of scholarly fascination with the English and Chinese languages. I admired his quick perceptions and ability to manipulate the rules of a language that he had never experienced in its native setting.

"Why do Americans say 'Have a nice day'? Are they sincere? Do they genuinely care?"

How could I not be charmed by the person who posed this question? He taught me the equivalent greeting in Mandarin.

"The Chinese usually say '*Shi fan le ma?*' when they bump into each other. It means 'Have you eaten?'"

My turn to ask about sincerity. But it made sense in a culture where food might be scarce. Where drought and hunger had been regular occurrences.

Professor Li became my unofficial Mandarin teacher. And one day, in those first couple of weeks, he lit a brilliant sparkler in the office to relieve me from the drudgery of yet another script about a geology conference on the Qinghai Tibet Plateau.

IN ADDITION to the broadcast journalism class, I was asked to conduct workshops on American media and society. Partly it was meant to improve the staff's English but also to enlighten them about their new target audience— North Americans. Although their signal had reached around the globe before, they now cared about reaching that strange mob on the other side of the Pacific with something other than slogans from the Cultural Revolution.

Since Liberation in 1949, there had been little or no contact with the US or Canada. Both countries recognized the Republic of China on Taiwan—a creation of Chiang Kai-shek—as the legitimate government, and both countries had fought China during the Korean War. Then, through a twist of geopolitical alliances during the height of the Cold War, Canada and the US began to see an advantage in cozying up to the Chinese. Canada recognized the PRC for the first time in 1970. Two years later Nixon made his historic trip to Beijing.

Not until the end of the Cultural Revolution in 1976 did China begin gingerly taking steps toward real US–China exchanges initiated by President Jimmy Carter. The first organized groups of American professionals and scholars began touring China in the mid-'70s. Most of those visitors—including several friends of mine—while eager to hear the "good news" about the Cultural Revolution and New China, also realized they were treated to a highly curated display. Model communes, model factories, model entertainment, model citizens.

If I was appalled by how little the English department staff knew about their audience, I reminded myself how ignorant most Westerners were about China—including my highly educated friends and me.

I was forced to contemplate the meaning of Plato's cave versus Mao's cave. Founding mythologies. Forms rather than substance. Enlightenment. In Plato's cave, characters are staring at the back of the cave watching the shadows on the wall formed by people passing the mouth of the cave in front of a fire holding certain objects. People staring at those shadows thought they were real. Only when the protagonists exit the cave and step into the blinding light, which eventually clears, will enlightenment and truth be revealed. One could compare this metaphor to the founding mythology for New China traced to the Long March and the Yan'an caves, where the Party had transformed, embracing a new direction and leadership as well as a commitment to rural, agrarian revolution. Truths about the losses during the Long March and the leadership struggle in the caves, along with the death toll among the landlord and rich peasant class during the organizing of the countryside, were kept in shadows. So perhaps there was a way to compare Mao's cave with Plato's. I wondered if I could find Plato's *Symposium* to reread the part about Plato's cave.

IF I had landed in a country of mysteries and shadows, my colleagues were equally baffled by me. It began with my national identity. I referred to myself as a North American. Born and raised in Canada, I then lived, worked and engaged in social movements in the US for sixteen years as a "green carder." For the Chinese, however, I was Canadian, since that was the country from which my passport was issued, and my Canadian-ness gave me some respectability.

The comrades reminded me repeatedly that Dr. Norman Bethune—a fellow Canadian—was revered as a model Communist in the People's Republic, having "selflessly served the needs of the people." Bethune had trained as a doctor and joined the Communist Party of Canada before working for the Republican cause in Spain, running a mobile blood bank to the front lines. In 1938, he had gone to China to set up battlefield medical services for the anti-Japanese revolutionary forces in Yan'an, where he had trained Chinese nurses and doctors. A year later, he contracted an infection and died. Professor Li informed me that Mao's famous essay about the selflessness and commitment of Bethune—written in 1960—was still required reading for all elementary school children in China. I could only be a disappointment here.

But my challenge was to help them understand the folks north of the Rio Grande. I suspected that the serious motivation problem among the comrades had to do in part with a feeling of alienation from their audience. The Cold War had prevented real knowledge from flowing between East and West. Then, during the Cultural Revolution, any association with Western culture could have led to severe punishment.

Although most of the workers had a satisfactory grasp of formal British English grammar, they had little or no exposure to the living language of English speakers in the New World. The department library offered nothing more recent than a few nineteenth-century British novels. *Newsweek*'s journalistic style was incomprehensible to them. Perhaps a blessing. When I played my radio documentaries and reports to illustrate techniques and provoke discussion, my comrades could not understand the accents of the interviewees: older Russian Jewish immigrants, black Vietnam vets, New York firemen, factory workers of Polish descent, a Nuyorican poet, a Haitian undocumented worker or a Southern domestic.

It wasn't only the difficulty of the voices but also the modes of expression. The assumptions of context. What hubris it was for me to think I could bring this material from home and have it mean anything to my Chinese colleagues.

Another part of the audience problem for the comrades had to do with listener feedback.

"Listeners don't usually say anything about the programming," said Xia Xia (pronounced "Sha Sha" and meaning "glorious sunrise"), a young staffer in the letters section. "They only want their frequency cards confirmed." Xia Xia and her colleagues handled a bewildering pile of listeners' mail.

"Many of our American listeners seem to be fourteen-year-old boys," said Fan Ling ("spirit soul"), looking at me as if I was secretly responsible for this peculiar phenomenon of American culture. Shy and nervous, Ling had the sweet demeanor of a self-conscious teenager, although she was much older.

"In the US, few people have shortwave radios," I explained. "Shortwave has been a hobby with young boys since the 1920s and is part of the fascination with the technology of radio rather than with the content of programming."

Ling looked at me, disappointed, her eyebrows bunching up. I, too, wished I had a sexier or more radical explanation. Since most radios sold in China had shortwave bands, this tiny subculture of shortwave listeners in the land of high tech seemed odd.

"Most Americans listen to radio in their cars while commuting to work," I tried to rationalize. "They want music and news headlines. I, of course, like to think they really want to hear intelligent documentaries, features and interviews." I laughed.

Xia Xia and Ling were eager to show me that, in addition to the steady stream of frequency cards that listeners sent in, there were also puzzling and comical gifts.

"What does this mean?" Ling's smile was tentative as she handed me a postcard of a motel in Palm Springs. I guessed that for someone who has sat in a dreary office six days a week for twenty years or more with periods of chaotic and even violent group confrontations, but without vacations or travel or a family car or a sexual revolution, the image of a shiny motel surrounded by palm trees and signs boasting a pool and TV must have seemed surreal. I laughed but had no answer for her. That postcard looked like an artifact from another planet.

Ling's desk was littered with recent offerings from the other side: photographs of a listener's children, postcards of churches, a package of Big Red chewing gum, a Catholic prayer on stiff paper with gold-leaf trim suitable for framing and a card enclosing a five-dollar bill with a scribbled note: "Go out and buy yourself a drink."

One afternoon, as I sat at my desk editing a script about a model worker who sold buttons in Tianjin, the usual office sounds of slow-clicking typewriters, Mandarin whispers and guttural spitting were suddenly overpowered by the screams of the Sex Pistols. I ran down the hall to trace the source. Walking into one of the large offices, I found eight comrades frozen in their chairs, eyes wide, as if in deep shock, while a tape deck blasted out punk rock.

"It's a gift from an American listener," frowned Leader Ma.

August 27, 1980, Journal:

It's Wednesday night, 9:30. Just finished listening to the wavy whistling, humming and buzzing of Voice of America, Radio Japan, Radio Moscow and Radio Korea. The cicadas have stopped screeching for the day. The erhu player has taken the night off. My next-door neighbor's baby is crying, and I can hear the faint sounds of an old Chinese documentary that is playing on everyone's TV. I'm also listening to my Eric Dolphy cassette, reminding me of another world that is giving me a lot of trouble in dreams.

When I turn the music off, it will be almost silent—few combustion engines in the distance, no garbage trucks, no emergency sirens nor eighty-year-old subways screeching at deafening decibels. No drunken revelers disgorging from a bar. Just stillness and quiet.

Beginning the fourth week and I still cannot pronounce the names of the two main streets near my apartment. That's symptomatic of the degree of foreignness I'm feeling. Language is the great wall, but I am studying.

It's been a historic week. They took down the giant images of Marx, Engels, Lenin and Stalin that loomed over Tiananmen Square. Foreigners refer to this as the exorcism of the real Gang of Four. Images of Mao have also been disappearing. Only one remains in the Square. Meanwhile, the other gang is still being blamed for backwardness, turmoil, disaster and chaos, or what used to be called the

Cultural Revolution.

In the four years since Mao died, what was once the Great Proletarian Cultural Revolution (with caps) became the Cultural Revolution (with caps), then the cultural revolution (no caps), then those ten years of turmoil and chaos. Now, in our radio scripts, this revolutionary and cataclysmic era is simply referred to as "1966–'76."

Earlier tonight I went out for dinner with a twenty-two-year-old student of my Montreal friends who teach in Guangzhou. She's home visiting her family. As we were strolling through Tiananmen Square, I asked her what she thought of them taking down the Big Four. She said, "Oh, they have their reasons for taking them down, and they had their reasons for putting them up." That is about the most reflective answer I've had to a million questions in China.

We ate at a local worker's restaurant. Government-run, of course, like everything. Crowded and noisy—a surprising relief from the controlled monotony of my days. It was also dirty. Some tables were bare, some had soiled plastic cloths. You get your own plates and chopsticks, but there are not enough chairs, so people stand at the table and eat, or they stand behind those already sitting, poised to grab the chair as soon as the lucky seated one finishes. They eat furiously without dropping anything from their chopsticks! Not even a slippery fried peanut! No thought of lingering over a meal to chat or savor the food or ambiance.

However, some young men—in their cerulean-blue cotton factory overalls— were getting drunk on beer served in big plastic pitchers. Two men with flushed faces played a finger game, calling out numbers while throwing out fingers in a steady rhythm that grew louder and louder. The winner always slugged more beer. From their crimson cheeks I gather the loser does, too.

Customers spit bones onto the tables, shoved with sharp elbows in lineups at the counter, waving their money and ration tickets at the service people to get attention. A riot of sound and movement. And it's fast. It began at 5:30 and by 7 p.m. the food had run out and chairs were stacked on tables.

It's not terribly enjoyable. Not even for anthropological purposes.

When employees cannot be fired because of the "iron rice bowl"—a guaranteed job for life—or when waitresses don't make decent salaries or tips, when there is no owner who stands to make a profit from providing services, why bother to make the place pleasing or have enough food? Aaaahhhh, for a little private enterprise and petit bourgeois fussing! What happened to "serving the people"? Does capitalism serve the people better? Not what I used to think.

And there's a shortage of beer in Beijing this summer. No one seems to know why. Too bad, because it's one of the seven words I know in Mandarin. Seems *funny that on BBC this morning they reported that British Columbia, Canada also has a beer shortage this summer! Must be other forces besides capitalism and socialism at work? Or play?*

After our dinner we went to the Beijing Hotel to take film to be developed. For the second time tonight, this young Chinese citizen had to fill in lengthy forms to enter a building. The first time was at my apartment. This is just a hint at the control mechanisms to keep the Chinese from fraternizing with foreigners.

So now I'm listening to Coltrane and wondering how to share this life of elusive flashes, rumor and information vacuum. Shortwave is my major source of news. There are no foreign newspapers.

THE REAL conundrum was that although I worked in a news and information agency, none of my coworkers spoke to me about anything going on in Beijing, the country or the world. You might have thought that the Gdańsk ship workers' strike would have meaning. Perhaps it was too dangerous for the Radio Beijing editors to comment on. All those hijackings of American commercial planes to Cuba by disgruntled Cuban refugees—seven so far? You'd think that would have propaganda value here, but given that Cuba was in the Soviet circle, they were enemies, so no mention. You might have thought that Israel annexing Jerusalem as its capital and Saudi Arabia, Iraq and Morocco threatening attacks might be a safe story. The World Bank just reported that the economic reality of third-world countries was bleak, as poverty was on the rise. Nobody at the office commented about any of this. Our scripts were silent on these world matters.

When I asked my coworkers questions about news events, the response was usually silence or giggles. At least they didn't turn and walk away like they did when I asked about what happened during the Cultural Revolution. What I was getting from my comrades was trivial. While I was concerned about the recent conflicts at the Democratic Convention concerning Carter's planks on abortion, the ERA, the Kennedy jobs program and health care, at Radio Beijing there was an information void. I had been trying to get different comrades, especially those who needed to exercise their English, to translate the *People's Daily* for me as a way to indicate that I needed information and they needed practice. They did it with so much distress that I had stopped asking. I tried to explain that reporters and producers needed a range of sources and discussions about issues and events, that it was vital for the development of the staff's language skills and consequently for the programming to discuss current events in English. Finally, Shadow Zhang came into the office and volunteered a piece of news: a Japanese woman had given birth to a fourteen-pound baby!

So while there were rumblings of big politics dancing in the wings in China and the US, I polished scripts about pigeon clubs in Shanghai. According to our radio reports, "backwardness" was the problem, devotion to the Four Modernizations—in agriculture, industry, national defense as well as science and technology—was the solution. Every place in China was "beautiful" and all roads led to "friendship."

I began to worry that I would grow very stupid in Beijing.

The People's Congress—the closest thing to a legislative body of representatives—would be opening in a few days at the Great Hall of the People, and for the first time foreign reporters would be allowed to go to a few of the early meetings where position papers were read. Radio Beijing's English department was going to send two comrades who had never covered an event before. Another colleague would interview a few delegates, also a first for her. It was all highly controlled.

After the flurry of questions during my first week, by the end of August no one asked me about anything, even though there was a presidential campaign going on in the US and President Carter was bogged down with the Iranian hostage crisis. Nothing. Not even about Ronald Reagan sending his VP candidate to Beijing to clarify his statements about commitment to Taiwan. No acknowledgement of any of it at Radio Beijing. Were they reading my letters? Had I revealed too much about their queries at the beginning? Other foreigners insisted that all of our telephones were bugged and letters read. I had a difficult time accepting that, hence I kept writing long, garrulous letters.

I also continued editing atrocious scripts. One day, while searching for one of my colleagues in our labyrinthine building, I stumbled into an interior room billowing cigarette smoke, littered with desks, clacking typewriters and men in shorts and sleeveless t-shirts pecking away at the keys. These, I was told, were the editors—"responsible members." They churned out the feature scripts to be translated into forty-nine languages. After only a month on the job, I blamed most of our problems on this group of serious-looking comrades.

Our efforts to send scripts back to the editors for more information were futile. If it was a local story, Leader Zhang, along with the translator, would spend hours tracing down more information at my request. The result was usually a remarkable improvement over the original. One of the puzzles for me was why this group of "responsible members" was permitted to continue churning out such horrible material.

It would be months before I understood the real-life journey of a Radio Beijing script and its place in the overall policy and propaganda machine in China.

August 29, 1980, Journal:

It's still very hot. Smart ones sit at their desk all day with hand fans. I can't figure out how to type and hold a hand fan. The special electric foreign experts' fan can't be used because it blows our papers all over the room. Today it's gloomier than ever. It rained earlier, and the hallways turned black. Outside, in the yard, the coal mountains get higher. Sand and lime, constantly sifted, are perpetually carted around.

Another extraordinary sighting—I was standing at my office window the other day and watched the People's Liberation Army unit, which seems to live on our grounds, doing bootcamp training in the dust below. Crawling on their stomachs with their rifles. I literally walked over and around them when I went out to the gate. Imagine if you had a division of the military practicing maneuvers outside CBS or NBC along Sixth Avenue. I'm wondering what war they are preparing for...?

Someone said I may have to send my rolls of film to Hong Kong to get them developed. Hong Kong—the service center for mainland China. My fridge will come from HK soon. Like all appliances, it is expensive—$400 US in the Friendship Store. That's a month's salary for me. And yet they sell them cheaper to foreigners. For a Chinese it would be more than a year's salary! But the locals are into TVs, not fridges.

Although my apartment has no kitchen, I need to cook and prepare some food for myself. I cut vegetables on my desk, cook simple things on a hot plate and wash dishes in the bathtub. I can buy milk and yogurt from the dining room. But everything rots and sours. So I need that HK fridge. Meat is bad and expensive. Chicken and fish are also expensive.

I also need to replace this portable typewriter that I picked up in Paris without realizing it has a European keyboard. Another item on the checklist for Hong Kong. Portable typewriters?! I cannot believe that's what I'm working on. At the office and home. Not since 1962!

I'm frustrated about Shadow Zhang. Everything I need I have to ask her for. If I talk to my apartment building interpreter about something I need, he contacts her. At the office, she makes my telephone calls. And she receives my telephone calls. No private life.

There's hope. Moon Festival is coming!

MY NIGHT-TIME reading was reminding me that the prescient idea for Mao was that everyone should learn from peasants and manual laborers. To be a worker-peasant-soldier was the epitome of right thinking, especially during the Cultural Revolution. It was Mao's way to challenge the overwhelming tendency in Chinese society toward bureaucracy.

That bureaucracy had traditionally consisted of intellectuals and literary types whose role was to mediate life between the ruler and the ruled to ensure that the ethics of Confucianism endured. Under Mao, that critical role—which might have challenged the power of the Communist Party—had been eliminated through persecution and class struggle or thought reform.

Mao's mistrust of intellectuals and professionals partly explained the Sino-Soviet split in the late 1950s. He had felt threatened by the power of the Soviet technocrats; in his view, everyone in China should learn from the commonest of laborers, from the peasants, while accepting leadership and authority from the Communist Party.

In 1980, the engineers were coming back—literally. They were coming back to Beijing from their rural banishment. I learned that most of the staff at Radio Beijing, like all urban intellectual workers and students, had been "sent down" to the countryside during the Cultural Revolution. Many students and young people had spent years working on communes and in factories far away from their homes in Beijing. The English department staff had taken turns spending one or two years at a time on communes in the provinces working in the fields, emptying latrines and feeding pigs.

Every day I was witnessing the effects of thirty years of political struggle. While I understood that this opportunity to work in such an agency in China would lead me on an extraordinary journey, I was also too close to the mind-bending routine and the sluggish, alienated work ethic among many of my colleagues to be able to stand back and see beneath it all.

Despite my concerns about putting this effort into a pathetic propaganda agency, I also recognized something in my character. I was trained by working-class Depression-era parents to put everything into the job at hand. Whether it was picking blueberries at age thirteen, waitressing at fourteen, making donuts at sixteen, being a telephone operator, a receptionist and a ballroom dance partner at seventeen or typing purchase orders at nineteen, I worked with diligence and enthusiasm. Executive secretary, researcher. Yes, I bored easily and kept moving. When I discovered the magic of radio and the satisfaction of working for political change, I worked even harder—that old Protestant work ethic was ground into my bone marrow. I was facing two years at Radio

Beijing, so I threw myself rigorously into the work. Trying to take it seriously. I didn't know any better.

So why weren't people working their guts out for their socialist vision in China? They had made a revolution! What happened?

Another frustration was gathering steam. I had wanted to document my experiences through regular reports by audio cassette to my colleagues at NPR in New York. Margot Adler had encouraged me to think about this and offered to edit them for broadcast on *All Things Considered*. There was already too much to write about, and it was all too confusing and overwhelming. I didn't know where to start. A China scholar friend in New York had warned me: "You either write a book after the first two weeks when you know nothing. Or it will take you ten years, because you know too much and you still won't trust what you think you know."

Beijing, 1980

Chapter Five

We Have Friends All Over the World
我们的朋友遍天下

As August's stifling heat morphed into September's clear blue skies, I bicycled at the end of every work day and on Sundays in search of something beyond the stupefying routines and scripts of Radio Beijing. I needed to prove there was something deeper and richer than my first dreary impressions of the city. A universe of surprising expression. A hidden sensibility.

Some days I was an explorer consulting my map. Yes, a map. Precious, since they were considered state secrets. Although crude, mine outlined the basic coordinates of the city. Streets and place names were all in characters—ideograms—which I had no ability to decipher. I could not *name* anything. Foreigners who had been in Beijing longer said that the Chinese had purposely made incorrect entries on the map to keep outsiders from learning the details of the grand design. But plotting intentional mistakes on maps was an idiosyncrasy of all cartographers that helped them identify maps as their own and perhaps claim copyright. I pedaled on.

From my bike I studied the course of a single alley—called a *hutong*—noting its interconnections with other *hutong*. Professor Li, my office mate, explained that the city was once a labyrinth of these alleys originally created by the exterior walls of courtyard residences. Since Liberation, the building of a ring road and new construction had played havoc with this iconic network of fine veins. (In another twenty-five years, this signifying network would almost disappear, in one case replaced by a Disneyesque stage set built just before the Olympic Games in 2008.)

During the Ming Dynasty, people of higher social class built their fancy mansions along the east/west axis, with the Forbidden City as center.

"The original courtyard residents wanted a gate facing south," Professor Li explained to me.

The closer they were to the center, the more affluent or important they were. The commoners, merchants and artisans built along the north/south axis, farther from the center. Since Liberation, the fancy courtyard houses had been divided time and again to shelter more families. I had glimpsed that congestion from my bicycle.

It was the networks of *hutong* near the Drum and Bell Tower north and west of the Forbidden City and those south of Tiananmen that I returned to again and again. These veins felt like a schematic into the heart of the city.

Some days I felt like a sociologist documenting the new street trades—entrepreneurs who had set up shop on the sidewalks: the shoe repairmen with their little stools, simple implements and jagged pieces of grungy leather; the tin man shaping useful items from recycled metal; the old woman who parked her sewing machine near the curb to mend those plastic zippered tote bags everyone carried. These were the tiny stirrings of private enterprise. Tentative experiments of Deng's Four Modernizations at the grassroots level. In this case on the hard earth or concrete sidewalk.

August 20, 1980 Journal:

Beijing is all sensual for me. Since I cannot speak, my eyes, ears and nose are working in overdrive. I am seeing more. Among my fellow cyclists, some have little WWII-era sidecars, where an infant face peers out of soft plastic windows. One bike is stacked in the back with leeks. A tag of fatty meat is mashed under a fender clamp. No wrapping paper. A Peking opera whines from a cassette deck dangling from a handlebar. The bicyclist sings along to the aria.

Sinewy legs push down hard and slow on the pedals of three-wheel bikes with platforms hauling loads of shoe boxes or a woman with her arms draped around a box marked "Black and White TV" in English. Even two-wheel bikes carry impossible cargos—multiple armchairs, a sewing machine, a table, a double bed!

I am distinguishing scents and odors now. The fecund smell of the wet, compacted clay after the summer rains, and now the dust as the winds clear the skies. The bitter burning of coal pollution, the strong hit of the public latrines on every block overwhelming the finer scent of garlic shoots mingling with cilantro passing by on bikes.

Weaving around the cyclists on the main arteries felt like the closest thing to walking the streets of Manhattan, watching the ebb and flow of humanity pedal by. What at first I perceived as passive resistance I now appreciated as survival. Bicyclists commuted long distances between work and home. In the heat and dust, breathing in coal pollution, a steady, slow pace made sense.

Deeper pleasures came from my solitary night riding. Although Professor Li and some of the other comrades had cautioned me that the streets at night were dangerous, they would not specify why. The possibility of danger excited me, since everything felt so regimented and controlled. I longed for a little unpredictable evil lurking.

Night riding was serene. The traffic was thinner, and I could look at the Chinese without them noticing me first. In daylight I had to keep moving. If I stopped in the street to photograph or just to peruse the scene, I drew a crowd.

Once, while bicycling around the old Qianmen shopping district, I stopped to buy a soda. Since there was no place to sit, I squatted, leaning against the front of a building. A crowd of about thirty pressed in closer and closer to watch me drain the bottle. Open-mouth gawking. I felt repulsion. But then I tried to imagine what I looked like to them—a tall, fair-skinned woman with a huge mop of red hair, a big nose—all of us foreigners were referred to as "big noses"—pink pants, a purple t-shirt and blue sneakers. I tried to imagine the conversations over dinner that night: "Is that who we're going to fight the Russians with?"

On an excursion to one of the new experimental peasant free markets— where they could sell their privately grown produce—the crowds jostled me and I felt taunted by the relentless gaping. By then I recognized the words children shouted at me everywhere: *"Waiguoren! Laowai!"* Foreigner. Outsider.

Only at night off the main avenues could I find the anonymity that was a daily routine on the streets of Manhattan. Down unlit alleys, I could see into windows of textile workshops or a bakery to watch workers mold doughy *baozi*—those large Beijing dumplings. I was invisible. Funny how I had no guilt about being the observer, the voyeur, the gawker. But when the dynamic flipped, I became agitated, uncomfortable, even incensed. Unconscious of the contradiction, I continued with my righteous observations as if I needed to devour with all of my senses to understand anything about where I was.

On those warm summer evenings, I watched middle-aged couples stroll along the main avenues, partly obscured by the shadows from trees. Young teenagers squatted under a street lamp, reading and reciting English. Older women hobbled on previously bound feet before lingering on the overpass to play with toddlers. Men with tired faces squatted along the curb, staring aimlessly into the orange glow of the street lights, sucking slow and hard on bitter-smelling cigarettes.

One early September evening with a nearly full moon, I was almost delirious with the vision of a sky sparkling like a glitter ceiling. In ten days or so, the country would celebrate the Moon Festival. Store counters were already heaped with moon cakes that I had been gorging on. Flaky pastry buns stuffed with sweet bean paste, nuts and lotus seeds. The Beijing version, Professor Li said, was flavored with hawthorn and wisteria.

The Moon Festival looms large in Chinese consciousness—linked to the fall equinox, with all its meaning for peasants. According to Comrade Yan, who sat behind me at the office, "The moon is so full then, so large, so close that the goddess Chang Er can be seen dancing on its surface." She chuckled and continued. "It's when poets wrote exquisite poems about drinking fine wine with beautiful women while searching for Chang Er in that brilliant globe."

Yan intrigued me. She produced the best English translations in the department—graceful, literate. I was curious about her because she was old enough to have been educated before the Cultural Revolution. She was very quiet and reserved, so I didn't feel free to ask her directly what she had experienced during the anti-intellectual movements of the past two decades. But I sensed that she might once have had literary ambitions.

On that particular September evening, after returning from another nocturnal bike ride, I sat on the stairs in front of the foreign experts' building, feeling the moon on my face, listening to the bristling of the poplar trees along the driveway and watching Victor pace.

Every night between 10 and 11 p.m., Victor was out here treading the concrete squares of the driveway, from the front door of our apartment building to the hut where the PLA soldier stood with his rifle. Back and forth, up and down, Victor paced. The teenage daughters of my Malaysian neighbors often played guitar at this hour, singing Joan Baez songs in their faint, high voices. Without their music, Victor's sleepwalk felt leaden.

Victor was an exile. Short, shy and in his forties, he lived alone. Originally from Santiago, Chile, where he taught Marxist economics, Victor now worked in the Spanish language department of Radio Beijing. He sought refuge there following the coup in Chile that deposed Allende's democratically elected regime. Pinochet and the military were in power in his home country, the Chicago boys had privatized the economy and a new constitution ensured the military would stay in control. Victor's friends disappeared, were imprisoned, were tortured or went into exile. It was ironic that he sought refuge in China, whose foreign policy now embraced the dictatorship of Augusto Pinochet because it was anti-Soviet. Any enemy of the Soviet Union was a friend of China's. And because his own government was his enemy, Victor could not make his presence known to the Chilean consulate in Beijing.

Victor was unhinged in the world without his country, culture, friends...or family. Bahdra said his wife left three years ago. He must have felt as though he'd been erased from history. After seven years in China, he spoke no more than a dozen words of Mandarin. He spoke no English. My tentative kindergarten Spanish elicited a forlorn grimace, then withdrawal. I was saddened by this because I wanted to talk to him about my Chilean friend in New York who had worked to bring the crimes of General Pinochet's coup and regime to light and expose American complicity in the overthrow of Allende.

Jaime Barrios, my friend, was close to Orlando Letelier, who was once Allende's ambassador to the US and one of the highest-ranking members of Allende's cabinet. Letelier was arrested and tortured after the coup. When he later moved to Washington, D.C., he lobbied for Congress to stop loans to Chile. In September 1976, Letelier and his American assistant were assassinated in a car bomb explosion, the work of Pinochet's DINA (secret intelligence service) agents. Jaime's New York friends had worried for his safety, since it was clear that DINA was operating in the US. Jaime was also one of my only New York friends who encouraged my decision to work in China.

Of course, Victor knew Letelier. I wanted to talk about all this with him, but he shied away from the language struggle. Perhaps his experience was too painful, or I represented the very power that had undermined Allende's government. After all, one of the DINA agents involved with Letelier's assassination and later prosecuted was Michael Townley, an ex-CIA operative. Perhaps Victor suspected me of being CIA, too.

Victor kept his head down. I never saw him go anywhere except on the deadly official trips organized by the Foreign Experts Bureau. Apparently there was only one person who occasionally came to visit Victor—an interpreter from the Spanish department. His shadow. Victor's pacing made me want to cry.

Of the dozen families and few singles who shared my apartment building—from South Asia, Africa and Europe—a number lived there in exile. They were Communist Party members who had fled dangerous political conditions in their own countries to seek a vision and safety in China. Some had been living in Beijing for ten or fifteen years. They raised children there.

One neighbor told me that for a decade during the Cultural Revolution all the foreign experts were cut off from almost all social contact with the Chinese. Even though he said the situation was much better, I never saw any Chinese visiting residents in our building. And my neighbors seldom went out. Their kids didn't play with their Chinese counterparts, even though our building was surrounded by hundreds of Chinese families with young children.

I was resistant at first to believing that the policy that forbade relationships between Chinese and foreigners during the Cultural Revolution was still resonating. Surely my neighbors would have had relationships with the Chinese if they spoke Mandarin fluently.

Perhaps the segregation we felt from locals was rooted in Chinese xenophobia. Was it Han chauvinism? After all, the Han ethnic group represented about ninety-five percent of the population. Or was it the lack of cross-cultural social skills, since the Chinese had been cut off from any relationships with Westerners for several decades? Was it mistrust after the century of horrible Western colonialism, when the Europeans had reigned supreme in special zones along China's eastern seaboard? Was it the Cold War or post-Liberation support by many Western nations for Taiwan? Or was it the Chinese Communist Party striving for ideological purity? Perhaps all of those things. I kept remembering that statement from Lu Xun, China's most revered writer, about how the Chinese only looked up to foreigners as gods or down on them as barbarians. Never as equals.

Whether they were circumscribed by privilege, segregated by Han chauvinism or government policy, the lives of my "foreign expert" neighbors seemed intolerably pinched and boring. Since I had come to work at Radio Beijing for two years, looking at their world frightened and saddened me. Only Yanna, a polisher in the Czechoslovakian language department and a neighbor in my building, had enough Mandarin, chutzpah and determination to fraternize with an interesting world of Chinese dissident artists. But Yanna was preparing to leave.

"WE HAVE Friends All Over the World" bragged a huge banner in English in the lobby of the Beijing Hotel. I had only been in Beijing a few weeks before I saw this as a shrill joke. Radio Beijing's scripts also harped on this theme. Friendship. It was a big lie. Although my coworkers were superficially pleasant and cooperative in the work effort, there were only a few words exchanged in any dialogue, especially if one other person was present. They treated me cautiously. I could never seem to move beyond a surface veneer to something more authentic, reflective or revealing of private doubts and fears, fantasies and phobias or jokes, that become the stuff of intimacy or true sharing. And they never referred to a government policy that demanded Chinese not have relationships with foreigners...at least, not in the early weeks of my interactions with them.

This social unease was exacerbated by the general vacuum of information. Nobody ever spoke voluntarily about anything. It was impossible to have a sustained discussion with anyone. I had to keep reminding myself that I worked in a communications institution. The effect became numbing and disorienting.

Initially, I rationalized it as my fault. I didn't speak their language. But then I was hired to ratchet up their English skills. So I felt as if I was in a funhouse of confusing mirrors. My Mandarin learning was stunted by my work schedule in English. Their often-hesitant English inhibited nuanced conversation. But, I suspected, the yawning abyss between us had nothing to do with sharing a language.

My efforts to initiate social situations with my coworkers were usually blunted. The worst part was the truncating of spontaneous gestures. I soon learned, for example, that I could never just walk into one of the offices and say to Liu Hui, whose scripts I edited, "Let's have lunch together today." Nor could I go into the office where another staffer worked and say, "Why don't you and your wife come over to my place for dinner one night this week?"

One day, during the famous Golden Season, I was feeling so high from the early morning sun and crystalline sky that I went into one of the big offices down the hall to invite a couple of the single women comrades to lunch.

"Let's bicycle over to the park and have lunch today," I said. Knowing how important their after-lunch nap was, I quickly added, "You can lie in the sun and sleep."

I was greeted with the usual bewilderment.

"Well, think about it and let me know later."

Within an hour, Shadow Zhang approached my desk to announce, "We understand you would like to go to a park for lunch." She explained that since it was a tradition of the department to go for a fall outing, the department would arrange for it some day that week.

My spontaneous enthusiasm was stifled. The idea was taken over and turned into a group production for the features section of the department... about fifteen people. Pleasant enough, but with section heads and the old

Long March veteran Party leader included, the conversation was guaranteed to never move beyond trivia and cliché. I couldn't help feeling that the translators acted like dutiful children in the presence of their leaders and that the masters of organization had also finessed passive participation and the flattening of fun. It also guaranteed that no comrade would be seen alone with me. The group was protection.

ONE NIGHT, a new face appeared at my apartment door, which I had left open to create a breeze. "Excuse me...hello..."

I turned down Miles Davis' *Round About Midnight* playing on my cassette deck.

"Where do you get laid around here?"

Now, I cannot remember whether I let out a laughing yelp or simply stood there looking stunned. I was working on a charcoal drawing. I wiped the black dust from my hands and ushered this stranger in.

"Hi. I'm Luisa." The husky voice plunked her abundant body into one of my plastic brown armchairs.

I fetched a couple of glasses and poured Luisa some Chinese rum.

"I just arrived to work in the Spanish section."

To my automatic questions she replied with a smoky accent, "I'm Argentine. Jewish. And a poet," as if somehow this identity would explain why she was this far from home. "It's my first day," she continued, "and it looks desperate. What do you do? I mean, what do you do for fun? For your soul?"

I waved my arms around the room. I had only been in Beijing for six weeks and every inch of wall space in my two rooms was covered with drawings of Beijing street scenes. The loads people pumped around on those three-wheeled bikes; the way backs curved or hunched over handlebars; portraits of people squatting at the curb or stretched out, snoozing on the clay boulevard midday; the chiaroscuro in the narrow alleys and doorways that led into the enigmatic world of the Chinese—the world from which I was excluded. My drawings had absorbed a lot of my spiritual energy—or was it libidinal?

I avoided Luisa's questions and ran down the routine in the building: how to get yogurt, milk and eggs from the kitchen, how to avoid eating in the dining room unless you liked lots of oil and overdone meat. "A couple of the hotels have restaurants offering different cuisines. There's Pakistani food at the Qingqiao."

She stared at her drink.

"There's a Sunday morning bus trip to the Friendship Store. Friday nights they organize a bus to take us to movies at the Friendship Hotel..."

Her eyes studied my walls.

"Look," I said, "the real story here is the segregation between foreigners and the Chinese."

Now my eyes were drifting. To a drawing of one of Beijing's eight-foot walls—those walls had become a metaphor for the alienation I was feeling.

Luisa seemed interested only in some privacy and men. I wondered why she chose China. Between sips of rum she told me about her adventurous past. Leaving Argentina during the "dirty war." Love affairs in Spain. Work in Japan where the misogyny was so great that they wouldn't give her birth control pills. Something was missing because this woman was adrift on the planet. But the rum was blurring rational thought. Here, where my synapses were in overdrive with fresh sensations, the wrestling match with a strange language and the nightly cramming of Chinese history, I was having difficulty retrieving details about Argentina's "dirty war." I kept listening. Luisa was provocative, energetic and romantic. Another passionate woman in China.

I recognized more than a little of myself in Luisa. Spontaneity and intensity combined with lunacy—and vulnerability. In New York I would have embraced her, encouraged her friendship, played off of her childlike emotions. But here, now, I was uncomfortable with her. I wanted to cover her up, shut her out. I was saddened by her, afraid for her. Listening to her open and raw sensuality, I realized that I had already begun to construct a carapace to protect myself.

Luisa's opening question, "Where do you get laid around here?" had shocked me. I had never heard a woman pose that query in exactly those words before, despite my generation's sexual revolution and my so-called liberated past. Perhaps she would never pose it in her native language. Sometimes we can blurt things in another idiom that would never feel appropriate in our first and most intimate, nuanced language. But I admired her for it. It was so wild for China and cut straight to the heart of what ailed so many foreigners—and maybe the Chinese for that matter—that I should have laughed hysterically and held her close. I regretted not exploring her past more, but her interests eluded me, and I was already embarking on a tortured soul journey trying to breach that wall to the Chinese. I had not come all this way to invest enormous emotional energies in foreigners, Westerners—even passionate refugees like Luisa.

Within a week, Luisa moved to the Friendship Hotel, "where the action is."

THERE WERE several ghettos for foreigners living in Beijing. Diplomats, journalists and UN types lived together in a luxurious series of high-rise prisons just east of Wangfujing Street and the Beijing Hotel. A few foreign experts, like me, lived at apartment complexes attached to our work units. But most foreign teachers and language polishers hired by the Chinese government, in this one-company country, lived in the giant Friendship Hotel on the far western edge of town.

Youyi Binguan, as the Chinese called the Friendship Hotel, was built during the '50s for the Soviets. When they left, foreign workers from other countries moved in. Behind the walls of this complex, you could find everything from a health clinic to a beauty salon. It was all there. And it was pretty. Trees, grass, rock garden. But it was still an outpatient prison.

It began at the gate attended by at least one rifle-bearing PLA soldier who made sure no Chinese passed without first registering at the guard hut, filling out a form with name and, especially important, work unit—*danwei*— because their *danwei* leaders would be informed of their presence at the guard hut. The Friendship Hotel resident then had to be called to come and fetch the visitor—sometimes a walk of several blocks.

Each apartment building within the grounds also had twenty-four-hour attendants on duty who made it a point to record and watch all who entered and exited. They could also enter any apartment at any time without knocking.

Since a copy of the form that a visitor signed to enter was also handed back at the gate when leaving, the guards knew how long visitors stayed. It was a law that any Chinese visitor could not stay beyond 11:00 p.m.

At the foreign experts' building where I lived—that I now called by its Chinese name, *Zhuanja lou* (pronounced "juanja low")—security was even tighter. Foreigners as well as Chinese had to fill in a lengthy form at the gate explaining their relationship to the resident they were visiting, and parcels were inspected. At night, if I returned home by taxi, the PLA soldier would leap out of his box and block the car, pointing his rifle at us. Faces in the car were searched, so usually I would get out of the car there and walk the rest of the way to the entrance, or everyone would have to fill in a form, even if they were only going to drop me off.

This segregation between the Chinese and me did not come as a total surprise. But nothing could have prepared me for the emotional trauma of living with the surveillance, mistrust and fear that reinforced it.

ABOUT A month after I had arrived, Zhang Wei, my efficient, humorless shadow, invited me to her house for lunch on a Saturday. Despite my conflicted feelings about her, I was thrilled. My ambivalence toward Zhang Wei was entangled with the contradiction between helpfulness and control. I felt it from the beginning. While she exuded the spirit of "serve the people" and expressed impatience with the laziness of some Chinese and dismay for economic and social problems, she didn't feel entirely enthusiastic about my presence. Now, she was inviting me to lunch. I was starved. Not for food, but for a genuine gesture of warmth and curiosity beyond her early hostile question, "Do you hate children?"

Wei explained that she lived with her husband, their young child, her parents and her brother. I knew that housing was crowded. I insisted that she keep it simple. After all, we worked Saturday mornings. I offered to bring something.

That Saturday morning, she didn't show up at the office. Now I knew it was going to be a major production. How could it not be? A foreigner invited to a comrade's home. When I arrived at her apartment at noon, the household was abuzz with preparations. Her brother and his girlfriend were in the bedroom standing over a table erected over a bed, making dozens of dumplings—*jiaozi*.

"Making and eating *jaozi* with friends is a Beijing tradition," Shadow Zhang declared.

As I watched them shape doughy, small circles, then place a spoonful of pork or vegetable filling on one half, then fold over and flute the edges, I thought perhaps I had misread the signs of friendship here in Middle Earth. Who would not be seduced by this tradition? When we sat down to eat, I was instructed to dip the dumplings in a mix of vinegar and hot pepper oil before popping them into my mouth. Of course, I dropped one on the floor and then squirted myself with hot filling from another. I read somewhere that the Chinese secretly enjoy it when foreigners humiliate themselves using chopsticks. I was eager to demonstrate that we North American hipsters were accustomed to eating Chinese food with chopsticks. But maybe not every dumpling. We all laughed at my ineptness. They were the most delicious dumplings I had ever tasted.

Shadow Zhang's husband was busy in a hallway kitchen cooking up a half dozen different dishes. Candied carrots, pickled lotus roots. It was more like a banquet than a lunch. I felt so honored yet guilty. It was all too extravagant. I had some idea how stressed my colleagues' economic situations were. Although I hadn't seen any interiors yet to evaluate whether this housing was typical or not, from my walk to work I could see broken windows and bare lightbulbs dangling. From the numbers of things stacked on the window sills, I knew space was cramped, conditions strained. I presumed that the office or Party had helped Zhang Wei with the expense of this feast. And my guilt was assuaged by the obvious reality that there would be leftovers to last them for several days.

Zhang Wei's family was gracious and cheerful, yet it was impossible to go beyond surfaces. Just like the office exchanges. What did I expect? I didn't share a language with her family. I was such an oddity. A single, thirty-seven-year-old woman without children traveling from the former Number One enemy camp all the way to Beijing to work for a couple of years. I had to be suspect—or a weirdo.

When I asked Shadow Zhang where her father was, she simply said he was working. That seemed strange, given the conformity of schedules and the uniform two-hour lunch break along with the preparation of such an abundant meal.

"What kind of work does your father do?" I asked.

Zhang Wei paused and screwed up her forehead. "Public Security Bureau," she said.

"Is that like the municipal or state police, or is it more an investigative federal police?" I queried, searching for the North American equivalent.

She hesitated again, wrinkled up her nose and said, "I don't know."

Her response cast a strange shadow over the lunch. My imagination could now run wild. Zhang Wei, highly intelligent, earnest Party member whose privilege of going off to England to study at the end of the Cultural Revolution probably stemmed from a father who was a high cadre working at the Public Security Bureau. So high up in the Party hierarchy that he could not be seen by a Westerner. Was I suspected of being a spy who might ask questions or take his photograph? Or maybe it was simply more innocent. He worked shifts. I would never know. Since I would not be invited to the home of another colleague for a long time, I interpreted that particular invitation as an official Party-sanctioned event with the most important Party member of the household absent.

ONE EVENING in early September I invited Professor Li and Shadow Zhang and both their mates to my place for dinner. I ordered chicken, pork and vegetable dishes from the building's kitchen, and during my lunch hour I bicycled ten miles back and forth to the Friendship Store on the other side of town to get wine, beer and other treats.

When I opened my door that night, twelve people were standing there—all from the features section of the department. I was flummoxed. I had to quickly order more food from the dining room and find chairs downstairs. But I was the only flustered one. For my coworkers, this situation, the rearrangement of furniture and space, was not problematic, as I would soon learn, because their tiny rooms were crowded. They used boxes and beds to sit, shared kitchens in the hallway, ate holding a bowl in their hands. Perhaps it was us Westerners who were too uptight about "conditions" or the aesthetic for entertaining.

The comrades weren't bothered by any of my last-minute frenzy to get more food or chairs. They seemed perfectly content to get a peek at my luxurious apartment and have a free meal of chicken and meat that would be too expensive for them.

Was this sudden appearance of twelve dinner guests, when I had invited two colleagues and their mates, a form of protection against being perceived as getting too close to a foreigner? The conversation remained superficial, and these mostly uninvited guests stayed only long enough to eat. It was all over before I could ask a meaningful question.

FOR THE first time in my life, the culture I was infused with was brought into question. Or highlighted with a yellow felt-tip pen. I, who had come from a society hooked on individualism and intimacy, wanted to have one-on-one relationships with a few of my Chinese coworkers. They, on the other hand, had a strong ideological and political history of collective organization. I understood that if I were to share some of my privileges as a foreign worker with one or two of the group, it would be considered unfair. And perhaps corrupting. Was I supposed to only engage with my colleagues as a community? A collective? But somehow social gatherings of the entire department only duplicated the social rigidities and cautiousness of the office.

Perhaps I was overly hung up about intimacy. Perhaps I was simply missing my close friends at home and honest, heartfelt conversation. Humor! A real connection with one human being. I was beginning to feel it would never be possible with the comrades from the office.

The prospects of friendship at Radio Beijing looked hopeless.

So I kept pumping bike. Thirty-five minutes of hard pedaling to the northwest university district took me to the Friendship Hotel to visit new

American friends—like Ron Dorfman, a journalist from Chicago. One of the founders of the *Chicago Journalism Review*, he was "polishing" at *China Reconstructs*. Then there was Peter Kwong, a Chinese-American historian from Hunter College in New York, whom I had met just before heading to China. He was teaching at one of the local colleges. At the Friendship Hotel we drank beer on the roof and traded stories about our frustrations with the skill levels of our young colleagues—mostly brought on by the collapse of schooling during the Cultural Revolution.

Through Ron I met Janet Yang, a Chinese-American from Scarsdale, New York, who had perfected her Mandarin at Middlebury College before heading to Beijing. Janet's parents, like Peter's, were originally from Shanghai. In China, she was translating and polishing for the Foreign Language Press. She lived in a workers' dormitory with a boyfriend, Wang Yaping, a local writer.

Chinese-Americans experienced a different reality in Beijing. They had more access to local Chinese citizens, naturally, but then, surprisingly, they were also paid less for their work than were Caucasian foreign experts and sometimes treated very shabbily when mistaken for native Chinese entering "foreigner" establishments, like restaurants, hotels and the Friendship Store. They always carried their passports.

At Ron's apartment we met his neighbor, Ahmed Kheir, a poet and founder of the Sudanese Communist Party who had lived in exile in Beijing since the 1960s. He was a polisher at the *Beijing Review*. A once handsome and brilliant man—according to my Sri Lankan neighbor, Bahdra, who knew him from international peace conferences in the '60s—he was now politically and intellectually diminished and a notoriously heavy drinker. She said he'd been in Beijing too long.

Sometime in September, Jane Eng, another foreign expert working in the English department, announced she was getting married. Chinese-American, Jane was a progressive attorney who had worked in New York's Chinatown. She spoke fluent Mandarin, lived in a Chinese dormitory, dressed native, hung out with locals and had chosen a *Beijingren* fiancé.

I decided to have a shower for her, since it would be an opportunity to invite the women from the department and—maybe—have some fun. *Perhaps, I thought, my female coworkers will shed their office armor once they are freed from its dulling context.* Sitting in a circle in my living room, balancing plates of food, they presented Jane with a gift and then acted out a Chinese ritual of pestering the bride to tell something about the romance: "Where did you meet? When did you first go out? When did you first kiss?" No, they didn't ask the obvious question that would flow from this in the West.

Jane played out the adolescent fun of it. I was hopeful that this playfulness would lead to relaxed conversation of a more meaningful kind.

But, like other Chinese social functions that were to follow, the speed and fury of the eating and leaving was dizzying. Within an hour everyone was gone. Every last morsel of food and drink was devoured. Nobody lingered to engage in conversation. Nobody used the opportunity to ask how I was managing to settle in or to invite me to their home and meet their families, even as a courtesy gesture. Office decorum was maintained except for the silliness. Two of the women came with their hair in rollers. A breaking trend.

If I found the comrades' cautiousness with me exasperating, I detected that they were also guarded with each other. At night I was reading newly translated short stories from the recent "scar" literature—tales of persecution of intellectuals, professionals and bureaucrats during the Cultural Revolution. The revelations were shocking—studies, careers and lives interrupted by banishment to hard labor in the remote countryside, husbands and wives separated from each other for years on end, children turning against their parents.

These new narratives did not reveal the worst physical crimes: banishment to prison labor camps, deaths from beatings, denial of medical care or abuses leading to suicide. That information was coming to me through Chinese-American acquaintances. Young Red Guards had attacked their parents. Husbands turned on wives. Students persecuted their professors and teachers. Workers tortured their bosses. Stories of these crimes were beginning to ooze out. Most insidious was the "ratting" or reporting on colleagues, friends, family and neighbors that had become a disease in the body politic.

I wondered how all this played out in the cosmos of the English department. Did the comrades harbor resentments toward each other after ruthless political battles and factional fighting during the Cultural Revolution that left enemies sitting next to each other in crowded offices for years with no hope of a job transfer? I tried to imagine criticism sessions when one individual was singled out for harsh interrogation and accusations while wearing a dunce hat and being held in the "airplane" position—bent over with his or her hands tied to a bar in the back. Class struggle—it was called. Thought reform. Purification. Confessions were demanded. Did anyone jump out a window at Radio Beijing like they did at Beijing University or *China Reconstructs,* where it was reported bodies were either dumped or people leapt to their deaths? Even Deng Xiaoping's son was left a paraplegic after being forced to jump from a high window. What had happened at Radio Beijing?

Why hadn't I asked Sidney Rittenberg more specific questions? My foreign expert neighbors who had lived here during the Cultural Revolution explained that Rittenberg himself became too close to Chinese power at the beginning of the Cultural Revolution—siding with one faction at Radio Beijing.

"That's why he ended up in solitary confinement for ten years," one neighbor explained. "Rittenberg was an idealistic, sloganeering, true believer who came back from shaking Mao's hand one day and suggested his colleagues wash their hands in a bowl of water with him to share in the glory."

Apparently, class struggle turned against Rittenberg, even though he was a Party member or perhaps because of it. Another shocking revelation to foreigners—attacks on Party cadres were endemic during the Cultural Revolution. My neighbors used Rittenberg as an example of how and why foreigners were not trusted.

"You must never get involved with their political movements," warned my neighbor, shaking his head.

It still left the mystery of identifying who were perpetrators and who were victims in the English department. Perhaps they were both. My neighbors mentioned one of the women comrades in the English department, an announcer, as having tried to take over Radio Beijing with Rittenberg. She was very unhappy these days. Perhaps that was why. The tide had turned. I knew she was trying desperately to leave the country. After committing more than thirty years to New China, Rittenberg had left for the US. My neighbors admitted that foreigners couldn't really know what was happening during those years, but it was "wild" and "frightening." They had kept out of it.

The new "Scar" literature also revealed that the persecution of intellectuals began much earlier during anti-Rightist movements in the '50s. Short stories now addressed the damage to families, relationships and careers that had resulted from the Hundred Flowers Movement[2] in the late 1950s. Most of my Western acquaintances—especially the new arrivals—were in a state of shock about these disclosures as the tragic tales tumbled out. Our fantasies about the revolution, about Mao and the Cultural Revolution, imploded. But then few foreign scholars and journalists had access during the previous thirty years to report on these events.

A few weeks after I had hosted the shower for Jane, she held her wedding celebration in the dining room at *Zhuanja lou*. The comrades arrived, ate and drank energetically. Within an hour they were gone. The bacchanalia of Western weddings or the elaborate and bountiful traditions of Chinese banquet weddings in New York felt far away and exotic compared to this stiff, arid, nonevent. Had the battle against decadence during thirty years of revolution sucked the life juice out of what should be the biggest festivity of a lifetime? Was celebration still bourgeois? Was it about the cost? Fiestas didn't have to be expensive to be joyful. Was the cautious restraint a reaction to the bride being a foreigner? A sprinkling of other foreigners would be in attendance. Was the reserve of Chinese guests evidence of their lack of trust toward each other? If they seemed too free and easy with one of the foreign experts, would a comrade report them to their section leader? Having a foreign friend, speaking a foreign language, owning foreign books, speaking too much with a foreigner—all were serious offenses during the Cultural Revolution.

When I went to a reception at the Canadian embassy, one of the consular staff told me I should watch the event carefully. At 5 p.m., he said, they will serve the cake. The Chinese will gobble it down and in fifteen minutes they will be gone. "No conversation of substance or informal ice-breaking. No lingering or relaxing or exploiting the situation for diplomatic purposes," he added. *Definitely*, I thought to myself, *no playfulness.*

From earlier readings about the Chinese Revolution, I remember how Mao encouraged the peasants to *speak bitterness*, to voice their complaints and sufferings—to the landlords, tax collectors and others who oppressed them. *Speaking bitterness* was the essence of class struggle or revolutionary change. It challenged one of the time-honored codes of behavior dictated by the Confucian ideal: to *eat bitterness*, to be non-complaining, to swallow sadness and anger, which may account partially for what Westerners often perceive as Chinese reserve.

Those who were now middle-aged had gone through three decades of class and ideological struggle, rectification, purification, routing out so-called "Rightists" and "enemies" or "black families"—those who may have owned land or worked for the Japanese, a foreign corporation, or the Nationalists before Liberation. Anybody with a whiff of a bourgeois past was labeled a "poisonous weed," a "monster" or a "demon." No wonder the men in the English department all chain-smoked at their desks while one leg bounced neurotically. Who might be labeled a "stinking black" next?

In 1980, it seemed as if Confucian *eating bitterness* was once again a respected virtue, perhaps a necessary response to the excesses of the Cultural Revolution, the last time when *speaking bitterness* was heralded and the furies it unleashed might have led to death.

Then I wondered if the comrades seemed dull and flat not because of eating bitterness but because their spirit was exhausted from thirty years of radical political shifts and fear of persecution with each new political campaign. Were they worn out from years of scapegoating, name-calling and political confrontations with life-shattering consequences? Had these brutal, hostile encounters done something deeper to the creative and playful spirit in the general population? Would I ever know the answers?

Would it matter if I could speak their language? I had learned how to do simple negotiations about directions, order a taxi, explain where I worked and lived. That was it. The only characters I knew were for men's and women's bathrooms and numbers from one to ten. Otherwise, I concentrated on Pinyin, the alphabetization of the characters that indicated how to sound them out, because I desperately needed to talk. And the sound of the language was seducing me. At least, the official version of it on the loudspeakers everywhere. Meanwhile, Professor Li drilled me on the "zhi" sound, and getting my tongue back in my mouth and throat to make that Beijing-accented rolling "r."

IN MID-SEPTEMBER, I began meeting with a group of foreigners in a weekly study group. Most were teaching at local universities or editing at one of the propaganda work units. A few were China scholars, like Nancy Jervis from New York, who taught at the Film Institute. There were also old China Hands—foreigners who had lived in China for decades—like Iona Kramer, a polisher at *China Reconstructs* who came to New China in the early '50s with her American-Chinese husband, a professor at Tsinghua University (the MIT of China). In 1970, they had been put under house arrest for eight years after her husband was accused of being a spy. He was eventually exonerated. Despite that experience, she was still a committed Maoist.

Some of the foreigners and scholars were fluent in Mandarin, like Helmut Opletal from Austria, who had been among the first Western students to study at Beijing University in the early '70s. He had been reporting for German language newspapers and radio.

An eclectic group, we were largely sympathetic to New China. All of us shared a commitment to understand the history, culture and language. Since we each had access to different tidbits of information through our work units and contacts, we pooled our knowledge. Those who could read Mandarin translated important editorials in the *People's Daily* or other Chinese papers.

The new foreign experts in the group felt caught in a frustrating contradiction. The government invited us to work inside Chinese institutions, then prevented us from having authentic relationships with our coworkers. Even those foreigners who had been in Beijing longer told troubling stories about their efforts to befriend individual Chinese. Our frustrations with the social segregation sometimes erupted into rants condemning the entire system.

"SHE'S FIERCE," said Shadow Zhang after Yanna, the Czech foreign expert at Radio Beijing, had been in my office complaining about some bureaucratic idiocy. Yanna's family had witnessed both the Nazi invasion and later the Soviet tanks rolling into Prague. They had fled to Vienna. Now Yanna railed against all forms of authoritarian control and bureaucratic incompetence but most especially against the policy that separated Chinese from foreigners. Her complaints were no different from those of most experts, but her voice was louder and more strident. I knew that Shadow Zhang had given considerable thought to finding the English word "fierce."

When Yanna referred to cadres as "animals," her jaw tightened and her eyes narrowed. I shuddered at the level of hostility she harbored for the Chinese system. I couldn't simply dismiss Yanna because she was also generous and I admired her determination to learn Mandarin and befriend a few interesting Chinese. And she had bucked the system by developing a close friendship with her interpreter from the Czech language department.

I, too, was distressed about things I experienced at Radio Beijing. I, too, was impatient with incompetence, disappointed in the content of the work and troubled by the suspicious atmosphere. But I wasn't ready yet to denounce, to call cadres "animals" or to insult my coworkers. And while I listened to the laments of other foreign experts with my head, my heart rejected the idea that people who work together six days a week will remain strangers because of a policy.

September 15, 1980, Journal:

The sun is sneaking through the poplar tree outside my window now. An English lesson is blaring from a radio across the courtyard. The buzz and waves of Voice of America's early morning News in Special English is humming through the walls from the apartment next door. It's 6 a.m. in Beijing, and I hear the sounds of China awakening from all the four-story buildings around me. I am heading out to do tai chi in a park with Bahdra. A young jogger is exercising in the driveway. The PLA guard shivers, blowing hot breath into his cupped hands, as he greets us outside the guard hut.

It's cool and clear. It'll be another dry and slightly dusty day. By afternoon it will be warm. It's the Golden Season in Beijing.

"SOON THE winds will grow stronger and the dust will be unbearable," Bahdra warned.

Already some people were wearing cotton face masks. Many bicyclists already revealed their long underwear—visible only as a patch of fluorescent fuchsia between the bottom of their trousers and the tops of socks. Clotheslines were flowing with Revlon-pink long johns. What a kinky secret about the Chinese!

Since I arrived in early August, crowds in the streets had gone from slurping slices of melon and spewing out the wet seeds to cracking sunflower shells between their front teeth. The streets and sidewalks—formerly slick with melon seeds—were now strewn with the cracked skins of sunflower kernels. Hands were perpetually cupped around a fistful of seeds and pockets filled with them. A right of passage between summer and fall.

In the quotidian of my Beijing life, I tried not to be sucked downward into the quicksand of my ignorance and frustrations as well as the melancholia for orange juice, Doux de Montagne cheese and very dry, very cold white wine. And maybe rum raisin ice cream.

I tried to take advantage of the two-and-a-half-hour lunch break, writing in my journal, cranking out letters home, studying Chinese so as not to sink into irrelevance. I kept acquiring more language books in some futile effort, as if finding the right one would ignite a torrent of Mandarin spewing from my mouth.

Without language my life was a muddled chain of miscommunication. Like yelling into the wrong end of the megaphone. To explain to the cook in the building's dining hall what I would like, I had to first find then explain it to the building's interpreter, who then interpreted it to the waitress, who then clarified it for the cook. It took thirty minutes to explain I would like a boiled egg a couple of times a week. If the building interpreter didn't understand my request, he would call Shadow Zhang at the office, so then the entire department would know I was asking for a boiled egg sometimes. My comrades at the office ate a garlic-laden noodle soup for breakfast, so my requests must have seemed bizarre.

My days weren't long enough. It took so long to do basic things, like wash dishes in the bathtub, wash everything else by hand in the bathroom sink, iron on my bed, cook on a hotplate, stand in long lines for produce and type on a cranky portable.

Too much time was wasted at the office doing useless work. I began to worry that my talents and skills were atrophying. I could not muster the clarity of thinking to write or the splendid energy to narrate a story for NPR. Reflecting upon what I had been producing before leaving New York, I realized that my life pattern was to turn away just as I was mastering a skill or achieving a new level of creativity. Fear of failure? Fear of success?

Yet I was in the midst of a crash course on Chinese politics. At the Wednesday night study group, we learned that the Party Congress underway downtown had been forging the new policies being pushed by Deng and his faction. That meant nudging out Hua, who had been chosen by Mao as his successor. Hua was resigning as premier, although he was still head of the Party. These were huge and signifying developments. Deng's crowd was calling for more democratic participation at the lower levels, a concerted effort to challenge an encrusted geriatric leadership.

The new economic policies Deng promoted included certain capitalistic measures: rewarding workers for their initiative and productivity, allowing some plants more control over profits and granting more autonomy at the local level. According to the China Hands at our study group, the pressures to make these changes were coming from below—unemployment, a black market and disillusionment with the Party after the manipulations and abuses of the previous two decades. Other problems were holding back the economy, like the shortage of higher-educated workers and management to push development.

Meanwhile, I kept pedaling. Forty minutes of vigorous pumping directly east from Radio Beijing along the Avenue of Eternal Peace, past the Forbidden City, through Tiananmen Square, delivered me to the Friendship Store to buy French wine, English cigarettes, ground beef, tomato sauce and spaghetti. On the return trip, just before Tiananmen Square, I stopped at the Beijing Hotel for *Newsweek* and the famous watering hole—well, the only one—in Beijing: "A milk bar—in the middle of a jewelry store," as Ron put it. There I could get a coffee made from an instant concentrate and chat with a few disgruntled diplomats. I already distinguished between the clusters of foreigners in Beijing. The diplomatic corps were the most unhappy.

"Beijing is one of the dreariest assignments in the world," a diplomat from Ghana told me. "Only Pyongyang in North Korea is worse."

So far I had discovered few, if any, in the diplomatic community who truly cared about China, who persisted in learning the language and mixing with the Chinese. Most seemed only interested in recreating their lifestyle in what they considered a boring village, yet they—along with the UN officers—lived in the most privileged ghetto of all in a heavily guarded compound of modern apartment buildings east of Wangfujing near Ritan Park.

Even within the diplomatic community there were divisions. Race and a wealth gap created a ghetto within a ghetto. The Africans were caught in a confusing situation. For years China's foreign policy was based on solidarity with the Third World and luring Africans from the Soviet sphere, but within China, racism was overt.

It began with ordering a taxi. If I wanted to see friends at the Beijing Hotel bar or the International Club on a Saturday night, or for dinner at one of the few hotel restaurants (there were no private restaurants, only a few pricey government-run ones for high cadres and tourists, and workers' restaurants, which were not conducive to "dining" nor finding wine) I would order a taxi from the one-and-only car service—a government operation, like everything else.

They grilled me. In Mandarin, of course. It was a hilarious and panicky exercise. I rattled off my memorized phrases, repeating them over and over in fear that I wouldn't understand if they interrupted to ask me a question, which they always did.

"*Wo shi Zhanada-ren*"; "I am Canadian."

"*Wo shi Zhuanjia*"; "I am a foreign expert."

"*Guanzuo zai Beijing Diantai, Guangbo Zhu*"; "My work unit is Radio Beijing, Central Broadcasting."

"I live at the foreign experts' building. I'm going to the Beijing Hotel..."

It never occurred to me that the suffering soul on the other end of the crackling phone line might not be able to decipher my tones. And that was the reason they kept barking what sounded like questions to me. After repeating my litany of phrases several times, there was finally an exasperated "*Dui, dui, dui.*" Yes, yes, yes.

The most important bit of info here was my nationality. It was common knowledge that callers identifying themselves as American, Canadian or Japanese received the quickest service. Africans had to wait. They were at the bottom of the list. And yet everyone paid handsomely for this service.

Several African diplomatic acquaintances told me that when they entered the Beijing Hotel with a Chinese friend or interpreter, those Chinese would inevitably receive rough treatment. The Chinese companion might be arrested. In restaurants, Africans were often treated rudely.

There were many fewer single African women in Beijing than men, which created tensions at the International Club and the Minzhu Hotel disco, where a new single foreign woman arriving on the scene would be rushed. It also encouraged Chinese prostitutes. The foreign diplomatic corps in general—largely men—seemed particularly desperate. Another downside to sexist hiring practices.

On my first Saturday at the International Club—at the end of my first week in Beijing—a diplomat from Toga offered me a drink and asked me to dance, calling me "Kale." I barely arrived on the dance floor when he said he would take care of me for two years. I could meet important people, have the key to his apartment along with an "American-style" relationship. He was overbearing and tenacious.

I was rescued from this oppressive entanglement by Ahmed, Ron's neighbor, who then kept bringing me "vodka" drinks. I eventually extricated myself and remembered getting home through the guard's gate, but I awoke in the middle of the night, fully clothed, on top of my bed in a pool of vomit. I could have choked to death. Grain alcohol. Desperate men. I would not be returning to the International Club anytime soon.

Fraternizing with diplomats for the first time in my life was a crash course in global power arrangements. Shortly after arriving I met Ahmoud, a Chad diplomat, at an embassy party and agreed to drive with him one Sunday out to the Fragrant Hills for a walk and then lunch in the city afterward. I felt like a naïve child being offered her first car ride with a stranger—eager to flee my predictable and confined world—yet apprehensive all the same. When Ahmoud arrived at my apartment building, he had another man with him in the car. To my reaction, he quietly explained that Chad was in the midst of a civil war; the other gentleman represented the rebelling faction. It was a complicated scenario between North and South. Libya was supporting rebels from the North while Germany and France were advising his president, since citizens of their countries had been taken hostage by those rebel forces. There was something about not being able to pay their bills at the embassy in Beijing. Now, a representative of that rebel force was sitting in a car I was about to get into—their campaign having been carried right through to their embassies abroad. It felt murky and messy. I disentangled myself from the plan. They drove off. The rebel with a sneer and Ahmoud, a pout.

With my beginner's Mandarin I had a very limited world within which to make friends. Prospects at Radio Beijing looked futile. There was the foreign community, but I had no desire to spend two years in China drinking myself to liver disease in the lobby of the Beijing Hotel or partying every weekend to disco music with a roomful of the dispossessed.

September 19, 1980, Journal:

I believe in my own power to find something here. Spirit. I know I need to study Mandarin, but after being pent up inside a dreary bureaucratic office all day, it is my bike that liberates me from my privileged cocoon. If only momentarily. Perhaps it is only a false feeling of abandon, the tease of adventure, this breaking away from the tiny, proscribed world of foreigners in Beijing.

Some days I felt like a philosopher on a bicycle quest for beauty and essential truths that might lie behind the walls of Beijing. They had become the metaphor for my distance from the Chinese. Sad walls, neglected walls, mysterious walls peeling centuries and layers of plaster and brick, crimson giving way to grey, and, I was sure, revealing secrets if only I could decode them.

I cruised the narrow alleys—*hutong*—more deliberately. I studied the walls more carefully. When I stopped, of course, I saw more. Somewhere along the wall was a doorway, arched, square or rectangular in thick petrified wood, with foot-high stone sills and doors patched with cross-hatching wooden slats. Oblong stones stood at each side of the entrance carved in the shape of mythical animals, worn blurry.

"These animals keep the evil spirits out," Professor Li explained when I queried him about what I had seen.

Inside the doorway stood another wall.

"To discourage harmful demons," he giggled. "The Spirit Wall."

Standing on the outside of these forlorn and shabby traditional houses that opened onto narrow streets, I noticed that one of the doors was often open partway, offering a slender glimpse into the world of the Chinese—courtyards overgrown with plants, enamel basins, stacks of coal, bricks, twig brooms and unrecognizable junk.

I could also now detect all the little extensions people had built from their homes—a three-by-five-foot shed made of rusted metal sheets. Tar paper on top. A stovepipe pushed out through the window. Add-on kitchens? Plants perched on top. A string mop rested against a wall to dry. Flour sacking blew in a doorway. A man washed clothes in a basin.

Only eight months earlier I had tramped around the streets and alleys of Mexico's famous silver towns—San Miguel de Allende and Guanajuato—staggered by the details of Spanish Colonial beauty with its Arabic influences. Centuries-old stone walls, high sills, carved door and window frames worn smooth, adobe walls painted white or ochre, burnt yellow or Moroccan blue, intricately designed wrought-iron doors, gates and balcony railings. Everywhere I looked seemed to offer up a feast of sensual pleasures. Bougainvillea tumbling down twenty-foot-high walls. Yes, high walls, too, but brilliantly colored and covered in flowering vines. Gorgeous courtyards filled with plants surrounding fountains. The historic centers of Mexican towns unfurled so much visual beauty that synapses in my brain had been permanently altered.

Somehow I had imagined that ancient Chinese notions of exquisite beauty—in architectural detail, furniture, silk fabrics and objects—would open my aesthetic ideas in another way. After all, I had seen the antique carved wooden furniture and magnificent blue-and-white-painted vases in the store windows where I grew up. But I had not imagined how much had been destroyed in China by occupation, by civil war, by revolutionary movements.

Perhaps I embraced a pile of contradictions. Lusting after beauty created for aristocratic classes while arguing for social equality. But in Mexico, startling beauty was generated by indigenous artisans. Creativity seemed to be embedded within the culture. What had happened in China?

I kept looking. Until my eyes hurt. On busier streets, doors opened directly onto the sidewalk. Over the window stretched a square of handmade lace crocheted with shapes of bamboo leaves or peacocks. A cornice above, red paint chipped and peeling, revealed subtle but intricate carving in geometric designs. It was once very beautiful. I imagined the residence of a former aristocrat.

Every ledge—under the roof, over the door, along the windows—was turned into storage: dilapidated baskets, a crock basin giving life to herbs. A pair of black canvas shoes was propped up against a window to dry. A bean plant twisted up a bamboo stick. On the step, a chamber pot.

"The old traditional houses have no bathrooms," Bahdra reported. "There are public latrines on every block in the old part of the city."

I could smell them when I turned the corner on my bike. And the first time I used one, stalls with no partitions, simple foot rests at the side of a trough, I mused about North Americans with all our neuroses about private bathrooms, padded toilet seats, silent flush tanks and floral scents. At night, from my bicycle, I had seen the honey-pot drivers in the street; those horse-drawn carts that collected human waste from the latrines to take to the surrounding communes as fertilizer.

I was seeing much more. A woman was hanging slices of eggplant on a clothesline to dry. An old man placed a birdcage with its yellow captive on a hook underneath the eve. A little girl sat at a miniature table doing her homework.

When I returned to *Zhuanja lou*, I felt chastened by the luxuries I had been provided. At night, feeling raw, lonely and privileged, I threw on a cassette of Coltrane or Ahmad Jamal and drew with charcoal a scene from the day that had imprinted its image on my brain.

One Saturday night, I spotted Luisa on the dance floor at the Minzhu Hotel shortly after her escape to the Friendship Hotel. She was twirling to yet another horrible canned Hong Kong disco beat. Her partner was short and round. They were dancing with abandon, her head flung back, laughing. I felt pangs of envy. Somebody explained that her dancing partner was one of the most isolated men in Beijing, since he was the Cuban Consul General.

Cubans, supported by the Soviets, were consequently considered enemies of the Chinese. Luisa's new dancing partner was a social pariah. I sensed that, for Luisa, that might feel edgy and exciting, maybe even sexually titillating. Now, if only there was some Cuban music around.

BY THE end of my second month in China, I completed what I noted as "The Disposing of Friends" dream series. All but the final dream involved various American friends coming to violent deaths in some macabre scenario. In the final dream, I rode on the back of a magnificent white swan, circling and gliding over the Caribbean islands, where my friends were supposed to be, but I could not find them. I was sad but resigned to their loss. Perhaps I should have called them the "Letting Go" dreams. In the final dream there were no other people on Earth.

But that wasn't waking reality. My emerging, tentative expatriate friendships were vital to soul and spirit. Despite this, I wanted more. I wanted Chinese friends. Although it felt hopeless, I kept running at that Chinese Wall.

Tianjin, 1980

Chapter Six

Stranger in a Strange Land
陌生地的陌生人

"Do you speak English?"

This ubiquitous greeting was yelled by young bicyclists and pedestrians in the streets. Perhaps a student from one of the language institutes, a worker, or an "unemployed youth" who was studying English at home by radio. For many, it was one of the only English phrases they knew.

This time the question came from an attractive, square-jawed, thirtysomething pulling up on his bike. My camera lens was focused on reflections of the Imperial Palace in the moat as the setting sun softened the light. I had rushed to this spot after work to capture the magical luminosity, but the deliberation of this stranger's voice broke through my concentration.

"My name is Liang," he began with forced enunciation. "I am an English teacher at Number Two Middle School. My school is famous. The best in Beijing. The majority of our students are admitted into university."

It was a staggering opener. But I understood the significance of his pride. Only a tiny percentage of middle school graduates could enter university, creating fierce competition and furious backdoor maneuvering. I had tapped into the anxiety among the comrades at the office regarding their kids' access to the best schools. It was unclear whether the limited spaces were a result of scarce resources or the damage to educational institutions during the Cultural Revolution or the Party's desire to control the size of the intellectual class. Most likely a, b and c.

Bicyclists and pedestrians hovered around us, staring. Liang suggested we continue cycling while we talked.

"Are you teaching in Beijing?"

"No, I'm a foreign expert at Radio Beijing."

"Would you like to meet with my students? They seldom have a chance to meet with a native English speaker."

At this I stopped. "I'd love to. How can we arrange it? When can I come?"

He hesitated, frowning. "The school is old. They would not like you to visit. They do not want foreigners to see it."

"But you just asked if I would like to meet your students..."

Once again, a dozen bicyclists had dismounted, clustering around to study us.

Liang reached for paper and a pen from his plastic shoulder bag. "We will meet in a park." He scribbled on a scrap of paper. "This is my name, phone number and address of the school. You should write to me, then call on the telephone to arrange a time and place. I can bring the class to a park."

We had attracted a crowd, faces pressing close, examining the slip of paper, looking me up and down, staring intensely at my face then my shoes. Always my shoes.

"I have to go now," Liang started off on his bike. "*Zaijan*."

He disappeared into the tide of bicycles before I could look at the paper and tell him I could not read or write those characters.

A few days later, I approached Shadow Zhang for help.

"This young teacher has invited me to talk with his students. Could you call the school for me to arrange a meeting with his class?" I was almost giddy.

Asking Shadow Zhang to call for me epitomized my dependence and frustration. I was a capable reporter and producer who had navigated strange countries, cities and neighborhoods alone—and I couldn't make a phone call by myself in China.

The telephone was a symbol of both my illiteracy and my lack of privacy. At the office, there was always an audience. In my apartment building, the phone hung at the end of the hall, where its ring was inaudible. Some of my neighbors spoke little English and could not pronounce my name, so if any of my new foreign friends called, my neighbor didn't know who the caller was asking for. And the foyer, where the phone was situated, was like an echo chamber, further accentuated by the yelling required by poor connections. If a resident or building worker was coming by they could listen in on your conversation. Other mysterious ears were listening, too. The clicking on foreigners' phones, whether at our offices or apartments, reminded us that the line was tapped.

This was not the first time I had asked Shadow Zhang to telephone a

Chinese acquaintance for me. There was the geologist who gave me his card at the airport. I detected disapproval in her face and body as she dialed his number at the university. Twice she told me that he was out. I persisted and asked her to call again. On the third try, she seemed to reach somebody, but she was talking rapidly in Mandarin for quite a while. She turned to me with a frown.

"He is too busy now to see you."

"But he gave me his card and wanted me to call him. Surely there will be a time soon that he can meet? Besides, you seemed to do all of the talking." Silence. "What was all that about?"

Shadow Zhang managed a smile while still frowning and left the room. Could I cope with this much suspicion and mistrust?

How could I have been so illiterate? How long would it take to have enough Mandarin to make calls for myself? I lived in a completely mediated world. And, I suspected, that was exactly what the authorities—all those "responsible members," those high cadres, the Party—wanted for foreigners like me.

Once again, Shadow Zhang was calling on my behalf. I detected from her conversation with Teacher Liang that something was wrong. It was the tone of her voice. She was taking too long to make a plan for a meeting. Nevertheless, a meeting was arranged for Saturday afternoon at Beihai Park.

Even though it was a raw, drizzly day, I was ecstatic. As I approached the park entrance on my bicycle, I could see Liang and a tall, gangly teenager waiting at the gate. They furtively escorted me inside the park gate.

"People will stare." Liang was visibly nervous. He introduced the young boy and apologized that the other students couldn't come.

"There is a school function this afternoon."

He looked over his shoulder as we walked slowly in the park.

"You must never call my school again."

Apparently, the boy's English was bad enough that Liang felt free to scold me in front of him.

"You must never tell the people at Radio Beijing that you are meeting with me again."

"But you gave me that phone number! I cannot read or speak Chinese—I needed help. What did Zhang Wei say to you?"

"She said you were a journalist and that I must be careful when I meet with you." He looked over his shoulder a third time.

"I'm sorry if I caused you any trouble. I didn't understand it would be a problem." My body was becoming very heavy. "Besides, I thought the situation was supposed to be more relaxed now between foreigners and Chinese."

"It is better now than it was during the Cultural Revolution," Liang began, enunciating each syllable distinctly, which made what he was saying even more distressing. "But it can change again." He forced a chuckle. "Of course, we are not going to talk about state secrets, but it is dangerous for us to meet with foreigners. I could get into trouble at my school if they thought I was meeting with a foreigner, especially a journalist. You did not tell me you were a journalist." Liang's voice was agitated and nervous. "Never telephone my school," he repeated. "And do not say anything to your comrades at Radio Beijing."

If it was such a risk, I wondered, *why was he willing to meet?* It was his idea for me to meet with him and his students.

The situation was Kafkaesque. My body felt like concrete; my feet, lead bricks. The drizzle turned into real rain. Every few seconds, Liang looked nervously over his shoulder. The rain fell harder. Hunching my shoulders against the cold, grey wetness, with eyes focused on the ground, I stuck to safe questions.

Liang told me he was married and had two daughters. He worked twelve-hour days at school and spent his summer vacations translating books from English into Chinese for his students. His students did well on the university entrance examinations.

"You must be very proud," I responded.

Secretly I wished I had a microphone to debrief him about his story. But I couldn't say that, since he was so frightened already about my being a journalist. While I was impressed by his commitment to his students, another more cynical voice whispered in my brain.

That's it, I thought, *he wants books from me.* But he didn't ask. Already I had grown skeptical about why any Chinese wanted to make contact with foreigners. Within a few sentences of being approached by a Chinese youth on the street, their friendliness transformed into a request, a favor, help with an application to a foreign university or to get something from the Friendship Store. We expats would prefer to think that they were actually interested in us.

The rain made the walk with Teacher Liang and his student more miserable than the conversation opener. We ducked under a covered soda stand and sat on the damp ground. I blurted out my frustrations.

"Look, I came to China to learn about this country, about the people, but it is impossible to really talk to people, to make friends. People are so frightened. Why?"

Liang's student looked awkward and shy. I assumed that he understood little or nothing of our conversation.

"You'll learn. You must be patient." Again, Liang warned me not to telephone his school or tell my comrades about what we discussed. Yet, on our way back to the gate, he asked if I would meet with his class on a Saturday in two weeks at one of the Children's Palaces. He indicated on my map how to get there.

Bicycling home, the cold rain searing my face, the prospects for a normal social life felt bleak. I wondered about Liang's life. About his fear. About his desire to meet with me. In the park, he walked close to me so that his body lightly touched mine. I found him physically appealing, and I guessed that he was attracted to me. I suspected that he was not only interested in my meeting with his students. Perhaps I was too hungry for affection. I was reading too much into the encounter. And he was married.

Back at *Zhuanja lou*, I poured myself a shot of whiskey and flipped in a cassette of one of the albums that had seen me through the early 1970s: Bonnie Raitt's second album, *Takin' My Time*, with cuts like "Everybody's Cryin' Mercy"—a Mose Allison song—and "Guilty" by Randy Newman. I loved her bottleneck guitar and melancholy voice about love lost, broken hearts, drinking too much and all the rest. That rainy night I sang along...

> Yes, baby, I been drinkin'
> And I shouldn't come by, I know
> But I found myself in trouble
> And I had nowhere else to go
> Got some whisky from the barman
> Got some cocaine from a friend
> I just had to keep on movin'
> Til I was back in your arms again.
>
> Guilty, baby, I'm guilty
> And I'll be guilty the rest of my life
> How come I never do what I'm supposed to do?
> How come nothin' that I try to do ever turns out right?

After interviewing Raitt in 1974 for Boston's alternative weekly, *The Real*

Paper, and for our *Women's Hour* on WBCN-FM, she introduced me to her manager, Dick Waterman, who was a source for tickets to all kinds of blues performances. Dick had been a major force in resurrecting the careers of long-forgotten Delta Blues musicians. Another world. A different life.

SIX WEEKS into my Beijing sojourn, I worried that my dependency was unraveling my self-respect. To regain some confidence, I asked to have the next Saturday morning off to visit Tianjin, a port city that my guidebook told me was only three hours by train from Beijing. Perfect. I thought the trek and distance might provide some perspective and prove that I could survive without the constant interventions of my shadow.

The guidebook promised interesting architecture reflecting the presence of the British and French in the nineteenth century as well as the fancier traditional Chinese merchant houses that clustered in such an important trading hub. Tianjin had been one of the colonial "Unequal Treaty" zones before Liberation. After the first Opium War (1839–42), the British had set up these free-for-all zones in major port cities along the China coast—Shanghai, Ningpo (now Ningbo), Fuchow (now Fuzhou), Canton (now Guangzhou) and Hong Kong—whereby foreign powers could live and play by their own rules with total disregard for Chinese culture, history, laws and interests.

While I wanted to purchase the train tickets myself, the Foreign Experts Bureau insisted that since a visa was required to travel anywhere in China they would be best suited to arrange for everything, including my overnight stay in one of only two hotels for foreigners—government owned, of course. And like other hotels for foreign experts, called the Friendship Hotel.

The foreign experts' office at Radio Beijing offered to do my banking and get airplane tickets for an upcoming trip to Hong Kong. It was helpful, but slow—forms and papers to be filled out—and it meant they knew my every move. If I allowed them to do all these things, which many foreign workers did, I would become a dependent child.

In the week leading up to the journey, Professor Li drilled me on a few basic phrases I would need.

"*Dui buqi. Wo bu hui shuo Putonghua.*" "I'm sorry. I do not speak Mandarin."

My colleagues were astounded that I would consider traveling alone.

Once on the train, I was separated from Chinese travelers because the Foreign Experts Bureau had insisted upon first-class tickets. The comrades argued that I wouldn't want the dirty bathrooms or grubby conditions of the second- or third-class cars. Privilege and segregation. Just as in the "good" restaurants in Beijing. To punish us or to ameliorate our guilt, we paid more for our special treatment and isolation.

As the train pulled into the station, I knew the guidebook writer hadn't visited the city recently. If I thought Beijing channeled Dickens' Coketown, I was wrong. It was here. Tianjin. Sooty, charcoal greys of a thousand hues. Smoldering sky, smoke-hued brick buildings. As I pitched out of the station toward my hotel, I coughed and wheezed past shantytowns of reclaimed stone from former colonial buildings, straw matting, wire and tar-paper roofs held down with chunks of coal.

Pedestrians took on the appearance of ashy ghosts in their faded blues. Children carried wheelbarrows filled with bricks and stone. Young men shoveled coal into ragged baskets that were then pedaled away on platform bikes.

"Do you remember they had a huge earthquake here just four years ago?" A Canadian businessman whom I had chatted up on the train pointed to a collapsed building on the outskirts of town.

"It was 8.2 and centered just north of Tianjin. The aftershock registered 7.2."

I remembered the news headlines. "I hadn't realized it was here. But I do remember the controversy. Didn't China refuse to allow the International Red Cross or any foreign government to help in the rescue operation?"

"That's right. Hundreds of thousands died. And since the timing coincided with the death of Mao and the arrest of the Gang of Four, this natural catastrophe was considered auspicious."

Nobody at Radio Beijing had mentioned the earthquake before I left. I gathered that none of them had visited Tianjin to see the consequences. Or perhaps it was another taboo subject. Shockingly, people were still living in the middle of what had been wide avenues. They had built a shantytown in the road that stretched onto the sidewalks next to bus stops. A crowd awaiting a bus could peer into the gloomy interiors of five-foot-high huts, little vestibules with a feeble plant struggling to survive. Here life is lived, exposed.

People sat in the narrow, crowded street washing clothes, dishes and themselves. A girl cleaned vegetables. A young man shaved a piece of lumber. An older woman sprawled on the ground hammering something. Children sat at little tables doing homework. All in the street.

Geographically situated at the confluence of a major canal and river near the coast, Tianjin allowed sea access to Beijing, which historically made it an important port and trading center for grain, food and silk as well as a military garrison. By the nineteenth century, it had become the most important port in Northern China. Western colonial superpowers were attracted to its strategic location and negotiated concessions from the Qing dynasty to control the most important land and trade along the waterfront.

Until the 1930s, Tianjin was the largest industrial and commercial city of Northern China, boasting an extraordinary cornucopia of Western architectural delights, including neoclassical hotels and ornate cathedrals. Most were severely damaged by the Red Guards in the 1960s. Those left standing were further undermined by the '76 earthquake.

Once-beautiful houses of wealthy merchants or colonial captains of industry stood shattered, gutted. Lone stairways ascended into the air. Squatters lived in the basements. Adjacent shacks looked as if they were built with the ruins of the original house. Other dwellings were made of canvas on poles. I could see inside. Only space for a cot, wash basin and bicycle.

Old people look dazed. A crazed man sat, nodding out. Only children had energy. Everyone else seemed to be drifting.

The old British and French colonial buildings—once monuments to classical architectural ideas—were dark, foreboding. Windows everywhere broken and dirty. A cactus poked out from a dilapidated bit of roof. Near a makeshift dwelling, an older man sucked a mouthful of water from a bowl then sprayed it on his spider plant, much like the voodou priests with their rum during a ceremony. A moment of tenderness in this otherwise violated city.

In the state art gallery in the center of town, another version of reality hung from the walls—Socialist Realist paintings presenting an idealized vision of Chinese life. No painting or sculpture revealed what I was witnessing in the streets nor what I imagine haunted local souls. Where was the social document of life in China today? The spirit? The challenging aesthetic? Where was the heartrending cry for a ravaged Tianjin?

Back out in the streets, two young men approached me—one a university student studying international finance, spoke English well. He explained why so many people were living in the streets.

"They are afraid. The earthquake was horrible. They do not trust any building. The government wants them to move to new housing far from here. They do not trust it. And they have relatives and friends here."

"Their community," I interjected.

"Yes. Their community."

He then asked me if I was Christian. This was not a casual question. The comrades at Radio Beijing had also asked me the same question. Perhaps testing to see if I was a covert missionary.

Some understanding of history was important. Protestant and Catholic missionaries, from Britain, France and the US, working to convert the Chinese during the nineteenth and early twentieth centuries, played a critical role in the establishment of the treaty ports and then used them as a wedge to reach farther into China. It was well understood by the Chinese that the missionaries had a parallel imperialist mission running schools and businesses, introducing Western products and ways. There was pushback. In 1870 Tianjin, the "church incident" involved the murder of French nuns, a French consul and several merchants because local Chinese believed the church was kidnapping and brainwashing their children. The Boxer Rebellion—a movement against the Christianizing efforts of Western powers—led to a brief takeover of Tianjin by the rebels in 1900.

This history flooded my brain while I chatted with the future international banker. I joked about Marxism and Maoism as religions. When I pulled out my camera to take their photographs, a policeman suddenly appeared, and the laughing students evaporated into the crowd. The cop wouldn't leave me alone until I tortured him with a litany of my butchered Mandarin phrases—the very ones that Professor Li had insisted I needed to have in my arsenal—"I am Canadian, I am a foreign expert, I work at Radio Beijing at Central Broadcasting, I am staying at the Friendship Hotel here, I am sorry I do not speak Chinese"—and put my camera away. The panorama was too depressing to photograph anyway.

In the search for somewhere to sit and reflect upon the dystopian landscape and maybe find a beer, I wandered over to the old Grand Tianjin Hotel. Overlooking the river, this former Astor House was now forlorn but functioning. The guidebook explained that the original building was the brainchild of a British Methodist missionary who arrived in Tianjin in the mid-nineteenth century. It claimed to be the first international hotel in China. In the late nineteenth century, it hosted diplomatic missions—including the first American consulate. Apparently, Sun Yat-sen (early twentieth-century Chinese physician, republican politician and revolutionary) *and* Herbert Hoover (US president from '29 to '33) both rested their heads there. In 1980, it offered succor to international business types, diplomats and UN elites.

Passing through the lobby decorated in a sober mix of socialist aesthetics, including shiny new wooden furniture with plastic covers, I headed for the once-grand restaurant. A German couple invited me to join their table. Over a delicious fish dish, the woman explained she was born and raised here.

"I had a Chinese grandmother. This was my first trip back since my family escaped in 1949."

"And what do you think? Do you recognize anything?"

"I am dismayed to see so much destruction still remains after the earthquake. It's as if nothing has happened to restore the city in four years."

"Did you find your old house?"

She looked at her husband and down at her plate. "I cried when I saw it. A complete shambles." She paused to take a deep breath.

"The conditions of the workers' neighborhoods are worse," her husband interjected with a screwed-up face.

"But everyone eats now," his wife emphasized, trying to sound cheerful.

On my walk back to my dreary "economical" hotel for foreign experts, another Soviet-inspired wonder, I pondered the troubling landscape. *OK, people might not be starved for food*, I reasoned, *but for life—an energizing spirit.* What would happen to people here? Would they ever experience something else? Or was I missing the critically vibrant aspects of this city because of my illiterate brief encounter?

Despondent from what I witnessed, I took an early train back to Beijing the next morning. So much for asserting my independence. Again, I was incapable of describing my experience on a cassette for NPR. Not enough information. How could I simply report what I saw? Another apologetic letter to Margot Adler.

THE NEXT Saturday afternoon, dizzy with great expectations, I soared along Chang'an Boulevard, turned left onto Xidan and pumped a couple of miles north to Xinjiekou. Liang was waiting for me at the entrance to an alley and led me through a web of *hutong* to the Children's Palace, which occupied a former mansion built around a courtyard. Children's Palaces, Liang explained, are neighborhood centers offering classes and activities for kids. I wanted to ask if they served only the elites, but we were already faced with a roomful of smiling faces.

A group of twenty young teens, polished and fresh, sat around a long table. They looked eager, bright and well-off. They all spoke English.

After Liang's formal introduction, I tried to loosen things a little and test their vocabularies, describing the geography of Western Canada, listing subjects I had studied at school and university, and some of my work history in the US. Somebody always knew the English word.

"Waitress!"

"Professor."

"Journalist."

They wanted to know about schools and student life in Canada and the US. I explained that although many more young people had the opportunity to go to university in the West, there was a growing concern about illiteracy. They were puzzled by the notion that watching a lot of TV might affect people's ability or desire to read. After all, they were the first generation and class of Chinese glued to their TVs every night.

"What do you plan to study at university? What kind of work do you hope to do after graduation?"

Half of the class indicated they wanted to be scientists, engineers or doctors. The other half wanted to become translators and interpreters. These choices reflected the current government policy: modernization. These would be the prestige jobs providing opportunities for travel and research abroad. Despite the talk of economic development, there was no mention of architects, designers, contractors, bankers or business entrepreneurs. The state still owned all the means of production.

"Nobody wants to be an artist? A poet? Musician? Historian? Philosopher or anthropologist? Why not?"

Lots of giggling.

"The technocrats are winning," I teased.

After Liang translated, more giggling.

"How many of you have parents who went to university?"

All except two raised their hands.

"Then the educated class is reproducing itself?"

They nodded slowly in agreement. One student, a girl sitting prominently in the first row who always knew the meaning of words I used, spoke up.

"China is a poor country. China is backward. That is why we have to work for the Four Modernizations."

It was a neat conclusion to almost any group conversation. I had heard this slogan dozens of times. Hearing it from this quick and clever young girl, I tried to imagine what it would feel like to utter these words. Did she really believe that the Four Modernizations were possible without the sons and daughters of peasants and factory workers going off to university with her? Or was I the one not thinking correctly? Isn't this why Mao and his cohorts made a Cultural Revolution? To challenge class hierarchies, privileges? To allow workers, peasants and soldiers to go to university? How could the goals of the Cultural Revolution have become so buggered up?

When it was time for me to leave, each child approached me to say "thank you" and present me with a little gift—a bookmark or a handkerchief. Their courtesy and grace were disarming. One young fellow rescued me from the emotional moment with a final question.

"What is the difference between disco and jazz?"

"She's tired. It's late. She must go." Liang pulled me away.

"Soul. Creativity!" I called back to him.

Finally, an unscripted moment. But he was being pushed in one direction while I was pulled in another.

I left feeling both grateful for the chance to meet with some of China's brightest kids, however privileged, and discouraged because only formal group contacts seem possible. Would I always be destined to meet with the Chinese in groups, where there could never be true reciprocity? The setup ensured that I would do most of the talking. They provided a few careful comments about China, but the group enforced restraint. There would be Party members present to ensure nobody revealed too much. And what kind of revelation could that possibly be? These were fourteen-year-olds!

How difficult would it be to break through the formalities and censorship, the inhibition and fear, and really talk to someone about the stuff of life or feel like I had made a real connection? Passionate sharing was what I was seeking. Passion. Where was it here?

Bicycling home, I thought about Liang. He seemed even more nervous today. His manner was overly formal, his speech forced. But when I asked the students how many had parents who went to university, Liang spoke up.

"My parents did not go to university."

"Mine didn't either," I told him and the class.

He shot me a look of disbelief and curiosity. I wanted to know his story, too. He wore Western-style hard shoes, but his face had the rich color of peasants and the wrinkles of someone much older than his age. Like someone who has spent long hours in the baking sun doing agricultural work. Did he suffer during the Cultural Revolution, or was he one of the student-peasant-soldiers who attacked the so-called Rightists or bureaucrats, professionals or educated folk who spoke foreign languages? But, then, he was fluent in English. It didn't fit. The one thing I knew for sure was that he worked very hard, and I had a hunch that even though I had no way to contact him, this would not be the last meeting with Teacher Liang.

"HUSBANDS AND wives should be compatible politically."

In early September, Judy, a journalist from Boston, invited me to give a lecture about American-style broadcast journalism to her graduate student class at the *People's Daily* Journalism School. These were China's future foreign correspondents. In return, I asked if I could interview them on audiotape— since they spoke fluent English—about romantic love, sex, marriage and divorce. A new version of the Marriage Law had recently been published, and I had proposed to the leaders at Radio Beijing that we should produce a program about it. I thought this might be a start.

Most of these students were in their late twenties and early thirties and had been married for a year or so. Compared to the cautious and reticent style of my colleagues at Central Broadcasting, this group seemed uninhibited—telling jokes, interrupting each other, disagreeing and laughing. Delicious laughter.

Interview for Radio
Gail: How do you define a good love or marriage relationship?
Ms. Fan: Political harmony and loyalty because of the pain and abuses of the past.
Ms. Wang: Yes, that is the very most important thing. Husbands and wives should be compatible politically. During the Cultural Revolution, husbands reported on wives and wives on husbands.

This information was not news to me, but hearing it from young Chinese husbands and wives felt poignant. In some ways too raw, too painful to pursue as a line of query. I changed course.

Gail: How do young women and men meet? At work? Through sports? Hobbies? I know there are no bars or churches!
Laughter.
Ms. Wang: There is still not much opportunity to meet each other. Maybe the man works in a steel factory. The woman in a textile factory. They work long hours. Factory. Home. Factory. Home. Sundays they have chores. They have so little opportunity to meet each other.

Mr. Li: So matchmaking is coming back. I have become a part-time matchmaker—

Giggles.

Mr. Li: Families of six girls have asked me to find a husband for their daughters.

More laughter.

Ms. Zhang: In fact, state-run matchmaking agencies are starting to help as..."go betweens." That's what we call those people—"go betweens."

Ms. Fan: Some factories are set up strictly for men or women—or married couples might get work assignments in different cities. That also makes it difficult to keep a marriage together.

Mr. Li: During the Cultural Revolution millions of young people were sent from the cities into labor camps, reeducation farms and factories in rural districts. Parents of "sent down" youth worry that their children will end up marrying somebody in a rural community or small village or another city and therefore will never be able to return to Beijing.

Ms. Wang: Intellectuals worry about this. Parents plead with their work units to have their children returned to the cities so they can find a mate in the city.

As I listened, I could hear the concerns of class, geographical status and privilege overpowering the egalitarian goals of the Cultural Revolution. I sensed that the intellectual elites based in Beijing believed that real opportunities for higher education and work only resided in Beijing. How different was that from the US, where many parents seem to think their children should go to UC Berkeley on the West Coast or Harvard, Yale and NYU on the East?

But we were on a different track here. My motivation for this interview had been the newly revised Marriage Law.

Gail: The original 1950 Marriage Law outlawed child brides, arranged marriages and made divorce easier. It stipulated that the marriage age for boys should be twenty and for girls eighteen. The new edition of the Marriage Law pushes the marriage age up by two years and emphasizes again that divorce should be easier. What do you think?

Ms. Yan: But, in fact, the government encourages young people to delay marriage and childbirth until they are in their early thirties, and young men and women need to have the permission from the government—their work unit—to marry.

Ms. Wang: The reason is housing. That's the greatest impact on decisions to marry. If you don't have a room, what can you do?

Mr. Li: Those young people who were "sent down" or banished to work in the countryside, many have been returning to the cities since the end of the Cultural Revolution and making the housing crisis worse.

Ms. Zhang: During the Cultural Revolution there was little new housing built, so the housing crisis is serious, especially in the cities.

Ms. Wang: Some married couples live separately in singles' men's dorms and singles' women's dorms!

Mr. Li: The government sometimes offers a honeymoon room that a newlywed couple can use for one month. *Laughter.* If they want to spend more than a month they have to pay. It is too costly. Then another couple is offered the room. *More laughter.*

Gail: I can see the potential for a short story emerging here. *Chuckles.*

Mr. Li: Another new thing is high-cost weddings!

Ms. Zhang: Brides now want thirty-six legs, four things that go round and three things that make noise—

Laughter.

Ms. Wang: Thirty-six legs refers to the furniture—tables and chairs, closet and bed. Four things that go round are a watch, fan, bicycle and sewing machine and the three things that make noise are: TV, radio and cassette deck.

Mr. Li: I say I have two legs. I walk on them. I am as poor as a church mouse! *Laughter.* Judy taught us this expression. Poor as a church mouse.

Mr. Zhao: The man is expected to get these things.

Gail: But I thought that traditionally in China it was the woman's family who had to put up a dowry and pay for household and farm property to entice the man.

Ms. Wang: Nobody can require a dowry or payment for marriage. That's not allowed in the Marriage Law, but it happens. Only now it's a reversal of the past. Now it is the man's family who needs to attract a girl.

Gail: Since the recent edition of the Marriage Law increases the age for men and women to get married, is there sexual education and access to birth control before marriage?

Laughter.

Gail: Why laugh?

Mr. Li: It's rare and it's a vice...for Chinese to have sexual relations before marriage.

Gail: Why?

Mr. Li: Our morality demands that. We are very strict on this.

Mr. Zhu: It's not necessary to have that kind of relationship.

Gail: But what do young people do? If they cannot get married until their mid- or late twenties, what do they do with all of that sexual desire and energy?

Mr. Zhao: Cold showers!

Laughter.

Mr. Zhu: This is bad in China...

Ms. Zhang: I have no objections to sexual relations before marriage since many people have practiced this in the West. But in China I think this is unrealistic for us to do so. If a woman has a sexual relationship with a boy before marriage and they break up, it will make it very difficult for her on her first wedding night when she does get married. Because she is no longer a virgin. If she confesses this to her would-be husband, her relationship probably would break up.

Gail: In the West, the morality of virgins came from the Christian churches. Where does morality about virgins come from in China?

Mr. Li: The ideas come from Confucianism. About 3,000 years ago.

More laughter.

Mr. Li: Because Confucius taught in his books that women should be obedient before their marriage to their fathers, then to husbands and later to their sons. Women should always be morally loyal to their husbands. Women weren't allowed to remarry, etcetera. It's social tradition. It's unthinkable to practice premarital sex.

Mr. Zhao: Except in minority areas, because Confucius was never there. *Laughter.* I spent time in a minority region, Inner Mongolia, during the Cultural Revolution. One family lives in a tent. Visitors spend the night. Sexual relations are common.

Gail: It is the majority Han Chinese who are so puritanical?

Mr. Li: The other day I read an article in *Chinese Youth* magazine. The title is "Cherish Your Virgin."

Giggles.

Gail: Sounds like the 1950s in Canada, where I grew up. It was a double standard because men were never held to this strict behavior. Is there a double standard in China?

Mr. Zhu: I think it's the same for women and men.

The men generally delivered more conservative attitudes about premarital sex as well as expectations during marriage and divorce. The women sounded more forgiving and broad-minded. Of six women in the interview, only two thought sex before marriage was wrong.

Ms. Wang: Especially in China because people rarely get divorced, so you really should be very prudent. That's my opinion.

Gail: Divorce was granted by the original Marriage Law. A new survey indicated most divorces were rooted in financial tensions or conflicts between wife and mother-in-law. Is it easy or difficult?

Ms. Fan: It's difficult because the whole family is involved as well as two work units. There is persuasion, mediation, then you need your work units' permission.

Ms. Zhang: I think it is still very difficult. For example, a woman who is divorced has a difficult time finding a mate. She must find a man who has been married before, usually. The man's family would have objections. They want him to find a woman who has had no relationships before.

Everyone addressed the generational war that was taking place in Chinese cities—between young people, who thought they should have more freedom to "play"—which meant dating—and parents still suffering effects of the Cultural Revolution when men and women could be persecuted, tortured or driven to suicide for having an affair. The youthful focus on play was considered by the older generation and the government a result of creeping Western influences.

I tried to raise a question about the new one-child policy and its potential to create a gender imbalance, as families preferred boys over girls. Already there were rumors about female infanticide and abortions until a boy was produced. But this subject was too uncomfortable. Nobody responded.

Gail: And to achieve the one-child policy—what about sex education and birth control?

Ms. Wang: On your honeymoon, the neighborhood committee will pay you a visit and give you some information about birth control and check on your periods. Birth control pills are not available to unmarried students.

Mr. Li: During the Cultural Revolution, sex and birth control education were considered bourgeois. Now an occasional book or pamphlet might recommend cold showers and exercise to inhibit sexual desire.

This interview opportunity, the students' candid and genuine responses, was a generous gift to me. Judy had alerted me that in exchange for being interviewed they wanted me to bring American dance music so they could learn some new steps after the class. I was enjoying the cycle of reciprocity—I give a lecture on broadcast journalism, they grant me an interview on tape, I am then asked to give a dance lesson.

I started out with Chuck Berry's "Maybelline" and then James Brown's "I Feel Good," "I'm a Sex Machine" and "Cold Sweat." The students wanted to watch me, study my every move. I insisted that they all get on their feet. They loved to dance. Was I corrupting them?

Dancing to James Brown reminded me that memory is not confined to the brain or mind but resided in the body as well. How could I ever share with this group of eager Beijing dancers the excitement of moving to this music in one of the first integrated clubs in Berkeley in 1965, the Steppenwolf, where I first danced with blacks and whites together?

"ARE YOU lonely?"

I was unnerved by the question. Even though it would seem to be the obvious query about my situation here. Except it was a young Chinese man posing it. Gao Yuan. He was the fiancé of Judy.

It was the October first national holiday weekend, when New China celebrated its founding. The three of us were on an overnight train from Beijing to *Taishan* or Mt. Tai, the most famous of China's five sacred mountains. Some scholars claimed it as the birthplace of China's civilization; others emphasized its meaning to Taoism, Buddhism and Confucianism. Confucius' home village was only forty miles away. For hundreds of years pilgrims had been climbing this mountain to honor its legacy of meaning as a place of rebirth, sacrifice and immortality. Although Taoism, Buddhism and Confucianism had supposedly been eradicated from Chinese hearts and minds, the pilgrimage to the mountain had survived.

In second-class open bunks, eating oranges and drinking tea, the handsome, angular-jawed Yuan got right to the heart of the matter. Wasn't I lonely living as a single person in Beijing, where there are so few foreigners and a policy that prohibits Chinese and foreigner liaisons? He knew that policy intimately.

Yuan and Judy met and fell in love at the *People's Daily* Journalism School, where he was a graduate student. They had applied for permission to marry, but the government kept throwing an endless barrage of obstacles before them.

An overflowing box of paperwork stood prominently on a bureau in Judy's Friendship Hotel apartment to prove their efforts. When I visited, she tilted her head toward it.

"Things aren't going well."

Like any engaged couple, they had to get permission to marry from the Party committee at their work units. And as Judy reminded me, the Party committee expected its wishes to be obeyed since it also controlled access to housing, promotions, transfers, passports and visas, along with a host of other goods and services, including entry to schools for children. The new Marriage Law did not guarantee freedom of marriage to non-Chinese. So Yuan and Judy were being put through hoops.

The government demanded proof that each of them had not been married before.

"I have tried in vain to explain that Americans don't produce that kind of documentation," Judy complained.

Furthermore, leaders at Judy's work unit had tried to discourage her by telling her that Yuan had made a previous girlfriend pregnant and therefore wasn't considered worthy of her. But Yuan and Judy were determined. And they had plans. They were applying to graduate schools in the US. Yuan wanted to write a book about growing up as a Red Guard.

Pulling out from Beijing's train station, we had been talking about Yuan's Red Guard experiences and the ideological fervor of that era. He did not address the often unfair punishment of teachers, how some betrayed their own parents, the humiliations, beatings and deaths as mob behavior, and how violence and a kind of gang warfare took over between competing groups of Red Guards. He had lived outside of Beijing; perhaps that had made the difference. While I acknowledged that the initial movement of egalitarian values was inspiring to us in the West, I was surprised by Yuan's description of the sense of adventure that so many young Red Guards like himself felt: "We traveled on trains around the countryside for free with other teenagers."

In such a conservative and puritanical society, I tried to imagine what this freedom from the constraints of family and school must have unleashed. Despite his regret about the excesses that he had since learned about, he still felt committed to the underlying goals of equality, collective decision making and anti-bureaucratic struggle. He, like millions of other young people, had been electrified by the thrills of participating in politics. It was something I, too, understood.

But now he wanted to know if I had been married before, and, if not, what kinds of relationships had I experienced with men. It was refreshing that a Chinese person was interested in my social history, even if that story withered in comparison to his Red Guard epic.

Our second-class "hard sleeper" tickets provided us with open bunks in a co-ed setting. Uppers and lowers. No doors. Sinks and toilets at each end of the car. The late-night dim interior lighting transformed Yuan's voice into the intimate warmth of a close friend, even though I had only met him once before. Perhaps because I was unaccustomed to anything other than impersonal chats with the Chinese, I felt surprisingly shy.

I knew that my answers might shock Yuan, but I craved frank and honest personal exchange. As I began to describe my romantic past to him, I found myself analyzing my own culture's obsession with psychological language, with sexual and emotional confession. At first, conversations in China without neo-Freudian language, without sexual and psychological signifiers, were disorienting for me. It took a while to identify this sudden loss in expression, but its absence in the new Chinese literature struck me immediately.

I had been reading contemporary short stories published in English, and their lack of a vocabulary for emotional landscapes, for sensuality and desire, for guilt and obsession, prevented characters from becoming whole. These lean narratives and wispy characters lacked a soulful, spiritual and sexual dimension. Perhaps my tastes were more anchored in a Judeo-Christian moral mind frame than I had ever considered. Hooked on seduction, guilt, taboo.

Yet it was a relief to walk—mostly bicycle—the streets of Beijing without being treated as a sexual object, and it was refreshing to live and pass through public spaces without constant reminders on every surface of the ingratiating positions in which women can be placed to promote consumption. Yet there was something unsettling in the absolute absence of all that. Navigating in asexual space.

"How many lovers have you had?" Yuan was not about to back off from this line of questioning. "Why didn't you marry?"

Judy was patiently listening to Yuan's inquiry, not attempting to impose discretion. Instead, she implied support with her radiant smiles.

It was now past midnight. We each picked out a bunk to continue our conversation horizontally.

"I once had another girlfriend before I met Judy," Yuan confessed softly.

It was a courageous admission for a young, single Chinese man, I realized.

"Did you live together?

"No. That would be too difficult."

"Do Chinese couples ever live together without marrying?"

"Rare. If people really want to get married and their work unit won't let them for some reason, they might live together. But not often."

"In the West the divorce rate is quite high," I said. "It's common for people to marry several times in a lifetime. What do you think about that? Is it something you think could happen to you?"

"No. We are so different. I believe in marriage and being married for life. Judy may want to have other love affairs. But I know I won't. I will be loyal to her forever." It sounded canned.

Judy laughed while hitting Yuan gently with a book. We were all too tired to continue on, but the conversation, however tentative, had drawn me closer to a Chinese person than I had ever been.

As I lay on the bunk absorbing the rhythm of the wheels on tracks, I wondered what it must feel like for lovers on a train not to touch. Yuan was in a bunk above Judy. And given the taboo of showing affection in public between husband and wife, I wondered how restrained and frustrated they must feel as a forbidden foreigner-and-Chinese couple. It demanded even more control. I wondered what each of them was thinking. Drifting off with the motion of the train, I ignored Yuan's last question.

"Gail, have you had any women lovers?"

At sunrise, our train pulled into the small town at the foot of Mt. Tai. A dense mist lifted gently. Occasional clear shafts of sunlight brought the mountain to life before us.

Groggy, we began our ascent, joining hundreds of young people and families. The pilgrimage required hiking to the top, where we would stay overnight, then rising before dawn to watch the sunrise before making our descent.

The mob of pilgrims pressed its way through the paths and stone stairways that spread out in every direction. Giant rocks shaped like smooth buttocks, gorgeous thighs and defiant elbows perched precariously in streams at the base, as if pushed there by some sexy god of the mountain. Pine and cypress forests enveloped the slopes. Squatting vendors sold apples, boiled peanuts, candied fruit, sodas and beer. Further up, jagged cliffs cut into the sky.

We stopped at a creek to wash ourselves, letting the mountain into our senses. Climb. Rest. Repeat. The ascent would take all day.

Confucius had made the trek to the top. Tablets along the way bore inscriptions of his poetry. China's emperors came to make prayers or sacrifices, searching for immortality or renewal from the many gods honored here.

Periodically, a set of stairs led off to a small temple, altar or pavilion. Many were in disrepair, evidence that Red Guards and the Cultural Revolution had taken their toll. In 1965, the government had forced the nuns and monks residing in the temples to relocate into secular life.

Recent pilgrims had left offerings of fruit, cookies, coins and cigarettes—signs that Buddhism hadn't been completely eradicated. Charming inscriptions humored us along the muscle-cramping hike: "Bridge Where One Greets the Faeries," "Spring Where the Dragon Meditates." I bought Buddhist incense papers from a crouching vendor and burned them for the spirit of the mountain in a little temple en route. I loved the relaxed distance from official, deadly serious, civil-servant Beijing.

Three and four generations of some families were making the climb. An old man with a cane, an ancient woman with bound feet, young parents with children. Some carrying infants. As the sun rose higher, our pace slowed.

Scaling worn stone stairs—more than 6,000 of them—we watched another cast of hikers pushing on ahead. Sinewy men stripped to the waists, torsos and arm muscles glistening, short trousers revealing compacted calves, balanced poles from their shoulders, weighed down with cases of beer and sodas, sacks of rice and coal, drums of cooking oil, oranges and cabbages. All for our meal at the mountaintop later. A humbling sight.

I watched the blissful Judy in her low-key Chinese clothes and slender Yuan with the dreamy eyes, the way they looked at each other without touching yet seeming intertwined in each other. I marveled at their self-discipline. Our conversation never strayed far from the magic of nature, the rapture of being there. Young people disentangled themselves from the crags and bushes carrying fistfuls of miniature maple branches—purple, crimson, cadmium yellow.

While still in the lower third of this mountain splendor, three men suddenly emerged from the crowd—or was it the bushes?—and pulled Yuan aside. Judy, hands shaking, pulled me close, not taking her eyes off Yuan.

"They are police, plainclothes police."

As we approached them, they jostled Yuan farther away. Judy, who spoke Mandarin, whispered to me that they were drilling Yuan.

"Who are these foreigners? Who are you? What is your work unit? Why are you with foreigners?"

"I am their interpreter." Yuan explained.

"Do you have a letter of permission to be with them?"

The magic of the day evaporated as the policy separating Chinese and foreigners snaked its way up the mountain on a holiday weekend. I had already guessed that my presence helped keep this excursion from looking like a romantic situation. After the plainclothes cops receded into the crowd as cunningly as they had emerged, Yuan fumed.

"We Chinese can only be servants to foreigners. I can only be with you if I am your servant." He hardly spoke for the rest of the climb.

We walked silently. We three. Wanting to be lighthearted, to leave behind the madness of suspicion, surveillance and segregation along with the humiliation, fear and rage they engendered. We had come to the sacred mountain to be restored and renewed, but the evil forces wouldn't let go.

The mood worsened at the top. By sunset, as almost 2,000 climbers reached the summit, thirsty, hungry and looking for a place to sleep, the clamber for resources began. As foreigners, Judy and I were assigned to share a room with cots in what constituted a special wing of a simple dormitory. Two nurses from Beijing were our roommates. Yuan shared a room with several men across a courtyard. But hundreds and hundreds of others planned to sleep on the dining room floor or outside on the ground. Long lines snaked to the bathrooms.

At the restaurant mayhem broke out. Long lines, hungry customers yelling for service, snarly staff, a shortage of food. Yet when Judy and I appeared, we were swiftly shuffled to a section of the dining room surrounded by a curtain. They had divided the dining room into two equal parts. Just as in the better restaurants of Beijing, foreigners were put behind curtains. In this case, a group of thirty foreigners, a tour group that had not climbed to the top but rather had been bused up were sitting at several round tables with white tablecloths, and as a multi-course meal was spread before them, hundreds of equally hungry climbers outside the curtain were creating pandemonium at the shortage of food and servers.

Judy and I wanted to refuse but were prevented from doing so by the cadre in charge of the restaurant.

Yuan refused on principle to join us. "I'd be betraying my people."

Yuan's anger and resentment boiled over. He screamed at us and the restaurant workers for creating this ridiculous situation. Keeping hundreds from being served something simple while a few foreigners could eat cooked food immediately.

I hated this privileged, quarantined policy and now began to see its infuriating unfairness from the Chinese perspective. But what could we do? We were trapped in our privilege. So we sat miserably eating our precious meal while dozens of young people sat on the floor outside our curtain. Some hungry climbers walked over them to get to the front of the lines while others were fighting their way out. Near riot. We quickly left.

I was so exhausted from the climb that it didn't really matter where I slept, but I still appreciated my guilt-ridden cot and some privacy. By 5 a.m., we were all roused to head to the rocks around the edge of the peak to join in the ritual of watching the sunrise over Mt. Tai. Confucius had done it and announced, "I feel the world is much smaller." Most of China's famous poets had shared this experience and left behind a canon of beautiful poems. Mao had reportedly sat here at sunrise and announced, "The East is red." The crimson, orange and yellow glow on hundreds of faces huddled in blankets was worth the journey.

Yuan told us what happened after we left the restaurant the night before. Apparently, some of the foreign tour group folks had lingered at their tables, relaxing and chatting, when the cramped diners outside who had been relegated to the floor decided to rip the curtains down and sit down at the tables and eat. The foreigners had been offended. According to Yuan, there was a rising tide of frustration about the special privileges of foreigners. Big character posters were beginning to appear around Beijing with complaints.

When we reached the train at the bottom of the mountain, we had to compete with the jam of young people trying to get on board, so we had to climb through the windows. No privileges to that!

Sipping my coffee early Monday morning I ruminated on the deep lessons of the weekend. I had experienced a meaningful pilgrimage and learned how young people traveled. I had also witnessed the absurdities of the policy separating the Chinese and foreigners. And the reach of surveillance to ensure it. I had learned something about Chinese civilization—building stairs and temples all the way up a mountain. To heaven. I wished I felt reborn.

THE FOLLOWING day, at 7 a.m., there was a knock at my door.

"Telephone," my neighbor called out.

It was Teacher Liang, his voice rushed. "I want to invite you to a movie tomorrow night. Please meet me at the Dongdan bus stop at six forty-five."

I had just enough time to mutter, "Yes...thank you...OK," and he hung up.

As we walked up busy Dongdan Street the next night, Liang scrutinized me up and down, as he had done each time we had met. It was less a body examination than a clothing inspection. At our previous meetings, I had worn my usual colorful wardrobe. Liang wore dark loose pants, a white Western-style collared shirt and an ultramarine blue cotton Mao jacket, the kind that almost everyone wore. The day I met Liang at Beihai Park, he said that I should wear Chinese clothes for our meetings.

"Why?"

"So people won't stare."

I understood that Liang's instruction was for his protection and mine. And when I had first arrived in Beijing, I had wanted to run out and buy some baggy pants and a Mao jacket. I now rejected the idea. In recent weeks my New York wardrobe had taken on more significance than ever before. I was developing a militant stance toward maintaining my identity in a perplexing environment. My clothes were the only link between my present and past. They were a symbol of my free spirit and flamboyant, playful self that felt so squashed here. They represented my defiance against the passionless landscape threatening to consume me.

The more I understood that I had to change myself into a Chinese mannequin to have a Chinese friend, whether it was to be acceptable in a xenophobic culture or to decrease the risk for a Chinese because of a government infected with distrust, the more I rejected that condition.

But here again I was forced to listen to contrary voices. That night, with Liang, I wore dark colors.

Strolling through the crowd of after-work shoppers, I detected a desire on Liang's part to be close physically. Since he was married, I was particularly curious about his intentions, inviting me to a movie, looking at me that way, pressing lightly against me as we walked in the street.

I recalled a recent conversation with another foreign expert.

"Chinese men like to talk about sex with foreign women."

Susan, who had been teaching in Beijing for a couple of years, was popping boiled peanuts into her mouth with chopsticks. I had been describing my shock and amusement at teenage boys who blew me kisses as I bicycled around the city.

"I never notice them blowing kisses to Chinese women," I said.

"It's because of the repression in their own culture," Susan explained, sipping a beer. "They have this image that Westerners just fuck all the time, without meaning, without love. Sexual liberation. They are just learning about it. Mostly through black market movies and pornography."

Since Susan spoke Mandarin, I appreciated her insights.

"So no matter how starved I am for affection and contact, and no matter how attracted I am to some guy...I can't trust what his intentions are," she said as a peanut slipped out of the clutches of her chopsticks. "They must all be as frustrated as hell. So the brave ones want to visit foreign women. Maybe they see it as an opportunity to practice," she added whimsically.

As Liang and I approached the theater, he pointed to a far door.

"You go in the other door. We should not go in the same door."

"But then what? Should we sit in separate rows?"

"No. I will come and sit down beside you."

Now this really was absurd. *We should go in separate doors and then sit down together? He really is giving himself mixed messages.* How often did an American woman go to a local Beijing movie theater alone and happen to sit beside an English-speaking local who will then translate for her? Why would she go to a movie alone if she needed a translator? What must it be like to be that confused? Or afraid?

Shortly after we sat down, Liang gave me a little parcel. I could see through the wrapping that it was books.

"Chinese language books," he confirmed. "But do not unwrap them here. There is a letter inside."

Now I was really anxious about his intentions. Was it part of a seduction? Did he want something from the Friendship Store? Did he want help to find a university abroad? Did he want out? Certainly this wasn't a "normal" way to make friends, or was it? Had I lost perspective? Was I the one who was confused? He was giving *me* books!

"Why didn't your wife come tonight?" I tried to be casual, sound relaxed, but I wanted to let him know that I had principles.

"She is at home with our daughters," he explained maintaining a matter-of-fact tone.

I wondered if he had told her that he was taking a foreign woman to a movie—which was just about to start.

Love at Luoshan. Everybody was talking about it. A love story between a mainland Chinese boy and an overseas Chinese girl in one of China's most famous scenic mountain parks. He was the son of cadres persecuted during the Cultural Revolution; she, the daughter of an ex-Kuomintang general. Acceptable characters and theme for the Ministry of Culture. Many recent films were addressing the wounds suffered by the professional, artistic and intellectual classes during the Cultural Revolution. Some victims were Party members. This story also promoted the new policy of friendly gestures to Taiwan.

Among the half dozen movies I had seen since arriving, this one looked familiar: melodramatic scenes, one-dimensional characters engaged in a simplistic conflict. Good vs. Evil. All resolved in a happy ending. The clumsy techniques were typical. Shots held too long for emphasis, fast zoom-ins to punctuate a heavy emotional moment, the overuse of corny flashback techniques.

Liang began translating word-for-word in a loud, stilted voice.

"It's OK. It's all right, I understand," I whispered, since it was also disturbing others around us. The story was so transparent it hardly needed interpretation.

When I left Liang at the bus stop after the movie, I thanked him again.

"I would like to meet your wife soon."

"Yes," he said. "We would like to have you to our house for Spring Festival."

That was five months away! What was possible in the meantime? Was that a way to discourage me from meeting his wife?

I hadn't even closed the apartment door when I ripped open the package to read the letter. It was a stilted, overly formal piece of jargon about Norman Bethune and friendship. He then wrote that he was a poor country boy who suffered a lot to go to university and become a teacher. Now that's a story I would really like to unravel.

If the letter was disappointing and curious all at once, the other enclosure was disturbing. It was a photograph of Liang and his two daughters that had at one time included his wife. Her sweater sleeve was still on the edge that had been carefully scissored off. What message was I supposed to take from this? Was he hinting loudly that he was a family man but free to have an affair? He had a lousy relationship with his wife? From what I had learned about the experiences of couples during the Cultural Revolution and the difficulties of divorce, perhaps he was trapped in a terrible situation. Or was this a cynical effort on his part to deceive me? Yet Liang was my age. It would be fascinating to share our life histories, to talk freely about our ideas, doubts, hopes and fears. Not just his fear of being seen with a Western journalist.

Way, way, way too complicated for me, given the little that I already knew. As much as I was intrigued by Teacher Liang, in this puritanical environment, combined with a government policy that forbids our friendship, I needed to let any hopes for a relationship with Liang—even the most innocent one—wither before budding.

I sunk into my brown plastic armchair feeling raw and lonely. I ached for real relationships with my coworkers. I craved mutual caring and physical contact. I resisted spending all my time in the foreigners' community. I was determined to penetrate China. To make Chinese friends. Yet here had been a glimmer of an opportunity, and I knew it was impossible.

I threw in a Billie Holiday cassette. I needed something jazzy and boozy, although I would really have liked to smoke a joint. Instead, I turned the lights down low, poured a glass of Chinese rum and opened my second pack of cigarettes for the day while listening to "Solitude," "Lover Man," "I'll Be Seeing You" and "As Time Goes By."

Alcohol and music always triggered the suggestion of deep thinking. The appearance of soul searching. That night it went like this.

I was learning over and over again how difficult it was to have any real relationship with my colleagues with whom I worked six days a week. The hope was that some friendships might have been possible *outside* of my workplace—a common perception shared by other expats, especially those working for propaganda agencies. But my first independent contact—Liang—had been warned about me and was fearful and would be too dangerous—perhaps too strange—to pursue. But I was committed to reaching beyond the walls of my prison. I kept thinking that learning Mandarin was the key to unlocking the mysteries of the Chinese and making Chinese friends. I did not want to end up like Bahdra.

In her late fifties, Bahdra has decided she was too old to master another language. She was dependent upon the English-speaking community and offered solace to the Sinhalese students studying at Beijing University. Although she was vivacious, warm, kind and identified with the underdeveloped and developing world, Bahdra didn't have a single Chinese friend. Bahdra had been in Beijing for four years.

As I looked around at those foreigners who did speak Mandarin, my theory about language as the wedge into the world of the Chinese wasn't holding up, either.

Marianne, the French department foreign expert, was thirty-five when she started studying Mandarin in her native Australia. On a deeper journey into the language and culture, she came to work in Beijing. In three years, Marianne had befriended one Chinese couple whom she saw every few months, and they were trying desperately to leave the country.

Yet Marianne wanted to study Mandarin at Beijing University after she completed her contract at Radio Beijing and urged me to join her.

"Allow yourself the pleasure and wonder"—her English vowels were all rounded and distinct—"of really immersing yourself in the language, literature and history." She then looked away and paused for a long time before continuing. "But then who would we talk to?"

It was not a mischievous question. I was beginning to understand that Bahdra, Marianne and I posed a dilemma for the Chinese. We were single women, well over thirty.

Bahdra was divorced. Her grown children lived in England. Marianne came to China with a boyfriend. But after a devastating breakup, he returned to France. At thirty-seven, without a past, present or prospective husband—or children—I was positively weird.

A few weeks after I arrived, Jane, the Chinese-American expert in the English department, came by my apartment to see how I was doing. I shared some concerns about how my age and singledom and my style might be difficult for the comrades and perhaps it would explain their aloofness. She told me that a number of the women in the office were shocked at my status. "What's wrong with her?" they asked.

I SAW myself thrashing about behind a glass window like a puppy at a pet shop longing for the sustenance of connection, warmth, sharing and touching. I harbored deep suspicions that aside from Party directives it was my very essence that was the issue preventing any human bonding here.

In the streets young children pointed to me yelling, "*Waiguoren, waiguoren!*" Foreigner, foreigner! I was an outsider, after all, without the language, without much understanding of Chinese culture and character. But how would I ever learn? Unless I had already learned the only lesson there was to learn—that it was impossible to penetrate the world of the Chinese. To befriend one of *them*.

While I pleaded guilty to ignorance, I was more resistant to the notion that my flamboyance, my independent, argumentative and temperamental nature, might throw up a smokescreen between my Chinese coworkers or acquaintances and me. Although I had suspected there would be trouble with my essential self before I went to China, once there I had difficulty accepting that I, who had learned to get love with my energy, exuberance, zaniness and laughter, was witnessing a recoiling by others, a shutting down. I was forced to question the unquestionable, that my personality, my personal style—my persona—might be repugnant to the Chinese.

Even my physicality—the most unchangeable part of myself—seemed problematic to my coworkers. Often while passing my desk, Liu Hui or Xiao Zhi would pull my long, curly hair back into a ponytail—an act of familiarity I would have enjoyed if I didn't listen to their comments that I looked better that way. In other words, like them. Despite the permanents that half the women in the department were sporting, even if their hair was short they would pull back any little excess and fasten it with elastic. One day, when I was wearing sunglasses, Professor Li said I looked better in them and should wear them all the time. So then it was my eyes. Or was I confused. Was it a compliment or an insult? Were my eyes too big? Too round? Or was he trying to affirm my style?

Even if I had speculated problems with my persona in Middle Earth, I had no foreshadowing of how I would feel when the ground began to shift radically beneath my metaphorical feet. Culture, character, personality, identity or values that had shaped and supported me were shaking. I felt as if I were being jettisoned into an airstream created by the buckling of two worlds. I had no control over when and where I would land—or if.

I became suspicious and defensive. I was losing respect for things Chinese before I even understood them. The furies rose in me, lashing out at laziness. I was impatient with what I perceived as ignorance or the lack of education among my coworkers who were considered *intellectual* workers. Although they were privileged cadres, chosen carefully to work in this sensitive propaganda unit, none seemed excited by world events, ideas or reporting. Analysis or critical thinking was definitely not going to be shared with me—if it was entertained by them. There was no "yes" or "no." Why didn't anyone care about quality? Efficiency? Creativity? Imagination?

The more remote my colleagues were, the more frustrated I became with the rigid regulations, traditions or routines, like no taxis at lunchtime because the drivers were sleeping.

Yet I found myself recoiling from social gatherings with foreigners whose deafening din of complaints and alcoholism would become contagious if I didn't withdraw. So I chose to spend time alone studying Mandarin, writing letters home, reading and drawing, bicycling around the back alleys of the city with my camera. All therapy. While I struggled within myself for a way to endure, a submerged rage was metastasizing. Occasionally it would explode. At work. In the office. With the comrades.

Unpredictable, uncontrollable outbursts against Chinese ways of doing things only further distanced me from my colleagues. Then, ashamed with my impatience, I felt naked, exposed, like in the dream. Although my hands weren't hooks...yet. While I could see my emotional volubility was childlike, I seemed unable to prevent this infantile disorder. I felt like I was in a glass box. No privacy, being watched yet ignored. My behavior regressed as I begged for attention and approval. On the other side of the glass, my comrades moved with slow-motion smiles, like tolerant lab technicians, an image that came in another dream.

In rational moments, I wrestled with the roots of my social problem. Was the fear and caution that I witnessed among my comrades really a result of Communist Party policy that they, too, loathed? Or were they convinced that all foreigners were spies and bad elements, never to be trusted? Was their response to me deeply rooted in the historical memories of foreign occupation, or was it Chinese chauvinism?

Then the worst began to happen: The comrades' response to me was repelling me. I felt increasingly numb when talking with people at the office. My alienation was undermining my empathy. Empathy! It's what fueled my journalism, my work, my politics, my life!

Perhaps I had exhausted that stream-of-consciousness rant about the comrades and me. I also had to admit there were times when I adored a moment of exchange with one of them. Tiny droplets of moments. Whatever. I needed to change the direction of my thinking by changing the music. I whizzed around on a cassette to find Leon Russell's "A Song for You," a poignant love song that made me feel lonelier than ever. I had shared it with guys I had thought I was in love with, but usually I listened to it by myself, filled with longing and desire. I belted out the lyrics of the first and last verses. I remembered where I was when I first heard it in 1973. On a jukebox in a bar in Boston. Nostalgia. Melancholy. Maybe it was just Leon Russell's voice, which, on this song, reached deeper into my soul than any other he sang.

I've been so many places in my life and time
I've sung a lot of songs, I've made some bad rhymes
I've acted out my love on stages
With ten thousand people watching
Now we're alone and I'm singing my song for you...

I love you in a place where there's no space or time
I love you for my life, you are a friend of mine
And when my life is over
Think of when we were together

When we were alone and I was singing my song for you...

I was a romantic, reckless fool. Listening to this song, I could not prevent an archeological dig of my romantic affairs. I always fell for types that were mysterious, unreliable, noncommittal, dangerous—men who enjoyed being bad boys. At least those who came before and after Carl. With Carl, the conflict was deeper and more complex. He had rescued me from falling away from university altogether. He had stimulated a much deeper intellectual journey as well as my political activism. He had encouraged me to write and supported my plunge into the women's movement only to have it backfire. As I grew more confident and critical, I wanted to flex my unfolding wings.

The relationships that followed were either superficial, inappropriate or fleeting. There were so many. So many. Since I had been in New York, there had been the restaurateur from Provincetown with the Sufi tattoos—a lingering crush from my Boston days—whom I guided around Haiti, introducing him to artists and voodou priests, curators and Bohemians, driving him from one end of the country to the other. Emotionally unavailable, he gave me a little plant in New York before he returned to the Cape.

The neurosurgeon I had met in Haiti on that trip was eager to date when I returned to Manhattan but went into hiding when I came down with hepatitis a month later—the sickest I've ever been. He picked up with another redhead and then invited me to their "announcement of their relationship" party. What masochism made me go? When she opened the door, I thought I was looking in a mirror. What a cad!

There was the whacky yet charming musicologist. What had happened to him? There was a multitude of four- or five-night stands. All interesting guys on one level—usually very smart—including a radical economist, a movie sound man, an attorney-slash-art dealer, a photographer, a cultural critic and author, a TV producer, an artist. With each I fantasized for a glimmering moment whether something more substantial might be possible. Then my work or someone else beckoned. Someone more dangerous, more unreliable.

There was the scriptwriter (aka bartender) who couldn't understand why women wanted "commitment," then the scriptwriter (aka drug dealer) from Berkeley who was writing a screenplay about wild and adventurous drug dealings involving tankers and small boats and raw fear. Autobiographical, of course. After going out a few times in New York, he had invited me to come to Berkeley to visit. When I took him up on his cavalier offer, I landed in the middle of domestic drama. He was actually living with a girlfriend. The crisis I had precipitated by showing up led to both of them moving out of the house while I stayed and visited other friends in the Bay Area. It came with sleepless nights because I knew his jumpiness wasn't just about the woman crisis. I suspected he had substantial amounts of cocaine stashed in the house and at any moment I could be implicated. Either with the DEA or competing dealers. Neither scenario appealed. He was the easiest of romantic screwball interests to forget.

More ambiguous was the ongoing four-year secretive affair with a network television executive who lived between New York and Washington, D.C. Spicy late-night phone calls, expensive dates, never knowing when the next liaison would be possible all kept the relationship piquant. He was a Southerner, more conservative than anyone I would seriously consider and twenty years older. And married. I reckoned it was a father fixation, since I'd never had a positive model for one in my life. Not that his desire to cheat on his wife was exemplary. I knew it was doomed and damaging to hang onto, but I was so needy.

At thirty-seven, I was at my hormonal peak. And now, holding a photograph of a man and his two daughters with his wife's image scissored off, I knew I was a stranger in a strange land. Another title to a Leon Russell song. I skipped that—I really needed to hear Ella Fitzgerald sing "Cry Me a River."

Beijing, 1980

Chapter Seven

The Comrades and Mao's Pear
同志们和毛的鸭梨

Whomever wants to know a thing has no way of doing so except by coming into contact with it, that is by living in its environment...If you want knowledge, you must take part in the practice of changing a reality. If you want to know the taste of a pear, you must change the pear by eating it yourself...If you want to know the theory and methods of revolution, you must take part in revolution. All genuine knowledge originates in direct experience.

Mao Zedong

"You're a millionaire!"

Shadow Zhang had just handed me a bundle of Chinese *yuan* wrapped tightly with a rubber band. It was the fifth of the month. Payday. Earlier, Zhou Hong had delivered little clumps of cash to every comrade's desk. Professor Li had recorded it all in a ledger. It was my turn. Seven hundred *yuan* in ten-*yuan* notes (about $470 US; in 1980, the *renminbi*—the official name for *yuan*— was pegged at $1.5 US). My monthly salary.

"That's a year's salary for a Chinese," Shadow Zhang taunted. "Please count it to make sure it's right." It was a command, not a request.

Yan stood up from her desk behind mine to come and take a look.

"You're rich!" she chuckled while straightening her blouse and pushing a recalcitrant hair behind her ear.

"You must save it," Liu Hui advised.

She had just slipped into the office to join the others, all riveted by this horribly awkward ritual. I resisted counting, knowing the bills had been counted many times already. They insisted, echoing in Chinese as I exercised my linguistic skills, drenched in guilt.

"*Yi, er, san, si, wu, liu...*" counting up to seventy bills. I was permitted to convert part of my salary into the "funny money" required to make purchases at the Friendship Store. Both the "funny money" and the store were privileges reserved for foreign experts and high cadres. My apartment and utilities, along with ration tickets and health care, were all part of my package deal.

The comrades were fixated on the seventy ten-*yuan* notes we were counting on my desk.

"What do you think about this?" I asked. "Do you think it's fair? It doesn't seem right, does it?"

"You are an expert. You are very capable and experienced." Liu Hui made it sound rehearsed. As if she was trying to convince herself.

Their laughter was forced and dry. This scene replayed itself with subtle variations every payday. I should not forget how much more I earned than my colleagues.

When I had first arrived, I had asked Ma Riuliu, the news section leader, how much Radio Beijing workers earned.

"The average salary is seventy *yuan* a month," he replied in a tone meant to end the discussion.

We were walking along the gravel driveway that led from the grounds of Radio Beijing to my apartment building. One side of the driveway was bordered by a row of dusty socialist realist buildings housing employees from Central Broadcasting. Several windows were broken, some exposing a single bare lightbulb dangling from a wire. The *People's Daily* papered the walls of one room. Through a few windows I could see lines of laundry strung from corner to corner. A rag mop was propped outside a window. A bunch of leeks leaned on the sill.

I knew that seventy *yuan* equaled about $45 US, but at that time I didn't have much idea what it would buy for the Chinese on top of their ration tickets for rice, flour, oil and cotton. I only knew that foreigners paid more in restaurants and for taxis and our idiosyncratic needs. Cigarettes, refrigerators, tomato sauce and booze were all burdened with heavy import taxes at the Friendship Store.

I was as bewildered by the bits and pieces of information I was acquiring about Chinese household incomes as Ma was the day he came into my office and asked how much an office clerk made in the US. It wouldn't have mattered what figure I quoted.

"Ma, it's difficult to understand the meaning of a salary unless you also know the cost of rent, or a mortgage, health insurance or subway fare, kids' shoes, a quart of milk, a long-distance telephone call, a babysitter, a trip to the dentist, a blouse, an electrical bill, a gallon of gasoline, your kids' college education." I caught myself before saying "a trendy hairstyle in a salon, a Tanqueray and tonic in a bar or a month's supply of birth control pills."

Leader Ma scratched his bristly crew cut and bunched up his face. His mouth skewed to the side when he smiled or laughed, perhaps an effort to disguise his big front teeth. In his forties, Ma's face bared the lines of what I imagined to be class struggle. His laughter felt strained because he was nervous and jumpy. When he talked to me, whether he was standing or sitting, he was always moving. Most of the men in the department exhibited nervous mannerisms. Legs constantly swinging from the knee. Feet tapping. Smoking heavily. Professor Li had a noticeable tic in one eye. It would be a while before I knew enough to anchor this nervousness in the legacy of political purification campaigns. Or maybe inhibited sex lives or cramped housing. Or a marriage that you could not escape due to lack of housing alternatives. Or the misery of working at a job you hated but could not change.

Meanwhile, Ma looked uncomfortable when he conversed with me. He laughed when he saw me coming, but I liked to think of it as a kind gesture. I liked Ma, even though he mouthed what I gathered was the correct political line. He was a Party member and a cadre. It was Ma who wrote the letters to me in New York, offering a job, arranging for my visa and flight.

Although Ma was a leader, he was unpretentious, unassuming and humble. He was unlike anybody I knew in a comparable position of authority at a media outlet in the United States. He lacked self-consciousness, ego. At least with me. In his English-speaking self. I had no concept of who he was in Mandarin with his Chinese colleagues. I witnessed what I thought to be different personas projected by other comrades when they switched to Mandarin to address each other. Brusque, curt, loud. But with me, Ma projected humility. Like the day he came to me asking about whether they should tap the AP and Reuters wire services contracted by Xinhua, the national Chinese news agency. Yet if I asked him a question about China, he turned and made a quick exit.

When Ma said the average salary of the Chinese was seventy *yuan* a month, I thought that meant almost everybody earned that. But from Yu, a translator at the Foreign Language Press, I learned that the overall pay scale stretched from eighteen to one hundred or more *yuan* a month, depending upon education and seniority.

I met Yu when I had visited an American friend at her work unit. She was more forthright in her responses than were any of my colleagues at Radio Beijing.

"A university graduate starts at more than twice the beginning salary of middle school graduates," she said. "Then, at the end of their first year, they leap to fifty-six. From there the scale goes up to sixty-two, seventy, seventy-eight, eighty-seven and a half, and one hundred."

"Who decides when you go to a new wage level?" I asked.

She let out a chortle before turning serious. "Well, finally it is a decision by the leaders. Based on how long you've worked, the quality of your work." She paused. "And how you get along with the leaders."

From Liberation to 1980, there had been little change in salaries. Then, as part of Deng Xiaoping's new economic policies, raises and bonuses were introduced as material incentives to crank up productivity.

I had just missed the excitement.

"Oh, it was so horrible," Marianne, my neighbor, described the tensions, animosities and breakdown of work in the French department at Radio Beijing during the entire spring of 1980, when "workers spent endless hours and days in meetings to decide who should get a raise and how much."

"To each according to his work" was the current political slogan, rationalizing the new pay scales. It was a flip of Marx's famous phrase "*from* each according to his ability, *to* each according to his need," although he wasn't the originator of this idea that had evolved within the international socialist movement and among early utopian thinkers. But here in 1980 China—after several decades of Marxist analysis blended with Mao's schemes, including ten years of Cultural Revolution slogans about "worker, peasant, soldiers" aimed at narrowing the gap between manual and intellectual work—the thinking about pay and the division of labor was changing again.

Since almost everyone in the English department did the same work, I wondered how they rationalized the differences. Although seniority was one basis for the pay differential and facility with English another, I was still puzzled by some individual salaries. Professor Li had been working at the radio station for almost twenty years. He spoke English better than any of the others. He earned sixty-two *yuan* (or *renminbi*) a month.

One day, when we were discussing health and nutrition in our office, I asked Professor Li if the Chinese took vitamins.

"The only vitamin I need is Vitamin M." His face registered mock surprise.

"M is for money."

I liked Professor Li's quiet sense of humor, his nervous giggle punctuating every sentence, even that tic in his right eye. When he explained some Chinese tradition or proverb, he would raise his eyebrows and open his mouth wide in mock disbelief, causing his glasses to slide down his nose. He did this the day I asked him why nobody had fixed all the broken windows in the apartment building next to the alley.

"That's the singles' dormitory, and they live three or four to a room." Professor Li looked at me as if I should have understood. "It's like the three monks. Do you know the story? One monk can carry a pail of water on a pole over his shoulder. Two monks can carry the pail on a pole between them. Three monks cannot figure out how to do it." He looked at me, raised his eyebrows, rounded his eyes and mouth, his glasses slipped and we both laughed. I harbored my own doubts or questions.

"When the state is the landlord, who is responsible for the broken window?"

Then forty-one, Professor Li had worked at Radio Beijing since graduating from Nankai University in Tianjin, "where Zhou Enlai studied," he was quick to add. That meant he was there during the Cultural Revolution. Like all the other comrades, Professor Li would not talk about those years. But he was willing to talk about money. That was safe because Deng Xiaoping's new policy touted economic and material improvement. I still didn't know why Professor Li was not earning more, given his talents, skills and seniority. Perhaps it was punishment for his behavior during the Cultural Revolution? Perhaps he had a larger living space? I was left to imagine all the possible answers.

But the official slogan "to each according to his work" was not how one bright young comrade at the office put it. She spoke privately: "It doesn't matter how hard we work, or how long, or how good our work is; what matters is that we get along with the right people." Some American workers would recognize that. But in socialist Utopia?

"LECTURE, PLEASE!" shouted Xia Xia. She and a group of ten comrades from the department began meeting at my apartment one night every other week for a discussion group.

Leader Zhang had suggested the idea. "It will help the comrades with their English," she had insisted. Her already-hushed voice faded to a whisper when she referred to the "comrades," as if she feared I might have a Cold War reflex to hearing that word. "Some of them have very little chance to talk to you during the day. You can talk to them about anything you wish."

Really? I wondered. *Anything I wish?*

Frustrated from the lack of communication in the department, I was ecstatic about the possibilities. This was our second meeting. Like the first time, we danced around picking a subject for discussion. They kept looking for me to lecture. I refused.

I suggested a revolving discussion leader. And a democratic approach to topics. The discussion leader would make sure everyone had a chance to speak. Then I caught myself by surprise. Was I really proposing all this to comrades from the People's Republic of China? Weren't they supposed to be the masters of collective organization? I expected them to have a superlative system for group discussion. Instead, silence. I wondered to myself if criticism, self-criticism and political education had worn them flat. Or raw.

More whispering and giggling. Then everybody spoke at once in Chinese, and then someone said in English, "You decide."

It was a repeat of the first session.

At that meeting, I had suggested that we each spend a little time talking about our personal, family, work and school histories. Their stories would put flesh on their bones and help me determine their comfort level in English. I would then describe something about my history to them. And they could ask questions. The differences could generate some interesting topics for further conversation. My grand theory of communication.

Each comrade delivered a few terse sentences in barely audible voices. Their age, where they were born, where they went to school and when they started working at the radio.

I prompted. "Are you married? Do you have children? How many? How old? How many people do you live with? Do you have relatives in Beijing? Who looks after your children when you work? What did you want to do when you were in school? Do you have hobbies? Do you belong to the Party? What do you hope for in the future?"

A few responded about their children. Most froze.

Total silence.

If I could have stepped back from this scene and examined it with leisure and reflection, I probably would have recognized some common group dynamics from my world. Who wants to be the first in a group to offer up personal information? Also, I, who had just landed from a culture of exuberant intimate confession to strangers, could not yet see that there was something deeply cultural in the Chinese reluctance to reveal oneself. I was simply exasperated at their guardedness. At that first session, I caved into the demand to lecture and talked about my family's immigrant history, my educational trajectory and a little of my experience working in New York.

At the second session, the group once again wanted me to lecture. I directed the conversation toward the responsibilities of a news organization.

"Nobody ever discusses anything newsworthy with me at work," I complained. "No one ever speaks to me about what is going on in the world." Their eyes all focused on the floor. "What do you think is newsworthy?" I was grasping at ridiculous abstractions here. "Or, perhaps easier, what kind of news interests you?"

I was hoping to trigger reflection upon the quality of journalism at Radio Beijing. While I also met with a similar group from the office to focus specifically on broadcast journalism skills, this was an opportunity to bolster that endeavor.

Chen Zhijan (Firm in Spirit) sheepishly spoke up. "At my wife's factory, people are all talking about a man who tried to poison his wife."

Someone snickered. I had noticed Chen's depressed demeanor before and was curious about him, but there was no time for those concerns at this moment because young Liu Hui chimed in.

"News is a mother who is sick."

"Well, those could be stories in a very local news outlet, but I am trying to get you to think about the responsibilities of journalists and your audience here. You want to reach North Americans. What do you think matters to them? What do you think they would like to hear about your country?"

Zong, a twenty-two-year-old from Nanjing, jumped in. "News is food prices, kids' education or getting into college."

Quick to respond, the articulate Zong had just spent two years at the London School of Economics as one of the first since the Cultural Revolution to study abroad. He also spoke in the deliberate verbiage of an Englishman— and with an "almost Oxbridge accent" that dripped with class and status. In 1980 Beijing—where I doubted anyone recognized the class signifiers—Zong's adopted accent was a bit comical. He was also single, well-built and handsome. I wondered for a fleeting moment if he was gay.

"Yes, those are common concerns for both Westerners and Chinese. The housing crisis and efforts to solve it? Unemployment—causes and remedies?"

Previously sagging eyes now reopened.

"Policies that affect families? New approaches to education? Conflict between teenagers and parents?"

Backs straightened.

"Who takes care of the elderly? How does your health-care system work? Who is making new music? What kind of stories are novelists, playwrights and filmmakers telling?"

Eyes were fully focused now.

"Are there new fashion designers emerging? What's the most popular show on TV or radio?"

Some easy laughter.

"Yes, your audience wants to know the same things about your country that presumably you want to know about them. How can we have this conversation in our work lives at Radio Beijing?"

Zong, who I suspected was the only one whose comprehension was immediate because he had recently lived among native English speakers, was the first to respond.

"But we only translate what we are given."

Awkward silence. Chairs squeaked. Eyes diverted.

I knew they were not the originators of the scripts, but in the broadcast journalism class I was agitating for them to develop critical reporting skills. Observation, interviewing and investigation. The importance of questions. Doubt.

I tried another tack.

"Well, should we discuss international stories that go beyond banquet news?"

Hush filled the room. We listened to the faint sounds in the hallway.

Oxbridge Zong plunged in again. "Let's talk about the Iran–Iraq situation. I'm really interested in international politics. Since I left the London School of Economics, I have had little chance to discuss these things."

"I hate politics!" declared the petulant Zhou. "I'm not interested in anything."

The glum-looking Chen spoke up. "Chinese hate international news. It's part of tradition." Chen, too, had studied English for two years in England but during the middle of the Cultural Revolution. I suspected he had a profound story to tell.

"Yes," added an older comrade, Huang. "We are egocentric."

I was shocked at this Freudian term popping up in China, where psychosexual analysis seemed so absent. From Huang's age, I suspected that he might have been exposed to those ideas before they were banned during the

Cultural Revolution or earlier. Then again, perhaps he had recently read an issue of *Newsweek*. Although it was too expensive for the comrades, and they were really not supposed to read this foreign publication, somehow copies originating from a foreign expert would make the rounds. Several comrades had already told me they found *Newsweek*'s writing incomprehensible. Too many popular cultural references that mystified them. I suspected that it represented too much consumer and celebrity culture. Too much sexual innuendo.

Back to China as egocentric.

"Perhaps this is something the United States has in common with China," I ventured. Zong laughed.

"We are the Middle Kingdom," Chen said, ignoring my offering. "The center of the Earth, but we should not cut ourselves off from the outside world."

This was promising.

Zong then ratcheted things up. "The comrades do not want to discuss ideas because they have been told what to think. The Party is politics. They do not have to think."

This was beyond anything I was expecting. Would they get into trouble?

Zong didn't let up. "Let's talk about the difference between capitalism and socialism."

Perhaps his two years studying at the London School of Economics had loosened his self-censorship. Unlike the others, he seemed fearless to talk about big ideas. I suggested we might break the subject down to manageable components, like housing under those contrasting systems. Or health care. But there was too much resistance from the group. Zong was disappointed. So I asked him what he meant by socialism.

"It's a system that provides improved material conditions," he responded.

"Given that definition" I chided, "the United States, Canada and Western Europe are socialist paradises." Everybody laughed.

Zong corrected me. "But the United States has many poor people."

I acknowledged that and explained that Canada was the more successful middle-class country. It was a blind spot for Americans who couldn't see or admit that other advanced industrialized countries had achieved more material well-being for working-class people, including Germany, France and the Scandinavian countries. They all had much lower percentages living in poverty.

Zhou spoke up. "I don't want to talk about politics or socialism."

Clearly this was a warning to move onto something else.

Xia Xia called out, "It is too complicated."

Someone else called out "Too big."

Yet another voice: "Another time."

"OK." I packed away my private musings about who in the group were Party members. "What do you want, then, for yourselves—in your own lives?"

"I want to improve my English to do my work better." Zhou was playing a disciplinary role by being a goody two-shoe. Safe.

"I want to improve my English." Liu Hui affirmed the direction while wrestling Dong Hua's hair onto rollers. "I'm not interested in politics."

"I want to improve my English so I can do a better job and earn more money," repeated the tall and gangly Xia Xia. The echo of responses could have been considered the correct Party line of the moment.

"I want to improve my English and become a professional journalist," declared the impatient Zong. "And get better training and earn more money. We all want more money." Zong was the only one who expressed real ambition in terms of journalism. But even he emphasized the common denominator: "We all want more money."

I knew from the scripts I was editing that the new economic policy in China placed new emphasis on consumer goods industries. Some workers were given coupons at their workplaces for discounts on appliances like sewing machines, refrigerators and TVs. Zong and the others were parroting this new policy.

"That's the main concern," gloomy Chen emphasized. "More money and housing."

Everybody laughed and repeated like a Greek chorus, "Yes, more money and better housing."

"So there's a subject which could lead to a story for broadcast. We could try to find a way to personalize the policy. Make it more human, more specific combined with policy directions," I pushed. But nobody was interested. It was the end of this exchange. The group quickly put away the extra chairs and left, as usual, en masse. Nobody lingered to have a more intimate exchange.

I was disturbed by their comments. Not because I thought the Chinese had enough material comfort. I had witnessed their economic stress. And I was beginning to learn about the social consequences of congested housing without facilities.

No, I was disappointed by what I wasn't hearing. I had asked what they wanted for their future, and there was no mention of any political, philosophical or spiritual ideal. Like freedom to create or change their world. No mention of freedom to change jobs, of more equality, democracy, happiness. No idealism about creating a better world for their children. Freedom of speech or association—not mentioned. All of this, I guessed, was too dangerous. They did express that they wanted to become more proficient in English, but Zong was the only one who expressed interest in becoming a better journalist.

Having grown up and lived in two major countries shaped by immigration, by the severing of ties with the old world, creating a culture defined by self-reliance, individual striving and the Protestant work ethic, how could I translate or understand what happened here? Was I stuck on the Western enlightenment and a particularly Americanized version of its values and ideals? Canadian culture encouraged communalism and cooperation—what's good for the community, while its southern neighbor placed more emphasis on individual rights and competition for success. I sensed that these bifurcated paradigms of my experience were useless in understanding what happened to character, values, ideals, goals and dreams in China.

At night I was reading about the "purification" movements that began even before Liberation, when Mao's cohorts were organizing the peasants in the countryside and continued as anti-Rightist campaigns after. These movements attempted to break down bourgeois thinking and behavior, replacing individualism and greed—as well as critical thinking—with collective consciousness and obedience to the Party. Had thought reform imploded? Did I really even understand the long-term effects of all that confrontation, struggle and indoctrination? Did I understand it in my own culture? How hegemonic ideas, values and perspectives were embedded in our journalistic enterprises, advertising, education, cultural products and expression?

How did ideology work? I used to think I understood it. After all, I had studied Antonio Gramsci and the Frankfurt School as a graduate student. I wondered if I should reread Franz Schurmann's *Ideology and Organization in China* that first appeared in the late '60s at the beginning of the Cultural Revolution. How relevant could Schurmann's work be, since he was never able to conduct research directly in China but only from refugees in Hong Kong? I remember that it revealed fissures between Mao and Party leaders, like Liu Shaoqi, over whether power should derive from the Party elite or the masses.

My disappointment with the comrades stemmed from their expressing purely materialist, prosaic desires. More money. No different from many of their counterparts in America. Somehow, it wasn't what I expected from the People's Republic of China.

ONE AFTERNOON, while searching for the translator of a script that was giving me a headache, I walked into one of the big rooms on our floor, where twenty or so comrades labored, to discover a haircut underway. A temporary barbershop was set up near the windows where Fan was wrapped in a plastic cape. The barber—Wang Zhenbang (Rejuvenate the Country)—was putting more creative gusto into this haircut than the translations he produced. I tried to imagine this scene in the offices at NPR or NBC.

To my astonishment, I was told, "The price is two cents!" When I responded, "The price is right," everyone laughed and repeated the new expression. I mused about stories I heard about Red Guards attacking young women with scissors during the Cultural Revolution, cutting off their long pigtails to leave just enough hair to pull back into two short ones.

Afterward, Professor Li told me that, like other workers, he received a bonus of one and a half *kuai*—the popular term for *yuan* or *renminbi*— a month ($1 US) for haircuts and the bathhouse, which cost fifteen cents.

"Once a week," he replied to my obvious question.

Li and his wife paid about five *yuan* a month ($3.33 US) for their two ten-by-fifteen rooms.

"We were lucky to get so much space," Li grinned. "My father was living with us when we were assigned housing. That's how we got an extra room. Otherwise four of us would be living in one room. My father left and returned to his village."

But like most dwellers in their 1950s tenements, they shared the toilet and the closet-sized kitchen with two other families. They, like other families, owned a little two-burner gas stove, like those propane camping stoves we used when I was a kid. Unlike me, they paid for their own gas and electricity. They didn't own a refrigerator.

Childcare and food were the two major expenses for Li and his wife. Food consumed almost half the monthly salary.

Li told me that they got some free medical coverage and they had to pay for some. The work unit pitched in about one *yuan* a month toward any medical expenses. While many of his coworkers had TV, Li did not.

These details came in dribs and drabs, as Professor Li didn't really want to talk about the facts of his life. He was a bit evasive when I asked about meat. "Not every day" was his careful answer. Nor chicken or fish, which I knew were luxuries. And it wasn't just about cost but the endless lines at the state stores and the new peasant free markets to get them. Those markets were outdoors, and it was uncomfortably cold already.

MY UNIVERSE of comrades included the China Hands who joined our regular Wednesday night study group with foreign experts. That's where I met Iona Kramer. Originally from Wisconsin, Iona went off to college in New York City then became a reporter for The *National Guardian*, a progressive newspaper founded and edited by Jim Aronson, my conduit to working at Radio Beijing. While in New York, she had met and fell in love with Gentom Wang, a student from China. In 1955, after they married, they moved to China to help build a new egalitarian society. She had been a polisher for *China Reconstructs* ever since while her husband taught at Tsinghua University.

Iona and her husband spent eight years under house arrest during the Cultural Revolution. They were released from confinement in 1978.

Now approaching sixty, Iona was more sympathetic to our complaints about the "system" than were the other old-timers. "I keep a shoe to throw at the wall, to defuse." She laughed. "It's vital."

I made a mental note.

Iona also attended a study group organized by another famous China Hand, David Crook. Like the other China Hands, Crook and his wife, Isabel, were seduced by the goals of the agrarian revolution and immigrated here to make a contribution to New China. Their path-breaking work led to the creation of the Foreign Language Institute, where they taught many future leaders, teachers and translators. Some of the China Hands had been part of the early efforts at Communist Party organizing from the 1930s in Yan'an. Others—Americans—had fled McCarthyism back home and had come to China in the early 1950s. Despite committing their adult lives to the socialist mission, many were imprisoned as spies during the Cultural Revolution.

Israel "Eppy" Epstein was perhaps the best known of the China Hands. Born in Warsaw, Poland, his family fled to Tianjin after WWI, and Eppy began his journalism career there as a teenager, eventually covering the Japanese invasion of China for Western news services. In the late 1940s, he moved to the US, wrote books and campaigned for an enlightened look at China, arguing that the Communists were the only future. He was blacklisted, like other Americans who sought a more sympathetic approach to the Communists. Song Qingling (Madame Sun Yat-sen) encouraged him to return to China to edit *China Reconstructs*, which she founded in the early 1950s. As editor in chief, he was also the boss of my new friend, Ron.

Eppy became a Chinese citizen and member of the Chinese Communist Party in the 1960s, yet during the Cultural Revolution, both he and his wife were imprisoned separately in solitary confinement for five years. Zhou Enlai personally apologized to him upon his release.

I had also met Eleanor Bidien when I first arrived. A friend in New York had met her while traveling with one of the first American groups to visit China after Mao's death. Eleanor was a translator and editor at Xinhua News Agency. When I telephoned, she invited me for tea. Her apartment was reminiscent of a petite Greenwich Village studio, bulging with books and cloudy with cigarette smoke. Coughing incessantly, Eleanor's gravel voice offered a haiku version of her story.

In the 1930s, she had joined the Communist Youth branch of the Party in New York City. By 1951, hounded by McCarthyism, she made her way to Beijing. Her husband, Charles Bidien, had been editor of the *Indonesian Review*, published by the American Committee for a Free Indonesia. He was killed in Indonesia during the horrible massacre of Communists in 1965. Eleanor had managed to stay out of prison during the Cultural Revolution, but she would not say what happened to her. While she seemed to manage a lower profile than some China Hands, the result was horrible isolation. When I grumbled about some things Chinese, Eleanor insisted that I understand the deeply conservative nature of Chinese culture.

For me, the enigma of the China Hands was their committed defense of the Chinese government—the Chinese Communist Party—after what they had witnessed and experienced. They seemed reluctant to discuss the dire consequences of the Great Leap Forward. Nor did they acknowledge the thousands of lives lost in the land reform movement in the 1940s or the suffering caused by purification campaigns since then. Nor the labor camps, the prisons, the persecutions. At least, they were not about to discuss these deep concerns with newcomers like me.

I thought I understood their idealism. Their passionate commitment to the goals of egalitarianism and socialism. The Chinese Revolution as documented at the village level by another China Hand, Bill Hinton, in *Fanshen,* and by David and Isabel Crook in their book, *Revolution in a Chinese Village, Ten Mile Inn*, was inspiring and breathtaking in its complexity. I had taken up reading both books again, following Eleanor's instructions to remember the task that the Party undertook to defeat feudalism and landlordism, to crush and break the centuries-old traditions of the countryside that kept a class of millions servile and broken.

"Remember that the Agrarian Law of 1948, passed by the CCP, was *as significant* to the death of landlordism during the Chinese Civil War as was the Emancipation Declaration to the defeat of slavery in the American Civil War," she emphasized, her eyes fixed on mine.

"And," she admonished, "remember the US government, with its brilliant founding documents, has interfered with democratically elected presidents in Guatemala and Iran, and collaborated to kill Lumumba in the Congo. Then ask again how people accommodate to a government with its ideals and realities stretched far apart."

"But what about legal rights, freedoms, rights to representation, to a fair trial, to free speech?" I asked.

"Freedoms all come at a cost," she replied. "The last era of unlimited freedom of expression here was experienced in the first frenzied years of the Cultural Revolution, and nobody wants a return of that. Freedom without protection. Who will protect you from the freedom and speech of others? How do we balance it? And as to rights, how long was it from the writing of the Declaration of Independence and the Constitution to the Civil Rights law? Almost a hundred years. And do blacks have full rights now? Are they treated equally as whites? How about women? How about Native Americans? And what about US imperialist wars, like Vietnam? What is happening in Central America now? How does the Cold War distort American freedoms and rights? Did any of these things cause you to renounce your government and leave?" Eleanor assumed I was a US citizen, but her question was still meaningful.

I mulled over Eleanor's situation. As a young Communist, she was blacklisted in the US. Discriminated against in finding work. In China, she had been provided with work, housing, food and cotton rations, health care and, most of the time, respect.

Pondering the China Hands, I admired how much they had embraced Chinese culture and language, but I had more difficulty with their steadfast support for the political and moral mission of the Communist Party, which seemed to have veered off course repeatedly. Then again, the China Hands had expressed deep affection for the Chinese, both urban intellectuals and peasants.

The China Hands had suffered during politically cruel movements of the past thirty years, but they had stayed the course. Their commitments and pleasure in language and literature kept them nurtured. And friendships with a few good souls. What could anyone ask for in life? They had been able to write books and articles, edit, teach and study.

Even if they had wanted to return to the West, I imagined that the paternalism and control that came with the Party system would make it difficult. Sidney Rittenberg was testing the waters. Others had tried leaving during the Cultural Revolution but had been denied passports by the Chinese government. None of the China Hands would mention that issue now.

After the long bike ride back home from the study group, I needed something profoundly familiar with emotional depth. I flipped in a cassette of Aretha Franklin's 1967 album *I Never Loved a Man the Way I Loved You*, totemic for a generation of blacks and whites. Taking us high and mellow at parties, I had used cuts from it in radio documentaries.

First up: "Respect." and I was dancing around the room then collapsed into a chair. I reflected about the study group.

Helmut Opletal was there. He said he was dreaming in Chinese.

Gerald was there—a Chinese-New Zealander. He said there was no place for him in China or in New Zealand. That it was the dilemma of certain overseas Chinese. He told us about a Beijing professor and famous artist who would not come to a party if foreigners were there. So despite the coming trial of the Gang of Four, fear of persecution and intimidation were still paramount. I had to keep remembering what had taken place here for the past thirty years. The factions that supported the Gang of Four were still in our midst. Still in our workplaces.

I was listening to Aretha's "Dr. Feelgood" while mulling over other issues of our discontent that the group tackled—problems we experienced in our work units with the lack of motivation. Someone suggested that the comrades' low energy and somnambulism was partly tied to the amount of protein in their diet. And...no coffee. The Industrial Revolution was fueled with coffee and sugar! But then there was a lot of adrenalin during the Cultural Revolution.

But to hell with it all. I was now listening to Aretha belt out "Let the Good Times Roll."

BY LATE October, temperatures were already plummeting, and there were no promises of heat in the office or at the apartment for at least another three weeks. Some locals were already wearing white face masks against the advance gusts of the Gobi Desert winds, which would bring a lot of sand our way soon. At work, we were all bundled up like snow people. My fingers were so stiff I could hardly hammer the keys. Some days I stayed home and worked near my hot plate, listening to Miles Davis, drinking coffee and smoking Guangming cigarettes. The only consolation was dreaming about a quick trip to the steamy South—Guangzhou and Hong Kong.

I needed to go to Hong Kong to pick up a different manual typewriter with an English keyboard. I also needed coffee. On the way I would visit Wendy in Guangzhou, where she was teaching. Just planning for the trip created chaos and confusion involving all sorts of folks because nobody knew the location of the airline office. The head of the foreign experts' office was away, and nobody else had that information!

A dozen colleagues sent me in as many directions in the city. I wasted hours on frustrating bicycle forays. One expat explained that the leaders really didn't want us to do these things on our own without the foreign experts' office controlling the entire process. Another issue might have been that since my coworkers never traveled—especially by air—they really had no idea how to find the airline ticket office.

October 10, 1980, Journal:

Suddenly cabbages are everywhere. Hanging from clotheslines, propped in window ledges and lining rooftops, laid out on the grounds of Radio Beijing— in the swimming pool used to air condition the TV studios in summer, on the sidewalks. As I bicycled around the city I kept snapping. Thousands and thousands of cabbages being dried for winter food!

In a letter from Mum yesterday, she said that a letter I had sent her with photos took five weeks, indicating that it had been opened.

"SO MUCH space" was always the first reaction of my coworkers when they came to my apartment for the discussion group.

"If I had space like this, I could really do good work and study more," said Zong, who resided in the singles dorm sharing a room with three others.

"Do you get lonely here?" came from the more reflective Chen.

It was the most poignant question any of my Chinese colleagues had asked. Caught off guard, I was speechless. Besides, the query was posed with an audience when it really demanded a one-on-one kind of response.

I cannot remember now how I answered. I only recorded his question in my journal. Probably I said I was used to living alone. In San Francisco, Boston and New York. How could I have complained about loneliness in Beijing, given my privileges?

But I realized both Oxbridge Zong and Chen had studied abroad. The disorientation, culture shock and loneliness were emotions they would have experienced, even though the first Chinese studying abroad during and after the Cultural Revolution usually lived in special living quarters set up by the local Chinese consulate, where they were watched closely by Party members. Perhaps they, too, were Party members. Perhaps that was why they could go.

At this gathering of our discussion group, I suggested we talk about housing, since they had all expressed the need for more and better living quarters last time.

"How is housing allocated? Who decides? Who gets priority? What factors do they consider?"

Oxbridge Zong always spoke up first. "We fill in a form. Where you work. What you do. How long you have lived in your housing. How many people live with you. Why you want to change."

The discussion seemed to end there. Nobody wanted to add more. As if they were exhausted by their conditions and stunted desires. Perhaps they would not talk because any revelation that might be considered negative could reverberate through Radio Beijing, their work unit or *danwei*.

The *danwei* was the major organizing principle in China. Everyone was assigned to a *danwei* for life. The *danwei* provided the infrastructure for tying people to the policies of the Communist Party. Information flowed up and down through it. Services and resources were distributed through it. Permission to travel, to marry, to have children, to divorce was given by *danwei* leaders. Resources like canteens, ration coupons for cotton, cooking oil, childcare and schools, clinics, bathhouses and now, with Deng Xiaoping as helmsman, subsidies for basic appliances. All were distributed through your *danwei*.

Even though cranes hovered above the skyline as dozens of new high-rise apartments pushed up like teeth above the gum line of the traditional cityscape, the crunch for housing was considered so enormous that it would be years before the living squeeze would be eased.

"The newspapers encourage young people to stall marriage until they have studied and begun working," Liu Hui explained. "Then you apply to your work unit to get permission to marry. If you don't have housing which you also get through your unit, you won't get permission to marry."

"If you're older," Zong added, "you have a better chance. Unless there's room in your parent's house, it's impossible."

"What about peasants?"

"No problem!" Zong exclaimed in a huff. "They have big houses! They can build them themselves!"

No new housing had been built for Radio Beijing employees for almost two decades. A thirteen-story building was now under construction behind the station producing, anxieties over who would get the new apartments. The tension permeated the rest of our session.

Bao Hong (Red), in her late twenties, had been married for a couple of years. She and her husband still didn't have a room together. After having a miscarriage when she fell from her bicycle on the way to work, she "borrowed" a student's university dorm room so she could live closer to work. Now she was trying to get pregnant again. Her husband still lived in a dormitory at his workplace.

How do they rendezvous for sex? I wondered to myself. Does the government provide sex rooms, like the honeymoon rooms for newlyweds?

"I want an apartment for my wife and baby." Fan Chaoyang (Toward the Sun) was petulant. Twenty-seven, he had recently studied in Ottawa, Canada, for two years. He and his new wife lived apart because there was no housing for them. She lived with her parents and he in the men's dorm sharing a room with several roommates. His impatience and anger were barely suppressed.

The Canadian experience, I suspected, had only made him more frustrated with conditions in China. Sometimes I felt that he wanted to avoid direct contact with me because he understood viscerally how far the Chinese had slipped backward in economic development and the price they had paid for the Cultural Revolution and other political movements in terms of material well-being and job opportunities.

After all the propaganda at home, in Canada Chaoyang had witnessed a social democracy that provided real services to people. Job mobility, housing choices, health care, accessible universal higher education, old age pensions, unemployment insurance. Freedom of movement. Freedom of thought. And that mess of a political system—democracy. He was guarded in sharing his thoughts about any of this. I worried about the disjuncture for him. He was very bright. Seemed eager for change. How long would it take? Did the Canadian experience simply leave him with longings and desires that could never be fulfilled?

There were tiny escape holes. Wang Dongfeng (Eastern Wind), one of our best announcers who was in his mid-forties, lived with his wife and child in two rooms with eight people. He had applied for a job transfer to a unit that was building new housing for its employees. There were hints that his request for a work and housing transfer was going to be granted.

And so my knowledge of the stress and concerns of my colleagues' lives evolved and deepened. During my nighttime bicycling, I caught glimpses of the blue light leaking from windows as families huddled around their new black-and-white TVs. Sublimation. Pacification. Stress relief. Soon it would foster desires. Old American sitcoms were now part of the TV schedule. Advertising billboards were sprouting on some of the downtown streets.

The discussion group with the comrades had reminded me of the Cultural Revolution slogan—"Serve the People." During that revolutionary movement, concern for the self, for goods and services, was criticized as bourgeois and reactionary. Yet it was clear from my tiny sliver of urban experience that some critical needs were unfulfilled. Clearly, the earlier task had been to feed a hungry nation, clothe and provide some kind of roof. I needed a perspective on 800 million peasants. Also on the enormity of the task coming out of a hundred years of corruption, exploitation and occupation. Wars with imperialists. Civil war. Revolution. But not long after independence and Liberation came the break with the Soviets, shunning their aid and expertise. The Great Leap Forward was a disastrous policy responding to the Soviet withdrawal. Economic productivity slid. And slid again with the Cultural Revolution. Model farms and factories, much touted then, were now being revealed as hollow shams.

By 1980, it was fashionable to criticize the Cultural Revolution years for their effect on economic conditions. Besides lamenting the dearth of housing, the comrades complained about the lack of services, the closing down of all the teahouses, restaurants and street-service industries like laundries, shoe and bicycle repair shops.

But serving the people was not just about providing services; it embodied a spirit of collective endeavor toward a better future. That spirit had been broken.

Older coworkers spoke with nostalgia about the "collective spirit" of the early 1950s, when everybody pitched in to help build New China.

"My parents, like many other comrades, went to Tiananmen Square to help haul bricks to build the Great Hall of the People," said Shadow Zhang. "In the 1950s and early 1960s, people helped each other. If somebody needed money, and if our parents had some, they just gave it to them. Now people only think about themselves. People have become selfish."

Perhaps she was forgetting the persecution that also accompanied those years. Would anyone have helped those who were attacked and tortured during the anti-Rightist and Hundred Flowers Movement of the late '50s?

Zhang Qiannian, the leader of the features section, shared her story. "I came from a business family. When the Japanese invaded, we first escaped to

Hong Kong, and then to Chongqing (the Nationalist Party capital during the Japanese invasion). I remember as a little girl the perilous boat ride we took at night from Hong Kong to the southern coast of China, where we then took a train and then a truck to Chongqing. I thought it was an exciting adventure. I was too young to appreciate the dangers of it."

In the mid-'40s, Leader Zhang's family had sent her to the US to study. While at Oberlin College, she met Liu, a student from Beijing who was active in the progressive movement, the anti-Japanese resistance part of the Communist Party.

"I never knew about it before. We fell in love and got married in 1949 and after Liberation decided to return and help build a new China. The spirit during those early years in the country was so different from today."

Shadow Zhang was one of the few in the department who was critical of the current emphasis on individual material striving and its potential effect on people.

"She's got a good heart," said Professor Li.

I assumed that Shadow Zhan been a Red Guard when she was in high school.

"She is a model worker," Professor Li continued. "She takes all her assignments enthusiastically, quietly."

Shadow Zhang, the younger Zhang, was efficient, competent and uncomplaining. She would visit staff members who were in the hospital or pay house calls to those who had been away from work for several days. Although department politics were never shared openly with me, I discovered it was Zhang Wei who tried to figure out what people were thinking and feeling about leaders, about relationships. And she would try to communicate this to the Party hierarchy. Yet that was, perhaps, exactly my discomfort with her. That she could not exactly be trusted. That she was a conduit to report everything to a higher echelon of the Party. Already, I knew how complicated this dual role of "taking care of" and "controlling" was becoming for me. How did the others feel about it? Did they ever know anything different? Could they stand back and see it?

Shadow Zhang was the only person in the department who got excited about the resurrection of Lei Feng in the fall of 1980. The first Lei Feng campaign appeared in 1964, about two years after this model soldier died in a tragic accident. He was heralded as a hero who worked hard, did good deeds and was devoted to the Party. Some critics have suggested that the first campaign promoting "Live Like Lei Feng" was meant to rebuild confidence in Mao after his ruinous Great Leap Forward policy led to massive starvation and deaths.

The Lei Feng campaign consisted of a countrywide tour of his physical artifacts, including his ever-expanding diaries. It also included photographs of him polishing the cars of high cadres, washing his comrades' socks, sewing on buttons and generally exhibiting revolutionary fervor, selflessness, modesty and obedience to the Party.

Susan Sontag, in her essay collection *On Photography*, commented that the Lei Feng photographs appeared to be false, since he was unknown at the time of his supposed good works and it would have been unlikely that anyone was around with a camera documenting him. Within two years of the first Lei Feng campaign, the Cultural Revolution began.

In the fall of 1980, the "Live Like Lei Feng" campaign was reemerging from the dustbin of history. Lei Feng was now seen as a means to resuscitate Mao's image from the calamities of the Cultural Revolution, to revive a more innocent spirit of the revolution he masterminded.

Perhaps the Party leadership saw the threat of cynicism and political exhaustion. They needed to jolt the citizenry into a new social discipline and obedience to the Party. I edited scripts about the new crusade. One manifestation in Beijing was a tree planting campaign. Some of the comrades snickered at the comeback of Lei Feng. But Shadow Zhang spent a day in the rain planting trees on boulevards in Beijing.

At least one comrade was openly skeptical about her enthusiasm. "Zhang Wei is the only one who mouths political slogans in the department," she remarked.

In our department discussion group, Shadow Zhang seldom spoke. I suspected she was there to report on the discussion to the Party leaders. Otherwise I couldn't figure out why she came.

When there is a scarcity of goods or services—when some get them and others don't—competition or corruption takes over. That describes what was happening in 1980 China. While there was a revving up of consumer goods production—bicycles, watches, radios, TVs, washers, refrigerators, fans—acquiring these items meant comrades had to apply to their work unit for the coupon to ease the cost. Since there were not enough coupons for everyone, leaders decided who would get them. A scholar in our study group explained that it was at that point when bribery and gift-giving could enter. This was when *guanxi* kicked in. Favors, gifts, bribes that bind loyalty of one to the other and become the means of getting access or something out of reach. *Guanxi*.

This was the point of corruption, discontent, disillusionment.

Apparently, contemporary short stories, letters to the editor and TV plays were addressing this disenchantment. That these cultural products had passed the censors meant that the Party was acknowledging the problem and, through Lei Feng, trying to tackle it.

Despite the concern for growing selfishness, I was moved by forms of social caring in the department. While one of the comrades remained in hospital after a serious operation, she was never left unattended. Each comrade signed up for a time slot to visit her because her husband lived and worked in another province.

EARLIER IN the fall I had convinced Leader Zhang that we should produce a program on the New Marriage and Family Law, but the effort to reach potential interviewees by telephone seemed insurmountable, even if the phone was functioning that day. Despite this, I had interviewed the students at the *People's Daily* Journalism School. After I told Leader Zhang about the content, there was never any reply.

Taking another tack, I pitched her on the idea of reading Lao She's *Rickshaw Boy* on the air. Lao She had been persecuted during the Cultural Revolution until he committed suicide by drowning himself in a lake. He had just been rehabilitated and a movie was in the works. The Party must have sanctioned our reading the novel for broadcast. No different, I supposed, than the gatekeepers at the US networks or the senior editors at NPR.

GIGGLES AND Mandarin whispers intermingled in my living room as a passel of ten comrades dragged their chairs in a circle for our regular discussion group. As I passed around sodas and cookies, I had to break through the chaotic shuffling and Mandarin backtalk. Were they gossiping about my amateur drawings on the walls? My messy apartment? Or ...?

"Come on. We're supposed to speak English here. This is for you!" Impatient, once again, I suggested that they determine the subject of our conversation. "Are you interested in American or Chinese themes?"

"American!" shouted Xia Xia. Several others looked at me expectantly.

The downbeat Chen began. "I would like to talk about the May Seventh Cadre Schools."

This was promising. I knew from discussions at my study group with China Hands that these were the farm "schools" that city intellectual workers were sent to during the Cultural Revolution. Not schools in the academic sense but education in the fields and factories. Thought reform through grubby labor, sweat and dirt.

"For one or two years, cadres had to do hard physical labor on a commune," Chen explained. "I was sent to Cadre School in 1973 for two years. It was a waste."

"Why?" I queried. "I thought that you were supposed to learn from the peasants. Did you share your knowledge with them? Teach them to read?"

"I grew up on a farm." Chen's face screwed up into a tortured look. "During the worker-peasant-soldier movement of the Cultural Revolution, I was sent to university. In 1971, I was sent to England by the government to study English for two years."

I was trying to imagine Chen, hot from the Cultural Revolution's emphasis on class struggle and political education, landing in London to study.

"When I returned," he continued, "I was sent to Cadre School, so I had no chance to use my English. I did not need to learn about physical labor. I grew up on a farm. When I came back from England, I had no opportunity to practice English or utilize the study."

Squirming in his seat, Chen's body and face took on their usual look of defeat. If the peasant who had the extraordinary opportunity through the Revolution to study in England was now depressed with what followed, something was terribly wrong. When Chen bit into Mao's pear, was it rotten? Had the Cultural Revolution zealots punished him by sending him back to the farm after his privileged educational opportunity in London? Was it factional war? Personal vendettas? Would I ever, ever understand?

I knew that in 1966, at the beginning of the Cultural Revolution, all of the universities closed. It was unclear when many of them reopened. In 1972, only two reopened in Beijing. But after several years of violent class struggle between Red Guard factions that included the persecution, beating, incarceration, killing and suicide of some professors and administrators, along with the destruction of books and facilities, the universities were decimated.

I felt grateful for Chen's courage to share his candid thoughts—the most dramatic and intimate revelation that any comrade had yet offered. He was inviting me to plunge into his tortured soul. My selfish complaints and disorders filled me with shame.

"We are supposed to learn from the physical work of peasants and workers. Not only theory from books," Xia Xia piped in. "I was sent to an army farm in 1974. Young people were sent to army farms. This was not too far from

Guangzhou, where I lived as a student at the Guangzhou Foreign Language Institute. We worked every day. Studied Mao's *Little Red Book*." She giggled. "We planted vegetables."

Zhou Hong said she had been sent to the countryside to Cadre School three times. In 1957, 1969 and 1975. Deconstructing those dates, I figured her first stint would have been during the anti-Rightist campaign in the late 1950s, the second one at the height of the Cultural Revolution and then just a year before the Cultural Revolution officially ended. Was she considered a Rightist despite her revolutionary name? But then I had to remember that people changed their names with the political moods. Choosing "Hong"(Red)" during the Cultural Revolution was hedging one's bets.

"I joined the Army and left home at the age of sixteen," Zhou Hong added.

This startled my assumptions about her being a Rightist. I knew she was a Party member, and I had picked up hostility toward her from other comrades. What had she done at Radio Beijing to elicit so much hostility and resentment? During the Cultural Revolution had she ratted on others? Had she been particularly punishing and cruel? She was stunningly beautiful, so I wondered if she had stolen a colleague's husband. I stifled my questions.

"Did you have much contact with peasants? Did you develop relationships with them?"

"Most Cadre Schools were separate from the communes," Liu Hui explained. "People had little contact with the local peasants."

But Zhou Hong had actually lived with a peasant family during one of her times in the countryside. "They treated me like their daughter." She had maintained contact. Most of the other English department comrades had never been back to visit the peasants they worked with or met.

Chen's face contorted with misery. "We had to do everything by hand. All the farm work we did was by hand."

"Yes," Zhou Hong confirmed. "Even when they had farm machinery in the sheds, we still had to do it by hand."

Why?

"So we can learn about physical labor," Chen added sarcastically.

"To punish us. We are intellectual workers," Zhou Hong added. "Intellectuals should do everything by hand. Physical labor is good." I sensed from these comments that Zhou Hong was a committed Maoist.

But I was confused by this stunning contradiction. Physical work was supposed to be good—intellectuals were supposed to learn from it—yet it was used as punishment. Many intellectual workers who were severely criticized during the Cultural Revolution were banished to the countryside to clean public latrines, to haul the honey pots of human excrement to the surrounding farms, to do back-breaking work, not to use their intelligence and training to improve the lot of peasants. There was something hypocritical at the core of this policy.

Zhou Hong chirped, "We brought culture to the peasants. They wanted us. We taught them and they taught us." It sounded like cant.

Chen contradicted her. "It was impossible to teach them to read. There were no books."

"And no paper and pencils in most villages!" Liu Hui confirmed.

"Newspapers were weeks late," said Xia Xia. "There was no information."

"The good people were peasant-worker-soldiers," said Chen. "Book learning was seen as corrupt and especially foreign languages."

"But you are all students of a foreign language! Were you punished for that?"

Xia Xia: "That's why we read Mao's quotations only." More giggles.

Zhou Hong disciplined the group. "The peasants were often very kind to us. They were very poor, but they gave us little things."

I tried to imagine how farmers looked at this experiment in social engineering. All these city slickers with delicate hands showing up to dig and hoe, haul and weed.

Shadow Zhang had been silent until now. She adjusted her glasses. "The peasants have a lot to teach us. They work hard. Their work feeds us. We need to learn from them."

Aaahhh, the perfect ideological outcome. And a truth, of course. *How must she feel about the fact that peasants are rarely mentioned in our broadcasts?*

I knew that Shadow Zhang and Zhou Hong were Party members, and I suspected that Liu Hui was as well. I wondered about Chen and Xia Xia. Perhaps only Party members could come to these discussions. It was ironic that the only person in the group from a peasant background was the most critical of the Cadre Schools. This was one of the major attempts to overcome the gap between the urban intelligentsia and the rural peasants, to bridge the gulf between intellectual and manual work while fusing theory and practice. I was surprised to hear the cynicism, dissatisfaction and bitter humor about this important Maoist program. Had a program meant to reeducate intellectual workers through manual tasks turned into a program using grubby physical work as punishment?

In an effort to explore or explode—I wasn't sure myself—the different ways that work was viewed in the Big Bad West, I took the floor that night and described all the jobs I had held since the age of thirteen. At least I would expand their vocabularies. I had been a babysitter, waitress, cashier at a drive-up hamburger joint, sales clerk in a department store, berry-picker, long-distance telephone operator, donut maker, a teaching assistant at an Arthur Murray dance studio; at a boathouse in Victoria I had been a fishing guide, tackle salesperson, ice-cream scooper besides filling outboard motor tanks. That was all by the time I had finished my first year of college.

As I started rattling off my "life list of jobs," there were giggles, but as I progressed, silence filled the room. Perhaps it all felt incomprehensible to them in a system where you are assigned to a job and workplace for life.

When they looked at me in puzzlement, I tried to humanize the list by telling little stories, like the one about my donut-making disasters when the manager of Eaton's, a prestigious department store in Victoria, had descended four flights of escalators to reprimand me—a sixteen-year-old—for creating a stink of deep-fried fat throughout the building with burning donuts.

Then there were the mishaps of waitressing. I had rushed too quickly in an old teahouse with a slanted floor; I had slipped and a whole tray of cups and saucers as well as pots filled with boiling water went flying across the room, slightly burning one customer and nearly missing another with the crockery missiles. I had been only fourteen.

Between years dropping in and out of university at Berkeley and graduate school in St. Louis, I had been an executive secretary, an environmental researcher and an assistant professor of sociology at Washington University. All of this was before my professional career as a reporter and a producer in radio and television.

I had bought my first typewriter at the age of fourteen after working at the Oak Bay Boathouse all summer. That typewriter became a metaphorical tool for the rest of my life.

My working history, I explained to my captive audience, had been a valuable education. While I had learned about corporate organizations, business practices, law offices, radio stations, telephone switchboards, management, money and the proscribed jobs for women—no small matter—mostly I had learned about the lives of other working folks, and that fueled my insatiable curiosity that propelled me toward the social sciences at university. My working history had also cured me of dull, repetitive jobs. Then participation in political movements fostered my desire to interview, document and report.

The comrades' brows were knitting themselves into squiggly horizontal lines and foreheads were creasing.

On a roll now, as if oblivious to their need to understand, I was reflecting on my own working and political history—that constellation of experiences that incited my search for understanding, my desire to re-mold the world and my commitment to confront injustices. I had bitten into a version of Mao's pear and been transformed.

I explained that as I developed new reportorial and production skills, my work took on new meaning. In the anti-careerist and collectivist spirit of the 1960s—partly influenced by the Cultural Revolution—I worked for alternative newspapers, community radio and television projects that embraced a critique of mainstream media for their inadequate reporting about contemporary power arrangements and the social and political movements challenging them. Those alternative media projects also addressed the exclusion of huge constituencies from mainstream institutions. Women being just one. During an era of Black Power, my work addressed issues of racism. I was also a participant at the birth of the environmental movement.

My comrades' eyes were drooping. I knew I was talking into a void, like a lone speech maker in Congress when the House is empty, but I was affirming myself in a place where my history seemed irrelevant and my desire to know where I had just landed was considered suspect.

I barreled on. I looked at their slumping bodies yet continued. It was they who wanted lectures, after all.

"Eventually," I said, "I needed to earn a living through journalism, and therefore I tried to bring that critical approach into the work of what we call 'the fourth estate' in the democratic process." Now I was sounding like a boring ideologue. But I couldn't be stopped.

"Giving voice to the voiceless." I spared no trope. "Speaking truth to power." People's faces looked more puzzled than bored at this triumphal announcement, but maybe it was a language thing. They started to squirm as if I were finished, but no, wait—I wasn't!

"This is my point!" I was almost yelling. "I never saw work—especially physical, routine, even mindless work—as punishment," I said. "Exhaustion, yes. Boredom, yes. But punishment, no."

China was forcing me to look at this history through a new lens. A more reflective one. Perhaps my intellectual and political choices meant I would have been a target of struggle in the Cultural Revolution. Uncomfortable thought.

Back to the tired comrades in my living room. Chairs shuffled, Mandarin mutterings grew louder. As usual, there was no time to discuss the huge chunks of information that had been shared by them and me. The comrades all had chores yet to do. They went to bed by 10 p.m. and were up again by 5 or 6 a.m. to exercise outdoors, listen to the news, study, do more chores. I would have liked to talk more—much more—with Chen, but the self-policing of this group meant there would be no individual side chats. I marveled at how they all seemed to squeeze out my door *en masse.*

While I was grateful for the bits and pieces I was learning about the comrades in our discussion sessions, the fact that no hint of a collegial friendship could result from these discussions continued to distress me. And I knew that their comments about this major campaign to flatten the hierarchy between intellectual and manual workers would never make it into the programming at Radio Beijing nor into my microphone. Too bad.

After the comrades left, I plunked a cassette into my tape deck...*Kind of Blue* with Miles Davis, Bill Evans, Coltrane and others. Perhaps the best jazz album of all time. I had been listening to it since it first came out in 1959.

I had to thank Gordon Detwiller, who in 1958, when I was in the tenth grade, introduced me to jazz. Although Gordon was a teenager like me, he had an old soul. We would stretch out on his parents' living room rug, listening to jazz albums, bebop and eventually cool—Art Tatum, Dizzy, Charles Mingus, Thelonious Monk, Roland Kirk.

In Beijing, on November 6, 1980, I poured myself a glass of Chinese rum and sat back in my plastic armchair, allowing Miles and Coltrane to wash over me while toasting Gordon—wherever he was. Somewhere between Vancouver Island and Galiano Island, I suspected. I hadn't seen him since 1963. I thanked him for expanding my senses to absorb this elixir for the soul. And once again—in this puzzling and frustrating environment—for keeping me human, offering transcendence. Jazz.

Xian, 1981

Chapter Eight

Journalists, Missionaries and Spies
记者，传道师，及间谍

November 4, 1980, Journal:

It is the beginning of November—the end of three months in Beijing—and I am sinking into a deep swamp of depression. My despair over the quality of the scripts and the lackluster attitudes of my colleagues deepens. The comrades' alienation fuels mine. Nobody but the leaders seems to care about the accuracy or quality of the final product. One of the Chinese puzzles for me is why the editorial department is allowed to continue pumping out such lousy material.

The overall absence of dialogue about the purpose or nature of this "journalistic enterprise" combined with the information vacuum is stunting my skills and torturing my conscience. My journalist's soul feels embattled. I need to keep reminding myself that my colleagues are civil servants. Not journalists.

What am I doing here, "polishing" propaganda for a society and system that I have nothing but questions and mounting concerns about? I am having a profound crisis about truth-telling.

*In my journalism classes with the comrades, I talk about **doubt** being a major attribute of good journalism. Questioning assumptions, viewpoints, the givens. Interviewing one more person to get the complexity of the story. Doing one more round of research to get it right.*

A few days before this journal entry, I refused to edit one of the scripts. It dealt with post-Liberation history, referring to the Hundred Flowers Movement as a positive moment for freedom of expression in China. I sought out Leader Zhang.

"I understand there may be different perspectives on the Hundred Flowers Movement," I said hesitantly.

Her eyes squinted at me.

"I don't want to imply that I know the correct history," I continued, "but this version seems seriously flawed and propagandistic and would be laughed at by any informed listener."

Her lips pressed closed as she raised own eyebrow.

"Perhaps," I suggested, "you should edit it." With that, she took the script and left the room.

This revisionist history was perhaps no morally different than American high school texts that failed to mention the Japanese internment camps during WW II or avoided describing the CIA's role in the overthrow of legitimately elected leaders in Guatemala and Iran.

I have no idea if the offending script was "polished" by someone else and aired. I had stopped listening to the broadcast, like all the other comrades.

One genre of scripts that I routinely turned back to Leader Zhang concerned China's ethnic minorities. Every script reporting on those non-Han groups began with, "These people are good at singing and dancing. They wear colorful clothing and bright jewelry."

I had early on asked for a map of China to tack up over my desk so I could have a visual reference to the geography of our scripts. This allowed me to at least see graphically where these diverse peoples lived. With their own languages, traditions and beliefs, minority peoples clustered or sprawled around the perimeters of China from the Mongolians in the North and the Uyghurs in the far-west Xinjiang region to the Tibetans in the Himalayan South and the Bai, Yi, Hani, Miao, Dong and Zhuang, who largely clustered in the southern-most regions of China bordering Vietnam. In our reports, each group was described as a cute freak show. A museum diorama.

The "exotic dancer" scripts—as I labeled them—always concluded by extolling the civilizing traditions and improved economic conditions that the Party (and the Han Chinese) had and continued to bring to these communities. I harbored doubts. But, then, I knew nothing of these peoples and regions and what had taken place there before and after Liberation. Given the racism that I had witnessed in Beijing toward foreigners with darker skin or the prejudice from urban Chinese toward swarthier, simpler peasants, I could not but suspect there were frictions and problems in those minority areas instigated by Han supremacy. Or, at least, complications.

Given the previous eighty years of raging debates among Western anthropologists about how to observe, document, report on, interact with, study, record and interpret other cultures, the whole business of the "exotic dancer" scripts seemed sad. I longed to share my concerns with Margaret Mead and Ruth Benedict.

The inability of the Radio Beijing editors to report on these ethnic regions with more rigor, I suspected, was rooted in an unexamined racism that results when one ethnic group is represented by almost a billion people. Our scripts claimed the Han comprised about ninety-five percent of the population. At the office, we had no research sources to verify that. I was always swimming in a sea of suspicious facts.

When I looked at the map over my desk, the area of Tibet and the western Xinjiang regions loomed like Texas and California on the US map, taking up almost twenty percent of it. Given the news that leaked to the Western press about tensions with ethnic Tibetans, I could only imagine that similar stress existed in other ethnic areas as well. If independence movements flourished, the People's Republic would lose a huge chunk of the map. I could see why headquarters would want to control the narrative.

Looking at that map triggered reflections about US and Canadian history regarding the indigenous tribes of North America. Growing up on Vancouver Island in British Columbia, I had a front-row seat to observe the outcomes. European settlers introduced diseases, alcohol and firearms, grabbed land and resources, waged wars, forced native peoples onto reservations. It was a sordid record of broken treaties, degradation of languages and cultures, abuse and lack of reparations. Canada had a better record than the US in making financial restitution, but the legacy of shattered cultures could not be fixed by money alone. Perhaps I had no right to speak up in China, where I knew so little.

The least I could do, however, was challenge the "singing and dancing" reports. Finally, my complaints were so vehement that Leader Zhang arranged for me to visit the Institute for Ethnic Minorities. In a large, forbidding office, with an aura of a mausoleum, in a polite and formal configuration with stiff cadres whom I suspected were Party functionaries, an acknowledgement was made that the scripts should be improved. The assembled group included a couple of scholars who said they had not done any work in those minority areas since 1958. Aha...the year of the famous Hundred Flowers Movement that punished intellectuals who spoke up. These rusty academics still had good stories to tell about shaman-like spiritual leaders who must be won over by the local Han cadres to appease the spirit of the valley before they could build an irrigation ditch. They all chuckled. These were Han Chinese scholars, of course. Han chuckles.

I marveled at all the potential stories. But nothing changed at Radio Beijing. The scripts still began with a line about "singing and dancing."

Not long after my meeting at the Minorities Institute, Fan, in charge of responding to listener mail, asked me which listener's suggestions to write into scripts, and I disqualified all topics unless we were going to tell the truth. I felt bolder as my tolerance for the scripts decreased. Fan walked away without comment.

Later that day, I told Zhou Hong to lock up the editors. We laughed.

I needed to laugh at something. I was still reeling from the news of Reagan's victory announced on Voice of America that morning. Not a surprise, but profoundly troubling, given his positions on almost everything and his partnership with the newly emergent Religious Right. But, I had to admit, American realities seemed so far, far away. It took all of my energies and emotions to keep my nostrils above the waterline in my tiny Beijing world. To prevent myself from drowning in my own ignorance, daily misunderstandings and the mysteries swirling around me.

At night and on weekends, I had no problem hammering out lengthy free-association letters to friends on my manual typewriter, reporting in vivid detail my observations and experiences, only to be constipated when it came to finding the voice for NPR reports. China was too big, my experiences and feelings too contradictory and confusing, my knowledge too fractured. How could I write anything that would fit neatly into an *All Things Considered* broadcast?

I knew my real dilemma was something else. How could I tell the truth and continue working here? How could I say I was working for an information agency at Central Broadcasting under the Propaganda Committee of the Central Committee of the People's Republic of China and be honest about the scripts and my coworkers without ending my contract immediately? How could I describe what I had learned about my colleagues' lives without hurting or betraying them? How could I render the physical environment without insulting my hosts? If I reported candidly, what would be the point of staying on? I was crippled by uncertainties about what I was learning and seeing and feeling, as if my view was obstructed, at least partially. Maybe next month I would start finding a voice and the confidence to write and narrate those NPR reports. Next month, the view might come into focus and the pieces of the puzzle would start linking up. But then, since I didn't speak Mandarin, how could I claim to have the authority to report?

Why couldn't I simply write a charming story about the adventure of buying and cooking a chicken in Beijing? First, the lady behind the counter at the Friendship Store thwacked a whole chicken across the counter—head and feet attached. No offers to decapitate or remove the feet. So I placed the lump-in-a-newspaper-with-feet-dangling in my bicycle basket and pedaled home, strategizing just how I would easily remove those inconvenient appendages. No such luck. My dull knife made the struggle on my coffee table monumental, brutal and messy. Then, to my dismay, all the insides were still intact. It took dozens of flushings to get it all to go down my toilet. By that time, I had lost interest in the bloody mess. But I persevered. Washing it in my bathtub before wrestling it into a pot to cook on my hotplate. Then I realized I didn't have all the ingredients and herbs I would need to make it taste like anything. In the future, I would leave the chicken preparations to the cooks in the building dining room. They were delighted with the gift of two enormous feet.

ON A Sunday in early November, I took a taxi to visit Don Murray, one of the few North American journalists stationed in Beijing. He was reporting for CBC radio. My Montreal friends had suggested I contact him. Don and his wife, Vera, lived in the heavily guarded diplomatic compound—totally separated from any taint of the Chinese. When I entered, I caught a glimpse of their kitchen and household maid. Luxurious. Privileged. Quarantined. Like most foreigners in China.

I was introduced to one of Don's Canadian colleagues visiting from Hong Kong. Most newspapers and networks had bureaus there and sent reporters to Beijing periodically to attempt to report. Brunch was surreal. Eggs Benedict, champagne and orange juice, bagels, smoked salmon, cream cheese and good coffee with cream—all courtesy of flights from Hong Kong. Several times during the meal, I fantasized about having an affair with Don's friend, despite his aura of self-importance. How ravenous I was for male attention. As my teeth sunk into a bagel and cream cheese, I also admitted to myself how starved I was for commiseration with intelligent, professional journalists. I missed my colleagues from WBAI and NPR.

Despite the Canadian conviviality around Don's table, I sensed a distance. Don and Vera's privileges were much greater than mine and already I felt uncomfortable with that extra gulf separating them from the Chinese—people like my coworkers. It made me more conscious of the ways my own material privileges might alienate my colleagues and thus inhibit any relationship.

I also felt judged. They were astonished that I, who had worked for NPR as well as ABC and NBC in the US, would choose to work at Radio Beijing, a major propaganda agency for the Chinese government. So while they were intrigued by some of the experiences I was sharing, I also felt them reacting to me as if I were contaminated. Not a real journalist. Like them. While I hungered for their insights and envied their access to interpreters, Chinese officials and travel around China, I found myself withholding some of my discoveries. Why should I give away any of my hard-earned knowledge? In this bizarre, censored and secretive environment, minor information took on a value, like money to be hoarded, exchanged or flaunted. "Foreign experts" had direct experience in China's institutions that these journalists did not. I also knew how frustrated they were, trying to acquire accurate information and convince officials or regular folks to talk into a microphone. Or talk at all.

I also suspected that they harbored beliefs about their own ideological neutrality that I didn't share. To my students at Rutgers University, I harped away about the myth of neutrality. The very stories we chose to report or that editors and executive producers approved or assigned, the people we chose to interview, the questions we asked, the facts or information we included, what we left out, the vocabulary we mobilized—all led to favoring some facts and perspectives over others. And if we included conflict, there was an assumption that there were only two positions rather than multiple perspectives on any event or policy. And furthermore, the pressures to create a narrative or force a story arc might imply an ending or resolution when there is none.

All of it was embedded in world views that were subtly—and not so subtly—favored at the established media outlets. The Cold War, communism, the military–industrial complex, feminism, homosexuality, pornography, civil disobedience, atheism, racism, militarism, imperialism were all seen through a particular lens in most American news outlets. Don Murray was lucky enough to work for CBC with a slightly larger viewfinder.

Still, I was jealous of them. They could spend all day researching, reading and studying Mandarin. Don already flexed the language.

The one thing we all had in common was that all of our phones were bugged—we could hear the clicking—and our mail was opened and our movements monitored. Don complained about how difficult it was to even get a telephone; then, once installed, it worked so poorly it was exasperating.

We marveled that there was no telephone directory. The only one available to foreigners was designed by the wife of Ross Munro, a former correspondent for Toronto's *Globe and Mail* who was here from 1975 to 1977. Don explained that Munro had revealed some of the secret privileged system of distributing information to Party cadres in every work unit. Munro was expelled from China after that series of articles in 1977. In the meantime, foreign reporters were dependent on Mrs. Munro's personal collection of phone numbers of foreign embassies, a few Chinese government trade entities and restaurants. From a Google search today, it is evident that Munro had Canadian State Department and Intelligence Committee ties. Perhaps the Chinese were not always wrong when they suspected Western journalists of being informants or intelligence gatherers, if not exactly full-time spies.

Sitting in the midst of this comfort and listening to these reporters' frustrations, I realized how very far away they were from the Chinese. Their salaries and conditions allowed them to recreate—almost—their Western lifestyles. While I had tremendous privileges compared to my coworkers, at least I was closer to their world and could not hope to replicate my old bohemian life in a Little Italy tenement. Or...maybe it was closer than I was willing to admit?

The next day, Monday, at the office, Leader Zhang was cool and distanced. Her face stern and disapproving. Her body rigid. I suspected that my visit to Don Murray's apartment had been reported, since I was required to provide full information about where I was going to the government taxi agency and then fill out a form to enter the fancy diplomatic and UN compound.

To blunt any suspicion, I enthusiastically reported to Leader Zhang that I had a wonderful typical Montreal-style Sunday brunch with a Canadian journalist. It was no use. She left the room. I got the message. I was a journalist. I was meeting with other Western journalists. I could not be trusted. Was Don tainted by Munro? Was I now part of their cabal of journalist spooks?

I decided I would stay clear of Don Murray for a while and any other of the tiny handful of foreign reporters stationed in Beijing. Already I was bending to the Chinese paranoia about them. I had received the message that any contact with them might discredit me with my coworkers. I did not want to betray the trust that Leaders Zhang and Ma had risked by hiring me, the journalist, although I sensed that some comrades, still Maoists or Cultural Revolution enthusiasts, were not happy with their decision to hire me. Like Shadow Zhang.

At least one Chinese-American foreign expert who worked as an editor at one of China's international publications was on the payroll of Fox Butterfield of the *New York Times* and perhaps *Time* magazine. She could translate Mandarin and interpret the culture. She dressed in local garb and so could pass as Chinese and had access to both official and underground Beijing.

I grew increasingly uneasy, however, about any association with journalists after a particular incident at Radio Beijing later in November. One morning, I noticed a booklet opened on Leader Zhang's desk. It was a collection of international reporting. A reprint of an article by Fox Butterfield of the *New York Times* was circled on the open page. It described how information was communicated from the Communist Party and the government to the workers, citing as an example the large meetings that each work unit organized where the latest government policy positions were announced. Butterfield told about a Chinese worker at Radio Beijing who had been prohibited from attending the large meetings because she had developed a close relationship with a foreign expert. This might have been yawned at anywhere else in the world, but in Beijing it felt like high intrigue.

I surmised the identities of both the Radio Beijing employee and the foreigner. I also had an idea of how the story might have reached Butterfield. Since the article was circled, I wondered if my department leader suspected me as the "leak." Again, I decided upon directness to forestall any suspicions. I told Leader Zhang I had been made aware of the article (since it had appeared in the *New York Times*) and asked her if she knew who this foreign expert was? Leader Zhang would not answer my questions or engage in any discussion about the article. For the next few days, all the comrades were standoffish with me. After a couple of weeks, the ice thawed. But this launched a pattern of cooling off and warming up that would intensify over the weeks and months ahead.

I knew, of course, that the foreign expert was the "fierce" Yanna in the Czech department. She had recently returned to Vienna. And I was the beneficiary of her much larger one-bedroom apartment on the ground floor, closer to the telephone.

Yanna had developed a friendship with Xiao Liu or "Martha"—her interpreter and shadow—whom I had met on several occasions. Anybody meeting Martha was immediately struck by her exceptional intellect. Already fluent in Czech, she was now studying English. Since Yanna had been hanging out with a dissident sculptor and had close contacts with Richard Bernstein, the first bureau chief in Beijing for *Time*, Martha could be implicated as well.

At the farewell party for Yanna, Martha indicated she would like to keep in touch with me for purposes of improving her English. Yanna recommended that I should befriend Martha, as she was very bright and "has nothing left to lose." Before leaving for Vienna, she had wanted to give Martha her bicycle. The leaders found out and nixed the plan. Yanna's furies at the Chinese never subsided.

One day, after Yanna's departure, I went upstairs to Martha's department during the morning work break, simply to say hello and perhaps arrange a time when we might have lunch or she could visit my office or even my flat, to have conversational practice. Why had it taken me so long to learn?

Later, she called my apartment building phone and said I was never to come to her department office again and I must never try to contact her. It was doubtful that we could ever get together because she was being "harassed." Her department leader had interrogated her about why and how she knew an expert from another department and the leader was going to report it immediately to the Foreign Experts Bureau. Martha had apparently been severely criticized and punished for getting "too close" to Yanna already.

Several weeks later, I bumped into her on the grounds of Radio Beijing. She was clearly nervous even about our being seen chatting for a few minutes. By this time, my sadness and anger were overpowering. Here was a person I wanted so much to know and it would never be possible. There we stood, like two stiffs trying to look like we didn't really know each other. We were just saying hello but exchanging so much desire, frustration and sorrow. At least, I hoped that the feelings were mutual for her. I thought my rage might explode my whole being into flames right there in the yard of Radio Beijing.

AT NIGHT, I kept reading to search for clues to all the suspicion of foreigners, especially journalists, and it was becoming clear—as if enlightenment was emerging from the photo tray of history.

Until the Opium Wars in the mid-nineteenth century, foreign colonial powers were restricted by the Canton factory system. Qing dynasty rulers—in power since the mid-seventeenth century—limited the trade activity of foreign companies and refused access for governments to proselytize and—some claim—to even learn the Chinese language on China's soil. The Western powers—primarily Britain and France—were confined to one port—Canton (now Guangzhou).

The Brits figured out how to break into the China trade by selling opium-laced tobacco. Until they pushed opium, China was disinterested in most foreign products. Since the West was greedy for Chinese silks, tea and porcelain, the only way Britain found to address the trade imbalance was by peddling more and more opium from their tobacco factories in India. By the early nineteenth century Qing dynasty silver coffers were emptying to sustain an insatiable habit. When they woke up to its destructive powers, they seized a huge opium shipment, triggering the first Opium War in 1839. Britain's warships delivered a quick victory. The Chinese government buckled.

A weakened Qing government was forced to not only pay reparations but also allow the unhindered trade of opium. Propelled largely by the British East India Company, the opium trade also had its entrepreneurial dealers—like the Scottish merchant powerhouse Jardine Matheson & Co., the names recognizable to anyone visiting Hong Kong today.

The Treaty of Nanking, the first of a series of unequal treaties that China signed at the conclusion of the first Opium War, opened up five "treaty" ports along the China coast for trade by Britain and other colonial powers, including the US, Russia and Japan. Within fifteen years, a second Opium War and another "unequal treaty"—the Treaty of Tianjin in 1858—further weakened the Qing regime, and together these treaties initiated the "century of humiliation" in China that ended with Liberation—the victory of the Chinese Communist Party—in 1949.

The unequal treaties that operated for most of that century allowed foreign companies to conduct all manner of business activities according to their own laws, out of reach of any Chinese regulations. Missionaries could then push into the interior of China.

While missionaries—mostly Protestant, mostly American—established medical clinics and schools, they became a spearhead for American business interests. One of the books I had brought from New York was *The New Empire: An Interpretation of American Expansion 1860–1899* by Walter Lafeber, who documented how American missionaries played a complicated role in opening up China for US markets and diplomacy during the latter years of the nineteenth century. Some had established their own successful import/export businesses. Others had become stringers and reporters for the Western press along with fulfilling their missionary duties. Lafeber pointed out that they had not only been people of faith but also believers in the superiority of their industrial and agricultural products. They had promoted American values and ideas through the very things they had consumed, imported for their own use then extolled to the Chinese. No wonder American diplomats referred to the missionaries as "pioneers" for American trade and business.

Missionaries were also associated with the opium trade whether they wanted it or not. They had relied on the opium trading ships for transportation and communication, and opium merchants had often been their bankers.

While some Protestant missionaries had organized an anti-opium movement, they were better known to the Chinese for smoothing the way to market surplus American cotton and agricultural foodstuffs to China. Some blamed the collapse of the Chinese cotton market in Eastern China for the rise of the Boxer Movement that unleashed its furies at the end of the nineteenth century.

Lafeber argued that the Chinese also saw the presence of the missionaries as an affront to Confucian patriarchal social order undermining their villages, traditions and control. Missionary promotion of a Western lifestyle was demeaning to Chinese culture. Given this, it should not have been surprising that the Boxer Rebellion targeted not only foreigners in general but American missionaries in particular.

> *"Somehow I had learned from Thoreau, who doubtless learned it from Confucius, that if a man comes to do his own good for you, then must you flee that man and save yourself."*
>
> Pearl S. Buck, *The Fighting Angel*

The Fighting Angel is Buck's biography of her father, Absalom Sydenstricker, who had gone to China in the 1880s. Even his name conjures the autocratic, sexist and unaffectionate Presbyterian missionary that she describes. Buck refers to him as a "fierce warrior" whose mission was part of the "astounding imperialisms of the West."

Yet American missionaries also represented ideas of individualism, women's rights and republicanism, ultimately destabilizing to Chinese society. Their ideas helped to propel the Republican and reform movements in early-twentieth-century China. The dialectics of history and imperialism.

But what did the missionaries have to do with journalists and with my experience in Beijing in 1980? Well, quite a bit, it turned out. During that wickedly imperialist Century of Humiliation, there had been a complex intermingling of foreign journalists, businessmen and missionaries. Sometimes in the same person. Some of the first Western journalists had worked out of the opium factories in Canton starting in the 1820s. William Jardine had launched the *Canton Register* to spread his free trade views, and his editor, William Wood, a Philadelphian, also had roots in the opium trade. Western editors and correspondents had fueled the imperialist effort with newspapers serving the interests and worldviews of their business masters.

After the two Opium Wars, foreign countries and companies operated by their own free-trade rules without interference from the Chinese government. In Canton, Shanghai, Ningpo (now Ningbo), Fuchow (now Fuzhou) and

Amoy (now Xiamen), foreigners created a decadent expat universe separate from the Chinese.

Few foreign journalists spoke up against the new arrangements. Most supported the extraterritorial laws, working as cheerleaders for Western business interests. Some worked with intelligence agencies, while others negotiated for their governments. Few spoke the language or understood the culture. The Boxer Rebellion was a wake-up call.

The fact that foreigners became targets during the Boxer Rebellion stirred world interest in China. When British and French troops retaliated and destroyed the stunning Summer Palace—known as the Versailles of China— George Morrison, the first full-time foreign correspondent in China, was seen looting some of the buildings afterwards. But in the new century, as revolution raised the prospects of a republican government, Morrison, like other foreign journalists, took sides. He would eventually advise the new government after 1912 and even negotiated on behalf of the Chinese government at the Versailles Peace Treaty meetings in 1919.

During the first decades of the twentieth century, the community of foreign reporters in China kept growing. Many of the American correspondents sent to China by the *New York Times* and other papers were "mish kids" (children of missionaries), witnesses to an extraordinary period of Chinese history: the collapse of the Qing Dynasty, the emergence of a new Republic in 1911, the May Fourth Movement in 1919, itself a response to China being abandoned by the Great Powers at Versailles and coinciding with the Russian Revolution. The seeds of a Communist movement in China had been sown.

The demands back home in the US for China news kept swelling. Now the China overseas press was attracting a more sophisticated pool of journalistic talent with better knowledge of China, some fluent in Mandarin. They covered the rise of the Nationalist Party—the Kuomintang—and its leading celebrity couple, Generalissimo and Madame Chiang Kai-shek. In his newspapers and journals, Henry Luce, a former "mish kid," wouldn't allow any critical reporting about the Generalissimo.

Reporters tumbling into China provided eyewitness accounts of the Nationalist slaughter of the Communists in Shanghai. Some had joined and recounted the story of the Long March by Mao and his ragtag Communist Army. Edgar Snow, Agnes Smedley and others had trekked to the caves of Yan'an to interview Mao and covered the revolution taking place in the countryside. Other reporters described the Japanese bombing of Shanghai and the rape of Nanking. Some were killed during the Japanese assault on the

Nationalist wartime capital of Chongqing. Snow and Smedley reported on the Civil War between the Nationalists and Communists after the Japanese were defeated during WWII.

But when Mao and his Communist Party team announced their victory in Tiananmen Square in October 1949, foreign journalists were mostly absent. The American State Department brought American reporting in China to an end. As the Cold War progressed, and war erupted with Korea involving China, the country closed down to most Western reporters. There followed an almost three-decade famine of reporting on China.

Not long before I arrived in Beijing, Canadian, European and American journalists had just begun to report after this long hiatus. The country was a closed book. Journalists were suspect. I was suspect. But I was invited. *Kafka,* I thought, *where are you when I need you laughing at the telling of your own stories?*

ONE NIGHT, after the cold shoulder from Leader Zhang, I was up late, listening to Yusef Lateef drinking black tea and thinking about the journalists who interviewed Mao and other Communist Party leaders during their retreat from the Kuomintang and the Long March. These plucky Americans had gone to the caves at Yan'an and reported on the idealism and concerns of this new breed of revolutionaries. Eleanor Bidien reminded me that Agnes Smedley had slogged for two years—more than any other reporter—in the conflict zones where Chiang Kai-shek's forces, the Communists and the Warlords were slugging it out. And then she had covered the supposedly unified war against the Japanese. When civil war escalated between the Nationalist and Communist armies after WWII, she was there as an eyewitness. Formidable Agnes Smedley. Poor farm girl from Colorado.

But her book, *The Battle Hymn of China*, was practically unknown while Edgar Snow's *Red Star Over China* defined Mao and his Party for Americans, for the West and for at least two generations of China watchers. Snow's book was the first one I—and so many of my generation—read about the Chinese Revolution back in the 1960s.

Eleanor Bidien gave me Smedley's book, along with the autobiography of Anna Louise Strong. From a New England Congregationalist background, Strong was the most highly educated of the trio that included Snow and Smedley. Strong was the more passionate true believer in communism and the most prolific writer. Bouncing back and forth between the Soviet Union, China and the US, she published books every year reporting on the Soviet system as well as Chinese Communist Party efforts to create agricultural communes. After a century of Western journalists touting the charms of the free-market from their beats in China, here were a handful, who, during the first half of the twentieth century plunged deeply into the battles for the future of China and saw hope in the Maoist plan.

In 2014, more than thirty years later, after a generation of new scholarship on China had been produced, through Google I could find an article by David E. Apter, an American political theorist and sociologist, published in 2005 that explains how Snow, Smedley and Strong shaped the thinking of Western progressives about China.

Apter postulates that these three reporters fostered the "founding myths" of the Chinese Communist enterprise by writing about the Long March and the Communist headquarters in Yan'an in ways that glossed over uncomfortable truths. Like the fact that only a tenth of the Army had survived the Long March. That there had been internal struggles that had taken many lives. That Mao had exhibited ruthless behavior even then against competing leaders. Purification campaigns had been part of the agenda from the beginning. And in class-struggle sessions in the countryside, thousands of landlords had lost their lives.

Yet these three journalists couldn't just be written off as propagandists. Snow wrote for the mainstream *Saturday Evening Post*. Smedley wrote for German and American newspapers and the *Manchester Guardian*. Anna Louise Strong's *Letters From China* were published in the US and England and were said to have influenced Eleanor Roosevelt.

From the mid-'30s, when it was still unclear which way the wind would blow, these journalists cast the Chinese Communist leaders and their ragtag army as heroic. Their mission as Biblical. The power that each of these writers had with an American audience was their ability to portray the Chinese revolution as a battle between good and evil. They shaped the opinions not just of a US readership but also in China, where their writing was credited with convincing thousands of urban, educated Chinese to join the Communist cause.

Cold War ideologues branded these three as Communists. Meanwhile, there had been other more mainstream American journalists working in Civil War China who had tried to warn anyone who would listen. Theodore White had also tramped to Yan'an to interview Mao. His articles for *Time* were rewritten by his New York editors to conform to the pro-Chiang position of his boss, Henry Luce. White had warned that the Communists would most likely win the Civil War and that they had the more admirable ideas and track record of social activism to help the largely rural peasant population. He was then attacked by anti-Communists in the US.

White was branded as a Communist sympathizer, along with a group of China Hands—foreign service officers and scholars, like John Fairbanks, who had argued for a more sophisticated approach to the Communists rather than a wholesale embrace of Chiang Kai-shek's Nationalist Party.

The tragic consequences of this dominant Cold War mentality led the US into wars in Asia that could have been avoided, along with lost lives and destroyed environments. One could argue that these wars were the result of anti-Communist forces in the US, who insisted on backing Chiang Kai-shek, the losing horse. As historians have since recorded, Mao, through Zhou Enlai, had reached out to the Americans from the caves in Yan'an. How different history might have been if the US had been responsive and crafted a relationship with the Chinese Communist Party at that stage.

In November 1980, my access to this information was limited. But as I struggled to unravel the interweaving of Western journalists, missionaries and spies while cleaning up my Beijing apartment, I needed some upbeat music. I found my cassette of salsa: Ray Barretto at the Beacon Theatre. First up: "Cocinando."

As I danced around my living room, I remembered the story from somewhere that Anne Louise Strong and Agnes Smedley had taught Mao and others to dance in Yan'an. Imagine having a phonograph machine in the caves—who brought the records? What music did they dance to? Those American girls!

OVER DINNER one evening in early November, Ron Dorfman reported that he had been invited to attend a "documents" session at *China Reconstructs*, where the privileged intellectual workers learned about the latest policy announcements before they were revealed in the *People's Daily*.

At this session, Ron said, a report indicated there was to be no more deifying of leaders, especially Mao. Former leaders were not to be glorified out of proportion to the facts, nor were "facts" to be invented to polish the image of contemporary leaders. Revolutionary leaders and others being criticized at any given time were not thereby condemned as evil persons, and their contribution to the Party and the people was to be recognized and respected.

Also, the news organs were instructed not to tamper with history to suit the needs of contemporary political struggle. I thought that somebody needed to tell the editors in that smoke-choked room at Radio Beijing. Here was an example of a major policy shift critiquing the cult of personality, meaning the Cult of Mao, and ending or at least tempering the brutalities of ideological struggle, critiquing the bending of information or "facts" to fit political agendas. Since every propaganda agency had these same "documents" presentations, why was I not included in these sessions at Radio Beijing? Was Radio Beijing more important—and therefore more sensitive—in the hierarchy of information/propaganda agencies?

Had my department leaders decided after reading all of my letters that I could not be trusted with this information? While I knew they were reading my letters, I still could not stop "reporting" in them. Letter writing was my couch. My safety valve. And none of the people I was writing to were journalists.

Shortly after this revelation, our study group with China Hands began looking at the Chinese press and the state of Chinese domestic journalism. There seemed to be some liberalization with more exposés of corruption. Exemplary cases.

But Ron and I wanted to talk about the "real" flow of information and communication. When Ron reported on the "documents" session he attended, the old China Hands and foreign experts who had been here for years described the communications system that channeled serious foreign and domestic affairs, economic reports, policy information and directives to certain workers. But they were cautious in explaining this, perhaps because this policy and politburo information appeared to a hierarchy of Party members—including some of the China Hands—before it appeared in newspapers, if ever.

This protective and secretive system of privileged information may have had its roots in the guerrilla struggle during the early years of the peasant revolution and civil war with the Nationalists, whereby information leaks might have determined not only the outcome of battles but also who won the hearts and minds of the peasants.

Thirty years later, it smelled of distrust and fear. Fear of the free flow of information. Were the Party elites afraid that information would unravel their power?

Since foreign reporters had begun working in Beijing, their contacts with a few overseas Chinese experts who had access to some of the special political directives and documents meant that information from this rarefied river of communication had occasionally appeared in the Western press. The Party's pushback was to republish the "Provisional Regulations for the Preservation of State Secrets," which had first appeared in 1950–'51, shortly after Liberation.

At our study group, Helmut reported that a newspaper item had appeared in the *People's Daily* earlier this year outlining the categories of information that must never be revealed: anything to do with the armed forces and national defense, state security and the police, foreign affairs and economic planning. What was most surprising to our assembled group was the inclusion of categories dealing with ethnic minorities, public health and culture.

Clearly, to enforce these regulations required a rigorous censorship campaign and compliant staff in the offices of newspapers and radio and TV stations. No wonder our "ethnic minority" stories on the radio all began with "These folks are good at singing and dancing." Nobody wanted to be responsible for revealing anything but the most uncontroversial information lest it be considered revealing state secrets!

Over a beer later, one knowledgeable expat described to Ron and me the hierarchy of *neibu* or "internal" publications. There were four tiers of information, increasingly exclusive, as you moved higher up the bureaucratic Party ladder. At the very bottom was "Reference News"—reprinted articles from the foreign press, including articles by Western reporters in Beijing. That was what I had seen on Leader Zhang's desk. Some believed it had a larger circulation than the *People's Daily*. Even though the sources were all foreign press, foreigners were not supposed to read it.

Moving up the ladder was "Reference Material," a more detailed collection of foreign news articles only available to high cadres at the work unit. Above that were collections of reports for the highest elites in the Party. In addition, there were document rooms in many agencies or work units that were only accessible to high-ranking cadres in that work unit.

Even though Munro had already exposed this privileged, hierarchical and secretive information system in Toronto's *Globe and Mail,* if I could ever get anyone to talk on microphone about this, it would make for a stunning NPR story. No hope.

November 12, 1980, Journal:

I agreed to meet with Francis, a visiting VP from ABC, at the Beijing Hotel. He was given my contact info from a friend at NBC. Am I risking trust again at Radio Beijing by seeing him? He and his wife asked me what to serve the Chinese TV people coming over. I suggested Peking duck and Tsingtao beer. Both out of reach to most folks here. The equivalent of caviar and champagne for us.

I told Francis they were lucky to have Dam Ping from our department as a translator. "She has a very colloquial command of English and is very bright," I said.

Francis quipped, "But she's a Communist."

Well, you're a capitalist! So what?! Of course, I didn't say that. "She spends her lunch hours reading Michener's Chesapeake," *I chuckled.*

The Americans! Especially the American mainstream media, who are so stuck in these simplistic paradigms! Where do I belong? Here? There? Somewhere in the whirlwind between?

From Francis I learned that ABC has begun licensing ten minutes of evening news along with Britain's Visnews to air nightly on the Chinese national news broadcast. Without a TV set, I had no idea. So all along my colleagues were watching as Ronald Reagan won the election, as the Pope toured Africa, political terrorism ravaged Italy and on and on. They were watching daily as I was desperate for conversation about world news! And nothing from them. Perhaps foreign TV news is also a state secret?

Not long after the encounter with Francis of NBC, Michael Weisskopf of the *Washington Post* invited me to dinner at the famous Russian restaurant. Despite my recent policy about not fraternizing with journalists, I caved. Perhaps the prospect of caviar and eggs, prawns Kiev, cold chicken and potato salad undermined my will. I had not eaten like that in months! Sitting in the cold, gothic interior of this former Soviet hangout, he pumped me for info. He wanted to know if I had access to the "documents" or "policy" sessions at Radio Beijing. When I explained that I didn't, he was clearly disappointed. Perhaps he wished he could leave immediately, that he wouldn't have to waste his time or money.

Afterward, we went to the Beijing Hotel for cognac and coffee. I was attracted to his type—smart, quick-witted, Jewish, perceptive, wishing he wasn't married—but then again I was put off by his comments about Asian women. Disappointingly traditional. Similar to the American consular guy I met in Mexico City earlier in the year. Only he swooned over the malleable Mexicanas. How he liked to buy them stiletto heels and dress them. Weisskopf seemed pleased that I was interested in his wife, Lilly.

A thought flashed through my head that he just might receive two paychecks. *The* Washington Post*...and...let it go. Let it go. Remember the assumptions about Smedley. Ruth Price's 2005 painstakingly researched bio of Smedley uncovered that in fact she did provide intelligence for the Soviets in her anti-fascist work against the Japanese while reporting in China.*

IN MID-NOVEMBER, I flew to Guangzhou to visit Wendy, my old high school friend. I needed to see her, her husband and kids to soothe my soul. Then I went on to Hong Kong for a frenetic shopping binge to stock up on vital necessities, like batteries and coffee. JR, my secret lover in New York, had arranged to have an American manual typewriter delivered to my Hong Kong hotel room. And since music was my spiritual salvation in Beijing, I needed a better audio cassette deck—a boom box!

My bosses at Radio Beijing didn't want me to take this trip. I carefully explained why I needed to go and that I would do my work in advance. Apparently, the department had held a special meeting and agreed it was OK. I tried to imagine the staff at NBC, or at NPR, for that matter, weighing in on a personal vacation plan for another staffer.

But then, a few days before I was to leave, Leader Ma came to tell me that I would have to come back in three days. I erupted.

"I have planned this trip for a month!" I argued. "I am going a long way and it is expensive. There are items that I need that can only be purchased in Hong Kong, and I want to see my close friend, who is working in Guangzhou. If I have to return in three days," I pouted, "I will cancel the trip."

The foreign expert office leader weighed in to explain the concerns regarding my trip. "If you go to Hong Kong, then all the other foreign experts will want to go immediately. And you only get one month off in one year, and if you stay away longer than three days, we will have to deduct the days from your month."

"OK," I said, "since I planned to go to Guangzhou and Hong Kong for *six* days, deduct three days from my holiday." At which point I delivered my first lecture on the foolishness of clock time.

The comrades who had to work a spirit-crushing six-day week took time off during work hours to do all of their personal business. They gossiped half the workday, were allowed one morning a week to read the *People's Daily* at leisure, got haircuts at the office, popped out to a peasant's market to buy vegetables and on and on. While I didn't begrudge my beleaguered colleagues the time they took off from work to do their stuff or try to derive some social pleasures at the office, when I was there, I worked intensely. So if I wanted some time off and finished the work in advance, what was the big deal? Of course, I didn't say it so bluntly. And, of course, this was heresy. I was reacting like a spoiled child. Knowing that the system infantilized us all didn't excuse my behavior. I had controlled my work schedule for years. I often worked twelve- to fourteen-hour days, but I determined my schedule.

So I compromised and agreed to return on the sixth day.

I loved digging out my summer clothes for the heat and humidity while realizing how much weight I had gained from the overabundance of oil and sugar in the food. On the plane I could barely curb my excitement at escaping from Radio Beijing—from my depression and anger with the work and the process of doing anything.

At the Fang Hotel in Guangzhou, I caught up on the news with my Canadian friends, Wendy and Glen, and their two kids, whom I loved. Five and seven, wearing little red scarves around their necks, they were babbling in Mandarin. Wendy was making waves with her theories for teaching English to Chinese teachers. Glen, a gifted and accomplished journalist, was teaching to packed classrooms. I envied their situation in the South, where things seemed more relaxed and at a university surrounded by admiring students.

Yes, the South. Sultry, funky, passionate, naughty. Far from Beijing. In Guangzhou, we stopped at a storefront teahouse. From the street we could see Buddhist altars nestled into little stalls. Bright-red incense papers to be burned on altars beckoned from the shops. There was much less presence of the state. A pickpocket tried to steal my wallet in the market. Near White Cloud Mountain, where they lived and worked, we bicycled through dreamy bamboo forests and lazy villages.

How good it was to be with Wendy. Friends since high school, we operated on a special wavelength all our own. I had tried to explain to the comrades at Radio Beijing why I had to visit her: "She ignited the spark of my desire to come to China."

On Sunday, I took the train to Hong Kong, first witnessing the infamous bathrooms in the Guangzhou train station—open troughs with periodic water gushing. At the border with the New Territories, we had to change trains by walking across the trestle bridge with our bags at Shenzhen—a tiny, nondescript village—to board the famous Hong Kong train. Shenzhen, since the mid-1990s, has become one of the biggest motors of China's economic boom with $30 billion in foreign investment and a population of 15 million by 2012. Unimaginable in 1980.

The buzz of arriving in the West in the East! I stayed at the famous YMCA hotel in Kowloon that looked across the river to the hypnotic glitz of neon lights on the Hong Kong side. I took the nickel ferries, feeling the strangeness of the frantic dash in the streets, skinny guys running around with briefcases, the driven purpose of it all, buy, buy, sell, sell. Hong Kong, the shopping mall for China and Southeast Asia. I luxuriated in the pleasures of professional and speedy waiters who smiled. Bacon and eggs and toast, orange juice and coffee. A cocktail in a bar. Dinner with a glass of wine.

Exhausted from the shopping frenzy, I returned to the hotel to watch English-language TV for the first time in almost four months and marvel at the glut of ridiculous stuff that was advertised. Sprawled across the bed, I gorged on foreign newspapers and news magazines. Voyager had sent images back from its approach to Saturn. The Polish government had recognized Solidarity. War had broken out between Iraq and Iran. And Reza Pahlavi, the eldest son of the shah, proclaimed himself the successor to the Peacock Throne. While I had heard some of these headlines on my shortwave radio, this was my chance to read more extensively about world news.

But my real mission in the hotel room was to wait. For the telephone to ring. For the promised call from JR from New York. When the phone rang, I knew it was morning his time. His voice was awkward and distracted. The conversation stilted. My anticipation, frustrations and needs were left to hang out shamelessly in contrast to the emotional flatness on his end. It was finished. Over.

When I hung up, I sank into a very dark place. Maudlin self-pitying. If I were a guy, I would have probably gone to a bar, ordered straight shots and picked up anyone with a smile and sass.

I had met JR while working on a documentary project for him. He was an executive at NBC working out of D.C. and New York. I had succumbed to his seductions. His journalistic arc interested me because he had started as a print reporter in the South during the Civil Rights Movement, moved into TV at NBC and PBS, learning along the way how to massage the network system that meant not rocking the boat—during years when women had little access or voice. Or respect. It was a guys' club. And he knew how to work it.

My infatuation with him centered on his fatherly maturity, his Southern demeanor and grace, an overabundance of confidence fused with a magnetic sexual energy. At a time when I was working a half dozen freelance jobs around the clock and barely making rent, he would take me out to dinner somewhere swell and listen. He liked hearing about my adventurous Haiti work and the magical radio series about storytellers. He was enthusiastic about my radio pieces for NPR, encouraging my values in journalism and my reportorial instincts. In the spring before I left for Beijing, he mediated with the executive producer of a new network magazine program for me to produce a couple of stories that I had pitched.

To his credit, he had never promised to leave his wife for me. He knew I would never believe that anyway. So this was an illicit, taboo affair that couldn't be shared with anyone. Perhaps I thought that by going to Beijing he might miss me so much he would beg to make the relationship more legitimate. I hungered to be cared for, worried about, pampered, soothed…fathered. I had been out there on my own for a long time. I needed to be loved. It was all part of my irrational, romantic, passionate history. In the end, my infatuation with him mimicked my pattern of obsession with dangerous men. Emotionally unreliable men.

The experience of being alone in China was ripping the mask away from any self-delusions about the advantages of my solo life, fueling my desire to share my life with someone. Intensely. More than ever I realized how alone I was yet how good I was—at times—at being alone. Each morning I could be filled with enthusiasm and energy. Only to be worn down by evening. Should I have worried about my capacity to continue this solitary dance? How had Agnes Smedley done it? How had Eleanor Bidien done it?

But I had a new manual typewriter with an English keyboard. JR arranged to have it delivered to my hotel by NBC's Hong Kong bureau chief.

Leaving Hong Kong, changing trains at the border again, walking across the trestles—this time carrying all my Hong Kong loot—to board the mainland train to Guangzhou and catch a flight to Beijing. So crazy. What a relief! And contradiction. I was seduced by consumerism and relished the escape from it.

My first morning back at the office, I brought a huge Guangdong papaya as a peace offering. We sliced it into little bites. I luxuriated in my thermos of coffee while confronting an overwhelming pile of scripts to be ripped apart. Aaaah, my $500 coffee! How could I explain this to anyone in New York? Flying more than a thousand miles for a decent drink and coffee? It gave me new respect for how the discovery and importation of coffee—and sugar—fueled the Industrial Revolution in England. In the eighteenth century, coffeehouses had popped up all over London…minds, bodies and ambitions in overdrive. Serotonin levels screaming. Hearts pumping furiously. All the big ideas in politics, math, science, nature, music and literature tumbled forth. And the evils of imperialism and the slave trade.

Immediately upon my arrival from my tropical getaway, my things were moved to a temporary studio downstairs before I would be moved to Yanna's apartment. No hotplate and no heat in the temporary studio. Shadow Zhang said they needed to paint Yanna's apartment and make repairs. In fact, they were replacing all the plastic wallpaper. I suspected they needed time to re-bug Yanna's apartment in anticipation of the Wild Woman. Me.

Beginning all over in another space. It was clearly time to make a new social horizon plan.

Mr. Chad—Ahmoud—invited me to a party at his apartment in the diplomatic compound. I hadn't seen him since the earlier situation with a representative of the opposition in the car with him and I had withdrawn from the scenario. Although he had described this event as being a dinner party with a dozen others, which was the only reason I agreed to go, when I arrived there was a Hong Kong floozy and six African men from various consulates but also my neighbor from Niger, Amadou. He was the only person I could really converse with in the group. I liked him and his wife, Fila. He had independence. She did not. I had bumped into him at the International Club hanging out with the cluster of African men without women. She always remained at home, cooking and taking care of their kids.

The floozy's body language was tiresome-looking, and the boredom of the Africans was palpable. I also read their despair. No one else showed up, even though there seemed to be food for fifty. We ate dried-out and cold chicken, pork and potatoes meant to be served hot and juicy. Was this leftover food from an embassy function?

All the French-speaking Africans began arguing over politics, so I studied Mr. Chad's home decorating aesthetics: pandas painted on velvet, lions fornicating on a postcard, anti-Imperialist posters, plastic flowers, crocheted doilies—just like those made by my grandmother for the Vancouver rooming house. Chinese kitsch. Mr. Chad drew me aside and began complaining about his financial and political distress. He needed money to run his electric generator. Is that why I was invited? Indeed, that was his next question. I asked him to order a taxi for me.

On the way home, I ruminated about all the wasted time when you are single. Time squandered exploring the social landscape. These thoughts were interrupted by the usual drama at the guard hut. For the taxi driver to drop me off at the front door of my building, he had to fill out a stupid chit at the hut. The cabbies always argued with the young PLA soldiers. This time the driver simply threw up his hands and sped his taxi to the front door. The soldier stood screaming and waving his rifle. Somehow the end suited another disappointing evening.

November 23, 1980, Journal:

Several comrades at Radio Beijing have said that I have the reputation as the best dancer in the capital. Now how would they know, since they do not go to the International Club or to parties with foreigners? Spies everywhere? But I'm amused. If only somebody would appreciate my mind!

"Do you want to find a husband?"

It would be several months before anyone in the office ventured questions about my marital status or desires. It came from Professor Li, whose sweet humor, along with his commitment to his work, had already melted my heart.

"Do you want to find a husband?" he asked quietly, peeking over his glasses in his usual way.

I had been in China long enough to recognize the potential of this otherwise innocent question. I wanted to answer honestly, but I also knew that I must proceed cautiously, not to endanger the promise of this opener and never again have the opportunity to tiptoe deeper into the forest.

"Well, I'm not *looking* for a husband," I started forthrightly. "But if I met someone who I really loved, perhaps we would get married."

Professor Li looked stunned and perplexed.

Oh, God! I thought I had been careful. Even more recklessly, I explained that in New York I had several men friends with whom I could do things—go to movies or dinners.

"We help each other, Li. We're friends, but we don't feel strongly enough to marry."

I wasn't being totally honest. But if this information troubled Li, honesty would have him running out the door. His face looked so strange that I knew I must keep talking, qualifying. Yet the more I tried to explain, the more perplexed he looked.

I told him that some years before I had lived with a man in a relationship "like marriage," but that when we had problems we couldn't resolve, we had decided to separate.

"We are still very good friends. Since then, I haven't met a man I wanted to marry."

The lines in Professor Li's face deepened as he squirmed awkwardly in his seat. He was perspiring. "But you should have a husband," he insisted in a low voice. "Would you like a Chinese husband?"

"I don't know. I've been here three months and I haven't met any Chinese men. I can't speak Chinese. I'm not looking for a husband. It takes time to make friends. At this point I'd just like to meet some men—and women—to do things together. But in China I think that's impossible."

Li was blushing and squirming uncontrollably in his chair. "We're so different," he muttered.

I knew what he was thinking. Or at least I thought I knew, so I went straight for it.

"I don't mean I am going to have sex with them. I'm just talking about making friends. Before you got married, didn't you have women friends?"

"No." He was shaking his head to make it very clear.

With that, the discussion was over. He was turning to his desk the way he always did when I asked a question that was off-limits or when we had reached some forbidden boundary in the conversation. Raising the issue of why Chinese and foreigners couldn't be friends despite the propaganda was definitely unsafe. Referring to sex was taboo.

And Professor Li would only engage in conversation when we were alone in the room, which wasn't often. That was a pattern with others as well.

What interested me was the question he opened with. Did he and the other comrades think I had come to China in search of a mate? Or was it a test to see how much I was truly a friend of China, if I were willing to marry a Chinese? Or was it the beginning of a matchmaking effort so that I wouldn't seduce a series of men at Radio Beijing and make trouble? Because Professor Li had also said I *should* be married. Does a single Western woman present a threat to the moral fabric of the Chinese community? Of the work unit?

When the subject came up again a couple of weeks later, I decided to have some fun with it. I asked Professor Li if he would try to find a husband for me. When he asked what qualities I looked for in a mate, I launched into an exhausting list of attributes that soon turned into a poster over my desk. One quality for every letter in the alphabet. *Adorable. Bold. Comforting. Dependable.* All the comrades contributed. *Funny. Gorgeous. Handy.* I suspected the poster provided release from a tense situation. It offered an explanation: "Gail's too fussy. That's why she's not married."

I learned how ostracized a single older man or woman could be. Comrade Wang, perhaps in his late fifties, an unbearably shy bachelor, told me in one of our encounters, "I'm an introvert. I need to change my history."

Shadow Zhang turned up her nose. "He had one chance and lost it."

"He loved a woman very much," Professor Li added. "She loved him. But they did not tell each other."

"Until it was too late," Shadow Zhang and Professor Li both said in unison.

Why were they telling me this? Did they think they'd fix me up with him?

Xian, 1981

Xian, 1981

Chapter Nine

You Are My Chairman
你是我的主席

A revolution is not a dinner party, or writing an essay, or painting a picture, or doing embroidery; it cannot be so refined, so leisurely and gentle, so temperate, kind, courteous, restrained and magnanimous. A revolution is an insurrection, an act of violence by which one class overthrows another.

Mao Zedong

November 27, 1980, Journal:

Today, everyone in the United States is celebrating Thanksgiving. Extended families in scenes of communal warmth and abundance along with unreal expectations and tensions created by duty. Petty resentments, festering wounds and old scabs can sometimes complicate the familiar pleasures of mothers and home. But this day is supposed to be filled with the celebration of family and friendships through cooking for each other, then stuffing ourselves silly.

On Thanksgiving Day in Beijing, 1980, clusters of sorry-looking Americans, and a sprinkling of folks from around the globe, are leaning over small Formica-and-chrome tables in the brightly lit "Milk Bar" in the lobby of the Beijing Hotel—a somber group nursing whiskeys and beers, Nescafé and sodas.

It includes frustrated businessmen. One of them, an American, I recognize from a few days earlier, when he was sitting with his head in his hands. He told me then that the Chinese he was negotiating with insisted his company take all the risks. He had no idea if he had a deal or not. Perhaps never would. Since China has no reliable legal system or agreement to international laws, the new opening to the West is fraught with unknown dangers. The foreign business community persists, relishing the potential for rivers of profits in the future. You can see the dollar signs in their eyes.

Slumped at another table are a few sleep-deprived and protein-starved students from Europe and the US. They are packed eight to a dorm room at the prestigious Beijing University. That's where the historic May Fourth Movement started in the early twentieth century and where Lu Xun and Mao studied.

Draped around other tables are exasperated journalists and a smattering of disgruntled diplomats from the Middle East and Africa. I recognize a Libyan consular worker whom I once met at the International Club. He slouches in a chair, looking bored with a woman who looks even more bored, a Hong Kong or Beijing hooker with a vacant stare.

A young woman pretending to be a waitress, practicing a big pout, ignores the signals from the businessman that he needs another drink.

All eyes are focused on a giant TV. We're watching history. It's China Central Television's nightly report on the trial of the Gang of Four. Tonight's report covers the first day that Mao's widow, Jiang Qing, is testifying. The young hotel staffers hover in the wings, laughing at her defiant protestations from the dock.

It's the first big international project for CCTV. They're beaming nightly news reports of the trial by satellite around the globe with Colleen Leung, a young Canadian Chinese from Vancouver Island, voicing the English-language version going out to the world. She's the first foreign expert working at CCTV.

During the days leading up to the start of the trial, the scurrying in Radio Beijing's hallways and feverish Mandarin whispering charged the air with nervous anticipation. Trepidation mixed with excitement. Would this work? Would the Cultural Revolution be put behind? Would the nation emerge with a sense of justice? Would all that political upheaval have been worth it? Would relentless class struggle calm down? Would the country move on? Could people trust again? Would society enter a stable period with leadership that focused on improving lives?

I was only imagining this set of questions, of course, because nobody at Radio Beijing spoke to me about any of it. It was the elephant in the room. But if the revolution itself was not televised, this political theater would be center stage on national TV for weeks. It explained the brilliant planning by the Party to subsidize TV sets for intellectual workers in the months leading up to the trial. Since their class bore the brunt of the consequences during the Cultural Revolution, was this trial meant for them?

A week earlier, everybody rushed home from work to watch the opening day's events. We foreign illiterates had to wait for translated news reports to appear or for fluent Mandarin-speaking friends to fill us in. That wouldn't come from the comrades at Radio Beijing.

In the Beijing Hotel bar, as the theatrics unfurled on the TV screen, I recalled the conversation from the night before at our weekly study group. The illiterates had been eager to hear about the trial proceedings from China experts like Neil Burton, who worked on official translations of Chinese political theory.

Burton was a fellow Vancouverite who had attended UBC a few years before I arrived there in the early '60s. At UBC, he had been ignited by Paul Lin, a Canadian Chinese born in British Columbia to immigrants. In the late 1940s, Lin had pulled out of a Harvard PhD program to help build New China. He then spent fifteen years in the PRC, working at Radio Beijing and teaching. Like so many others of his class, he was sent to the countryside to do menial labor during the anti-Rightist and purification campaigns in the late 1950s. In 1964, just as I was fleeing Vancouver to ride a cultural and political wave in San Francisco and Berkeley, Lin returned to Canada. Interesting timing. He missed the Cultural Revolution! At McGill University, Lin established the East Asian studies department and then became a linchpin in the negotiations to normalize relations between Canada and China in 1970. I could not help wondering how he had interpreted the most violent years of the Cultural Revolution (1966–'69) to the Canadian government. Perhaps he too was in the dark, since by then he was in Vancouver.

Lin had arranged for Burton to study at Beijing University in 1973, the same year that Helmut Opletal had arrived as a student from Vienna. Burton went on to work at Radio Beijing polishing scripts. If I thought about how awful most scripts were in 1980, what must they have been like then? All slogans from Mao's *Little Red Book*? Or promoting model communes and factories that were by 1980 being dismantled or discredited?

Burton, like other China Hands, rationalized much of what we foreign experts found troubling about the recent past in China, yet I found him, like some of the others, inspiring. We illiterate newcomers were trapped in a potent contradiction. Since our Chinese coworkers would not talk to us about anything important, we needed these mysterious ideologues. Their insights and experiences were critical for us. I was trying to resist using the word "apologist," loaded with its anti-Communist flavorings, to describe them.

Burton was at Radio Beijing in September 1976, when Mao died, and at this night's meeting, he brought his cassette recording of the announcement of Mao's death on the English-language broadcast, accompanied by a funeral dirge. In the background we could hear the wailing and sobbing of the comrades in the English department. We were all stunned by this. I tried to imagine my colleagues—subdued and restrained these days—letting loose with such histrionics. Were they fearful of reprisals if they didn't sob enough? Did they feel it their duty to cry over Mao's death, despite the suffering unleashed by his policies or actions during the past twenty years. Were they truly sad?

Now my thoughts flooded with memories of the deaths of revolutionary and transformative leaders from a world I understood better. I remembered where I was when I heard about Martin Luther King, Jr.'s assassination in 1968. The shock of King's death was mired in a period of violence—the reactionary response to the nonviolent Civil Rights Movement and the rise of the Black Power Movement. Like JFK's demise, this was assassination, not natural death. Medgar Evers, Malcolm X, Kent State, Jackson State, Fred Hampton in Chicago, Bobby Kennedy. All of that shocking and outrageous violence—including the Vietnam War—was going on at the same time as the madness of the Cultural Revolution in China.

Burton played his cassette of weeping Radio Beijing comrades as a prelude to discussing the Gang of Four trial, since it was directly after Mao's death in 1976 that the Gang of Four were arrested.

Following his time at Radio Beijing, Burton was assigned to work as a polisher at the official agency for translating government documents. He had just worked on the new Code for Criminal Procedures. More than anyone else in our group, he was equipped to talk about the significance of the trial and its legal trappings. Burton had been a supporter of the initial ideas of the Cultural Revolution, but he was now in favor of Deng Xiaoping's radical new focus on material progress and development. That wasn't true of other China Hands, who seemed to express more concern for Deng's materialist direction than for the crimes and excesses of the Cultural Revolution. Perhaps it was a protective mechanism. Many of the China Hands had been sent to the countryside or imprisoned. Who knew which way the drama would turn next? Would protagonists and antagonists switch again?

Burton recounted what had taken place so far at the trial as revealed in TV coverage and the *People's Daily*. Jiang Qing and three of her associates were being accused of treason, persecution of others, attempting to seize power and training a large militia to challenge the regular army, among other crimes. They were being held accountable for the persecution of more than 750,000 people, of whom more than 34,000 had died. There was much suspicion that these figures were a very low estimation of the crimes.

Also included in the trial were Lin Biao's associates, who were accused of an assassination plot against Chairman Mao. Lin Biao had been one of the top military commanders in the victory of the Communists during the Civil War. During the early years of the Cultural Revolution, Mao had identified him as his successor. Then, in 1971, he had died mysteriously in a plane accident.

Burton explained that the trial was meant to be the first major step to rectify the lawlessness that had reigned during the Cultural Revolution when warring factions of Red Guards—encouraged by the Gang of Four—could interrogate, humiliate, berate, punish, persecute and even kill people accused of class crimes. the Trial indicated a return to the rule of law. Law schools were being established at several institutions, new societies of lawyers were being formed, but the most important development was the right of political criminals to defense. The fact that there was anyone willing to defend the Gang of Four and their cohorts was a significant step. In the past, nobody would have taken on this responsibility for fear of being implicated themselves.

"The trial is significant in the continuing political struggle between major factions of the Party," claimed Helmut, who read everything and had an array of contacts in the dissident community. He believed the trial provided a platform to address past political errors and that the prosecution was trying to separate these errors from actual crimes. "The challenge," he said, "is how they are going to pin everything on the Gang of Four without implicating Mao in the crimes."

Burton insisted that the trial was a way to deal responsibly with the history of horrible political persecutions and derailment of the socialist enterprise. I harbored doubts.

Back at the Beijing Hotel bar, the TV reported that the previous day, when Jiang Qing testified for the first time, the judge had asked her about the plots.

"I cannot remember," she responded. Later she asked to cross-examine one of her cohorts who had confessed to his crimes. When the judge refused, she shouted: "This trial is a parody of justice!" The judge then ordered her to be removed from the courtroom.

After watching the trial reports in the bar, it was time for the complexity of Thelonious Monk. Three decades later, I cannot identify the album I popped into my player that night. Was it the one with John Coltrane? I remember listening to a few of his own compositions—*Monk's Mood*, *'Round Midnight*, *Epistrophy*—brilliant, soulful, essential. Music to mull over the unfolding of history, actions and their consequences. Repetitions in semitones, bebop as a reaction to the crowd-pleasing big bands. Deconstructing the classics. The dialectics of jazz and history.

While the Gang of Four were standing trial for all the offenses of the Cultural Revolution, murderers and abusers were still sitting at their desks in work units around the country. At *China Reconstructs*, where Ron worked, we learned that a dozen people had died during the early and worst years of the Cultural Revolution, supposedly from "suicide by leaping from fourth-floor windows." After an investigation, it was found that all of them had been beaten to death beforehand. Then the first investigator had turned up dead. Eventually some people responsible for killing their coworkers had been sent to jail...for a while. These were all rumors, of course. No way to verify. Now there were new rumors that the perpetrators who had served jail time were back at their desks sitting beside people they had formerly persecuted. Ron said that every time he tried to ask one of his colleagues what happened at *China Reconstructs* during the Cultural Revolution years, that comrade left the room.

While Monk soothed my soul, I laid awake wondering who were perpetrators and who were victims at Radio Beijing. Maybe some comrades were both. What must it be like to have no choice to change your workplace after going through class struggle accusations, attacks and perhaps physical punishment? To have to sit next to each other forever? A sort of purgatory!

Was I sitting next to a perpetrator? A victim? Would I ever know?

A number of expats were picking up political tensions in our work units—although nobody at Radio Beijing would refer to or talk about anything that mattered. Helmut said there were rumblings that major political maneuvers for control were taking place. Deng Xiaoping and his colleagues were trying to demote Mao's chosen successor, Premier Hua Guofeng, and his allies. The Leftists (Mao's cohort) were being sidelined to make way for economic advancement.

"Premier Hua will not come through the outcome of the trial with much power left," claimed Helmut. "He is associated with the 'whateverist' movement—whatever Mao did had to be right."

In our study group, we pondered whether the Cultural Revolution was an effort by Mao to prevent the emergence of a new class of Party bureaucrats, capitalist roaders and bourgeois educators, or if it was purging his enemies within the Party—or both.

ON A dismal winter evening in late November, Ron and I stopped at the Beijing Hotel for an after-dinner drink. We recognized a cluster of Africans gathered at one of the tables. Ahmidou, my neighbor from Niger, and the consul from Togo, a staffer from the Chad embassy and others—regulars in the bar. Everybody was getting drunk. Empty and half-filled quart bottles of Beijing beer littered the table along with shot glasses of Chinese brandy. Nothing unusual—except for the fact that two Chinese men were sitting with them. If local men did any serious drinking with foreigners, it was at official banquets, where endless platitudes of friendship were expressed alongside much competitive drinking. Each toast was followed by slugging back a whole shot of strong Chinese liquor.

What were these guys doing here? The only Chinese permitted entry to the hotel were usually high cadres who had special permission. This bar was not their venue.

One of the men had a slender, puckish face and could have been in his late twenties or early thirties. At first glance, he sported the Hong Kong look with a down jacket and double-knit pants. The mainland giveaway—his shoes. The only style of black leather, hard-soled, lace-up footwear available in the PRC. His companion looked younger, had broad handsome features and wore a long black woolen coat, not the regulation padded green army variety. Along with a white shirt and dark wool pants, he was attired in the high cadres' costume for dressing up Western. He, too, wore the PRC-brand black leather shoes. Something about these two looked important, maybe diplomatic, except for their crimson faces. Neither, it seemed, spoke English, and this collection of Africans understood little or no Chinese. Everyone was smiling and laughing a lot. The Africans disguising their confusion and the Chinese relishing in it.

Too tantalizing to resist, Ron and I joined the table.

Ahmidou addressed our puzzled looks, tilting his head at one of the strangers. "He said he was a history professor at Beijing University."

Ron responded, "I think he's Sihanouk's son."

"He's a cop," someone snorted.

This was typical of the mystery surrounding mainland Chinese who occasionally showed up somewhere unexpected.

"Definitely looks like Sihanouk's son," Ron insisted.

We had heard on the BBC that the Chinese were harboring Norodom Sihanouk, the former king and then executive ruler of Cambodia, as the complex conflicts and horrors of Cambodia marched on. After the Vietnamese invasion of Cambodia in 1978, Sihanouk had gone to the UN in New York to make a speech against Vietnam. Afterward, he had sought refuge in China. Vietnam was friendly with the Soviets, and that was enough of a litmus test for the Chinese, who saw any friend of the Soviets as their enemy and any enemy of the Soviets their friend.

We had heard rumors that tensions were brewing—but apparently things were always in turmoil between China, Cambodia and Vietnam with the Soviet shadow. In the bar at the Beijing Hotel, we were considering the possibility that Sihanouk's son might be sharing our table.

I sat next to the younger of the two enigmas, the one in the long black coat that he hadn't dared to remove. He said his name was Ming. My Chinese vocabulary at that point permitted me to explain where I worked, where I lived, where I was from and how long I had been in China, and then I could ask a few simple questions about directions, bathrooms, taxis, some foodstuffs and prices. Right out of the beginner's' Chinese book for diplomats' wives.

When I first started studying Chinese, I had been frustrated by the vocabulary of this silly text for people accustomed to servants, but knew I had to start somewhere. Just practicing the tones in the simplest greetings had seemed like a lifetime project. Recently, my motivation for learning Chinese had been waning, since there seemed little opportunity to use it. I had degenerated to memorizing lists—numbers, days of the week, months, seasons, objects around the house, items of clothing and food. Nothing that mattered when I was suddenly confronted with a native with whom I could have a conversation.

Ming said he and his friend, Song, were professors at Beijing University. It sounded fishy. Why would they be in the Beijing Hotel? Intellectuals wouldn't want to attract the plainclothes police roaming around and stationed at the front door. Maybe they were cops or informants. But then why would they be getting drunk?

Between their few words of English and our skimpy Mandarin, we deduced they were out for an evening trying to game the security system that separated foreigners from Chinese. Dressing up in Western clothes, passing the guards at the door, drinking with foreigners. Ming was exuberant in his attempt to communicate with me and asked me for my phone number. Nothing so bold had happened since I had met Teacher Liang in the street, so I promptly complied. Then he somehow communicated that we should meet in front of the hotel the next day, Sunday afternoon.

That night, sitting in my darkened living room, drinking a glass of whiskey, smoking yet another cigarette, I listened to Otis Spann's piano blues. "Dust

My Broom," "Must Have Been the Devil," "The Blues Never Die," "One More Mile to Go," "I Gotta Feeling." While Spann's piano magic massaged my soul, I pondered who Ming really was, merging that curiosity with my intense yearnings to understand Chinese political history. My theory was that if I could grasp that history, I might learn something profound about Chinese character. Such as "Will Ming show up?" That question kept banging up against other thoughts about what I was learning about recent history.

To tell the truth is revolutionary.
Antonio Gramsci

Just a few weeks before the trial of the Gang of Four commenced, our study group had gained access to the transcript of another signifying trial, that of Wei Jingsheng. In 1978—two years after the deaths of Mao and Zhou Enlai—a group of poets began plastering posters on a wall in central Beijing, testing the political waters. They were from a generation of ex-Red Guards who had felt manipulated and then punished for their enthusiasm for the initial ideas of the Cultural Revolution. They had poured into the streets after Zhou Enlai had died in 1976. On April 4 of that year, the date of the Qingming Festival, when Chinese honor the dead, people came by the thousands to leave posters and wreaths of flowers in Tiananmen Square honoring the leader whom they revered as being "on their side" amid the cycles of cruelties during the previous years. By commemorating Zhou Enlai, they were making a radical statement.

Before his death, Zhou Enlai had been quietly resurrecting Deng Xiaoping. The Gang of Four, witnessing this outpouring of support for Zhou, saw the hand of Deng. They sent police with clubs into Tiananmen Square, cleared all the posters and flowers and arrested hundreds, sending them to labor camps and prison. Mao died later that year, and within months the Gang of Four was arrested.

Two years later, a group called Beijing Spring started plastering posters on walls in downtown Beijing posing questions about the Cultural Revolution. Questions supported by Deng's group, then on the ascendancy within the Party. Some members of Beijing Spring were former Red Guards. Others had been arrested during the Tiananmen incident in 1976 and had just returned from labor camps and prisons.

Small crowds had begun following the wall poster dialogue when Wei Jingsheng, another ex-Red Guard, had changed the tenor by posting his provocative call for "Democracy as the Fifth Modernization." Deng's Four

Modernizations would not work without this fifth, he had argued. Large crowds had then gathered along Chang'an Avenue near Xidan in what was about to be termed the Democracy Wall Movement.

Zhou Enlai had first promoted the idea of the Four Modernizations back in the early 1960s. That Deng Xiaoping was picking up the pieces in 1978 as he consolidated his power was a sad comment on the fifteen intervening years when China had fallen far behind the rest of the developing world.

Someone in our study group brought a translation of one of Wei Jingsheng's posters: "We want to be the masters of our own destiny. We need no gods or emperors and we don't believe in saviors of any kind...we do not want to serve as mere tools of dictators with personal ambitions for carrying out modernization....Democracy, freedom, and happiness for all are our sole objectives."

Wei Jingsheng, along with other activists, was publishing a magazine called *Exploration*, spelling out these ideas and arguments, stating their guiding principles as "freedom of speech, publication and association as provided by the Constitution."

Exploration was one of a number of magazines being published in 1978 on mimeograph machines. *Beijing Spring*—like the group that started the wall posters—was considered officially sanctioned by Deng's cohorts. *Exploration*, the magazine associated with Wei Jingsheng's group, was not.

According to Helmut, foreign journalists and foreign experts were able to meet and talk freely with the Democracy Wall enthusiasts. Some were even invited to visit the homes of activists. Wei Jingsheng was particularly eager to converse with foreign journalists. Perhaps it was this contact that aroused the Party elite. After Mao's death and the arrest of the Gang of Four, the Party had permitted Chinese to listen to the Voice of America and BBC broadcasts, which had been banned during the Cultural Revolution. Chinese dissidents had access to those reporters and through them could reach a larger Chinese audience than with wall posters. This development more than anything else had worried the Party bosses.

Government news outlets began criticizing Wei's arguments. Cognizant of what this would mean, Wei and his *Exploration* crew had rushed out an issue that asked: "Do we want Democracy or Dictatorship?" On wall posters, Wei had dared to suggest that Deng Xiaoping was not interested in democracy but was going to become yet another dictator. That's when the police pounced. Wei, along with thirty others, had been arrested at Democracy Wall in March 1979, and this new movement of free expression ended.

Wei's trial had taken place in October of '79, less than a year before I arrived in Beijing. I remembered vaguely the *New York Times* reporting it. My timing in China was unfortunate. The crushing of the Democracy Wall Movement had set the tone for my experience at Radio Beijing. It helped to explain the atmosphere of silence and fear. Why nobody wanted to be seen talking to a journalist. The contradiction of my hiring grew ever more confounding.

Some of Wei's fellow dissidents had obtained a recording of his six-hour trial, made a printed transcript and distributed copies at the Democracy Wall when they were arrested, too. These transcripts were circulating in Beijing among the foreign press, and we were now reading it in our study group. Wei was accused of giving military secrets about the China–Vietnam border war to foreign journalists, even though that information had been published in the *People's Daily* and was available to anyone who could read Chinese. He was also accused of counterrevolutionary activities, ridiculing socialism and calling Deng a dictator. He was found guilty of these crimes and sentenced to fifteen years in prison. Given that there was supposed to be a new atmosphere of openness in the Deng era, Wei's trial and sentence were discouraging.

In the government criticism of Wei Jingsheng and his fellow activists, prosecutors had claimed that some of them had dined in restaurants at the invitation of foreigners, and that this had impaired the state system. Wei had replied by asking whether Deng Xiaoping's dining with the Japanese emperor hadn't also impaired the state system.

The trial of Wei Jingsheng and the period of the Beijing Spring and Democracy Wall, along with the trial of the Gang of Four, provided so much information about China's political history since Liberation that once again my brain hurt. And my soul felt tortured.

I would toss and turn at night, pondering what it felt like to be an ex-Red Guard and feel so duped. To feel that the values that were so important fifteen years earlier had been manipulated and undermined. I worried about what it meant that this new democratic movement, which felt so reasonable, so thoughtful, so significant, was squashed...what had that meant to my colleagues, the comrades? If anything?

The arguments offered by the Beijing Spring group and Wei Jingsheng resonated with new democratic possibilities. The *Beijing Spring* writers had argued against the cadre selection system that created a bureaucratic hierarchy that was either sludge on one hand or corrupt and cruel on the other. They had argued instead for a slow democratic process while educating all Chinese citizens to participate equally—a kind of consciousness-raising process rather than radical systemic change whereby heads rolled. Yet history shows us that power seldom gives up without violence. That was Mao's argument about dinner parties and revolutions.

In 1978, the Beijing Spring group had asked which road led to progress and democracy. Some of the wall posters had suggested Yugoslavia as a model. Others had queried, "How much free speech is appropriate given the abuses of the past?" How much truth? Whose truth? Consciousness raising, challenging bureaucracy—what did Marxism–Leninism mean here now? If the Party was the State, how could there ever be equality? It seemed as if the Party had recreated the ancient bureaucratic state of China. Cadres chosen by the Party rather than representatives chosen by citizens.

But it hadn't been this discussion of democracy that had raised the ire of the Party bosses to punish Wei Jingsheng and his supporters, because the Beijing Spring group had also wrung their hands over democracy—how and what kind. No, it had been Wei's insistence on free speech, and calling Deng a dictator—but especially his relationship with foreigners—that had sealed his fate. And that fact pierced my heart.

Then, in January 1980, right after the Wei Jingsheng trial and just eight months before I arrived in Beijing, Deng had given a major speech in the Great Hall of the People to 20,000 officials calling for the abolition of the right to put up wall posters.

October 25, 2014, New York Journal:

I have reached the age that the obituary pages of the New York Times *are often my first news take of the day. It is not just obsession with dying, legacy and salacious curiosity—it is often the only place in the "news" where history is discussed. Today it is Chen Ziming, who has just died at sixty-two. He was an editor of* Beijing Spring *back in the late '70s and then a decade later an organizer of the Tiananmen Square Movement. He was in and out of jail and house arrest for more than a decade—first for criticizing the Gang of Four, then for involvement in the Tiananmen Square Movement.*

Ming was waiting in front of the Beijing Hotel at the corner of Wangfujing and Chang'an Boulevards in the midst of millions of padded bodies heading to the major shopping district. How thrilling to meet a Chinese man outside of the regulations and control of my work unit. The excitement and anticipation felt like junior high school.

I had bicycled to the hotel. As a crowd gathered to stare at us, we began walking my bike along Chang'an heading west. With dusk descending, we could walk together without attracting too much attention. Since we were both bundled up in bulky coats and pants over long underwear, it was difficult to see Ming's body type. Wearing a hat with earflaps, only his round, youthful face was visible. He was definitely cute.

Ming was shocked that I bicycled, and perhaps this loosened him up. He explained that he was a student at Beijing University, but I couldn't figure out what he said he studied. He was twenty-six, and, after an hour of walking in the sub-zero temperatures, that was all I could comprehend about his life. While he seemed old for a student, I knew that "sent down" youth would be older as they returned to Beijing and entered universities.

Ming repeated words over and over again, as if his own familiarity with their sound would help me to comprehend. I was clueless. I would search for the English equivalent and call it out, but there was no way to know if I was right. We then had the idea of pointing at things and naming them in English and Chinese: bicycle, wheel, bell, truck, the Great Hall of the People, the telegraph office, sky, street lamps. It was overwhelming. Our only release was to laugh and try again. Despite our shared illiteracy, I could detect a seductive sense of humor in Ming's animated gestures.

When we arrived at the corner near Radio Beijing and my apartment building—several miles from the hotel, where we had started—Ming jumped on a bus while indicating with hand signs that he would call. I went home and hit the Chinese books. Now I had a reason to study. And I had some idea of the vocabulary I needed. I began listing words and phrases.

Where is your family?

Do you have brothers and sisters?

Where do you live?

What do you study?

What would you like to do professionally?

What happened to you during the Cultural Revolution?

Were you sent to the countryside?

What do your parents do?

Were they persecuted?

What do you do for fun?

What music do you listen to?

Who is your favorite writer?

It was daunting.

Meanwhile, in case we bewildered foreign experts were not busy enough trying to deconstruct the trial of the Gang of Four or decipher the implications of the crushing of the Democracy Wall Movement, in the fall of 1980, China was experimenting with local elections for the first time since 1949.

So while I worried about the growing influence of televangelist Jerry Falwell and his Moral Majority organization, along with New Right operatives and fundraisers like Richard Viguerie and Paul Weyrich and the effect they had on the Reagan victory, China was dipping its toes into an experiment at the grassroots level by allowing elections of representatives for local district councils. Deng Xiaoping and his faction were cautiously promoting secret voting and encouraging a range of candidates in a new experiment with making local district representatives more accountable.

Although the elections were meant to be for all county districts throughout the country, it was the students in Changsha and Beijing who were testing the limits of the new election laws. Perhaps it was no surprise that it would be Beijing University—with its critical role in igniting political change in the early twentieth century—where multitudes of candidates were now organizing exciting campaigns including posters, packed meetings, passionate speeches, question-and-answer sessions with lively debates, all promoting a wide-open discussion of national and international issues along with the worthiness of socialism, capitalism, democracy and the Communist Party. All of this was witnessed by Helmut, who had been taking photographs of wall posters scrawled with "What do you think about socialism?" He reported from campus that there were demands for democracy and intellectual freedom. There was talk of forming a citywide union. Perhaps Beijing Spring had succeeded after all!

My journalist self felt pulled in two. Reagan's pitch had been sunny optimism along with the slogan "Get the government off our backs!" (a pitch that might have done well in China) while Carter seemed like the dour moralizer who couldn't manage the economy or the hostage crisis. I wanted to discuss these issues with my colleagues. For me, the enormous influence of the Religious Right in the American presidential election was as significant as the elections at Beijing University.

Silence.

Not surprisingly, Radio Beijing wasn't covering any of the local election activity.

"Why isn't Radio Beijing sending a reporter to Beijing University's big meetings and the final candidates forum for the election?" I asked Leader Ma.

"Xinhua isn't covering it. *People's Daily* isn't covering it. And the new election law does not say that campaigning is permissible, so we are not going to report on it."

"But every international news agency in town will be there," I argued. "It will be reported everywhere in the world and the only interpretation people won't have will be the Chinese perspective."

"It is the nature of Western media to report sensations, and they can do what they want," Ma Riuliu and Leader Zhang said, one echoing the other.

Later that night, I talked to Ron about it. We concluded that they didn't know what the official line was yet—and nobody wanted to take the responsibility for doing something that might get them in trouble later.

Our study group felt hopeful for a new generation searching with enthusiasm for paths to reform, raising profound questions about how much and what map to pursue. These young people weren't jaded from the Cultural Revolution and Democracy Wall Movement but rather seemed to be discovering their full potential in active political engagement, questioning everything. Just as generations of activists all over the world in previous times had done. Or were we foreigners once again—like our reading of the Cultural Revolution—getting it all wrong?

One foreign expert suggested that the elections were a way to address the "middle problem." Middle-level cadres who were fearful of making any changes.

When I raised the issues of initiative and motivation with the study group, China Hands reported that the *People's Daily* was filled with such complaints. Middle leaders did not want to rock the boat in fear of higher-ups. Maybe it was a problem of higher-up leaders, too.

As I thought about my complaints at Radio Beijing, I could only sympathize with the department leaders because they seemed locked in a frustrating situation. After devoting a lifetime to building New China, they had been victimized during periods of "purification" and now looked behind them to a younger generation that was less educated and more disillusioned as a result of the Cultural Revolution. On the other hand, these cadres had difficulties with those above them. A calcified layer of bureaucrats who were divided between their commitment to the Party, to Mao, or to saving their own necks, depending upon which way the next tornado headed.

I could only guess at the frustrations of Department Leader Zhang. She worked overtime every day. She was trying to implement changes: sending young staffers to do more interviews and to originate more creative programming. Several times she said to me, "Gail, please put your criticisms in writing so we can give them to the top leaders. Maybe they will listen to you because you are a foreign expert. They do not seem to listen to us."

The veteran revolutionary who oversaw the English department for the Party—who neither seemed to understand radio nor English—arrived late, spent his days reading the *People's Daily* and left early. He may have been a brilliant peasant-soldier-revolutionary during the Civil War, but he was now ill equipped to lead China into a sophisticated technological era.

I also saw the dissatisfaction of the younger staff members, who felt there was little real opportunity or incentive for them to explore their creative potential or to affect decisions in the department. Yet they all knew that their well-being was dependent upon how well they got along with their immediate leaders. So who would raise their voice to say, "We should be covering these election activities?" Most wanted to go to school in the West.

Later, when I asked Ming about the elections, his response was flaccid. He seemed apathetic, cynical. "There are radicals and reformists," he said. "The Party will squash them all."

It took an hour to look up all of those words.

Global politics sometimes ruffled our tiny proscribed world of foreign experts. One Sunday afternoon, my Turkish neighbors, a quiet and serious couple in their mid-thirties, knocked on my door. When I answered, they looked like their dog just died. Except there were no dogs in Beijing.

"Do you have time for tea?" Nilsu, the woman, asked.

In their apartment, while sitting at a table set with cookies and strong tea, embroidered doilies (like my British grandmother's—were they universal?) and brightly painted bowls, they spoke softly.

"We are exiles. We had to flee from Turkey after the recent military coup."

What they did not say is that they were activists...Leftists. But I filled in the blanks. In a pleading voice they explained that since they had observed diplomatic cars picking me up and dropping me off and that—to their eyes—I seemed to have an active social life, they would appreciate if I would never tell anyone that they existed. Not by their names, not by "there's a Turkish couple living in my building." Diplomats from the military government were installed at the Turkish embassy on the other side of town.

"Our lives could be in danger," Nilsu emphasized.

I wondered what it must feel like to have to ask a stranger to do this. Their reality was sobering. Not much different from our Filipino neighbors. They had been in exile in China for years. If I ached at night from the barrenness of this social landscape, I could not imagine their caged and frightened lives.

Now Bahdra was miserable. Since there was a growing Tamil political movement in Sri Lanka, the Tamils had convinced Radio Beijing to hire a Tamil foreign expert to translate, polish and narrate the scripts in the Tamil language alongside Bahdra, who narrated in Sinhalese. Bahdra was from Colombo, the capital, which was adamantly Sinhalese-speaking and Buddhist. The new Tamil family were Hindus. This appeared to be an ethnic conflict in our building.

"In the past, the Tamils have been badly discriminated against," explained Bahdra, "but since the 1978 Constitution, they have more rights and are claiming them."

She explained that armed guerrilla Tamil groups were claiming half the country's landmass and already there had been terrorist attacks in Colombo. Bahdra, who had been a lifelong international peace activist, was despondent about this conflict. She was terribly depressed about the broadcast in Tamil and never spoke with the Tamil family who lived in our building.

I was forced to acknowledge that I had only read about coups and conflicts in foreign countries. And while I had sometimes taken strong positions in protest, I had never been forced to live with the consequences of a civil war or a military coup. Once more, I was humbled by my privileged ignorance.

One day, Ming called at the office. Two other staffers lingered in the room, so I felt suddenly self-conscious and resentful. It was a mistake to give him the office number, but then he should be the one to worry. It was impossible to have a natural conversation on the phone and no way to disguise that this was a Chinese calling. Ming's English was not good enough for me to pretend otherwise. Long silences greeted my carefully articulated English suggesting where and when we should meet. But then I slipped up and repeated the information in Mandarin. My office mates perked up with curious faces. Hilarious. Two intelligent adults, repeating the same simple phrases over and over, making mistakes, checking to see if the other understood the meaning and all the while having an audience who could be potentially dangerous. Given my earlier experiences with Shadow Zhang, never again would I allow anyone from the office to mediate my phone conversations.

We met in front of the Beijing Hotel again, then took a bus to a park with a frozen lake, all the while feverishly looking up words in our dictionaries. When I saw skaters on the ice, I looked up the word for skates. I pointed a finger at myself. Ming looked at me in disbelief. As we negotiated to rent clip-on skates, he was concerned I wouldn't find any in my size.

"Too big!" he whispered, laughing, pointing at my feet.

We eventually joined the mobs skating on the lake.

I hadn't skated for years, and my rental skates offered no ankle support nor toe picks on the blades, so I was slipping and sliding all over the ice with no means to stop. After two falls and lots of laughs, we headed for the cafeteria at the lake, a huge room with big tables surrounded by young people having fun. The specialty here was borscht. A remnant of the Soviet period. He went to order and pay. I felt unbearably self-conscious in this room filled with hundreds of eyes focused on us. Would he be approached by plainclothes police, like Gao Yuan on the sacred mountain? Since Ming was younger than I was, I wondered what was going through their minds.

It wasn't possible to consult our dictionaries discreetly, given the congestion, and Ming grew visibly uneasy. Suddenly he jumped up to indicate we were leaving. Had he exhausted his courage to be seen with a foreigner? An older woman with red hair? He probably wasn't prepared for the fishbowl inspection by a mass of his contemporaries. As we left, he gestured that he would accompany me back by bus to Radio Beijing. All of this communication, of course, took frustrating amounts of time with miscues and misunderstandings.

On the bus, he drew a diagram and then indicated on my heavily worn bicycle map where he lived. I should come tomorrow night, Sunday, after dark, wear Chinese clothes, a hat and a mask across my face. I was astonished. Did he live alone? Yes. Even more astounding. How had he managed that when so many families were crammed into small spaces and young married couples, in particular, were waiting for a room or apartment? His parents must have been very high cadres. These were all questions I had no time to ask—we were at my bus stop, and I jumped off.

The following day—my one day off—I went to the Friendship Store to purchase something discreetly for one of the comrades. Although individual coworkers rebuffed my invitations for lunch or dinner, soon they arrived on my doorstep to ask me if I could buy something for them at the Friendship Store. I made the purchase and discreetly gave it to them at the office and never had contact with them again. I fulfilled similar requests for maintenance people at the apartment building with the same flat results.

In the beginning I hoped that some of the favors I did would lead to even tentative friendships, especially with my coworkers. The young, single staff members were the most careful in their dealings with me, yet each would one day pull me aside in the hallway when nobody was around to ask if I would write a recommendation for them to go to school in the US or Canada. When I completed the task, our communications would revert back to little more than eye contact and a half-smile in the hallway.

Nobody could blame the Chinese for a little opportunism.

After returning from the Friendship Store, I edited an application for one of the comrades to send to a university in the US. She would not talk to me openly in the office. This was all "backdoor" and secretive. At least I was useful for something.

If my colleagues were too terrified to make a social call to my apartment or go out to dinner with me, at least somebody was willing to struggle with the effort of hanging out. I shuddered with excitement getting ready to bicycle to Ming's apartment.

Even though he was ten years younger, how could I resist this opportunity? By this time, I had acquired loose army pants, which I wore over a pair of my blue jeans. On top of three sweaters, I wore my old man's cotton padded jacket. I could barely move with this bulk on my bike, and it was at least a three-mile ride in frigid temperatures to his street corner.

Furious Gobi Desert winds pounded coal dust and sand into my face while my hands turned numb even through my gloves. I pumped relentlessly driven by the wicked naughtiness of this bold adventure. Not just risky but illicit. Defying a government policy that forbade relationships between foreigners and Chinese, we could face serious consequences. Loss of housing, access to university, job placement and promotions, maybe even jail for Ming? Deportation for me? Despite all this, I was driven on in brutal weather by curiosity. And lust.

Through my tearing eyes, I spotted his lump of a bundled mass beneath the eerie light of a streetlamp at his corner. He smiled when he saw me swathed in Chinese disguise. But apparently my getup wasn't enough. Looking over his shoulder, he motioned me to follow him to the *back* of his building. Fear rippled through me as we were plunged into darkness. Was the decision to come here to his apartment building going to be my unmaking? No time for doubts. He beckoned me toward the fire escape.

After climbing up the unlit and cluttered stairway in silence, we landed at the fourth floor. He turned to me and made arm gestures to indicate that we would not be going through the door—instead, we would go through the window. My mind raced with the worst possible images of rape, death and dismemberment. Then, I asked myself why would it make any difference going through the door or window? As I plunged headfirst behind him through the window I only felt the thrill of getting away with something outrageous—and illegal. It all happened so fast.

Once inside his eight-by-fifteen-foot room, I felt like a criminal. I was in forbidden territory. There was a conspiratorial feeling with Ming that heightened the physical tension between us. When he turned on a dim lightbulb hanging from the middle of the ceiling, I could see a single bed, a closet, a desk and a chair, along with a few books, a pair of boots, a guitar and a bamboo recorder. As I took off my hat and mask, he pointed to a few oranges in a bowl and cubes of tea and cocoa he had bought for the occasion. He then gestured to a hot plate, which he explained that he had fixed that day. That fact took at least ten minutes of dictionary consultations.

He plugged in the hot plate and left the room to fill a saucepan with water from a bathroom out in the hall. When he returned, he explained through our frantic dictionary routine that he shared the bathroom with another young man who lived across the way. He asked if I needed to use the bathroom, and indicated he would have to clear the way and watch for his neighbor. I sincerely hoped I didn't have to pee while I was there.

The room had a depressing aesthetic and smelled of that odor I associated with teenage boys. Body excretions on the sheets mixed with dirty socks? After shedding my bulky coat, I perched tentatively on his bed to watch him make tea.

I could not believe I was actually inside a young, single man's apartment in Beijing. First of all, most single men his age either lived with their parents or in a dormitory. So this felt surreal—and suspicious. I wondered if he really lived there or if this was a den that different Chinese men shared for liaisons. There was that body excretions smell.

I had prepared questions to ask how it was he could live alone in this space when I knew married colleagues with a baby who could not get a room to live together. Although I found it not simply puzzling but shocking, I didn't have the vocabulary to express those reactions. We were locked into the perimeters of a pedestrian, slender vocabulary offered up by our little dictionaries. I did know the meaning of the next word he used.

"*Guanxi*," he laughed. The complex of connections between families and friends that implied loyalties, favors, duties. I was just beginning to learn about how it worked. Perhaps like "I'll scratch your back if you scratch mine."

Somehow I still had it confused with *hou men*, the "backdoor," which was the only other way to get what you wanted. If you had the connections.

He explained that his parents were high cadres, which I had already surmised. Like a hinge, he bent over at the waist with his arms stiff behind him, as if I should have known what this posture signified. I was stymied. He kept mimicking this posture, becoming increasingly perplexed that I didn't understand. His charades were becoming more antic as he made facial gestures of misery. He kept hinging at the waist with his arms agonizingly pushed up behind and looking at me in frustration.

He pointed out a word in the dictionary. "Airplane." More like a fighter bomber. Finally! I got it! During the Cultural Revolution, this was the humiliation posture, when victims—particularly high cadres and professors—were forced to wear a dunce hat along with a sign around their necks screaming out their class crimes while being pushed into the bent-over position with their arms tied straight up behind their backs—like an airplane. Well, to Chinese eyes. This was what his parents experienced during the Cultural Revolution. *Definitely high cadres*, I thought to myself.

Before the Cultural Revolution, Ming explained, he and his parents had lived in four rooms. Red Guards forced them out of their house. He and his mother were moved into one room and his father sent to the countryside to do physical labor.

Now his parents were back in Beijing, living in two rooms with hot water—a luxury. He never explained where his parents worked—he only pointed to the word "factory" in the dictionary. He, too, worked in a factory—but now only at night—so he could go to university in the daytime.

Despite all of the missed cues, a mischievous sense of humor surfaced from Ming's kinetic charades. To watch his animated face and antic gestures was such a relief in the midst of so much control. In mime, he acted out how Red Guards stabbed him in the butt with a rifle. Then it took ten minutes of clumsy dictionary work to explain that at the same time his motorbike was smashed by Red Guards. This would have been at least ten years earlier. To have a motorbike then would have been very luxe, and he must have been very young. Was I understanding the words? Did I have his age right? No time to stop and clarify.

He didn't ask me a single question about *my* life. Even though I had grown accustomed to this invisibility from the comrades at work, I hungered to be investigated by Chinese acquaintances out in the world. I wanted him to be interested in me! Instead he asked me about the men I was with the night we met at the Beijing Hotel. I sensed he wanted to know if I had slept with them. A growing feeling of unease washed over me. But then the tea was ready.

He explained that he had a girlfriend—she had gone to university in another city and then wrote him a letter. Dear John letter stories always bored me. Perhaps because the script was so predictable. He had been sad for the past year. His narrative included a new twist, as he also expressed sadness and loneliness in being an only child. That reality had never really bothered me—I relished having my mother's undivided love—but he was not interested in my story.

Sitting on the bed that served as a couch, working our dictionaries and sipping tea, he suddenly pounced and pressed his mouth on mine. A flat, forced, closed-mouth kiss. No finesse. Next, he was groping me through my bulky clothes. It was all very awkward and jerky. He began to unbutton his pants. I pushed him away, and we struggled a little. I didn't know how to say anything that might humor things. Instead, I jumped up and put my coat on. Not a seductive situation at all. Too bad. He was handsome and athletic-looking now that I could see him without his coat.

He flitted around the room, fidgeting with things. Oh, oh—a spurned lover in an unknown context could turn dangerous. My eyes darted around the room, searching for potential weapons. A bamboo recorder?

But then he pulled his coat on, and his pants revealed that he'd had an orgasm. He tried to cover up the evidence and helped me back out of the window. This was so crazy and awkward. Such a deflation of expectations. I suspected he would only accompany me down the stairs, but he bicycled most of the way home with me in the icy winds, repeating "Sorry," then, before turning back to his place, he indicated that he wanted to get together again.

Bicycling on alone on a desolate winter night, I felt conflicted. His lack of sexual experience wouldn't have bothered me if he was even a tiny bit romantic and had some skills of seduction, but his behavior indicated he simply saw me as an object to practice on. Yet, somehow, despite all that, I still wanted to spend more time with him. I was using him, too. Anthropology. Besides, there was something in his humorous approach to things that delighted me. And I felt like a delirious outlaw.

ONE DAY, during my long lunch hour, while photographing on busy Xidan Street, I spotted a used table in a secondhand store. After the shopkeepers' insistent efforts to tie the table to my bike, which I knew wouldn't work, fueling my already overwrought attitude about inefficiency and my inability to relax in China, I insisted on hiring a pedicab driver. I should have just laughed at the whole episode. I had lost my sense of humor. Time to see Ming again.

On the way back to my apartment, I bicycled alongside the pedicab with my table. An older man dressed in the usual padded blue uniform maneuvered his bike next to mine.

"I work at Radio Beijing. I have seen you there," he said. "I heard you have a degree in sociology."

"Yes," I stuttered, surprised not only at his perfect English but also at his knowledge of my resume.

"I studied that too—sociology, psychology. I work in the accounting department."

"Did you study abroad?"

"No."

"When did you study?"

"Well, I'm sixty." He gave me a knowing look.

I was supposed to figure out that, if he was sixty, he studied before Liberation in 1949. I was more curious about how he knew I studied sociology. Did the entire staff at Radio Beijing—thousands of them—discuss my background and daily comings and goings?

But then I thought about what it meant to be working in the accounting department when you had a degree in sociology and psychology. He had a story to tell. Would I ever be able to uncover it? Not today. He was peeling away from me as we approached Radio Beijing and disappeared into the sea of bikes entering Central Broadcasting.

The following morning, Voice of America and the BBC were abuzz with curiosity about what was happening to Hua Guofeng, Mao's hand-picked successor. Was he being put out to pasture? Would he be replaced as Communist Party head? Criticism had just appeared on the front page of *People's Daily* about him, which was apparently a sign that he would soon go. When I arrived at the office, I asked several comrades whom I sat next to every day what was happening to him. One was the Party secretary in our department; the other, Shadow Zhang, was also a Party member. Both looked at me with befuddled expressions.

"He is the head of the Party," Shadow Zhang proclaimed.

End of discussion.

Given this deadly intellectual context, it was easy to rationalize getting together again with an adolescent. Even if he was beyond the normal age for adolescence. The following Saturday, I met Ming at the Moscow Restaurant for an early dinner. The Chinese section of the restaurant filled an auditorium-sized room overflowing with animated young people crowded around square tables. Warm. Vibrant. Noisy. And the prices were cheap. Worried that Ming might be embarrassed to be seen with me in that goldfish bowl, I suggested the barren, colder and pricier foreigners' section. At least it would minimize peering eyes. There we could bring out our dictionaries and proceed with the cumbersome process of learning about each other. Well, at least, learning about him. It was my first official dinner date with a Chinese man alone, and it was agonizing and hilarious.

As we slurped borscht and nibbled chicken Kiev, Ming mocked the "crude" habits of the Chinese—spitting out sunflower seed shells on the floor, spewing bones out on dining tables, spitting in general and wearing sunglasses while swimming. His humor infused me like a drug, slowly dripping happiness into my veins. I howled when he told me about the difference when Chinese young people ate in restaurants versus eating at home.

"In restaurants, they say they aren't hungry and eat delicately. At home, they wolf everything in sight. In restaurants, they save face by leaving food on their plates," he explained through dictionaries and mime. I couldn't figure out how to ask him whether these were the privileged kids—children of high cadres. I assumed they were.

He defied this behavior by eating heartily in restaurants. So did I. Perhaps that was why he told me. He devoured bread, butter and jam. Said he loved it. Really?

I learned that Ming was studying economics. "Marx and Keynes." He also worked as a watchman at a factory at nights so he could sleep on the job. He acted out how his boss didn't like that.

After dinner, I brought him back to my apartment. I had no deep feeling for him, only a sense of exploration. He was fascinated by the drawings on the walls, my books, the music cassettes. I played the *Kind of Blue* album. Miles Davis. John Coltrane. Bill Evans. Cannonball Adderley. Cuts like "Freddie Freeloader" or "Blue in Green." Simple, piercing deep into the libido. I tried explaining its significance in the jazz canon. The bestselling jazz album, the simplicity of the approach. Modalities. I even tried to explain "sexy" and "cool." But that was way too complicated for our language skills.

The pacing of the music was so dreamy, I offered to draw him a hot bath. Both the privacy and the hot water were too luxurious to refuse. To his astonishment, I joined him in the tub, then dried him off. I rubbed lotion on him. He kept freezing. He gestured repeatedly to the door, referring to the soldier with a gun at the guard hut. He acted out the police knocking on my door in the most charming way. His whispering made me wonder if he thought the room was bugged. Gradually, carefully, I calmed him. He relaxed. Then, just as I knew that he would never know me, nor I him, sparks began to fly, and I could forget for a moment where I was and who I was with. Or whether this was behavior included in Mao's dinner party or revolution. Pirouetting. Twirling. Twisting. Heaving. Vaulting. Cleaving in two. Bursting.

Afterwards, as hearts calmed, he murmured, "You are my chairman."

I've been called a lot of things in the heat of the moment, but "You are my chairman"? I could learn to like this kid.

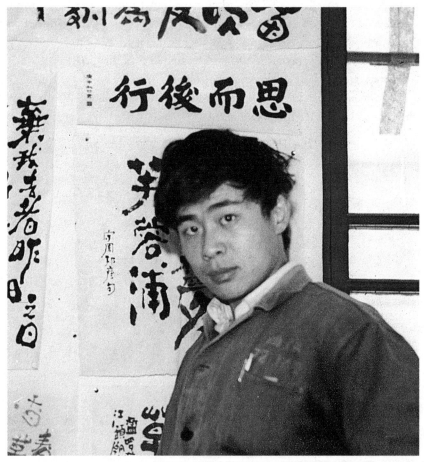

Shi Yung, my calligraphy teacher, at an exhibition of his work. Beijing, 1980

Chapter Ten

A Hundred Flowers—Blooming and Scorched
百花---盛开与枯萎

"Do you love her?"

"I am not sure. We are together a lot. Is that how you say it?"

Shi Yung crouched over some old *People's Daily* issues fanned out on my living room floor, his fingers clutching my new bamboo brush with goat hair. I watched carefully as his arm curved in a graceful arc to create exaggerated strokes of calligraphy.

Shortly before I had left New York, a choreographer friend, Ruby Shang, brought a visiting dance student from Beijing to my apartment. Like most Americans in 1980, I had never met anyone from Beijing. When she suggested I look up her brother, an art student in the Chinese capital, I was delighted. Now I would have one—yes, one—social contact when I hit the ground! After I arrived and met Janet, a Mandarin-speaking foreign expert, who revealed she had a telephone, I asked her for help to make the call.

By day, Shi Yung studied at the Central Academy of Arts and Crafts, where he lived in the crowded dorms. At night, he worked part time in the design department of a rug factory. Too wary to come to my apartment, he suggested we meet at Janet's in an all-Chinese building. When he said that he was studying calligraphy, I asked him if he would teach me. If I learned something about the artistry of the characters, I reasoned to myself, memorizing them might seem less daunting. And, more importantly, I sensed that secrets of the culture might be revealed through learning how to reproduce those intriguing forms.

After several months of bureaucratic wrangling, Yung finally obtained a letter of permission from his school and another from the Foreign Experts Bureau at Radio Beijing allowing him to come to my apartment once a week to teach this ancient craft. I was not allowed to pay him for the classes. Instead, I could help him improve his English conversational skills.

When I first met Yung, I was immediately drawn to him. Beyond his beautifully sculpted face and lean frame, his comfort with foreigners was refreshing. He combined qualities I hadn't encountered in my tiny world of Chinese acquaintances—a dignified assurance of his Chinese identity along with curiosity about Western contemporary ideas. His tendency to laugh a lot carved an imprint of grooves on his face. To me they created a map to his spirit. He was also the first mainland Chinese guy I had seen in tight pants.

First we bicycled to Lulishang Hutong to find brushes, bottled ink and a beautiful porcelain blue-and-white calligrapher's bowl for mixing ink with water. Later, he said, I would graduate to rubbing an ink stone on a black rock tablet to forge the right consistency for loading my brush.

For our first class, he demonstrated a range of voluptuous strokes used to create characters, making generous gestures on my old newspapers. I prodded him to talk about his past.

"My father and mother are intellectuals. They suffered during the Cultural Revolution."

This mantra among the intellectual caste, I had come to realize, was now politically acceptable by the Party. I wasn't sure whether this generality about his parents represented the limits of his vocabulary or a reticence to divulge details to a stranger. I pressed him to talk about himself.

"I was a 'sent down' youth. Young people from the cities—millions of them—were sent to the countryside to work on farms and in factories during the Cultural Revolution."

My study group had been wrestling with understanding this strategy. Had it been a way to defuse the Red Guard infighting and horrendous gang violence during the early years of the Cultural Revolution? Was it meant to reeducate and indoctrinate young people through agricultural and factory work? Or was it a plan to control future intellectuals and break their hold on bureaucracy? Mostly likely, all of those things?

"I was sent to a rubber plantation and factory in Yunnan province, which borders Vietnam. I hated the rubber plantation." Yung seemed reluctant to provide more details about the experience. "I taught myself English by reading *Jane Eyre*."

Apparently, *Jane Eyre* was one of the few foreign novels permitted by the cultural czars during the Great Proletarian Cultural Revolution.

Presumably, Yung's politically connected family pulled strings or called in old debts—*guanxi*—or went through the back door—*houmen*—to get him back to Beijing and into art school. Now he was applying to universities in the US and sewing his own blue jeans. We concentrated on strokes.

"Here," he demonstrated. "Before you begin with the brush, you mix the ink and you think hard about what you are going to do. It is like meditation. You need to see the brush as an extension of your arm."

Squatting on the floor, Yung showed me how to load just the right amount of ink and water on my brush to begin. As he shaped strokes with determined, fluid gestures, it looked deceptively easy. As I took the plunge, copying his strokes on my old *People's Daily* newspapers on the floor, I learned it wasn't simply about physical dexterity.

"It is an art," he insisted. "The amount of water and ink, your approach to the paper, the pressure, the speed. It is all determined by the idea, the word, the spirit of the character and must be practiced carefully."

On my hands and knees, the whole exercise was surprisingly pleasing. Like learning how to give pleasure to another's body. But then again, there was so much discipline, like learning the rules of a sonnet, a fugue or a tango. I sensed that I was embarking on a long journey to learn the secrets of a complex, exquisitely elegant craft. Although initially I hoped it would help me remember characters, it was the visual thrill of the ideograms created by this complex of lines, dots and marks that seduced me.

"There is a very strict order to the strokes," Yung instructed. "And each stroke requires a specific direction and pressure. Sometimes it begins fat and ends thin or the opposite. You must know just when to lift off the page."

I made such a mess of it. My movements were all wrong. It felt like I was learning how to swim and I was having trouble breathing.

"With practice you will improve," Yung encouraged, his eyes glistening with empathy.

Watching his profile as he turned to form a horizontal mark, his prominent cheekbones and full lips looked like carved jade. I had been in Beijing only four months and already Northern Chinese faces—with their high cheekbones— had become my ideal of sensual beauty.

Squatting over the papers, spilling ink and water, I couldn't help feeling the semblance between my ineptness at calligraphy and my general artlessness in China. Eventually, after repeating a single line many times, I was beginning to see and feel the mysterious poetry of this art form, the eroticism of a stroke.

I queried Yung about his latest girlfriend. "Are you having an affair?"

"I guess so."

"What do you mean? You guess so? Are you in love? Are you having sex?"

Yung laughed and blushed at my questions. I knew my probing was far too direct for Chinese sensibilities, but I was fed up with small, safe talk.

"I really like her. But I have difficult...having sex with...and love a woman... who has so many affairs with men."

Now it was my turn to be shocked with his forthrightness. I wondered whether it was easier to get to the point in a foreign language.

His new girlfriend worked in the film industry. I had met her a couple of times, and she struck me as being very Western in her style and behavior. Fetching, bold and playful, she seemed to be defying the prevailing earnestly sweet look.

I was eager to pursue this discussion with Yung so I could understand something about young people in Beijing, even if I knew that Yung could hardly be considered a regular guy. He was from the privileged intellectual class. From Janet I had learned that Yung's father, rehabilitated since the Cultural Revolution, was a leader of one of the cultural agencies.

"He runs the department that gives permission to foreign journalists and filmmakers to work in China," she had explained. "He's a major gatekeeper."

"During the anti-Japanese movement in the 1930s and WWII," Yung said, "my father produced plays and traveled around with theater troops. My mother was a singer. But they suffered during the Hundred Flowers Movement in the late 1950s when artists and intellectuals were persecuted. Then again they were punished during the Cultural Revolution."

Yung wouldn't provide more details.

"No, that's too much," he corrected me as I doused my brush in a mix of water and ink.

I was lost in a reverie about how many characters a Chinese child learns in the first few years of school simply to continue studying—something like 5,000. But in the old official scholar examination system, contestants had to memorize thousands and thousands of characters to absorb the whole body of literary and philosophical works with their myriad elliptical meanings. Since the 1950s, the government had promoted simplified characters to improve literacy. Of course, basic writing was different from the craft of calligraphy.

Yung was studying with some interesting masters of calligraphy, and he brought me examples of how the strokes and styles of famous calligraphers had evolved.

"In great calligraphy, style and shape are bound to meaning. It is a journey," he insisted.

I knew Yung had practiced this speech in English. And I loved it. But I couldn't resist steering our chat to a more prosaic altitude.

"What happened with the other one?" I had previously expressed impatience with Yung's description of an affair with a colleague at the rug design company. He spoke of it in overly romanticized language, describing his lover in idealistic, virginal terms, despite the fact that she was married. Her marital status made the relationship dangerous and, I presumed, more torrid.

"She is married to the son of very high cadres," he said in a whispered confession, as if my walls were bugged, which I increasingly suspected was true. "They could make trouble for me," he mouthed quietly.

Risky, courting disaster. It was not clear who had pulled away first. Now there was the new love interest.

As he watched me begin the intimidating process of a sequence of strokes—in their strict order—he talked about his new romance. My stroke was jagged. He sounded confused. While I made wobbly shapes on the newspaper, I couldn't help feeling compassion for the heartaches ahead as Yung navigated this new romantic terrain. I worried about what was in store for Chinese men and women as new images of Western sexual liberation began hitting them. The form without the content. Women, especially, were going to get burned. Then again, it was Yung's girlfriends who seemed to be exploring new turf, experimenting with forbidden boundaries. Contradictions.

"That's beautiful! Dynamic!" Yung cheered my progress.

While practicing a single stroke over and over again, I could see how this obsession with perfection could become a lifetime vocation. I no longer remembered the meaning of the character I was deconstructing but was seduced by the design, the artfulness, the sensation, the Zen...the tension between erotic impulse and strict order.

As our lessons continued, Yung brought copy books and rice paper for me to graduate from the *People's Daily* papers. While I labored over the voluptuous curve of a stroke that began with a strong gesture but lifted like a feather off the page, Yung said he would like to see a book about Matisse. I promised to ask a New York friend to send one.

"Last year," Yung explained, "after years of only permitting Socialist Realism in art, they removed Impressionism from the 'decadent' list. This year they removed Post-Impressionism. At this rate," he added, "China will always be about a hundred years behind the art movements of the West. At my school we have some reproductions of Western modern art—up to the early '60s—but my professors say it is bourgeois and bad."

He corrected my efforts at a stroke that began with a light, wispy touch then fattened to a strong, bulbous end.

"The attitude is changing," he continued. "Now they know that there are very good things, new things. You have to know them, then you can judge. Before what was wrong was that they judged modern art without understanding its context." He said that he and his classmates at school didn't argue about art very much because they knew there were Party members or informants among them.

Yung admitted that he understood very little about the meaning and intent of modern art. "That's why I want to study in the US to see what it is."

At Ron's suggestion, Yung had applied to the Art Institute of Chicago and received an encouraging response—however, not final. I told him that most Westerners shared his bewilderment about modern art. He looked shocked. When I laughed, he looked even more puzzled.

It would be several years before Serge Guilbaut's book appeared—expounding a tale about how the US State Department used abstract expressionism during the Cold War to promote American values, especially "freedom," abroad. Perhaps the Chinese Art Police were right to be suspicious of the subversive ideas that were attached to brush strokes and flung paint.

IN EARLY September 1980, Yanna, my feisty Czech neighbor had taken me to an exhibition of a dissident artist group called Xing Xing, pronounced "Shing, Shing," translated as "Spark Spark" or "Star Star." The idea behind it was a play on a famous Mao slogan: "A single spark can cause a prairie fire." Or, in the spirit of multiple meanings, Star Star represented stars in the night sky showing a new way or stars as beacons in an endless night.

"You could say that every artist is a star; it means we are each individuals," said Ma Desheng, one of the members of *Xing Xing*. "It challenges the uniformity of the Cultural Revolution."

As Yanna and I roamed the exhibit, she explained that this group of artists had emerged since Mao's death in 1976 and had been active participants in the New Democracy Movement.

"Most of these artists are from the Cultural Revolution generation," she said. "Which means they received little formal education and no art training.

They worked at other jobs."

According to Yanna, after being denied an exhibit in the official bastion of socialist art—the National Art Gallery—these artists hung their paintings in a park. When the police closed down that exhibition, the group organized a protest march setting out from Democracy Wall with banners that read "We Demand Democracy and Artistic Freedom." Finally, in the fall of 1980, the ideological gatekeepers at the National Art Gallery relented, and they were invited to show their work.

A sign at the gallery entrance stated, "Art must combine our free liberated spirit with the inspiration of creation." It also explained that these artists "have the courage to explore"—a reference to Wei Jingsheng's banned journal, *Exploration*.

While Yanna worked her way through the hundreds of excited visitors, greeting some of the artists she knew, I perused the work. To my Western, unsophisticated eye, many of the pieces looked like competent student emulations of late-nineteenth and early-twentieth-century European paintings. Impressionist still life, landscapes and portraits, a sprinkling of abstract pieces and nudes. The subject matter was mostly personal, the mood sad or wistful and on the surface the tone was nonpolitical. Yanna pointed out that the exhibit represented a break with orthodoxy by embracing banned genres and subjects and that made it very political.

She dragged me through the crowd to meet one of the more mature artists, Yuan Yunsheng. "He is famous for painting a mural at the Beijing airport in 1979. It depicts the water splashing festival in Yunnan," she chuckled. "The cultural bosses were outraged by two nudes in the work. At first, they covered the nudes with a curtain that people could peek behind. Then they were boarded over."

"I guess that's why I missed it when I arrived," I laughed.

Yanna's real mission here was to show me the sculptures of Wang Keping, who was now being mobbed by fans and journalists. His wooden pieces were provocative. Working in a traditional Chinese medium that had been lost for centuries, using the natural knots and gnarls of wood, Keping fashioned simple forms critical of Party bureaucrats and the Great Helmsman himself. The largest piece, called "Idol," depicted an oversized face, recognizable as Mao—and Buddha. One eye was shut, the other open.

"He wants to see who's praying to him," Keping said, with Yanna translating.

Watching Keping beam at Yanna while she translated, I guessed that their relationship blossomed beyond friendship. He exuded a warm, tender quality. I felt a pang of jealousy.

Along with several erotic carvings, another taboo genre, Keping's work included totem-like heads with corked mouths and blackened eyes. About one, called "Silence," he said, "They are people who can see but are not allowed to look. They have mouths but are forbidden to speak. This is what happened to the grassroots democracy movement in China."

Two of the youngest members of Xing Xing were Ai Weiwei, nineteen, and Yan Li, twenty-six. I wouldn't really learn about these two until they emigrated to New York and I interviewed them and other Xing Xing members in 1985 for a feature *Village Voice* article about dissident Chinese artists arriving in New York.

Ai Weiwei's father, Ai Qing, had been one of China's popular poets during the revolutionary movement of the '40s. Like many other patriots, he had spent several years in jail for his efforts in the anti-Japanese war, then went to the liberated zone of Yan'an to join the Communist Party and write political poetry. But even in those years, this independent and outspoken poet was at odds with the Party. Like many other writers, he produced less and less after Liberation. His criticisms grew, and by 1957, during the first anti-Rightist campaign, he was purged.

"He was charged with not writing what the Party wanted him to write," Weiwei explained when I interviewed him in New York.

First, Ai Qing and his wife were sentenced to two years of hard labor, then the family was banished to the western edge of the Gobi Desert. During the Cultural Revolution, Ai Qing was again severely criticized—because he had been branded a Rightist in the past—and sent to an even more remote village to clean out latrines for seven years.

Yan Li was a painter and poet, and part of a group known as the Misty Poets from the late '70s New Democracy period. He was only twelve when the Cultural Revolution broke out. Students ransacked his grandfather's house, and three years later his grandfather committed suicide. Yan Li's parents, both scientists, were sent to the countryside for nine years. Despite his history in the highly dangerous Communist Party underground in Shanghai during the '40s, Li's father was now accused of being a spy because of Party criticisms leveled against the grandfather. While in the countryside, Li's father became ill and was denied medical care. When he returned to Beijing, there was no job for him. He died at age fifty-four.

Both Ai Weiwei and Yan Li were marked by who their parents or grandparents were.

Li felt hopeless. "I cannot change who my grandfather was," he said.

Weiwei seemed to have absorbed the defiant spirit of his father: "I have always been a rebel."

When Weiwei's family returned to Beijing after the Cultural Revolution, he began studying painting with a friend, joined the Xing Xing group and was swept up into the New Democracy movement.

"It was a movement from the heart," he said in a faraway voice. "People expressed themselves freely. Even though the country had been through a terrible experience, they felt there was the possibility to make a new start." His face became strained as he continued. "With the jailing of Wei Jingsheng, those hopes were smashed. It was the biggest disappointment for young people in China. Our spirits collapsed."

Yan Li was also involved in the New Democracy Movement. Missing out on schooling during the Cultural Revolution, he educated himself while working in a factory. He began painting and writing poetry, then joined Xing Xing. "It was a period when the strongest need was for free expression," he told me. "Not intellectual analysis so much as expression."

But these interviews were conducted in the freedom of a New York living room five years later, not the whispering, secretive, constricted, self- and other-censored Beijing of 1980, when it was Wang Keping who seemed the most provocative and outspoken.

In the several months following the September 1980 show, foreign journalists had been reporting their visits to Keping's tiny apartment, where they could see a piece called "Backbone of Society," a head with eyes closed, nostrils jammed, mouth tightly shut, a bump on the cheek.

"That's a cancer," Keping thoughtfully explained. "The indifference of these officials is the cancer of our society. They are bad cadres."

In many ways he was speaking within the legitimate parameters expressed in the *People's Daily* of the moment. In 1980 Beijing, the Party was concerned about corrupt cadres: middle-level bureaucrats who were gaming the system and blocking development.

Another of Keping's sculptures, a self-portrait fashioned from bamboo, depicted a creature with the body of a man and the head and tail of an ape. Above him was the spine of a book understood to be Mao's *Little Red Book*.

"It was such a weight on us, we regressed into apes," Keping's voice, normally soft, receded into a whisper.

Wang Keping's pieces were curious in a country that for thirty years had promoted socially uplifting art—even more curious coming from someone who was the son of a Communist Party writer and who himself had been a Red Guard in 1966. In the spirit of that time, Keping, at seventeen, had burned foreign magazines and books, helped to destroy a church and its artifacts, criticized teachers who spoke foreign languages and denounced Western art as decadent.

By the late '70s, Keping was a scriptwriter for China's Central Television. When his Party bosses refused to produce his scripts, he turned to sculpting whatever chunks of wood he could find as a way to concretize his ideas and feelings. His openness to foreigners, welcoming them to his studio, caused some of us concern, since other Democracy Wall activists were in jail for such openness—especially with Western reporters. The gentle-voiced Keping would insist he was unafraid: "The Chinese people have been afraid for too long." Repeatedly he would tell friends and reporters, "Art should not be made to serve politics, and politics should ensure full artistic development."

This statement could set the whole house on fire. For more than thirty years, the intellectuals, writers and artists in China had been ensnared by Mao's famous *Yan'an Talk on Literature and Art*, whereby he laid out the principles for socialist art in China: Art must communicate with and please the masses; artists and intellectuals must change their consciousness. Art must be positive rather than critical. Art must serve socialism.

I remember first reading those lines when I was a political activist at graduate school in St. Louis in the early '70s. I thought it sounded inspiring. The deep purple walls of my apartment were covered with Soviet Cubist-style poster art from the '20s, along with Cultural Revolution images of the Helmsman surrounded by eager, rosy-cheeked Red Guards with fists raised next to psychedelic posters from Fillmore Auditorium concerts when Janis Joplin, the Paul Butterfield Blues Band, Jefferson Airplane and Muddy Waters might have all been on the same bill. All of it was potent art for me at that moment of my life. It was all triumphant in one way or another.

In China, for many artists and writers, Mao's Yan'an talk was a recipe for the crippling or silencing of creativity. One of the artists at the Xing Xing show told me while Yanna translated: "Mao's Yan'an talk has been a yoke on artists. Each artist must work out what he feels is right."

Mao's Yan'an talk wasn't the only yoke for artists. Communist Party control and censorship of the arts took a punitive turn during the Hundred Flowers Movement in late 1956, when the Party encouraged intellectuals, artists and writers to come forward with their criticisms and concerns.

"Let a hundred flowers bloom and a hundred schools of thought contend," the slogan chimed.

Mao insisted the movement was designed to promote the flourishing of the arts and progress of science. When intellectuals took advantage of this opportunity to speak their minds, they were immediately smacked down, purged, punished, and sent off to "reform through labor " prison camps. Again, in the late '60s, when I read about the Hundred Flowers Movement, I remember being staggered by the brilliance of the idea—and the metaphor. Now I was learning what followed. The "scorching of flowers," as one Xing Xing artist put it.

From Shi Yung I learned that since the end of the Cultural Revolution, art schools and academies had reopened and once again offered courses in Chinese traditional ink painting of birds, fish, flowers and horses as well as academic oil painting in the Socialist Realism style of mid-nineteenth-century Russia. Modern Western styles, as Yung had carefully explained, remained taboo.

"What about Socialist art?" I asked.

"For many years we were taught that art and literature must serve the people, serve the purpose of politics," he explained. "I am not crazy about what is art's function in politics. I'm not interested, but I think art can serve the people because it is art. It can give people very good ideas or refine them. That's art's function."

It sounded a bit canned.

"When I think of Socialist art in China, I think of the poster art produced during the Cultural Revolution," I egged him on.

"That's not art," Yung replied. "That's a slogan. I don't think people need slogans all the time and they will hate it if you give them slogans all the time. That's why art has improved a lot since the downfall of the Gang of Four."

Still seemed canned. I knew by now he suspected my rooms were bugged.

Yung preferred to talk about the spiritual dimension of centuries-old Chinese traditional paintings. I could hear the echoes of French Impressionists.

"Our teachers tell us not to pay attention to the exact nature of a thing," Yung explained, "just to paint what you think of it, how you appreciate that nature. When the artist paints bamboo, for example, they don't just sit there and copy a bamboo plant. They study the plant a long time and capture the spirit so you can get the feeling of it. When they paint, they paint freely, spontaneously. Bamboo is considered to be like a gentleman. The knot of the plant is called *jie*, which means nobility. All the good things in a man. Also, the empty core of the big bamboo trunk is called *xuxing*. That means humble, modest. So many artists paint bamboo again and again because of that."

Yung's voice became misty when he spoke about traditional Chinese art. The silence in the room enveloped us. Nobility and modesty. A key to the ideals of Chinese character.

These conversations were bringing an intricate cosmos into view. I felt like I was standing at the edge of a jungle at dawn as the light intensified. An experience I once had in Mexico. The profusion of psychedelic details emerging from the dark, undifferentiated mass.

While practicing my dots and strokes, I learned more about Yung's history. That when his father was subjected to class struggle during the Cultural Revolution, it meant Yung could not be a Red Guard. When Yung was sent to Yunnan for reeducation through labor, he was only fifteen. With other schoolmates from Beijing, he worked for six years, thousands of miles from home.

"You cannot imagine how isolated that place is...so far away from family. I was so lonely. We worked fourteen hours a day. When we got back to our beds at night, we collapsed. It's difficult to describe how depressing that time was because we had no idea when we could go home again."

Yung described the shock he and his classmates felt at the poverty and lifestyle of the people who lived in the region. "We saw how rural people live, how they suffer, how they take life as it is. They think that's just natural. For us, life was so hard there. Harder than you can imagine. You have to get something to support yourself, for your mind and spirit. Or you cannot stand it."

For Yung, it was painting and drawing "to not be so depressed" and teaching himself English.

"My father sent me that book, *Jane Eyre*, and I learned English by looking up every word in the dictionary. You know how difficult that book is. I had to look up every word and still I didn't know what it meant."

Yung's laughter was short and shallow. When he laughed or frowned as he told me this story, deep lines fanned out from his eyes. A loneliness grooved in his face. I, who had felt so forlorn in Beijing, was now forced to acknowledge the despair of others. Some of Yung's less resourceful classmates had committed suicide or escaped to join the Burmese army.

"It was good for me," Yung added. "I trained myself. So that now I can stand any kind of hardship."

I was clutched by regret that I had not been examining my soul more thoroughly nor strengthening myself creatively—at least not enough—in the face of emotional challenges in Beijing that, of course, withered in significance as I learned more about what so many Chinese had experienced.

At the end of each session, Yung would encourage me to write an entire poem on rice paper. He brought me books so I could copy simple ones with my shaky strokes. One time, he composed a short piece about loneliness and self-knowledge, but mostly he chose love poems—pure kitsch.

I saw Yung as a 1950s-era young man discovering the forbidden pleasures of the opposite sex or a Victorian artist wistful about the purity of virgins all mixed in with a wise old soul. As I wrestled with the spirit stroke of a character, we shared our love histories and attitudes about sexual liberation. Each of us struggling with something utterly new.

As our lessons continued—with Yung bicycling several miles across town to be at my apartment by 7 p.m. and leaving by 9 p.m. in order to not be locked out of his dormitory—our discussions while practicing calligraphy roamed from the Taoist spirit of a brush stroke to the difference between jazz and disco. These evening sessions with Yung, our efforts with brushes and ink, our conversations, generated the only grace in my life in Beijing, initiating me into Chinese culture while nurturing a tentative friendship.

The author at the recording of Lao She's *Rickshaw Boy*, Radio Beijing, 1980

Chapter Eleven

Little Miss Cultural Imperialist
文化帝国主义小姐

My glorious new rooms on the first floor allowed for the most voluptuous southern light to deluge my space. Normally it is northern light that artists prefer, but there in the geographical equivalent of North Dakota, as winter descended, southern rays were vital not just to my creative juices but to my very survival.

The new apartment was spacious with slanty floors that bounced and shook. After reporting that the plumbing refused to function, three substantial take-charge lady plumbers barged in—without knocking—and hacksawed the brick wall, leaving a giant hole so I could look from my living room into the toilet bowl. They solved the problem, and I hung a textile over the hole in the wall.

One Sunday in early December, I invited Ming over for brunch to bask in that light. This time he lingered over my calligraphy, which I had plastered on all the walls, purposely smothering the new plastic wall paper. While tacking up my beginner's efforts, I wondered where the bugs were implanted.

I think I made scrambled eggs on my hot plate. Maybe toasted bagels. Cream cheese? Could I get that at the Friendship Store? My notes don't indicate. All I recorded was that he stared at it but would not touch it. If I was trying to seduce him through food, I had failed. I should have ordered a recognizable dish from the dining room.

I shifted the focus to music, and he relaxed a bit. I fast-forwarded on my cassettes, playing some of my favorite romantic ladies—Esther Phillips, Bonnie Raitt, Etta James, Phoebe Snow. As I began to translate Phoebe Snow's "Teach

Me Tonight," there was a knock. Zong, the cute guy with the slight Oxbridge accent from the English department, stood sheepishly at the door. What a surprise! Countless times I had suggested he come by and it was never possible. Why now? His timing was intriguing, awkward and suspicious. What else could I do but invite him to join us for brunch?

Ming's face turned crimson and his body language screamed embarrassment. Perhaps he thought Zong was my boyfriend. Acting superior with his English fluency, Zong claimed that he dropped by to ask for help identifying a number of universities in the US and Canada. Since he had never had the guts to communicate with me in private or come here before, I suspected that the building spies—especially Xing, the building manager and Number One Spy—alerted someone at the English department to check up on me because I was entertaining an unknown Chinese man. Zong was working the day shift in the news section, a meager three-minute walk away. It was all too fishy. While mulling over his real reason for coming, I suggested a potential list of universities.

It all happened so quickly. After noting my suggestions, Zong exchanged something incomprehensible in Mandarin with Ming, then jumped up and left to return to the station. No queries about me or my life. Ming decided to leave as well. Zong's visit had rattled him.

My desires and needs were left hanging like gaping wounds. Two men with whom I could have flirted all day had just walked out the door! My only day off—my only day to hang out and enjoy dictionary dialogues. I felt like sobbing while clawing my eyes out and banging my head against a wall or drinking an entire bottle of wine by myself.

There was only one way to transform those self-destructive emotions and resurrect what was left of my humanity and self-respect. I fumbled with my stack of cassettes until I found Al Green's "Let's Stay Together," then Marvin Gaye's "Let's Get It On." Both songs provoked a profound nostalgia for a mythic romantic past.

At least with Marvin Gaye and "What's Going On?" I could continue in a more political vein. I needed all the soul music I could lay my hands on. Why hadn't I brought more Motown and R&B. I picked up the pace: The Supremes' "Stop! In the Name of Love"; Junior Walker and the All Stars' "Shotgun"; Gladys Knight and the Pips' "I Heard It through the Grapevine." I was on my feet, dancing around my living room.

Ah, the power of music—and this music, especially—and all its associations with my years in San Francisco and Berkeley. The first big party I had attended in 1965, where I was the only white person, at a boyfriend's apartment; he worked for the Congress of Racial Equality, an important organization in the Civil Rights Movement. Then, in St. Louis, all-night dancing parties, fueled by beer and pot after demonstrations and political actions of all kinds. In Boston, on the jukebox at St. Botolph's, the restaurant where I had waitressed. All memories melded together while I shimmied around my living room—alone.

Let's face it—Ming is an ignorant kid. I was making a mistake pouring my out-of-control libido and soul hunger onto him. *Move on. Don't know how to think about Oxbridge Zong. Gorgeous. Brilliant. Gay?*

December 4, 1980, Journal:

Judy called. She has been given permission to marry Yuan, but he has not yet been given permission to marry her.

We talked about the news on the BBC this morning. Four American churchwomen—a lay missionary and three nuns—have gone missing in El Salvador. It is suspected that they have been kidnapped and killed by death squads in the military.

ONE NIGHT the following week, the English department comrades assembled at my apartment for our regular discussion group. The comrades were giggling and gossiping in Mandarin while looking around at my amateur drawings and calligraphy on the living room walls. I mentally ticked off who was there: Xia Xia, Oxbridge Zong, Depressed Chen, Shadow Zhang, Shi Heung, Zhou Hong (Red), Mei, Chou. I was growing impatient. We only had a short time, and yet they took half an hour to settle down. I realized that they didn't have any relaxed time together without the presence of high cadres to watch over them.

Everyone looked at me expectantly, as if I were going to deliver a lecture. I had been dealing with a variety of American themes and concerns. I sensed that they did not really care about the subject matter. Maybe all they wanted was to hear an Anglo blabber.

Also impatient, the eager Oxbridge Zong, with two years at the London School of Economics and bad British food under his belt, wanted to talk about "history and truth." My God. How I wished!

"How about the trial of the Gang of Four?" he called out.

I knew this provocation would sink like a boulder in a lake. Silence. Sullen looks. I looked at him with a shrug and arched brows. I kept thinking about his visit to my apartment the previous Sunday and daydreamed about how I could convince him to come by more often.

No time for those thoughts. I had to pack away my fantasies about him.

We were supposed to talk about religion and spirituality. The group had agreed to that last time. Again, Zhou was having her hair put up in curlers by the one who never wanted to talk about politics, and the stiff, formal Shadow Zhang was looking worried and piped up.

"We want you to sing Christmas Carols."

I was ready to give it up or fall apart. What was it that Beckett's character said? "I can't go on!" *Pregnant pause.* "I will go on!" I ignored her.

I had given them an article from *Newsweek* to read about the new Religious Right in the US versus the spirituality of the New Age movement of the 1970s. I tried to get it copied but couldn't—only one copier in all of Central Broadcasting and it was reserved for the highest of the high—so comrades had to pass it around. A recipe for evasion. The few who had read it couldn't understand the language and references. Well, that was a beginning. I did my best to explain fundamentalism in all religions—the impulse or desire for certainty, for simple answers—and then a little about the nature of the American Religious Right, although this was a new phenomenon. I was only learning about it myself. I briefly described the constitutional guarantees of separation of church and state and why it mattered. I would have relished talking about the cult of Mao as religion but knew it would make them too uncomfortable. How self-censoring I had become.

I had asked them to come prepared to talk a bit about Buddhism and Taoism, presumably religions they knew. I asked them why it was important for broadcast journalists to understand world religions. Everyone looked down except Zong, who barked out: "So we know our audience better!"

Ah, the teacher's pet. If only I could get to really know him. Impossible. At first, a few comrades would talk to me briefly when I was alone in the office, but even that had ended. Unless they wanted help with foreign university applications.

I explained that in the English-speaking regions of the world—their broadcast audience—religion was a significant part of life for many people. Sometimes a defining part. Not just culturally, but it could shape politics, legal systems and ethics. Their audiences would have an interest in how religion was considered in China, and journalists were expected to report on it dispassionately, responsibly, without necessarily being believers or prejudicing one religion over others. Their eyes glazed. Was it political conditioning, or was I that boring?

"What about Buddhism?" I asked. Delicately.

"I am not interested. Buddhism is for grannies," scoffed Xia Xia.

Giggles.

"But wait a minute. I saw so many Buddhist altars in Guangzhou and in October on Mt. Tai there were temple offerings along the stairway. They were left by young people."

More giggles.

One of the comrades had gone to an encyclopedia to look up Buddhism and Taoism and parroted a short sentence about each. Well, that was something. They all professed to know nothing. Were they serious? Or was that political correctness?

"The way Buddhism is dealt with in Radio Beijing's scripts is embarrassing and inadequate," I declared. "On the *Travel Talk* program, some of the most precious sites our scripts promote are temples."

Pause. No reaction.

"And even though the western region of the country is home to Islamic minorities, the one script on Islam that crossed my desk was abominable."

Silence.

In the end, I caved into Shadow Zhang's request and sang "Joy to the World," "First Noël" and "Jingle Bells" into a recorder for her. *I can't go on! I will go on.*

"Perhaps a beer will help me remember all the verses."

"Beer and tea don't mix," warned Shadow Zhang.

At least I was not being asked to sing "Do-Re-Mi" from *The Sound of Music*, the one Western song everyone sang endlessly here.

I offered to give a presentation—talk and music—about the history of the blues at the next session, breaking my rule about not lecturing, but the date was just before Christmas.

"It will be my Christmas gift to you." Did that make me a missionary?

Smiles and chuckles! I wasn't sure whether the enthusiasm was for the subject or because I would give a lecture.

December 10, 1980, Journal:

Sitting stunned, listening to VOA playing Beatles music and reporting John Lennon's murder by a crazy assailant in Central Park two days ago.

Ron called right away. "Do you realize we are living amidst a billion people who have never heard of John Lennon or Jesus Christ, whom he is supposed to be more popular than?"

This morning at work, Zong talked to me in private about some of the universities he's considering from the list I had provided. What do I think about this one versus that one? All the best young minds in the department come to me separately for help with Canadian and US universities. They are competing with each other.

On my Saturday afternoon off, I took a bus to the Friendship Store to finish my Christmas shopping to send to Vancouver and New York. Silks for Mum, a hat with furry earflaps for her husband, Cy. I had arranged for a beautiful chop— those intricately carved stamps to seal letters with melted wax, this one cut from jade—for my dear friend Karen. It will be the symbol of Dumballa, the snake spirit. Important in the voodou pantheon, her subject. Should be an exhilarating exercise to figure out how to ship the packages.

On the bus coming home, everyone was staring at my boots. These cheap red cowboy boots with heels have garnered a steady gaze since cold weather arrived five weeks ago. I admit they're fun, and even in New York they attract some attention. After all, that's why I bought them! But here? Wild! I haven't yet dreamt about parading around Beijing with nothing on but my red cowboy boots.

IN MID-DECEMBER, we had our first snow. The leaves had long since gone. The air was smokier than ever. Buildings, sky and people all turned a monotonal grey. Shoulders hunched more than usual over bicycle bars. We all looked like padded pandas in our four, five and six layers. Every other day, the Gobi Desert blew a little closer. The city felt severe, punishing, desolate.

During December, my letters home revealed a soul and conscience in turmoil. And an emotional state that was unraveling. Already there was too much of China in me and around me. Too much that was just outside my grasp. Too many half-perceptions, misunderstandings, bizarre moments and longings for my own culture. But just as that yearning turned to self-pity, something in China lured me back— a private moment, finally, with a comrade, whom I wanted to support in some way. Perhaps a moment or space to express compassion for a coworker. Then I might find solace in creating a beautiful ideogram, only to become agitated by some stupidity, and then feel guilt and shame for my fury and temper tantrums.

It was a cycle.

Just as I arrived in the office, all positive and recharged, some dumb piece of propaganda with no information that could be checked would consume hours of time, and then I wouldn't be able to get a decent telephone line after forty tries, and suddenly a blood vessel in my head felt ready to burst.

One morning, I awoke thinking I was having a heart attack.

Two days earlier, I had been assigned a new translator from the department who spoke poor English. Shadow Zhang had turned cold and disinterested. She did not want to be my interpreter anymore, she said. I suspected the Central Broadcasting censors had been reading my letters, where I referred to her as my "Shadow" and "Party Informant."

Chou, the new one, "needs the experience," Leader Zhang said. I liked Chou, but it meant that I had to explain everything twice—at least. First to Chou, then to Shadow Zhang to explain to Chou because Chou could not understand.

Second tantrum: Since international newspapers were nonexistent or prohibitively expensive, I was trying to send away for a subscription to the *Manchester Guardian*. It had already consumed several hours of explanations. First I went to my new interpreter and then to Shadow Zhang. Neither knew what a money order or bank draft was. Then I went to the foreign experts' office, where, after a half-hour discussion, I was sent to my apartment building office, where after another half-hour discussion, I was sent to the accounting department at Radio Beijing, where I needed to provide the explanation from scratch (through interpreters) and was asked if I really wanted to spend my foreign currency. "Why not *renminbi*?" I said—to myself, of course—"Nobody outside China takes renminbi, and it's none of their business!"

But everything was their fucking business! If I was going out on a date with a diplomat. If I had friends over for lunch. If I wanted a lightbulb. My entire work unit was informed. I had no private life. Another expat explained that everything we foreign experts did was discussed by the entire work unit. Everybody in Beijing seemed to know WHO the Canadian was! And where I was going. Or where I had been.

The total lack of privacy forced me to reflect on our fascination with communal living and work in the 1960s. Was it the lack of privacy that caused most North American communes to wither away? In Beijing, I was completely starved for privacy. I was an only child, after all. And, I admit, a bourgeois individualist. I came to really understand that in Beijing.

I was also stridently independent. In the late '60s and early '70s, I had participated in working collectives but soon discovered that a few individuals did all of the work. Since the age of nineteen, I had done everything for myself. No family connections, certainly not through university alumni. I was the first in my large extended family to go to university. There was no family money. I was a self-made person in the West. In 1980 Beijing, that was either reactionary or selfish or subversive.

More emotional turbulence. Exasperation. After weeks of asking for simple electrical and door repairs, I came to realize that it would probably never be done for two reasons: One, if the building maintenance people did something for me, they said, other neighbors would ask for repairs. Two, they seemed reluctant to interrupt their afternoon chess games. There was no reason to work hard, since there were no rewards.

While I had problems with the material incentive system that turned us Westerners into competitive, selfish manipulators, I felt that China could use some revamping on this issue. I turned it over and over in my mind. Daily. Hourly. There was just so much human waste. So much bungling. Ineptness. Yes, finally, I admitted, backwardness.

On my worst days, in my foulest moods, I tormented myself over whether it was worth the effort to stick it out. But as soon as I gave voice to that, I felt guilty and sad for the comrades who did work hard, applied themselves and had to put up with the bureaucratic blockage and hassles. I constantly wondered how they ever made a revolution.

My only refuge was listening to jazz and reading. I played Miles Davis' *'Round About Midnight* album while reading Lu Xun's *The True Story of Ah Q*, a novella that was serialized in a Beijing newspaper in 1921 and 1922. The story was revolutionary at the time because Lu Xun wrote in the vernacular and in the accessible short novel form while critiquing feudalism and Chinese traditions. It was a moral tale meant to inspire a consciousness change among readers. My reading was motivated by the opportunity to interview Gladys Yang, famous for her translations of the Chinese classics into English.

Earlier, I had suggested we interview Ding Ling, a famous writer. Given the new "opening" and publishing of honest short stories, along with the sense that writers should have more freedom, I had convinced Leader Zhang that we should interview some of the older rehabilitated writers, like Ding Ling.

From my readings, I knew that Ding Ling had been animated by the spirit of the May Fourth Movement in 1920. She had written some sensitive stories about an emerging women's consciousness, elaborating on their desires for more freedom. In the '30s , she was imprisoned by the Japanese and then escaped to the Yan'an caves and Communist headquarters. One of the expats told me that after Liberation her writing took on a Leftist moral tone. Perhaps not enough. She was persecuted in 1957 and imprisoned during the Cultural Revolution. My source said Ding Ling had been disciplined and censored for writing about sexism in the Communist movement and the need for a better understanding of women's situation and their need for rights.

I asked if Dam Ping, one of the brightest young comrades with her head always in Michener's *Chesapeake*, could arrange for an interview with Ding Ling. We could do it together. Dam Ping explained that she had tried before and that Ding Ling was condescending, but perhaps if a foreigner were there, she would be amenable. Somehow, that interview never transpired; instead, I had the opportunity to interview the famous translator Gladys Yang.

Leader Zhang and another comrade accompanied me to Yang's apartment. Then sixty-one, Yang was head of the Beijing Women's Federation. Born in Beijing to British missionaries, she moved to England as a child and became Oxford's first graduate in Chinese language in 1940. That's where she met her husband, Yang Xianyi, also a noted translator. They returned to China in 1940 during the Japanese occupation. After Liberation, the Yangs became translators of Chinese literature for the Foreign Languages Press. What Gladys did not say the day of our interview—but an expat friend explained later—was that during the Cultural Revolution, both Gladys and her husband were arrested and jailed on suspicion of spying. Gladys spent four years in solitary confinement.

Apparently, after the Cultural Revolution, the Yangs returned to their formidable translating projects for the Foreign Languages Press, only to learn in 1979 that their son committed suicide in London. The China insiders claimed that she had become an alcoholic.

My journal notes about our meeting reveal my contradictory reactions. Although gracious she seemed guarded and self-censored. The formal and stiff seating arrangement at her apartment, along with the presence of numerous family members, friends and my colleagues, was not conducive to a candid or deep interview yet she was articulate and perceptive at times. She was animated about the women's movement that had emerged in the West during the previous decade and reported that she was translating some of the Chinese women writers of the pre- and post- Cultural Revolution period.

The lack of any available research for the interview contributed to my distress in trying to pull her out. My colleagues provided little or no information about her. Too dangerous to decide what was acceptable, I gathered. The interview never really engaged me, and I doubted it would interest an audience. While I was honored to meet her, my questions were probably too basic and unchallenging. Perhaps she was bored, too.

I went home determined to read more of the Chinese classics. Only then would I understand something about where I was. While I had purchased the multiple-volume set of the eighteenth-century mega-novel, *A Dream of Red Mansions* or *Dream of the Red Chamber*, China's equivalent to *War and Peace*, it was too much work to keep track of all the characters. Instead, the modernist, Lu Xun, intrigued me.

This time, I read *A Madman's Diary*, a story portraying a man's descent into madness as a metaphor for a society imploding from feudalism and Confucianism, reminiscent of Nikolai Gogol's *Diary of a Madman*. Both in the form of a diary, both addressing oppressive systems. Written at the time of a collapsing Qing dynasty, of republican voices calling for a critical examination of the Confucian order, Lu Xun's madman was meant to energize the reader to act.

Reading Lu Xun inspired a closer examination of Confucianism. An expat friend had encouraged me to understand both the positive and negative aspects of Confucianism. The positive—its core of humanism and ethics— insisted that a good Mandarin must speak out when the government becomes unethical. And within Confucian philosophy, the central concern was with the family, not gods or an afterlife. It argued that humans are teachable, and individual ethics can be cultivated and improved, whether through self-education or the communal enterprise.

Ah—Chinese existentialism!

The downside involved rigid hierarchies of power, control and the abuse of obligations. Confucianism combined with a concubine system was tough on women until they became the dreaded mother-in-law. I was just skimming the surface, but I wondered whether in challenging Confucianism the Party tried to break the control of the family. Did it exploit the communalism of Confucian ethics? Or build on it?

Meanwhile, I felt driven by my own ethical responsibility to raise tough social issues in my discussion sessions with the comrades. Sometimes I felt as if I had wandered into a foot-sucking bog.

One evening, I ventured into an entangled issue that was buzzing in the US and Canada—pornography, violence and free speech.

I described the proliferation of pornography with the development of videotape technology and introduced the conflicts in the intersections between sexual liberation, misogyny, rape, constitutional rights to free expression and feminist responses. I thought the comrades might find the controversy intriguing, since the official Chinese line associated the West with the evils of pornography. And particularly since there were rumors that porn tapes were

Coal mountains on Radio Beijing grounds with worker housing behind. Beijing, 1980

Endless shoveling of coal. Tianjin, 1980

Chang'an Avenue, Beijing, 1980

Beijing, 1980

Hanging eggplant slices to dry. Beijing, 1980

Card game during a work day. Beijing, 1980

Cabbages drying, Beijing, 1980

Cabbages drying for winter food. Beijing, 1980

Cabbages, cabbages everywhere. Beijing, 1980

Dried cabbages were primary winter vegetable. Beijing, 1980

From the train window in the south. April, 1981

Waiting for the sunrise on Mt Tai. October, 1980

Wang Keping in his home studio. Summer, 1981

Peking opera actor making up backstage. Beijing, 1980

Chinese New Year, Xian, 1981

Chinese New Year decorations, Xian, 1981

Wang Keping and friend at Old Summer Palace Be-In. April, 1981

Author with English department comrades at Radio Beijing. 1981

Author with Zhang Fan. Beijing, 1981

being smuggled into the country from Hong Kong.

No one said a word. Everyone looked painfully embarrassed and uncomfortable.

What was I thinking? Was I insensitive to cultural differences? Was I the advance team of cultural imperialism? But then, I argued to myself, they work in a news and information agency. Since they were all staring at their feet, I dropped the subject.

Unabashed in my unselfconscious missionary work, I agreed to give a "class" on broadcast journalism to those infamous editors in the smoke-filled room, the ones whom I had decided were the key source of our problems. Leader Zhang translated.

When I conjure up the scene today, it feels comical and sad and wrong. When I first discovered this room back in the heat of late August, the guys here—no women—were all in shorts and sleeveless undershirts or "wife-beaters." Now, they were bundled in double sweaters and army pants over long-johns, coddling glass jars filled with hot water in their hands. The room, as usual, was cloudy with cigarette smoke. Crossed knees supported bouncing legs. Their lips curled into ironic, almost mocking smiles, exposing nicotine stained teeth.

I listed my main points of concern. I knew that Leader Zhang was trying to smooth my brazen edges through careful translation. In the process, I was giving a lecture about reporting, about differing truths and the importance of doubt. I could almost hear some smirks. Somebody should have stopped me.

These guys conjured all the scripts for Radio Beijing—information that reached the world whether it was truth, lies, half-truths, fantasies, propaganda or legitimate information. Whatever. The scripts were from their country, their system, their perspective. Who was I, Miss Know-It-All, from the land of the former enemy, to sit here and tell them what I thought they should be doing with the scripts and stories? Was I having an out-of-body or out-of-mind experience?

Thirty years later, as I try to grasp just who I was back in 1980, I am embarrassed that I did this. The hubris. Back then, I forged on, suggesting some story themes that would catch the attention of a Western audience. I recommended interviews with real people. I critiqued a few scripts that I had saved. I could hear the unease in bodies rearranging as chairs creaked, faces crinkling, Mandarin whispers and quiet chuckles. My final act was to point out an example of a story that I had rejected because it would be ridiculed by a Western audience unless it was reconceived.

The "Tianjin Button Salesgirl" script. It was propaganda designed for a Chinese audience, where I had no judgment about its effectiveness. Aimed at the West, it was pure comedy. The Communist Party recognized there was a major problem of attitude among people in "service" jobs—salesclerks and waiters, especially. These government workers—with their iron rice-bowl jobs—could care less if they recognized a customer's presence, delivered any service or information. Their snarky expressions and disdainful postures were ubiquitous, turning their customers into screaming, waving idiots trying to be recognized and served. So the Party had decided it needed to set up a positive example of a great service worker, hence the script on the "Tianjin Button Salesgirl." She was humble, smiled sweetly, was polite to her customers and eagerly helped them find different types and sizes of buttons. She was efficient in every way.

If China had "Saturday Night Live," this would have made a great skit, since it was the diametric opposite to everyone's experience. As reporting it was sad because I knew the Tianjin Button Salesgirl was made up. She did not exist. Like Lei Feng, she was pure propaganda designed to improve the behavior of Chinese salesclerks. Was this, I wondered, an indication that the editors and top brass at Radio Beijing believed that their real broadcast audience was mostly mainland Chinese studying English? Not foreigners light-years away?

Reactions were contained. A few Mandarin comments in the background. I was now sweating visibly. There were no questions. I wondered afterwards whether that roomful of editors let out a huge howl of laughter after I left the room. What did I know about their true mission? Little Miss Cultural Imperialist.

December 19, 1980, Journal:
Lunchtime—the depressed Chen, who wouldn't be seen talking to me at the office, came over to ask for help with the Friendship Store and funny money.

ON A Saturday afternoon before Christmas, Ming and I exhausted ourselves in icy winds, tramping around Beijing's secondhand-store district looking for used ice skates. People sold used skates in the street, but they didn't have the kind that I needed—laced high to support the ankles and picks on the toes. We created a small sensation everywhere we went.

When we stopped for a snack at a sorry place, a beggar—perhaps mentally ill—was scouring for scraps. A gigantic man with an elephantine face, Frankenstein-ish, was sprawled across a table in all his layers. There was the sound and sight of endless spitting amid dirty tables. Three cadres from a factory sat eating and drinking robustly. I recalled a profusion of greasy diners and dives I had stumbled into from Bozeman, Montana, to the Bowery in Manhattan. I marveled at how these "workers' restaurants"—government run, like everything—were invisible to me when I had first arrived.

While all the patrons, whether sitting upright or not, stared at my boots, my Mexican jewelry, my hair, Ming brought me a *baozi*—Beijing's famous pork-stuffed bun—and a sweet drink. Then we were off again.

Next we headed to the Palace Museum at the Forbidden City. It was closed. Ming tried using his connections to get in. He always used the privileged connection approach. It was who you knew. But it didn't work there. Nobody was around.

He knew the cook at the Sichuan restaurant, so we went there. That was how we could get beer. He never asked what I wanted, but that day I suggested a beer. While we nursed our bottles, he told me that Japanese women were the most beautiful women in the world, "but no breasts like Chinese women." He must have practiced that sentence at home. I wondered why he would spend precious dictionary time on these boring clichés.

He almost passed out on the hot chili fish. That probably meant he seldom ate Sichuan cuisine. Nor fish. Way too expensive. I gleefully ate the chilis, sweating out my cold, mentally noting my observations.

I thought about my peculiar attraction to Ming. It wasn't intellectual. We could barely communicate at prekindergarten level. It wasn't about shared values. I suspected a huge gulf between us. Was it all physical? While his wide cheekbones, smooth skin and glistening eyes were appealing, it was what he did with his face that captivated me. He sculpted his face into exaggerated gestures like the one mimicking his boss's anger when he discovered Ming sleeping on his night job. Molecule by molecule, I was learning a little something about one character in this strange landscape.

When we returned to my apartment, I decided it was time for him to know something about me. I told him a hugely simplified story of my life. Haiku in Mandarin from the dictionary. All these years later, I cannot imagine how truncated or made up it was. I must have prepared it ahead of time. My journal records that he had absolutely no response. It was probably incomprehensible to him. No questions. No hint of curiosity. This was why I needed to break this off.

Yet I was still curious about his daring recklessness to come to my apartment and sneak me into his. I had little idea of who he really was, but I knew he was a bad boy, defiant. If my comrades were timid and terrified of a system of ratting, Ming was undaunted.

His risk taking and delight in comic performance, my sense of abandon without deep feeling, suspicions about his character, the meaninglessness—all of those jumbled feelings washed over me while I was with him. I rationalized to myself that, despite the emotional void, he was a research project.

He was also secret. And forbidden.

Although I was only vaguely conscious of it, I was also acting out a magnanimous desire—a moment—when an older woman could get carried away with the project of initiating a younger man—the hormonal wickedness of it. The illusion of control.

We opted for hot baths and fooling around. One would have to really stretch to call it foreplay. I mused to myself whether I should write a guidebook about The Clitoris while in China. His sexual inexperience was matched by his ignorance about birth control. Another writing project.

At one point, we could hear footsteps outside my door. Ming froze. We listened silently. They approached. Stopped. Waited. Then scurried away. We made silent giggles. Then we heard someone outside my bedroom window. Since it was the ground floor, it was tempting, I suppose, for Peeping Toms. In this case, Peeping Comrades. Party informants. Our bodies frozen like marble sculptures; we listened. I got up to make sure the curtain was carefully drawn. Lusty schemes now deflated. Ming left in time to take the last bus.

December 21, 1980, Journal:

I haven't been this happy since I left New York. I have been going through all the blues cassettes that I brought, as well as my radio documentary, "Classic Women Blues Singers," and am grateful that I thought to include Paul Oliver's The Story of the Blues *in the boxes of books I schlepped from New York. I've been making notes for tomorrow's class for the comrades about the blues...*

To clear my head in the middle of the day and ruminate about how to present this music form that was so maligned and misunderstood in China, I biked to the location that gave me more pleasure and contemplative focus than anywhere else: Temple of Heaven. Perhaps because it attracted fewer people than the Summer Palace parks. And the temple itself was more startling and brilliant against the sky—its colors and contours more densely packed—than the grandiose Forbidden City structures.

While strolling around the perimeter, I figured out how to bang out the basic rhythm of the blues, that deceptively simple 4/4 beat that musicians and singers slid all around in every which way. I had already been practicing how to play a bent note on the harmonica I had bought the previous week. I was thrilled to share a music that I loved. The challenge was to explain its deep significance in American culture as the mother lode of jazz and rock 'n' roll, given that all of these musical genres were prohibited and treated as degenerate and evil. My task was formidable. Should I have been more concerned that my determination to change perceptions was yet another form of cultural imperialism?

My boyfriend of the late '60s, Carl, was responsible for educating me about the blues as that revival exploded around us. We heard Muddy Waters and B. B. King at the Fillmore Auditorium in San Francisco in 1968. Then Sonny Terry and Brownie McGhee in a Berkeley club in '69. By 1970, we were driving on weekends from St. Louis to Chicago to hear the masters of Chicago-style blues—Buddy Guy and Junior Wells—at Theresa's, a funky little corner joint on the South Side, where you descended a few stairs to enter and paid your money into a paper bag at the door. A buxom housewife from around the corner, with her hair in rollers, would squeeze out of one of the booths and belt out a staggering version of "Sometimes I Have a Heartache," one of Big Mama Thornton's songs. My 33 rpm record collection stored in New York included many giants of the tradition. Delta and Chicago blues masters like Howlin' Wolf, Elmore James, Willie Dixon, Sonny Boy Williamson, Otis Spann and more. I brought cassette copies of many of them to Beijing.

NEW FACES filled my living room, as English-speaking comrades from other departments—and even other work units—came for my blues presentation. I was nervous but hopeful.

I began by trying to define what the blues *meant*. That the music and the song lyrics decried heartache, discrimination, a sense of loss or failure, frustration or poverty while at the same time celebrating love and sex. It could wail with complaint, suffering or longing, but then it could also jump with joy. It could moan a story of woe or flirt and tease. At several points, I stopped to define words like "heartache," "discrimination," "moan" and "flirt." Generally people looked engaged, although there were some smirks and downcast eyes at the mention of "sex."

So far so good.

Then I tried for a little geography and history—African influences in instrument and vocal stylings. If spirituals and work songs were the musical accompaniment to slavery, then the blues was a creation after the Civil War of the descendants of those slaves in the South, especially the Mississippi Delta. Rural guys, tenant farmworkers, cotton pickers or maybe lumberyard men playing acoustic guitar accompanied by harmonica and washboard. I needed to explain "acoustic" and "washboard."

My first mistake was to play a snippet of Robert Johnson's famous "I Believe I'll Dust My Broom." The poor quality of that early recording and his vocal style made the words unintelligible. The comrades looked stressed.

I changed to a snippet of Son House's "Downhearted Blues." The voice was clearer, and I could call out the lyrics as well. I pointed out the slide guitar using a knife or bottleneck to create coloring in the notes. Its roots in Africa. In a portion of a piece by Lightnin' Hopkins, they could hear the creativity of the guitar.

Foreheads crinkled into frowns. I could feel moisture accumulating on my face, under my arms.

I demonstrated a bent note on my harmonica. Then I played a segment of Sonny Boy Williamson playing harmonica on "Sugar Mama Blues."

Faces in the room looked amused and then judgmental as mouths moved into sarcastic smiles.

I soldiered on, sampling some of my radio documentary, "Classic Women Blues Singers." With roots in the minstrel shows, these women performed an urban, glitzier blues with backup bands. They roamed the cities of the South in the '20s and '30s.

Next up, Bessie Smith's "I Need a Little Sugar for My Bowl." Second line: "I need a little hotdog for my roll."

Faces looked sober and puzzled.

I tried to explain the *double entendre* in the lyrics.

Some looked stunned, some mollified, others confused. Frowns deepened.

I tried for some cross-cultural comparison. "It's like all the multiple meanings in a single character in a Chinese poem. Didn't all those classical Chinese poets write about wine and women?"

Nobody commented.

Oh God! I wanted to suck in my breath. I had not predicted how embarrassing these particular lyrics could be in a puritanical culture. I decided against playing Smith's "I'm Wild about That Thing." Instead, I switched to Bonnie Raitt singing a Sippie Wallace song, "Women Be Wise," and deconstructed the lyrics. It was also an example of the enormous impact the blues had on contemporary rock musicians.

Nobody asked any questions or offered verbal reactions. Only funny looks. Nobody seemed to enjoy the music. By now they were shifting in their seats, looking at each other, growing increasingly uneasy. I imagined they all wanted to run out of the room.

By now I felt trickles of sweat down my back, at my temples. I picked up the pace. I needed to get up the Mississippi!

I explained how the blues traveled up the river to Chicago during the Great Migration of blacks from the rural South to the urban North from the '20s on.

As an example of what happened to the blues with this journey, I played Elmore James' version of "Dust My Broom." Despite the squirming and creaking of seats, I persisted, emphasizing the electrification of the guitar and the ability of these musicians to make their instruments "talk." They invented feedback and distortion. I tried to define that and draw their attention to it in "Rollin' Stone" by Muddy Waters, whereby the guitar mimicked the human voice; his moaning implied the instrument.

I caught myself. Was there electronic music being made in China? Somebody said yes, from Taiwan.

Time was running out. To hear a bit of great blues piano, I put on "You Can't Lose What You Ain't Never Had." No time to explain the lyrics.

Finally, a little of B. B. King's "The Thrill Is Gone" as an example of how sophisticated the music became with electrification and the urban Northern experience.

By then, people were looking so distraught that I decided to turn it off and—dripping in sweat—break down the musical structure. The rhythm—a twelve-bar measure with a 4/4 beat. Chord changes. Those bent notes. Then the repeating of lines of lyrics. AAA or AAB. To hear it all clearly, I played a cut by Junior Wells on harmonica with guitarist Buddy Guy. I spoke of authenticity. Of poetry. Of the profound influence on jazz and rock 'n' roll.

Silence.

Finally, I asked if anybody had questions or comments.

Professor Li bravely spoke up. "This music sounds rough to us."

Others laughed in agreement.

Li continued. "It is rough-sounding, not fine or smooth like a violin or flute. It is country music like the Shang, a traditional instrument, a kind of horn, played in the countryside." I remembered that his father worked in a musical instrument store before he retired.

Some wrinkled their noses at the very mention of traditional music.

"The voices are too rough," someone called out.

I knew then I had failed to convince anyone to change their minds about the expressive genius of the blues. The pleasures of listening to it. Perhaps the lyrics were too difficult to grasp from these strange-sounding voices. I remembered that none of my colleagues could understand the American voices in my radio documentaries.

I asked how I could hear the Shang. Professor Li offered to arrange for me to attend a rehearsal of a Shang band soon.

Then it was over. I barely recalled people leaving my apartment. Probably they all squeezed out the door at once. As usual. No lingering. No one with a secret desire to learn more about this banned music. I suspected much of their response was fueled by racism. It was their general reaction to anything African.

Earlier in the week, when I had told Eleanor Bidien about my plan for the class, she said it couldn't be done. Well, at least my passion for the music came through, sweaty armpits and all.

ANOTHER DATE with Ming at the Moscow restaurant. This time, we sat in the Chinese section. Again, he didn't ask me what I wanted and ordered to show his control or maturity. Perhaps it was status.

He knew the cook and a waiter who brought coffee. Terrible Chinese coffee. But I was left wondering just how high up the ladder of authority, prestige and power his parents perched. Who was he, really?

Back at my apartment, I felt torn between my need for affection and my boredom with him. I suspected that if we had shared a language I would recoil from him. How frustrating not to be able to exchange political ideas, philosophies, books and life experiences. With nuance. His negative attitudes about the Gang of Four were stereotypical. He was completely negative about Mao as well. *How common was that?* I wondered.

Despite the chasm of illiteracy, his kinetic mimicry always undermined my resistance. Like his comic routine, acting out the cat-and-mouse games of the police watching for Chinese who meet with foreigners. I needed the levity.

Yet, each time I saw Ming, I swore it would be the last. I didn't like his attitudes—snobby and cynical—toward so many ordinary folks in the streets and parks.

He was also sexist. His whole riff about preferring Japanese women because they were obedient, feminine and soft. That American women were too brazen and free. What was he doing with me, then? And he *never* asked questions about my life. I was a nonentity to him.

Despite all of these reservations, Ming was the first non-English-speaking Chinese person I met independently without interpreters, mediators or shadows. Or so I thought.

He was illicit. And that was a turn-on. Somehow.

That night, we just ripped into each other. Passion without soul. Lust without any sweetness. Shouts and sighs as we rode then galloped to an ecstatic death. Rebirth and death again.

He was like a drug. You argued against it, then hated yourself for caving into it afterward. Despite his shallow concerns, spoiled situation and sexism, I would arrange to see him again.

December Dream:
I am working on a jigsaw puzzle. It turns out to be about China. I am working on it for a year only to discover that half the pieces are missing.

Tianjin, 1980

Chapter Twelve

Dreaming of Sugar Plums While Deng Lays Down a New Line
梦想蜜桃，邓布下新策

On Christmas Eve, Leaders Zhang and Ma gave me permission to leave the office early to attend a cocktail party at the American embassy—an effort to be normal in an abnormal context. Meaning a chance to wear pantyhose and high heels for the first time since I had arrived five months before.

I hadn't seen so many Westerners since I had left New York. I guessed there were perhaps 150 lost souls milling about the room. They included diplomats from other embassies, UN folks and journalists happy to have a grown-up setting in which to drink. Michael Weisskopf from the *Washington Post* was working the room with his wife, Lilly, at his side.

Western journalists were still in Beijing the day before Christmas because the trial of the Gang of Four had suddenly closed down after a hint that Jiang Qing raised some issues that went too far. All the journalists were in a state of suspended animation. What did she say? Surprisingly, there was no news in the Chinese press after days and days of endless evidence against this evil lady. The comrades at work still would not discuss anything about the trial. The only certainty was that nobody liked Mrs. Mao. The suspension of the final trial verdict, along with Hua's mysterious disappearance, had the foreign journalist community imprisoned. Rather than leave for Christmas week vacation, they were glued to daily releases from China's official news agency, Xinhua.

At the Christmas party, I noted how many guests looked disconnected, probably wishing they were back home. Only Judy and Yuan were radiating joy in the middle of the room. After a two-year struggle and a carton of official documentation, they were married earlier in the day. A gaggle of us swarmed like bees drawn to honeysuckle, smothering them with hugs and kisses and making toasts with rum eggnog. Their victory was a salve for the rest of us frustrated with the policy that separated the Chinese from us *waiguoren*.

Later, a fresh-faced twentyish fellow stood next to me. In an almost whisper, he mouthed, "You are the loveliest woman in the room." I was so flummoxed that I could not compose myself. How could these words tumble out of such a youthful mouth? Had he been binging on romantic novels? Why didn't I whisk him out of there and take him home right then and there?

Instead I turned into that self-conscious version of myself, smiling graciously, thanking him sweetly, saying something like, "How kind you are" or "Flattery will get you everywhere" or some such rusty phrase from the singles' bar scene on the other side of the world. Smugly, I touched my fingers to my abundant hair, secretly pleased that I had used henna to cover the few grey hairs starting to appear, and that I decided to wear one of my '40s vintage dresses. Finally, there was an occasion for the wardrobe I lugged from New York, along with the bronze eyeshadow.

He explained he was a student from Boston studying at Beijing University. Into the awkward pause, I commented on the magnificent production of Lao Tse's *Teahouse* that I had seen the night before, courtesy of the Foreign Experts Bureau at Radio Beijing. But then whatever magical potential the future might hold between this much younger man and older woman was interrupted by John, a New Zealand diplomat, breaking into our tentative explorations, querying the student about conditions at the university.

I left the student, whose name I hadn't yet ascertained, and sashayed off across the room, acknowledging a few more acquaintances, thinking I would work my way back once Mr. New Zealand had moved on. But when I turned around, the student with the golden tongue was gone, people were moving on to their Christmas Eve engagements, including me. Joe Meyer, from the Canadian embassy, offered me a lift to my next destination, the home of someone I hadn't yet met: Kirsten.

This was my first visit to the UN compound in Beijing—and I was stunned. A modern, spacious apartment, a workàble kitchen, attractive bathrooms, built-in closets, furniture transported from home, duplicating the lifestyle of professional Western elites in New York. As I arrived, Kirsten and her guests were lighting candles on a Christmas tree. A glass of mulled wine was pushed into my hand.

The formality of the occasion took me by surprise. A traditional German Christmas Eve dinner. At an elegantly set table with silver, linen and cut glass, we gorged on goose, champagne and chocolate sauce. I, who had been dressed in my padded Chinese clothes for more than a month, bicycling against bitter winds, shivering in my freezing workspace, typing while wearing woolen gloves with the fingertips cut off to counteract the chilblains that had turned my fingers purple and swollen—yes, I felt out of place in this fancy Western universe. Yet grateful to be included.

I learned that Kirsten was with the UN's Development Program, working with $16 million in funding and technical expertise to help the Chinese gear up with computers for their first big census.

"The census project is critical to future development aid to China," she explained. "And foreign trade. They need a reliable system of counting."

I chuckled to myself about the Western technocratic obsession with statistics, as if they solved all problems. But wasn't that one of the things I hated about the Chinese scripts? A love affair with numbers? They would dance well together.

There was a silly Austrian at the table as well as a very strong, commanding Danish woman, Siri, who worked with UNFPA—the population agency at the UN—and her nervous husband, Robert. Nervous, I guessed, because I was here at his invitation. I had met him on the dance floor at the Mingzhu Hotel disco. He was attractive, wonderfully playful, shared a progressive '60s-era North American politics and was presumably single. When I learned he was teaching video production at the Economics Institute, I suggested a lunch date. While nibbling on chicken with boiled peanuts, I learned he was married, had two kids and was sure I would like his wife, so he generously invited me to this Christmas Eve party. Since I adored his French Canadian humor, I accepted.

I tried to ease the discomfort for everyone of being Robert's "pickup" from the disco. I joked about his line, "If you like me, you'll really like my wife!" In fact, I was intrigued by both Siri and Kirsten and hungered for contact with such strong, accomplished women. But they were insulated in a completely different universe in Beijing. My head was spinning from the opulence I was experiencing. I couldn't help thinking about the contrast with other Christmas Eves in my life.

The previous December, while traveling around Mexico by bus, I was severely poisoned by some street food a couple of days before Christmas and spent what felt like near-death moments in a crummy hotel room in Aguascalientes (Hot Waters) before moving on. On Christmas Eve, still feeling dreadful, I made the mistake of taking a second-class bus that took forever to reach a coastal town that turned out to be all booked for the holidays. On the bus, I struck up a conversation with an older retiree from Arkansas and his young Mexican wife, who were returning from a market town. Echoing the Christmas story, they offered me a place to stay for the night.

As we trudged up a dark village road with their baskets of supplies and my travel bags, I began to regret the easy decision to go with them. When we entered their pitch-black cement block house with a corrugated tin roof, they fumbled for matches to light a lantern. Adrenalin shot through me. Fight or flight? Had I trusted them too much? Would they kidnap me? Rob me? Murder me? Bury me in the yard?

Instead, they showed me to a straw mattress on the floor in a back corner. I slept with my clothes on—just in case. After a nervous night, I awoke not only to the crowing roosters but to Mr. Arkansas barking orders at his *mujera*.

She had left a basin of water near my bed. I felt guilty for my initial fears and suspicions. When I entered their simple living space where she was washing his hair over a basin on the table, a picture emerged: American macho guy living on modest social security checks with impoverished sex-slave-slash-domestic-servant. She was willing to comply because she was desperate, and an extra dollar here or there probably trickled to her family. As he continued to harangue her, I thanked them profusely and made a quick exit. With my bulky bags on my shoulders, I stumbled down the hill, dodging threatening dogs, toward the highway, then the beach. Christmas.

I know now it was the decorum at Kirsten's that surprised me. The formality. The restrained behavior. I didn't need more of that, given the passionless environment of my life at Radio Beijing. It made me nostalgic for more exuberant North American approaches to celebrations. The ones I remembered at my grandparents' rooming house in one of Vancouver's working-poor neighborhoods with all the aunts, uncles and cousins, the whirling Christmas tree invented by my grandfather, the women all running in and out of the kitchen with bowls of steaming mashed potatoes and turnips, a platter of turkey, pitchers of gravy and cranberry sauce and, later, homemade plum pudding with hard sauce and mincemeat pie, artifacts from a culture that had survived the horrendous disruption of leaving English and Scottish villages in the early twentieth century for the brutal Canadian prairie.

Meanwhile, kids, sneaking chocolates, ran chaotically on all that sugar. My uncle, the singing cowboy and circus performer, Alberta Slim, would start yodeling, provoking my mother to put on an old 78 record to dance what she called "dirty boogie"—really big band swing—with her youngest brother, Bert. Noisy, sweaty, hectic, high-spirited. It included spats, tears, angry outbursts between sisters and one of my uncles trying to trap each woman in the stairwell to steal kisses.

In another memory vein, some Christmas Eves after my mum had remarried had been painful. She—who always worked from 9 to 5—would for weeks before Christmas shop for gifts for all the relatives, wrap and mail those gifts, write dozens of letters and cards to friends and family near and far, bake cookies and fruitcakes, make mincemeat, then dollop that into pies and tart shells, decorate a tree, hang boughs of pine, spruce and cedar around the house, suspend a branch of mistletoe in the hallway, loop lights around the windows, pin cards on the curtains, shop for and prep the turkey and trimmings for Christmas Day, as well as make invitations—composing rhyming couplets—for the Boxing Day open house for neighbors and friends.

Then, on Christmas Eve, she would come home from work, put on one of her party dresses with a brilliant rhinestone broach, smooth on creamy fire-engine-red lipstick and then sit on the couch by the fireplace and…wait. Wait for my truck-driving, heavy-drinking stepfather to come home from a roaming drunken fest with his work buddies. The Christmas before he got cancer and died, I was fourteen and sitting, dressed up too, in the living room with Mum. She poured herself a Canadian Club with ginger ale and prepared a little plate with cookies she had baked. I watched her spirit wilt. I was old enough to recognize the work she—and I, as her apprentice—put into creating these rituals, guaranteeing a celebratory Christmas mood. The waiting game fueled the loathing I had for a man who had mostly been trouble for me and disappointment for her.

I should have appreciated the gentility and effort, the generosity and goodwill at Kirsten's. Perhaps it was just that the lights were too bright. The effect of the candles was negated. When they all left for midnight mass at the newly restored St. Joseph's Catholic Church downtown, I begged off. My brain was reacting to riches that I hadn't consumed in months. My IQ was dropping in tandem with the fats and sugars pulsing through my veins, making me very sleepy. Plus I was facing a houseful of guests for a very different kind of fiesta the next evening at *my* apartment. I wrestled with myself during the goodbyes whether I should invite them all and felt guilty after deciding against it. I was worried I wouldn't have enough space, food and drinks. And while I was intrigued by Kirsten and Siri and adored Robert, somewhere deep down I feared they would judge my bohemian entertaining efforts.

The next day, Christmas, I was up early for a frigid bicycle ride against the gritty winds to the Moscow Bakery, which was closed, then to Sanlihe Post Office to pick up a parcel from Jason, an artist friend in New York, then to the Minzhu Hotel to buy wine for the party, peddling erratically home while balancing all the bottles. Back home, the party prep began while listening to Hamiet Bluiett and Schubert cassettes from Jason.

Shi Yung arrived first and was shocked to see me in a party dress, stockings and heels rather than my winter uniform of padded pants and layers of sweaters. We talked about New York City while standing on chairs fussing with some colorful Chinese paper cut-out decorations, looping them across the room. Even when I nudged him, he never discussed politics. Never asked about the American political madness. In my high-spirited mood, I had to force myself to remember that the room was probably bugged. His behavior indicated he knew it.

I lined up cassettes of jazz, blues, R&B and Motown, playing Billie Holiday, adjusting the volume, lighting a dozen candles as others started to arrive: Martha, Yanna's former interpreter, with whom I was not supposed to have contact; the sculptor, Wang Keping, and a couple of his Chinese girlfriends; Michael Weisskopf and his wife, Lilly; Canadian journalist Don Murray. His wife, Vera, had gone home for the holidays while he—like all the foreign journalists—was stranded here, waiting for the trial verdict. Then my Filipino neighbors and their two kids arrived, along with my French, Sri Lankan and Indian neighbors as well as Fatima and Ahmadou from Niger with their kids. Guests squeezed in—the Laotian family, Colleen Leung from Vancouver Island who worked at CCTV, and a friend of hers, then a few of the comrades from the office: Professor Li, Shadow Zhang, Leader Zhang and her husband. Peter Kwong appeared, then Duska, an Eastern European student at the university whom I met through Helmut. A new acquaintance, Paul Rice, a student from Texas working at *China Reconstructs*, joined us. Ron was back in Chicago for the holidays. Next, Wan Yaping, Janet's boyfriend, entered with some Chinese women friends. Janet was home in New York.

Everyone brought something to eat and drink. Sweets, savories, homemade, store bought. I had ordered turkey, duck and beef dishes from the dining room. There were treats prepared by Muslims, Hindus, Christians, Jews, Buddhists, atheists and agnostics—a multicultural potluck! With Esther Phillips crooning "What a Night," we kept shuffling the dishes on the table, passing bountiful plates around along with a potpourri of alcoholic choices.

Bai, an intriguing Beijing intellectual I had met through Yanna, arrived by climbing through a back window on the first floor of our building to avoid the scene at the gate. He said he had come to Yanna's parties and always used that entry. Perhaps entering through windows was not so unusual after all.

The women friends of Yaping and Keping disappeared shortly after arriving. When I went to get more cold beer out of the bathtub, I discovered they were all taking showers. They spent the rest of the evening with wet hair. It must be such a pleasure to have hot water in a more private context than the bathhouse. I tried to imagine this at Kirsten's.

My apartment oozed with music, laughter and chatter in multiple languages. Everyone seemed to be radiating a rosy glow. The only caveat was that Ming was held up for twenty minutes at the guard hut. Peter, who entered easily after showing his American passport, told me the guards were grilling Ming. I stormed out of my apartment, marching down the hallway in a fury, found Xing, the building interpreter/spy/informant, ranted about police states and "no other country in the world would do this!" Yes, waving hands and screaming—what a way to lose face. But Ming then appeared at the door, and the combination of rich food and warm vibes massaged by whiskey and wine softened my edges.

Somehow, this roomful of souls managed to recreate the atmosphere of my fiestas on Mott Street. Predictably, I spun around the room filling glasses with spirits while introducing strangers to each other. My Filipino neighbors, exiles who had lived in the building for almost ten years, announced with glistening eyes that it was their best time ever in Beijing. I felt that miracle of human connectivity and celebratory magic for the first time since leaving New York. I regretted not inviting Kirsten, Siri and Robert, but with children and a UN universe, they would have had more luxe options.

Perhaps celebrations are always about our need to overcome our essential loneliness. Certainly this gathering of exiles, wanderers and locals, revealed our commonalities. Our basic desire to expand our hearts, see the best in each other and embrace despite the peculiar conditions of segregation and isolation in Beijing.

The following morning, exhilarating in the afterglow, simultaneously exhausted and hungover, I flipped in the new Schubert cassette. While emptying ashtrays, sweeping up the scraps, munching on leftovers, cleaning all the long black hairs out of the bathtub, I reminisced about the night before. The delicious sensations of it. That's what I love about cleanup after a party. The replaying of conversations, reflections upon surprising encounters and accidental discoveries. Mostly I loved hanging onto the abundance of feeling that a great party generates.

Later, I bicycled to Beihai Park to walk alone in the frigid air, clearing my head while watching the skaters. Today I was filled with hope. I could look at that forbidden world of the Chinese and think that maybe, just maybe, someday, we could shatter the glass wall between us.

That night, Ahmadou dropped by with a potent gift, a specially painted and woven leather talisman from Niger to hang on my door to keep the evil spirits out. I would have liked to have a talisman that would encourage some naughtiness to enter.

He said some Chinese men were arrested at the guard hut today. Who could it be? I wondered. All my guests got home safely the night before—I hoped.

The party glow didn't last long. Waiting for me at the office the next day was a frowning Shadow Zhang. The interrogation began. She wanted to know who all the Chinese guests were at my party and how I had met them. I had predicted that, as my shadow and earnest Party member, Zhang Wei would be curious about my contacts outside the office. To prove that I had nothing to hide, I had invited her. I had not anticipated her relentless drive to gather information. She seemed to know that Wang Yaping was the youngest member of the Writers' Committee. Did she get dossiers on everyone who visited me? She wanted to know how I had met him and Ming. She revealed that she knew Ming was at university, but she asked which one. How late did he stay? Of course, she probably already knew from reports at the guard hut. She commented on Ming being drunk.

Oh, it was so tedious. What other countries had these infantilizing surveillance policies? The Soviet Union? North Korea? Albania? Professor Li said nothing about the party but sat silently at his desk listening to Shadow Zhang's cross-examination.

I rejected all the scripts that morning. Thank God it was Saturday, a half-day.

The next day, a Sunday, I met Ming at the park near the skating rink. We decided to walk rather than skate as I needed to exhale from the grilling by Shadow Zhang, I needed Ming to humor me. We headed to the Moscow Restaurant again for tea.

Our communication was improving as our vocabularies expanded. We had become incredibly swift with dictionaries and babble in baby talk. There was always new information.

Today he revealed that since he only earned forty *kuai* a month, his parents helped to support him, to his and their embarrassment. It was a sweet admission.

He wanted to talk about studying abroad. He asked specifically about Shi Yung and how he was applying for schools in the US. He always referred to my friends, even when he had only met them once. Was he a plant? Was he intelligence? Police? Was he reporting everything?

Since he only asked me about male friends, I also interpreted this as a form of chauvinism. I had noticed in meetings at Radio Beijing that women, even if they were leaders, took a backseat to men. Sexism appeared to be ingrained in the body politic despite the earlier revolutionary slogan "Women Hold Up Half the Sky." In fact, I saw that women held most of the brooms. In the street. And in the hallways at Radio Beijing.

As Ming and I slurped our teas, he related how during the first years of the Cultural Revolution it was good to steal cups from this restaurant and take them home but not now. I loved the little story fragments he told. I was never enthusiastic about seeing him, but then I always enjoyed his comic nature when we were together. Afterward, doubt returned.

As we left, I bought chocolates to take to Martha's later. I gave Ming little cakes to take home. He promised to call during the week.

After two months of estrangement, Martha showed up at my Christmas Party—safety in numbers—and then to my delight invited me to her house for dinner to meet her family. My first visit to the home of a Chinese acquaintance for a meal without it being approved and paid for by the Party.

She had drawn a map and explained I should get a taxi to a particular corner and then walk the rest of the way. When I pulled up on my bicycle where she was waiting outside, she laughed with surprise. I handed her a bag of oranges and chocolates.

"Thank you. Thank you. You should not bring gifts. I am so sorry that our apartment is so small, and now it is very crowded," she said. "My family are all visiting from out of town. Because my mother is sick in the hospital."

When we entered I saw that she shared two rooms and a closet-sized kitchen with her mother and sister and two young nieces. That seemed a fairly generous ratio of people to rooms given the reality in Beijing. The rooms were so stuffed with furniture and beds that it was difficult to judge the size. That meant they probably had a larger space before the Cultural Revolution and had to squeeze stuff into this smaller apartment. Now, because of her siblings coming to visit their mother in hospital, she explained that five people were sharing one double bed. Three adults—the sisters and two kids, dovetailed. Another sister and brother were on single beds in the other room.

Our conversation was lively since Martha was fluent and could translate. Her visiting brother worked in the Shanxi coal mines. Now in his late twenties, he went there originally as a "sent down" youth in the mid-'70s to learn from peasants and workers. He lived in a singles' dorm at the mines. Like so many others, he was trying to get back to Beijing. To do so, he had to trade jobs with someone. First, it was enormously difficult to find someone willing to trade. Then, in order to convince someone to swap, he had to pay a commission, which could be in the form of a TV or cassette recorder. It would be a great expense for him.

The visiting sister worked in a factory in a remote village in Sichuan province. She volunteered to go to the country during the Cultural Revolution and decided to stay and marry and had a family there. But she sent her two kids, aged six and eight, to Beijing to go to school, a statement about the quality of education in rural China.

This was their first opportunity to meet with a foreigner. They were all eager to talk. The kids tried out their little bits of English on me. I regaled them with my snippets of Mandarin.

Martha's brother and sisters were eager to learn about the US and Canada. What about poverty, technology, health care, alcoholism, food and conditions? They were also relaxed about my questions about China. I wanted to know how they viewed the trial of the Gang of Four. I also shared some of my concerns about China's uncritical embrace of new technologies and the need for more equal access to education for economic development. It was a free-flowing conversation between people who were excited to know about the world of the other, far from the informants at our respective work units. We were not sharing state secrets because none of us knew any, but we were enthusiastic about learning about the histories, thoughts and experiences of the other.

We compared the health systems of the US, Canada and China. While I shared my concerns about the privatized health care system of the United States as compared to the national health plan of Canada, they shared their frustrations about how difficult it had been to get their mother into the hospital recently. There weren't enough hospitals, so they were overcrowded, and the family had to use backdoor connections to get in. *Houmen*—the back door. The Party offered the biggest back door of all. This explained why so many Chinese now wanted to join the Party. It provided access to better housing, job mobility, raises, promotions, access to better schools for their kids and opportunities to buy special commodities. Corruption it would be called elsewhere. Recently, the government—the Party—had opened up some of the special foreigners' stores to high cadres, but not to regular folks. So the Party was constantly creating structures of hierarchy and privilege. Some rationalized this as rewarding hard-working, responsible cadres.

Martha said that Radio Beijing helped with the extra expenses involved with her mother's hospitalization. I was intrigued by that. The down- and upsides of how the system worked in the midst of scarcity.

The only part of our conversation that might have caused twitching for the ideological police was about "democracy." They asked whether I thought it worked better in the US or Canada. Brilliant question.

I laughed. "It would take me a month to answer! But, for starters, there's too much money influencing the democratic system in the US. Too many people are excluded from running for office. And it is curtailed by a two-party system. But the constitutional guarantees—separation of church and state, the checks and balances system of executive, legislative and judicial is critical as well as the Bill of Rights. Yet those rights must be fought for constantly. The recent election of Reagan seemed to violate the separation of church and state when churches became political precincts. But I think that education, engagement, organizing and civil society are all critical to democracy. Not just voting."

Of course, this speech needed much clarifying of concepts for Martha, and I was never sure if everything was translated correctly. My perpetual dilemma. "Civil society" took a lot of explaining. The concept was nonexistent in the present articulation of Chinese society.

I asked about the recent local elections in Shanxi. Martha's brother said it was a farce. His comrades at the mine filled out their ballots and elected themselves. They also felt the trial of the Gang of Four was a sham. That it didn't indicate a new, more just China. He said that coworkers felt that the legal process of the trial collapsed as the judges harangued the defendants. Surprisingly, that was the Western journalists' critique, too. Were they parroting the BBC or did they really believe that?

There was no question that they believed the Gang of Four were guilty of heinous crimes, pain and suffering. But they also wanted to see a new legal system at work, and at least some were disappointed.

Martha's brother also asked about Wei Jingsheng, the leader of the New Democracy movement, who was in jail. He asked about his age, and I surmised he was calculating whether he would have been a Red Guard. I realized how complex the whole phenomenon of the Red Guard movement was. I thought about Gao Yuan's story.

Martha's sister, the one who lived in the countryside, was younger but looked older. Life was much harsher in her rural community, I suspected. She said in her factory the comrades talked openly about discontent.

"The leadership encourages it sometimes and discourages it other times," she said. "The factory is having difficulties because it is remote from transportation. It's increasingly difficult to ship goods out. It's a major problem throughout China because of Mao's insistence on decentralization. Production is scattered everywhere."

"But wasn't that supposed to be a great idea? More sustainable? Fair?" I asked.

"It depends upon great roads, railways and communication system," Martha added.

They explained that, during the Cultural Revolution, the infrastructure broke down from political factional fights as well as the attack on expertise.

It was an unusual opportunity to meet with a family of seemingly ordinary workers, although given Martha's job at Radio Beijing, they probably came from an intellectual family. They had not mentioned their father—where he was, who he was, what his position was. Perhaps he was a high cadre who hadn't survived the Cultural Revolution? These siblings were clearly idealistic at one time, which explained their grievances now.

The freewheeling conversation took place as we sat on beds at a folding table crammed with all kinds of cooked and cold treats, spicy peanuts, fried, puffy shrimp chips, cooked vegetables and rice with little bits of pork.

Cradling my tea cup, I never wanted to leave, but the translations soon became wearying for Martha and conscious of the children's bedtime, I gently peeled away from this cozy familial scene. Martha wanted to bicycle with me part way back to my apartment building, but although I loved this Chinese tradition—hosts accompanying guests part way home—I discouraged her. She had already worked so hard to make this meal happen and translated all evening.

Pedaling home in the bitter cold, I felt as if I had a warm blanket wrapped around me and Demerol flowing in my veins. As I approached my apartment building, that comforting cocoon evaporated, replaced by regret and sadness that the sensation experienced with Martha's family wasn't possible with my colleagues in the English department. The people in my office had not said one thing about the trial. I had stopped asking. I didn't know whether I would be capable of "hearing" them anymore.

BRILLIANT STREAMERS looped from the ceilings and corners of the room. "Happy New Year" was scrawled in pink chalk on the blackboard. Judy's journalism class had invited me to join them for their New Year's celebration—the night before New Year's Eve. They had powdered the floor.

"For dancing!" someone shouted.

Another student insisted I share a plate of boiled peanuts, sunflower seeds, little strange-tasting cakes and lovely candied fruits. Someone else offered apples, pears and oranges.

A school leader delivered a painfully long speech in Mandarin. The students bristled with exasperation at this formality. One young man simply translated it as "best wishes." Everyone laughed.

The students insisted that the foreigners sing a song for them. We were hopeless. None of us knew the lyrics to anything beyond the first line. So we sang something idiotic: "Row, Row, Row Your Boat," encouraging them to join in the fun of staggered choruses.

Then they sang for us. Beautiful, elegant harmonizing. First a traditional song, then a revolutionary one. Someone translated. Humbling. It stirred memories of how much my family used to make our own music before the proliferation of electronic music and amplified sound systems. At my parents' parties, there was always someone who played the piano while everyone sang.

My reveries were interrupted by a handsome guy—perhaps in his mid-'30s—singing "Old Man River" with a deep bass voice. Paul Robeson came to mind. Someone explained that the singer was with the People's Liberation Army choir. He approached me eagerly while Yuan translated.

"I want to come to your apartment to learn popular American songs."

How bold! I wondered to myself, *How long would I have to wait?*

Then the real celebration began. There were two big cassette recorders—one with muffled sound, the other with no volume. I brought some disco and R&B cassettes, since Judy had warned me that the students had insisted that I should teach them the latest moves.

As I started with Gloria Gaynor's 1978 hit, "I Will Survive," the students yelled out, "Teach us! Show us!"

I took the floor with Judy, Yuan and another expat. Gradually, we brought them all to their feet.

Somehow I remember playing George McCrae's "Rock You Baby," the Bee Gees' "Stayin' Alive" and then "Shame, Shame, Shame" by Shirley & Co.

They wanted to find the beat—a fantastic sight!

Was I corrupting them? I had seen some older couples dancing tango in the park, practicing fancy moves. But the kids were focused on disco. What would happen to China when everyone started to tap their toes instead of dreaming of Lei Feng?

AFTER ALL the stroke-inducing calories of the previous week, something quite sour was happening at the office. It was a jolt. After all the human warmth of the holiday season, frosty winds were rustling through the hallways at Radio Beijing. The mood was icier, stiffer, more fearful. Perhaps my letters home were read out loud to them in secret meetings. But no—I thought it was something bigger.

Rumors were flying in the expert community about Deng's December 25 speech. While we were dreaming of sugar plums, Deng was laying down a new line. Ron had returned from Chicago, and one of his colleagues reported that Deng had cheered the gathering speed of economic transformation.

"But," Ron said, "Deng's speech turned out to be more significant for the part of it that had to do with culture and democracy."

It put all the rumors into perspective. Deng was sounding autocratic. He threatened to bring out troops and establish curfews to fight reactionaries and dissidents. The troops would confront strikes and demonstrations. The government was going to go after black marketing and prostitution. "Fight until death" was one of the phrases he used.

At the Wednesday night study group that week, Neil Burton had the text of Deng's speech. He translated some of it for us:

—"The main point is to adhere to the leadership of the Party, without which the country will fall apart. Without order and discipline and the leadership of the Party, we cannot have socialist democracy and we cannot have effective reform. So we cannot tolerate speeches attacking the principles of the leadership of the Party.

—"Some illegal organizations are very active; we must be on guard against this, especially among the youth. Students cannot go on strike or have demonstrations without permission from higher authorities...

—"The Party has made mistakes, but it is wrong to say we did nothing right...Chairman Mao's merits come first, his mistakes come second. If we stress his mistakes too much, we will damage the image of the Party and of socialism and of the country.

—"Newspapers must not exaggerate the failings of the cadres. We shouldn't give people the wrong impression, that we have a bureaucratic class.

—"We must struggle against bourgeois liberalism and out-and-out individualism. We must continue friendly relations with the West and learn business methods, but in the ideological sphere, we must struggle to the end.

—"We must emphasize stability and unity. Some people always want to stir up trouble using the methods they used in the Cultural Revolution. Some are talking about a second Cultural Revolution."

Burton reported that some youths who went to the border areas and had not been permitted to return to their homes in the cities were stirring up trouble. There were illegal magazines and pamphlets.

The speech continued:

—"There are still contradictions among the people ('class enemies'), and we must punish these bad persons appropriately. We must mobilize the people to struggle against these bad persons."

Now I understood the chill in the office. A strategy of fear was at work once again. It revealed that ideology was not cohesive. If the late '70s witnessed a cracking open of doors to allow breezes into their claustrophobic spaces—a little freedom of expression, wall posters and journals discussing democratic reforms, breathing space for writers and filmmakers, more openness to Western ideas of economic development—people had allowed too many gusts of fresh air. They had carried it all too far. It was time to slam those doors shut. Get tough.

THE FOLLOWING Saturday, hundreds of Radio Beijing comrades trudged toward the big auditorium. In the English department, the offices were eerily empty except for two colleagues at their desks in different rooms.

"What's up?" I asked Xiao Yian, the youngest staff member.

"It's a big meeting for all staff where they are reading Deng's latest speech."

"Why didn't you go?"

"I'm at the bottom salary level in the twenty-four levels, so I don't go."

In the other office, Dam Ping was at her desk, still reading Michener's *Chesapeake.*

"Why are you here rather than in the auditorium?"

"I am not interested," she replied with her usual indifference. "The speech is about a new crackdown on all the criticism." Her disdain was now palpable. "It is all repetitive information that I have access to in other forms."

"I hear that one of the new 'get tough' policy lines will restrict relations between the Chinese and foreigners. How could it get any more restrictive?" I searched her face but couldn't wait for a reply. I barreled on. "I cannot understand why my coworkers, who have more reason than anyone to spend time with me, come to my apartment, do things together, are so frightened of passing the guard hut at my building."

My exasperation had worked up to a fever pitch. I had never spoken this bluntly and directly to any of the comrades about my frustrations.

Dam Ping looked at me calmly. "No matter how much the comrades may want to be your friend and talk to you, have you to their house or become close to you, they risk losing everything...their housing, their children's access to good schools or to university, their pay raises. During the Cultural Revolution, people lost everything. The risk is too great."

I appreciated Dam Ping's guts to tell me straight what nobody else dared and what I had already figured out. The Cultural Revolution was over, but then it really wasn't. Nobody could trust that things couldn't change course again.

THERE WAS yet another big Radio Beijing-wide meeting as well as political education departmental meetings in the largest office on our floor to discuss Deng's speech. This was big. All the comrades were avoiding me. They knew I was filled with questions. Nobody dared to risk being seen with me. The dark hallways filled with Mandarin whispers and secrecy.

I called Don Murray. Since I was being frozen out of information at Radio Beijing, I thought I might as well commiserate with a journalist I respected. We met for coffee at the Beijing Hotel.

"It fits," he said. "The speech hasn't been published yet in the *People's Daily*, but we've been watching the shift in language showing up in papers around the country."

All week I felt alienated from the comrades because of their inability to talk to me about the speech, to be forthright and honest about it.

"What does Deng have to say?"

"Oh, nothing important," was one incredulous reply.

My response—becoming a pattern—was to reject a number of the scripts that week. One on prisons that was laughable. Another idealized miners.

I struggled anew with my principles. Openness, honesty, candor. Truth. Doubt. And with conflicts, like freedom versus self-protection. I felt hostile and suspicious all week.

When I met with Siri and Robert for dinner later in the week, they were ignorant of these developments. They lived in a bubble and had no independent contacts with *Beijingren*.

SHI YUNG and I had arranged to bicycle to Wangfujing on a shopping trip. He was eager for political conversation on our bikes—it was safe to discuss politics in English while bicycling. For me, this was proof that he believed my room was bugged. I asked him about Deng's speech.

"It is like the beginning of the Cultural Revolution—scary. The students are upset. I am tired of political education. It's Marxism, nothing else. Dialectical materialism. There's a joke at school about materialism. Cadres are the only ones who have it."

He was waiting and hoping for the Chicago Art Institute acceptance. Ron, while home in Chicago over the holidays, had lobbied with the Institute folks on his behalf.

Meanwhile, my discussion class with the comrades was canceled. Perhaps they could not be trusted. I might have asked uncomfortable questions.

January 10, 1981, Journal:

The drawings on my walls are now keeping company with a variety of calligraphic poems given to me. One is a beautiful poem about my journey to China by the husband of a colleague as a thank you for a book of Muriel Rukeyser's poetry that I gave them and they loved. We are not allowed to be seen talking to each other at the office, so this is all finessed discreetly. Another is by Yung, a line from a Sung poem about the sun at the end of the river. And a piece of calligraphy by another comrade's husband...a Tang poem that is still too complicated for me to explain. They have given me these poems in advance of the Chinese New Year. I am deeply moved and angry at the same time that this system prevents me from having normal relationships with these comrades in particular.

I've had a cold for two weeks and am feeling awfully tired all the time. Most of the foreigners are sick with flu, colds and exhaustion. Much to do with the horrendous pollution. A brew of coal, ash, dust and sand. Have to wash my hair every other day. My comb is black at the end of the first day.

MY RESPONSE to the iceberg at the office was to pursue another flirtation. For weeks, I had been smiling at a cute guy who made his presence felt occasionally as I walked onto the Radio Beijing grounds. He stopped to chat briefly one day, exercising his primitive English. His name was Zhu Yi. He offered to help me with my Chinese. That was my hook.

I suggested he come by my apartment. Three times we made what I thought was a date and he did not show up. Then, on a Sunday at 8:30 in the morning, he was at my door. I was still slopping around in pajamas and excused myself to throw on pants and a sweater; I ran a comb through my hair and a brush past my teeth. It gave him time to examine the chaos of my apartment.

Zhu Yi coughed nervously. I had a hangover. I made tea while flitting about the sitting room, emptying ashtrays, shuffling my drawing papers, tidying calligraphy implements, clothes, dirty dishes. I opened the window a crack to let out the stale air.

He sat poker-straight, and we exchanged banal remarks about the weather, his age—twenty-six. I worried about how old I looked this morning—probably fifty-six.

"What do you do at Radio Beijing?"

"Repair recorders. Recording and broadcast engineer."

"Oh, one of the maligned engineers!"

His eyebrows knitted together in a way that I knew meant he didn't understand.

"How long have you worked there?

"Ten years."

That would mean he started at sixteen? In 1970. But I didn't ask about that. I was too busy calculating dates and ages. He would have started working at Radio Beijing in the middle of the Cultural Revolution. Maybe he was older than he was letting on. Or was I missing something here?

"You were assigned to work at the Radio at sixteen in 1970 during the Cultural Revolution?"

No response.

Now he studied intensive English every morning. Translated ten pages every night. That's why he was so busy. I could appreciate it.

Turns out he was a cadre's son. Really?

"My father works in government—"

"Doesn't everyone?" I teased. "What kind of work does he do in government?"

"No English," Zhu Yi giggled.

"What about your mother?"

"She lives at home."

"Where do you live?"

"In the dormitory. Three roommates."

Eventually he asked why I wasn't married. I knew this was the burning question among the hundreds of workers at Radio Beijing who knew about me. I tried to explain the complexity of Western relationships. He was swimming in quicksand. I suggested more meetings.

"I want, but no time."

"I'm busy, too," I shrugged.

"Please do not tell anyone at Radio Beijing about my visit."

"I understand. Because I have other Chinese friends."

"Yes, but foreign."

"Chinese, too."

His jaw dropped and his eyes opened wide. I didn't have the vocabulary to explain or qualify. This was the problem. There were never any nuances possible with someone who spoke as little English as I spoke Mandarin.

He was on his way to an early-morning movie screening and left without making a future plan, which I hated because we could only make a date then by telephone, which was compromised and difficult. Yelling into the receiver in the echo chamber of a public hallway on a bugged phone. All this frustrated energy on these cadres' sons. And never knowing whether we had really understood each other correctly. No subtitles.

Also, no subtleties. That deliciously flirtatious and playful talk that two people pursue when they share all the same signals and codes. Through the language barrier our conversation was reduced to blunt facts. I was too illiterate to deliver a grand riff on the tension between my Dionysian and Apollonian selves. Only a minuscule fraction of my personality and essential self could be expressed, and I was certain even *that* was misunderstood. Conversely, I could only grasp ragged fragments of those I had met. I found it impossible to pose an interesting or playful question: "Have you ever wanted to murder your father or sleep with your mother?"

Then I thought about the foreigners I knew in Beijing. Was our communication any deeper? Better? Richer? Well, with Ron, partially, and with some of my women friends, somewhat. How I missed my girlfriends back home—all of them so different yet critical to my sense of identity and the juggling act between my intellectual, political, creative and emotional selves.

LATER THAT day, I met Ming, who was dressed in his Western coat and shoes—the ones he was wearing the night we had first met at the Beijing Hotel bar. The costume was designed to pass inspection by the guards at the Friendship Store. He managed that but not without having to fill out a form. He indicated that he was my guide or translator. Our plan was to buy a TV for him.

He didn't seem to understand the importance of handing me the envelope of money before we were inside the store. As we approached the counter, I was afraid he would never give it to me, and I was becoming irked because he shouldn't even have been with me as I made the transaction. It wasn't as if he needed to pick out the brand or features. There was only one kind. I thought he was going to wait outside in the car. Not being able to communicate made me so frustrated. We could both get into trouble if it looked like I was shopping for him.

At the last minute, as I was touching one of the sets, he handed me all the money—in *renminbi!* But they only took "funny money" there. Every high cadre's son should have known that. Surely this artificial currency especially designed for foreigners—and very high cadres—to use in the Friendship Store was a constant subject of conversation among his set. If Ming thought I would trade my "funny money" for his *renminbi*, he needed to negotiate this with me in private before we ever got to the store. So this was a doomed mission.

I tried to exit the store without it looking obvious what had just happened. We walked—each in our own fumes of fury—toward the bus. I didn't know how to hand him his money back discretely in the street while he, clearly upset, kept pointing to my purse. I scolded him in a jumble of Chinese vocabulary that I didn't know I possessed. His cheeks turned crimson.

We cooled down by walking blocks in the frigid air and then stopped at a local restaurant. The only free chairs were at a table with some friendly cadres who worked at Xinhua. Ming was wound up too tightly to display any social graces, if he had any. He was either too young or simply too spoiled. Or embarrassed to be seen in such clothes in a local place. Or frightened to be seen with a foreigner. Especially an older woman.

What was I doing with this kid? Learning conversational Mandarin, of course, and about Chinese character and culture, of course. Well, maybe only a sliver of that. Was there an easier way?

In the restaurant, a big man in an army uniform made obscene gestures trying to get my attention. Was I considered a prostitute out with my pimp? A beggar stumbled through the restaurant. This was the second one I had seen recently. Perhaps he was mentally ill.

After lunch, we kept walking. Ming was determined not to see me for three weeks until he studied more English and I learned more Chinese. I was fed up, too. He talked about his factory. There was only one cadre on the night shift, he said. What did that have to do with anything? Or did I misinterpret a word or phrase?

That evening, wallowing in my grumpy mood I admitted to myself that I didn't particularly want to be Ming's "Chairman" anymore.

January 14, 1981, Journal:

The comrades may not risk being seen talking to me, but they do not hesitate to ask for my help on the sly. Zong keeps wanting more help with American university applications; Su requests a recommendation for a University of Hawaii fellowship; the accountant wants a sociology book. I presume he could earn extra money translating it given that universities are beefing up their academic departments again.

The depressive Chen approached me privately at the office to ask another favor. He looked sheepish, then defiant; he wanted a gallon container of cooking oil from the Friendship Store. I think it's in anticipation of Chinese New Year coming soon. I told him I could not do it today. I will need a car for that and they will suspect if I bring something like that back. They know I'm not using that much oil. I have to think about how I'll do it.

Comrade Wang Qiang asked me to meet next Tuesday night with a doctors' group to whom he teaches English. He wants me to talk about the American health-care system. So these are the moonlighting gigs going on. I wonder how much he is paid to do this workshop. One comrade at the office whispered to me in private that he is trying very hard to get into the Party—it's a road to connections, "back doors," advantages.

"An opportunist?" I ask.

The confiding comrade smiles.

The quotidian of daily chores keeps devouring more creative time—like washing clothes by hand. Draping them around my apartment. It's so arid now everything dries quickly. panties, sweaters, long pants, blouses, socks.

ON A Friday afternoon in mid-January, somebody at Beijing University sent a car for me. I had been invited to give a lecture on the history of jazz.

On the way, I ruminated about the remarkable history of China's most prestigious university. How it spawned political and literary movements of the early twentieth century. Then, in 1966, Red Guards there took the lead in the new movement that would become known as the Great Proletarian Cultural Revolution by challenging administrators and then denouncing "capitalist roaders" in Party leadership, like Deng Xiaoping. Professors were humiliated and tortured. Some committed suicide. The school itself was shut down for at least four years. My radical American comrades knew little or nothing about this in the late '60s, when we were extolling the driving ideas of this potent movement.

Now, with Deng in ascendancy, the university was taking its former place as a leading intellectual institution, struggling with the neglect and ideological wars of the '60s and '70s . I felt so honored to be invited to speak there that my hands were shaking as I shuffled my lecture notes and organized my cassettes at the podium. I had spent the previous nights lining up particular cuts of music. In a shabby auditorium, I looked out at some 200 curious faces.

More than thirty years later, I seem to have forgotten how exactly I presented a history of jazz in ninety minutes while playing short segments of music along the way. Pre-digital, pre-Internet, pre-Pandora. I was completely dependent upon the selection of music on audio cassettes that I brought from New York for my personal use.

I do remember the broad outlines—beginning with Louis Armstrong— probably as a way to talk about the mother lode in New Orleans and his particular pioneering of vocal phrasing—then playing "Take the A Train" by Duke Ellington as an example of the big bands era. Then something from Art Tatum, who defined a new complex piano style, then probably part of a Thelonious Monk piece. What did I say? That he was a genius? How did I explain bebop? Dizzy Gillespie, Charlie Parker, John Coltrane, Max Roach and Miles Davis? I remember wishing that I'd had enough cassettes with me to take one single song from the American songbook and show how each of these musicians interpreted it differently.

I relished announcing the names of these giants out loud in this "sacred space" in China. The Chinese government had done so much to demonize jazz, blues, and rock 'n' roll that I wasn't sure whether any of what I said or the music I played could really "be heard." I should have been chastened by the experience at my blues presentation for the broadcasting folks. But that had been my idea. Beijing University had invited me to give this presentation on jazz. Perhaps somebody at the blues presentation had made the connection. I no longer remember.

"These composers, arrangers and performers," I slowed down my voice into the microphone as the room hushed, "mean as much to many of us in the United States and other parts of the world as Beethoven, Bach and Mozart. Jazz is America's classical music."

I knew that would disrupt some received wisdom, since Party cultural gatekeepers were now enthusiastically embracing European classical music after it was forbidden during the Cultural Revolution.

"These giants of jazz," I continued, "have created a rich legacy. Musicians try to emulate them all over the world. This is the best of what the United States has to give to the world culturally. Well, there's also dance."

My most vivid memory of the evening was looking out over that sea of youthful, eager yet puzzled faces while playing Billie Holiday's "Strange Fruit," hearing it echoing through the auditorium and thinking that perhaps this was a historical moment as I explained the meaning of the metaphor—and wondered how well my comments were being translated.

I have often wondered in the three decades since if anybody who was there that evening had their skull cracked—like mine was exploded by hearing many of these jazz musicians for the first time during my high school years in the 1950s. Did playing these icons of jazz in 1980 Beijing change the way any of these students heard, thought about or made music?

Several students rushed to the podium as I was packing up.

"Can you explain improvisation? Is it annotated?" they were bursting to know in their brand-new English.

I had touched on it, how every musician might interpret and riff on a song differently on different nights, depending upon the imagination of the group. I had spoken about phrasing and sliding around a note or a beat, like Billie Holiday and Louis Armstrong. I couldn't get very technical about what bebop was doing in response to the big bands of the '40s because I wanted them to hear bebop rather than say too much. I had simply run out of time.

No time to answer questions. I was ushered out by some "leading cadre" and whisked into a car to be taken back to my apartment. No hanging with the students.

When I got back to my apartment, I sat in the dark smoking, drinking a glass of whiskey and still buzzing from the excitement of speaking about music that nurtured another dimension of my soul, my spirit. An obsession with the creative force. The well of humanity and imagination. The ironies of that particular creative enterprise. Jazz. Its roots in Africa, the tortured and creative African experience in the Americas. The complex rhythms. The deep rivers of influences. West African, Cuban, Latin American, European classical and folk music themes. All this while listening to Erroll Garner bang out tunes from his *Concert by the Sea* album. I hadn't played him for the students because I had to make impossible choices, and he was considered a bit schmaltzy by some.

How crazy I was to have attempted this. Was I perceived as spreading degeneracy? That's how the government tagged this musical tradition. But then why would they invite me?

On the third or fourth sip of whiskey, I also began the regretting game that booze and music sometimes induced. I regretted that I had given up playing the piano, imposed when I had moved from Victoria to Vancouver into a little apartment in a fourth-floor walk-up in the West End. Mum had paid for shipping my piano on the ferry. But there was no way this old upright could be wrestled up the stairs. There it was, out on the street...at night. My soulmate. A pleasure object that had absorbed my loneliness, my teenage libido, my jealousies, my happiness, my broken heart, my desire for fame, two to three hours a day for the previous six years. Practicing daily since the age of five and taking all those Toronto Conservatory exams. The moving company paid a hundred bucks to take it away. It was like having my hands cut off and my heart cut out.

Erroll Garner. "I'll Remember April" was my favorite on the album. I was inspired to get the sheet music after hearing his lush piano style in ninth grade and then remembered my frustration that I had been taught to sight-read music rather than feel my way through chording, to play by ear. Garner may not have been a jazz great, but I just loved how he massaged a piano, his phrasing and all the grunts and murmurs that the microphones caught while he was playing. To push oceans of sensations through people's bodies, transfix their very beings, to heal souls by playing music. I could not think of anything more satisfying.

Then came "They Can't Take That Away from Me." I changed my mind. That was my favorite on the album. I was soaring with nostalgia, lost opportunities, happiness...it was all a muddle. I was drunk.

ON JANUARY 25, 1981, the judges at the trial of the Gang of Four finally passed down their sentences. It would take a couple of days for the details to reach us. And I made no notes other than it had finally concluded. In letters home, I reported some of what today can be garnered from Wikipedia.

Sitting in my Manhattan home in October 2013, I can Google the Gang of Four trial and find this from Wikipedia:

> As the trial went on, Jiang became increasingly defiant. On December 24, after the Chief Judge summarized the charges against Jiang, she suddenly stood up and loudly accused the Chief Judge of being a "fascist." She claimed that "the real purpose of the trial is to vilify Chairman Mao

and the great Cultural Revolution initiated by Mao." Obviously she was "defending" herself by cloaking herself in Mao's mantle. When the Judge reminded her to "rationally" defend herself, Jiang became even angrier. "This trial is only a show trial. I do not bother to defend myself." Jiang then announced that it would be "more glorious to have my head chopped off" and dared the court to execute her.

On December 29, 1980, after the testimony of forty-nine witnesses and the showing of more than 870 pieces of evidence, the trial finally came to the end.

Summing up the case, the chief prosecutor acknowledged Chairman Mao's "great contribution" to China, but also noted that Mao was responsible for the "plight" of people during the Cultural Revolution. He argued that the Gang of Four (particularly Jiang) cannot escape punishment by raising Chairman Mao as a "shield." He then cited some remarks of Mao in 1974 and 1975, trying to demonstrate that Mao disagreed with the Gang of Four on many issues. He then demanded the death sentence for Jiang.

Upon hearing this, Jiang immediately began to shout, "Revolution is glorious! Revolution is no crime!" Again, she was dragged out of the courthouse.

On January 25, 1981, the sentences were handed down. Jiang and Zhang were sentenced to death with a two-year reprieve. Wang was sentenced to life imprisonment. Yao received a twenty-year imprisonment sentence. There was no appeal process.

I suspect this Wiki entry was submitted and reedited by Chinese Communist Party editors. Letting Mao off the hook is the clue.

ONE SATURDAY afternoon, around the time of the trial verdict, Ming called. I broke the hiatus from him by inviting him over for dinner the following day, a Sunday. As he settled into one of my armchairs, he said he was depressed and talked about the breakup with his girlfriend. Again. She was a medical student and he had been broken-hearted for a year.

"I don't understand. She has such a cold heart. Now all my classmates are going away on their vacations to their girlfriends' parents' house or to travel, and I don't have a girlfriend."

He was pleading for sympathy. The Spring Festival vacation was looming. Like Christmas and Thanksgiving combined, emotional pressures were building to be part of a family and—I was learning—be with a friend, beau, girlfriend, fiancé. I couldn't say "lover."

"My friend, Sung, is going to his girlfriend's house for Spring Festival. I'm all alone."

Somehow this felt pathetic. His whine did not arouse my sympathies. Our usual disjointed conversational pattern unfolded. He suddenly picked up my book about the Rastafarians.

"What does it mean?"

It took me about an hour to explain some simple things about Jamaica, Haile Selassie, making music about world revolution and smoking weed. Wild thoughts, I imagined, for a high cadre's son.

He told me he had been studying for exams. Our conversations always took these wild turns. I believe it came from the exhaustion of trying to comprehend not only the language but also quantities of radically new information.

"What do you want to do after graduation?" I asked. "Will you teach?"

He screwed up his face when I remembered the Mandarin word for "teach."

"I do not know which *danwei*. Work unit."

I tried to imagine what he might do if he were in the US or another economic system with his particular set of talents. At least, how I understood them. Stand-up comic? Real estate developer? Car rental agency manager? Sales rep?

I told him I wanted to go to Mongolia and Tibet. He sneered.

While sipping tea and wolfing English biscuits from Hong Kong, I delicately tried for a little conversation about economics, since that was his major. "I think the new economic policies are a bit confusing. What do you think?"

He nodded his head in agreement slowly. As if a vocal answer might have been picked up by bugs in the room.

He squirmed with discomfort, so I went to the bathroom and turned on hot water in the tub. Perhaps I wanted to wash away the boredom and cut to the chase. We left a trail of watery footprints to my bedroom. I wished it were a path of rose petals and romance. Instead, we lathered each other in lotion, as much to prevent our skin from cracking from the dryness as for foreplay, which still partly eluded him. My dictionary didn't include the Chinese word for sex or foreplay, so it was impossible to talk about it. I wanted to think it was unnecessary to talk anyway. That somehow I could guide him through the erogenous zones and their pleasures. I mischievously speculated—to myself, of course—whether I should introduce him to spanking or tying up.

There was no love or even tenderness between us. It was as utilitarian for him as for me. Each in our own self-absorbed, clutching need to satisfy what was throbbing in our bodies. For a moment, we could transcend our separate selves to merge in an intense state of being. Eros. Thanatos. Dying briefly together. Again. And again. And what should I have made of the fact that he continued to call me "his Chairman"?

After Ming left that night, my mind roamed through my Beijing life. I realized I no longer had separation nightmares. I had somehow let go of at least parts of my New York life or built a hard shell around it. And there had been a breakthrough of sorts in my reflections on this experience. I now understood that this distance, navigating a journey far from my own culture, from my comfort zones, this immersion in a society and culture so foreign to my own, had been vital to excavate who I was and where I came from. It forced me to struggle with all the big organizational schemes, concepts and values—socialism, capitalism, democracy, individualism, communalism, independence, freedom, along with the public and private parts of life.

On a personal level it was a confrontation with surveillance, mistrust and puzzling denial. I tormented over how to understand character and personality here while realizing for the first time that I was shaped by my Canadian roots to trust, be open, curious, empathetic and cheerful. My American years had pushed me to be engaged, radical, critical. My forays to Haiti and Mexico had complicated my sense of history, injustice, beauty, the human spirit. New York had toughened me. Taught me about irony and the hurtful aspects of competition. The profound loneliness together with the quest for social connection in Beijing had driven me to some strange and sometimes dark places. I was still discovering, still plunging, diving deep.

Two days later Ming called.

"I cannot meet you again."

He had memorized and rehearsed this in English.

"Dangerous," he said. "*Gambus*—high cadre leaders—say. I cannot meet you," he repeated.

I was surprised that my first reaction was not concern for his safety but rather relief that we would stop using each other. I knew that he would be fine. Even with his naughty boy streak, he had too much self-interest to get into trouble. And highly connected parents.

I should have been deeply troubled that he had been warned away from me. Two days before, Zhu Yi had run away when he saw me. Yung had canceled our calligraphy classes. The Deng line was solidifying. I had no control. It made my heart feel like a block of ice. Yet about Ming I was wistful. Anthropology lessons were over. My stand-up comic gone. I was nobody's chairman now.

Children's used book stall, Xian, 1981

Chapter Thirteen

Solitary Walker

梦想蜜桃，邓布下新策

Secluded meditation, the study of nature, and contemplation of the universe force a solitary person to search with tender concern for the purpose in everything he sees and the cause of everything he feels.
Jean-Jacques Rousseau, Reveries of the Solitary Walker

January 28, 2014, Oaxaca, Journal:

I am near the end of two glorious months in Oaxaca, Mexico. My cell phone is loaded with attempts to record the kaleidoscope of nature's palette here in the Sierra Madre mountains. The high desert and tropical flora in the garden push my serotonin levels through the roof—biznaga and prickly pear cactus, agave, palmetto, and Huaje *trees—that give Oaxaca its name—with their delicious pea pods. Flor de mayo and pomegranate blossoms are breaking open. Closer to the house, dozens of succulents and violet trumpet vines, along with technicolor bougainvillea, are all carefully cultivated by Virgilio, who arrives with his burro bearing firewood from higher up the mountain. The only urban sound comes from the emergency siren of a little red Honda racing around the mountain ridges delivering fresh tortillas. It has been an inspiring retreat for studying Spanish, hosting old friends, making new ones, soothing my arthritic joints and remembering, reflecting and writing about a faraway place in another era.*

It's also the dry, dusty season throughout Mexico. Early this morning, on my daily hike up the dirt road into the mountains, a neighbor teased me about "come el polvo"—eating the dust. Back at my desk, I flip on a CD of Chavela Vargas, and while she cries out a song of melancholia, I muse about my heart's history and another dusty place I visited more than three decades ago.

ON THE first day of the New Year's holiday in February, 1981, my train pushed southward and westward from Beijing, exposing a monotonal landscape of grey and beige and brown. Was all of central China the color of baked mud? Well, in winter, anyway. Homes were built into the clay hills. Cave houses. They said they were cool in summer and gave protection against wind in winter—and they were cheap. Like those sod houses on the Canadian prairie that my mother told me about. Studying the moving vista out of the train window, I remembered the mythic stories of Depression-era Saskatchewan that were fed to me, along with Grandpa's sops—torn, stale bread, butter, boiling water, pepper and salt—and I wondered what kinds of stories parents and grandparents here reworked and repeated to children with their grain porridge. All the while, I was listening to the tunes blaring from the train's crackling speakers. I knew by now that they were either patriotic or sentimental. And although I still could not interpret most of the words, I had grown to love their sounds and musical themes.

I was nibbling from the tin of *kim chi*—pickled vegetables—prepared by one of the comrades in the office who grew up in Harbin, near Korea, where her husband was born. She had brought it to the office for me the day before I left for "the long train journey." Thinking about this surprising act of kindness, I ruminated about my comrades and the change in the weather at the office. The temperature plunge in mood and attitude toward me since the turn of the year contrasted with this thoughtful gift. The enigmas of China.

I had visited Eleanor before leaving, taking her a Chinese New Year's gift, wanting to let her know that I was venturing out on my own. In her book-crammed apartment, she sat statue-like at a table by the window. Winter light highlighted the landscape of crevices on her wrecked face as blue cigarette smoke encircled her body. She seemed suitably impressed and, I suspect, a tad envious. She was no longer physically capable of adventurous travel. And besides, she would not contemplate it without the Party organizing the trip and some collective accompanying her. My self-initiated, self-organized effort perhaps reminded her of a dimming independent past.

The Foreign Experts Bureau organized all travel for us aliens. From local excursions to the Great Wall to monthlong summer journeys to another province. Friends who had taken their longer trips said they were well intentioned, meticulously planned. All too controlled, too paternalistic for my taste. I could not imagine group travel. I wanted to be free to discover for myself. To get lost. To change course. To meander. To encounter.

I had always been a lone ranger, a "solitary walker," in Jean-Jacques

Rousseau's sense. He wrote about a series of rural walks at the end of his life in 1778, when he was in his seventies, in exile, when his friends had deserted him. He understood that the solitary impulse was the desire for self-understanding.

I had no idea about these essays when I was living in China. I came across them when researching the life of Mary Wollstonecraft for a screenplay that I wrote about her, many years after returning to New York. But I identified immediately with her embrace of the concept. It went back to my childhood. I was an only child. From the age of six, I walked at least a mile home from school by myself to an empty house. Latchkey kid. On those walks, I learned to observe, smell, touch, explore, deviate, reflect, dream and evaluate safety. Once in the house, I created an imaginary universe.

I had been a solitary walker in every city I lived in across the North American continent. And throughout Mexico. A *flâneur*. Breathing in the visual and aural sensations of a place while considering new experiences yet acknowledging one's essential loneliness and yearning for connection.

Perhaps I saw this solo trek to Xi'an in early February 1981 as allowing me the distance to consider the ice flow that had overtaken the hallways at Radio Beijing. As I looked back over the months since I had arrived, I remembered an initial polite and pleasant reception, but it had turned more aloof and cooler as the weeks and months wore on. I was convinced it was because they were reading my letters. Then, after Deng's speech on December 25, the comrades had become bone-chillingly distant, yet with tiny cracks of kindness.

Before leaving for Xi'an, I tried querying Eleanor about the current climate of relations with my colleagues. She always—always—defended whatever the policy dictated. I had grown weary of her apologetic stance. Was she simply being cautious with me? But then why did I think she would be any different than the comrades at the office? She had adopted China as her home. She had lived in China through all the anti-intellectual movements. How did she manage to escape persecution? Or did she? Did she know that her apartment— like those of all foreigners—was bugged? Or, my worst fear, did she mistrust me? Did she, too, suspect I could be playing dual roles in Beijing? One, as North American broadcast journalist, the other—spy?

The weekend before my journey, I had purchased a cornucopia of sweets, mandarin oranges, fancy dried fruits and little favors that seemed to be the fashion for New Years to make a gift bag for each of the young children of my English department comrades. Professor Li had compiled a list of some twenty children. I wrapped each packet in red and gold paper while sampling far too many of the candies.

On Monday, I delivered the packages to my coworkers, thawing the ice a tiny bit. That evening, while I was washing dishes in my bathtub and sorting through the clothes to take for my five-day journey, a comrade suddenly appeared at my door.

"Where's my gift?" she demanded.

I had seldom seen this woman, I did not know her name and her child must have been missing from Professor Li's list.

"I have a five-year-old son. Where is his gift?"

"I'm terribly sorry, it's an oversight," I said, stalling for time, glancing at my food supplies, "and I'm not sure I have enough treats to make up another package."

She wedged herself into my apartment and waited. As I excused the mess and offered her a seat, scrambling for a solution, I felt increasingly indignant. I could never have done that. But I didn't live under her circumstances, and I guessed she wanted as many treats for her son as possible. But, still, I was irked by her behavior. This was what thirty years of socialist ideology had led to?

I pushed a little bag of fruit into her hands and wished her a Happy New Year. She said nothing and left. At least *she* wasn't afraid to pass the guard hut and show up at my apartment alone.

As I mulled over this minor drama, I realized how ignorant I had been when I had arrived here, swollen with my 1960s fantasies and the mission to search for the New Socialist Man or Woman. What the past six months had taught me was that almost every kind of character type familiar to me as a Westerner was evident here as well. The selfish, the selfless; the greedy and envious versus the fair, modest and kind; the moral and generous contrasted with the ambitious, opportunistic or unethical. Only the braggart was missing. Shakespeare would feel inspired. What a fool I was.

As the prospect of their New Year's vacation loomed closer, the comrades were exhibiting increasingly giddy behavior. I assumed that for them it was time to be embraced by family around the preparation of elaborate meals. There would be luxurious days outside their deadly workplaces—a vacation from Party bosses, political shuffling and jockeying for favors. My solitary travel plan was incomprehensible to them. Their questions and warnings about my traveling alone grew more pointed.

"Won't you be lonely?" asked Fan.

"It will be dangerous. Aren't you afraid?" Liu Hui shook her head.

"How will you manage without speaking Chinese?" asked Oxbridge Zong.

"You must be very, very careful," warned depressive Chen.

"Hooligans are everywhere," said Professor Li.

Meanwhile—despite the general aloofness at the office—during the week leading up to the New Year holiday requests from the comrades and trades people at my building were ratcheting up. One of the car drivers for Radio Beijing wanted a gallon of cooking oil—a highly rationed commodity—and offered to drive me to the Friendship Store. I was incensed. I had never once used the Radio Beijing cars to go to the Friendship Store. In fact, whenever I really needed them in a pinch, they were never available. The drivers were always on their long lunch break or sleeping or having dinner. I always bicycled or took a bus or hired a "private" taxi. I felt resentful that I was being asked to do this favor for a class of workers who were already more privileged than my colleagues in the department. I acquiesced and bought two gallons of oil. One for Chen and one for the driver.

Then the electricians in my apartment building wanted me to purchase cartons of cigarettes from the Friendship Store for them. When I delivered the contraband, one of them struggled with some English questions.

"What economic class—you—in United States? What think Marxism, Leninism, Mao? Why not married?"

More pertinent questions than fell from the lips of any of my comrades in the English department—so-called intellectual workers! I can't remember how I responded—we didn't share enough of the same language to do justice to his line of inquiry. And the situation was rushed. I must have said something about my dismay at the policy preventing authentic relationships between foreigners and Chinese because of what the electrician said next.

"We are now friends. You can come to my parent's house and not hide who you are."

I was flummoxed. *Right*, I thought to myself cynically.

"Thank you," I said politely. "I would like that."

He then disappeared, never to be seen again. Was he reassigned? Punished for talking so freely to a foreigner? Was my room really bugged? Or was one of the people with him that day a Party informant?

ON THE train winding to Xi'an, I was booked in a "hard-sleeper." Second class. I had insisted with the Foreign Experts Bureau that I did not want first class. Instead, I wanted to be in the section with eight sleeping berths to a unit and a seating area. Open. Co-ed. It would be a twenty-two hour journey with my travel companions. I had been assigned an upper sleeping bunk with a PLA soldier below. A father and his son were opposite. Everyone was studying English. None had ever spoken with a native English speaker before, so there was an eagerness to practice. Shyness and boldness. Restrained excitement.

"How tall are you?" the young boy asked.

"Why are you traveling alone?" his father wanted to know, the question that I now imagined was on every Chinese person's mind. All these years later, I cannot fathom how I answered at the time while fumbling through dictionaries.

I had been told by other foreign experts that the only place in China where the Chinese would talk freely with us was on the trains. No bugs? No Party snoops from their work unit to rat? I was enjoying the pressure to flex my beginner's Mandarin, to look up words, to listen more carefully.

I was already censoring my questions. I didn't want to frighten them or raise suspicions that I might be a spy out to steal state secrets. I stuck with the easy stuff: "Where do you live? Your age? How many children? Where are you going? What kind of work do you do?" I was soliciting boring facts. Of course, I would have rather been asking them what they thought of everything. About the trial, about dismantling the communes, about the New Democracy movement, the elections, the new movies addressing wounds of the past. Too dangerous. But also beyond my vocabulary to understand their responses.

My travel companions struggled with the fact that I was Canadian but lived in the US. I was enjoying the Chinese in ways I hadn't before. We all seemed to be electrified by the opportunity to learn about each other.

In the night, I woke slightly to discover the PLA soldier tucking in my wayward blanket. In the morning, a child tried to sneak some oranges into my basket while I wasn't looking, and another young PLA soldier gave me a chunk of his precious tea leaves. It was the first time I saw how tea was compacted into large discs and broken off in little chunks for brewing. These acts of kindness made me feel guilty for doubting that the New Socialist Man and Woman existed. But, then, I didn't see them making those gestures to each other.

The first day on the train the chef came to check three times to see if I would like something special for dinner. While I knew I was receiving privileged treatment, I felt I could never suffer from neglect in China. When I indicated I liked chicken, he reappeared to ask how I would prefer the chicken to be prepared. The young train attendants were more interested in my boots—as always.

Strangers on a train. When I tried to reciprocate the generosity of my traveling companions by offering to buy them a beer for dinner, they all refused. The old problem. They could not take anything from a foreigner, although nobody presented it that way. They were also all shepherded to the dining car separately from me. When my meal was cooked, I sat alone in the dining car. Segregated again. The only foreigner, it seemed, on the train.

I complimented the cook. "*Hen hao, hen hao*," I said. Very good. Very good.

He politely responded, "*Bu xing, bu xing.*" Don't mention it. Not so good. You are too generous.

He disappeared, and I was left clinking my chopsticks. Drinking my beer. Making notes in my journal. Isolated. Privileged. Solitary.

Back with my fellow travelers, I sat next to an army doctor who spoke a little more English than the others. Plump. Forty. Just two years older than me, she was traveling from Beijing to Chongqing to celebrate the New Year with her family. This was her first opportunity to speak English since studying it in middle school. As I calculated, that would have been before the Cultural Revolution. We did our best to share our family histories.

She told me her husband—also in the army—was in Philadelphia for a year studying heart transplants. I wondered for a flash who would have access to new hearts in China, given the need to use the "back door" to gain entry to the hospital. Her sister lived in San Francisco and her brother was getting an engineering degree somewhere in the Midwest. She was vague about the details.

"They make those choices," she struggled with English. "I choose to stay."

She had two teenage sons living in Chongqing with grandparents, which might have explained why she stayed behind, although she worked in Beijing. Her eyes searched mine as if to see if I understood what revolution and political upheaval did to families and love relationships.

We sat close. Smiling. We looked up words in the dictionary feverishly and searched each other's faces for clues, as if there was information in an expression that could not be found in words.

Exhausted by the effort, for a while we sat silently. My mind traveled to the things unsaid. Veiled histories. Imaginary conversations. Thoughts about what we would need to know, want to know, about each other, the trust we would need to cultivate to become real friends. A gradual sharing of stories and ideas, doubts and desires, frailties and regrets.

What music would I play for her? Would we trade chicken recipes? I wondered what she would think of my '40s-era vintage dresses, like the one I wore to the Christmas party. She was wearing the standard People's Liberation Army uniform in that tropical green with the vermilion details. The pants and jacket were padded against winter's ruthlessness. Her officers' cap rested on her bunk. Would she be butch to my *femme fatale*?

Finally, my mind rested on the question that I always wanted to know about her generation. What happened to her and her family during the Cultural Revolution? If she was forty now, she was twenty-six when that movement exploded. Perhaps she was in medical school. That's when her sons were born. Did she participate? Was she persecuted, or was she a persecutor? Or both? Was she ever expected to deny medical care to victims?

But I had already learned to restrain the impulse for that line of inquiry. Given that members of her family had made it to the US and seemed to want to stay there, I assumed she was in the dreaded "black" category. They would have been victimized by their class backgrounds. But what did I know? Nothing. And I could not ask.

Now her round face was beaming at me. Perhaps she was trying to communicate something more intimate. I told her I was unmarried and had no children. I had learned to quickly follow that information with some explanation. This time, because my work was demanding—long hours, I mumbled.

Through a sympathetic smile, she whispered, "You are free."

I wanted to hug her—it was the first enlightened response to my situation from a Chinese person. And it would be the only time that any Chinese acquaintance suggested that my single status might have had merits. Or was no better or worse than any other situation.

I would be getting off the train before her, and if this had been elsewhere in the world, we would have exchanged addresses, phone numbers and promises to keep in touch. But we didn't. I knew that once she was back at her work unit in Beijing, I would not be allowed to contact her or see her.

IT WAS before dawn when I trudged my way out of the train station in Xi'an. I felt like I had been catapulted into a war zone. A cacophony of explosive bursts, like machine gun fire, flames leaping, thick smoke interrupted by spraying sparks. Clusters of rowdy teenage boys roamed the streets. Were they drunk? They were igniting long ropes of firecrackers. Some stoked scattered fires. Their kinetic bodies, padded against the cold, twirled like menacing shadow puppets, flickering silhouettes against the blazing orange haze. Faces momentarily flashed with light from the flames. This was the prelude to New

Year's Day. The sun wouldn't rise for several hours.

As I aimed into a black void beyond the fires, my knees were shaking. I was afraid for the first time in China. There was not much consolation in having memorized the crude map in the guidebook and the dot locating the foreigners' hotel when the route ahead was a dark fog, a daunting black hole. Was I making a bad move? Was my solo travel luck going to run out right there and then?

The comrades' warnings ricocheted in my brain: "Watch out for hooligans." My shoulder bags were heavy, and my boots had cowboy heels. No real mobility if there was trouble.

I stopped to ask a youthful couple directions to the hotel, hoping beyond hope that my Beijing-accented Mandarin pronunciation was intelligible here.

They kept me headed into the dark abyss while fireworks rang in my ears. My heart thumped as I stumbled down uneven pavement that I could not see beneath my feet. A little further on, I queried another huddled group because I distinguished a woman's face. She physically recoiled as I asked her directions, perhaps out of fear I couldn't see in the murk. Her reaction frightened me even more, since she seemed to be wearing an army cap and was with two others. One of them looked to be a man—impossible to be sure in the dark. And I was a lone woman in this ghostly scene exploding with a cascade of blasts, releasing smoke, but no light. They confirmed the direction to the hotel on my mental map. I kept pitching forward in an ever-darker, more sinister landscape. No streetlights anywhere, the fires receding behind me.

I was startled by whispers in English and Chinese. Someone on a bike was following me. His voice sounded middle-aged. His indistinct murmurs meant the same in any language—you knew it was sexual and desperate. I tried to ditch him by walking more briskly, but he seemed to know where I was going, and the turnoff was even more deserted. Suddenly, some teenage kids appeared. They also followed me. Maybe they would be a foil. Safety from the desperado. They'd check him. But what were their intentions?

Finally, I saw the dark hulk of another Soviet-style fortress—the Friendship Hotel—behind foreboding iron gates. Padlocked! Now what?

I shook the huge gate and called out. The kids called out as well. They weren't trying to kidnap me after all. And the desperado had disappeared. Eventually, a sleepy night watchman emerged from the shadows to unlock the gate, his pace unhurried, and led me across an unlit, spooky courtyard to the equally eerie—and padlocked—hotel. I rattled the door gate and called out again. Eventually, I heard the somnambulant footsteps of an attendant.

Once in my cheerless room, I dropped fully dressed on the bed but awoke in a few hours. The sun was up. New Year's Day! The fears of the night before had melted with the brilliant light at the window. I was excited by the prospect of new adventures. The hotel was deserted, like the Friendship Hotel in Tianjin, with its ambiance of an abandoned prison. Was I the only guest? Too bad. No flirtations in the dining room.

The sun was blinding. To a background of torrential eruptions from firecrackers, crowds ambled in the streets, strolling aimlessly, faces and bodies relaxed as if time had stopped. Pubescent girls were showing off bright padded jackets in a riot of orange, peach, red and pink. Younger girls sported red beads, colorful bows in their hair and red dots in the center of their foreheads. A sign of happiness.

Children looked ready to burst with their beet-red cheeks. Some with rashes. More skin problems were evident here. Contaminated water?

Peasant entrepreneurs pushed bikes festooned in brilliant colored bits of paper, dripping with psychedelically colored toys, decorations, fireworks and candles on long sticks. A rapturous vermilion blasted everywhere. The town backdrop of grey and beige highlighted the foreground of eye-popping color. I bought crimson candles and trinkets to take back for the comrades' kids.

After seeking out the Drum and Bell Towers, I headed for the other highlight in the guidebook, the Shaanxi Forest of Stone Steles Museum. Just as at the museums in Beijing, the educational information was disappointing. But the effect of thousands of steles—vertical stone tablets, like headstones in a graveyard—was powerful. Their potency was magnified by their covering of ancient calligraphy commemorating famous people, history and poetry. I mourned my illiteracy. One young chap was copying the ancient style of calligraphy in a notebook. Another was making a rubbing on rice paper—a pre-Xerox approach to making facsimiles. He spoke some English and explained that he was copying a Daoist philosopher's words.

"Desire is root. Cause. Make suffer," he claimed.

While pondering that thought, which could have as easily come from a Christian text, I met Harry, a German. He had overheard this young man's translation and indicated that in his guidebook it described Daoist philosophy as believing in no gods, no rules. The young man nodded his head in agreement, identified himself as a student and seemed eager to communicate with us about the ancient wisdom written here.

Suddenly another man—a little older—appeared, and the young student quickly gathered his paper and rubbing stone and disappeared. Plainclothes police here, too? Shades of the Mt. Tai experience with Yuan and Judy. Like that time, this plainclothes policeman dissolved from the scene like a fade out in a movie.

Enlightenment opportunity gone. Back to Harry.

He explained he was an engineer working with a polyester plant outside Beijing. I found his uncritical support for China surprising; then he admitted that the "workers do stuff when they decide. There's a lack of strong management." Given the situation at Radio Beijing, I found this surprising. Again, I was reminded of the difference in working for a sensitive propaganda agency so close to the center of power.

Harry was staying at a fancy hotel newly built on the outskirts of Xi'an and offered to pick me up the following morning to visit Xi'an's famous archaeological riches. Harry was rather remote yet generous to invite me.

He had a guide and driver. The next morning, we visited the imperial tomb of Qin Shi Huang. Now—more than thirty years later—this tomb is world famous. Pieces from this excavation circulate around the world's major museums, drawing the biggest crowds ever recorded at the British Museum.

In February 1981, the excavation was at its early stages. Local farmers had discovered this mother lode of Chinese funerary archeology in the mid-'70s while digging for a well. The life-sized terracotta warriors, cavalrymen, each unique in features, dated back to 200 BC. It was the archaeological highlight in China and the draw for a fledgling foreign tourism.

As usual, the didactic material frustrated Westerners. Guides could only describe its measurements—not its cultural or historic significance. Maybe there was no agreed-upon take or analysis. The guide-book claimed that Qin Shi Huang was the first ruler of a united China. That might have competed with Mao's legacy.

During the three decades since my visit, extensive digging has revealed an entire army along with many other nearby sites of funerary objects. Dying big. In 1981, the excitement was just beginning.

We proceeded to the famous Huaqing Hot Springs built at the foot of Mt. Lishan by an emperor in the 700s to bathe with his concubines. It gained fresh significance for being the location where Chiang Kai-shek was captured in 1936 by a former warlord and forced to join in a united front with the Chinese Communist Party to oppose Japanese imperialism in China.

Passing through villages as we returned to Xi'an, I photographed bicycles with hanging rows of red cellophane lanterns about to tip over from their wares. Old men with wispy grey beards and baggy, watery eyes shuffled along, slightly bent over, hands clasped behind their backs. Their traditional padded black pants were tied tight at the ankles, and their cotton-insulated grey jackets were tied at the waist with thick fabric scraps twisted like rope. Most wore little black beanie caps under big beaver-skin hats. Some squatted at the side of the road while dragging on long skinny pipes with tiny cups, their dirty, long fingernails stained brown from years of smoking homegrown weed.

Harry moved on, and for three days I wandered the streets of Xi'an alone, periodically perusing the guidebook, which claimed it was the capital of eleven different dynasties and at its peak, a thousand years earlier, it was the largest city in the world. Not Angkor Wat? It didn't matter. The streets were more engaging than this question of history.

Travelers somehow like to think we are the first foreigners to gaze upon a place, when centuries of wanderers, particularly in Xi'an, have scribbled journals and letters from this place, one of China's oldest cities. Here the Silk Road began, which for centuries was an artery of cultural exchange between East and West. I kept expecting to see a camel caravan emerge from the dust, bearing incense and myrrh.

In the northwestern part of the city, I discovered the Hui community. This minority neighborhood looked poorer, dirtier and funkier. Streets were not constantly swept as in other parts of the city. Smells of earth, animals and manure entered my brain. Goats were tethered in front of houses. There was little of the otherwise ubiquitous blue or green uniforms. Men wore white crocheted Muslim caps. Young girls revealed pierced ears.

I picked up an entourage of some twenty-five kids who followed me as if I were the Pied Piper. As if I were the most exciting thing to happen in the neighborhood for at least an hour.

Passing food stands offering raisins, sesame seed candy and walnuts. I stopped at a street vendor to sample a stew made from dates, raisins and spices. Definitely not Han Chinese ingredients or flavors. No one objected to photographs.

There were more food carts here than I had witnessed in Beijing. At one I bought roasted beans. A little farther along, I perched on a bench to eat a deep-fried unleavened bread while at least thirty faces—mostly belonging to kids—crowded around to watch me make it to the last bite. Unlike Beijing gawkers, this audience wanted to engage, with smiles and giggles. Most likely I thanked the vendor too enthusiastically and complimented him the wrong way while wishing them all Happy New Year—in my rough Mandarin. More smiles and laughter.

Then, just as I turned a corner, a mosque loomed with hundreds of men, all ages, filing in for prayer service. White cloth skullcaps. They had very different facial features than the Han. As I marveled at this visual thrill, a man at the door beckoned me in. Would I be breaking sacred laws? But he kept motioning me to enter. A strange sensation, since there were no other women there.

Such an exuberant display of religion shocked me. The minority scripts at Radio Beijing had never mentioned this. When my pageant of children refused to quiet down, I left quickly. In my awkwardness, surrounded by boisterous kids jockeying for positions close to me, my roasted beans fell to the ground and the children took great delight in picking them up. Every single one. I would have left them there, but they insisted.

As I wandered to the main west gate on the other side of town, I lost my parade of Hui kids. Were there invisible boundaries separating Han and Hui ingrained already in young children? Before I could analyze just where that boundary might have been, my camera tugged me toward a different set of kids—all Han, I suspected—sitting around a little open stall featuring used children's picture books laid out on the ground and watched over by an older, kindly looking man. Kids perched on miniature stools, arms draped around each other's shoulders, engrossed in well-worn books. They were so focused that they never noticed me. Nor my camera.

On my way back to the hotel, mellowed by the late afternoon light highlighting the raw beauty of this ancient capital, I felt...happiness, yes, happiness. I remembered Virginia Woolf's comments on beauty and happiness: "Too much beauty for one pair of eyes. Enough to float a whole population in happiness if only they would look." Did the locals see it or feel it anymore?

After four days of wandering, noticing, photographing, I concluded that the provinces looked funkier and looser than the streetlife in Beijing. Even the body language was more relaxed outside the capital. Young people looked punkier, as if Lou Reed had recently performed there, breaking through the black market diet of cheesy Hong Kong disco and Taiwan schmaltz. I saw one young kid with back-combed, sprayed hair. I decided to do a photo series on young men's hairstyles.

Young women wore shoes with elevated heels. Men sported long hair, mustaches, turtlenecks, Western collars and jackets, tight pants, bellbottoms and sunglasses. Of course, in Beijing, they wore sunglasses at night. In Xi'an, just as in the capital, they all studied my shoes. Who was observing whom? I wondered, *When personal cameras become more accessible in China, will the Chinese be photographing Westerners' footwear while the outsiders document their coiffures?*

On the train back to Beijing, I mulled over the conflicting lessons of traveling alone. There were the obvious advantages: I could absorb unhindered and control my schedule. I could try to be discreet. I could observe, uncorrupted by a travel companion's reactions, desires or needs. When traveling with somebody else, they become the focus, not the world beyond. Alone, I was forced to engage with a strange world. I could marinate observations and experiences. But the final result was profound loneliness. There was no one with whom to share the experiences. Nobody to bounce off the insights, nobody who would laugh, cry or wonder with me. Nobody to question my interpretations. Nobody to linger with over a meal at the end of the day.

Mexico had tested me to the limits. In a society structured around family commitments and gatherings, I was the only person sitting alone in a restaurant during Christmas and New Year's. On buses, in the streets, at hotels and restaurants, I had to be so careful, so nunlike that I felt like I was inhibiting my personality, my outgoing, expressive style in order to disappear. To not attract unwelcome attention. To not signal the wrong impression. Of course, with my big mop of red hair in any dark-haired country, I could not exactly melt into the wallpaper.

In a Zona Rosa café in Mexico City, a young, conservatively dressed Mexican woman approached me to say—in English—how envious she was that I could sit there alone. Impossible for Mexican women in 1979. When I invited her, a stranger, to sit and have coffee, she graciously declined, bought a cake and left. After four weeks and seven provinces of Mexico, I became so lonely, so bored with myself, that I was eager to return home.

I was evading the language issue. If I were fluent in Spanish or Mandarin, how different these solo explorations would be. Layers of texture, digging beneath surfaces, excavating meaning from conversations with strangers, allowing myself to be a *flâneur*, available for the next story to unfold, being able to tell jokes. But would anyone really linger in a long conversation with a single female in her late thirties traveling alone without assuming certain possibilities? In Mexico, men gathered in public places, not women. My ass was pinched in the best neighborhoods. Hands were all over me in the subway. Perhaps I was fantasizing about the doors that might open with fluency. Perhaps I would need to slam those doors shut.

But at least in Mexico I had the opportunity to take up with American and European male travelers whom I understood and envied for their freedom to explore with abandon. Despite invitations to join their journeys, I decided to keep true to my solo mission: learn, watch, listen and absorb a culture through my pores. If I took off with one of them, that might end.

Besides Harry, the German engineer, the only foreigners I met in Xi'an was a small group of Tanzanian students. They were studying at a local university and had a woeful tale to tell about their Chinese girlfriends, who had been arrested and sent to jail for dating these outsiders, Africans. We commiserated about this absurd government policy, and I carried on.

Arriving back in the capital, everyone looked rich, a bit fleshier and refined. And I resigned myself to a life of diminished expectations.

FOLLOWING THE New Year's Spring Festival vacation break, the social climate at the office grew even more severe. I could barely arouse anyone to listen to my Xi'an impressions. Ron said that a friend from People's University claimed there was a new instruction to reduce contact with foreigners after Spring Festival. Apparently, the leader of Beijing University had been dismissed for not being tough enough on student demonstrators and critics. The newspapers had been ordered to stop printing so much criticism of Mao. Voice of America reported that yet another editorial in the *People's Daily* argued against freedom of speech and the press.

I faced a fresh stack of dismal scripts.

My only salvation was a notice from the post office that I had a parcel. The following day was my birthday. *What could it be?*

After bicycling back from the post office against powerful headwinds and coal grit, I dashed into the apartment and ripped open a package from that Other World. Audiocassettes! A note explained that my dear friend, Karen, had hosted a party two weeks prior for my birthday and passed around a microphone to record the madness.

I poured myself a whiskey and sat back to devour four hours of a celebration with New York friends. The microphone captured all the natural peaks and valleys of any party—at some moments engaging and hilarious and at other times forced and a bit boring. The crucial essence of each person was revealed. I loved it. Matthew made rum punches. Erin reported on culture, always focused on what Lou Reed was up to. Beth took the microphone into the bedroom to relate something personal. Merle made a witty anchor; his wife, Danielle became sick and retreated to lie down. Karen fended off Merle's teasing advances. Both howled with laughter. Bonnie described the endless deterioration of social programs under Reagan. Some hogged the microphone, others shied away from it. Matthew and Karen argued about Judy Chicago's Dinner Party installation. I knew the situation, the people, the talk so well, but it sounded so far away from my life here. Then the morning-after chit-chat between Karen and Beth. Self-reflective, intimate, ruminating on love, life, work and politics. I named them the Love Tapes. I wept.

Returning to the English department, I shared a packet of glitter from Matthew. Comrades took turns showering it on everyone who entered our little office. They weren't sure whether they really understood it, but who could resist the magic of that look? And now there was glitter stuck to the heavily worn floor boards at Radio Beijing.

The next night, on my actual birthday, Ron organized a dinner party that included a whole lamb with a flower made from a gigantic radish bursting out of its neck. About thirty people were there—foreigners mostly—playing music on my boom box, dancing and singing. It was a good time.

Other New York friends had sent packages of cassettes—blues, jazz, punk and John Lennon. My big problem was how to control the uneven power supply for my cassette player in the late evenings. There were jolts of 240 volts, maybe even higher at night, so I plugged everything else in to suck up the juice. Who could listen to Bessie Smith or Billie Holiday at double speed?

February 24, 1981, Journal:
The BBC reported this morning that Prince Charles was engaged to Lady Diana Spencer. Canadians will all be yawning at this news while the Americans will be giddy with delight. A new fairy princess!

In late February, I worked at home for a few days to escape the freezing, cave-like conditions at the office. I had some heat at the apartment. At night, I was reading voraciously—from Victor Navasky's *Naming Names* to Solomon's *Chinese Political Culture*. From the Chinese classic *Dream of Red Mansions* to Husserl's *Phenomenology and the Crisis of Philosophy*. All stacked beside, around and in my bed as a bulwark against Beijing mind rot. This project was only possible because I had no TV or telephone.

The larger challenge of trying to understand the contemporary political and social landscape of China limped along. One evening, a neighbor dropped by to ask if I'd heard the rumors of big character posters. One outside Radio

Beijing the previous week attacked the Central Committee and praised the Great Proletarian Cultural Revolution, accusing folks now of the Liu Shaoqi road; in other words, the Capitalist Road.

Meanwhile, there were still indications that some workers and students were pressing for a little more democracy at the grassroots level. But since Deng's "Christmas speech," there was evidence the Party was pushing back for control against strikes and students who won elections. The students tried to bypass party approval, which triggered warnings in the press and speeches about anarchy, Western decadence, the importance of discipline and socialist democracy—not bourgeois democracy—and lots of heavy-handed propaganda about uplifting cultural production.

Also, new economic experiments—the closing of some factories, dismantling the communes, trying to let market forces guide—were creating uncertainty and anxiety. It was unclear what the social and economic fallout would be.

The famous Red Star Commune, just outside Beijing, once had a thriving business producing tractors, necessary for mechanization of agriculture. Since the new policies, they could no longer find customers. The government used to take care of that. Their old customers could not afford their tractors because the government used to subsidize them, so the factory closed, and they were lucky to find a few local orders for metal chairs or some other small product. This information came from a young Texan friend, Paul Rice, who worked weekends on the commune. He reported that many male commune workers were beginning to contract out on day jobs in the cities.

We outsiders predicted that economic chaos would be part of the transformation until a solid direction was worked out. The plan—part market system and part state control—had to be unsettling, even if beneficial in the long run to increasing the standard of living and implementing modernization at a faster pace.

How all this felt to the peasants, who still seemed to do the bulk of their work by hand, was the litmus. Common opinion seemed to indicate that rich peasants were doing well while poor and middle peasants, as well as factory workers throughout the countryside, were eking by.

February 27, 1981, Letter to Karen:

Well, honey, it's 9 on a Friday night and it don't mean nothin' and I'm sittin' here listenin' to my arteries harden and my skin crack.

Finally stopped drinking coffee and persimmon tea and hit the 75 cent bottle of Chinese wine that the kids drink. The music tapes you sent have been played at dawn as I stand at the refrigerator with my sweatpant leg shoved up to my knee and my big wool logger's socks hanging loose around my ankles, my mascara still smudged under my eyes, my hair bunched around my head, my mouth feeling like a tar pit, and I stand listening to that phrase in Debussy that I once used in a video piece about the landscape artist, Rackstraw Downes, with his painting of redwood trees in California. All the while, I'm eating yogurt from a little crock, knowing it's not low-fat yogurt and that I've gained so much weight from the volume of oil and sugar in the food here. And what will I do? But, yes, music does restore.

Tonight, the wine I'm drinking comes in a Coke-sized bottle with a cap on it, and it's called Pu Tao Jiu Mei Gui Xiang, and I have little idea what that means—and I've been here seven months. I oscillate between periods when I'm ravenous to learn Mandarin and other times when I'm ideologically resistant. I've been defiant this week. It comes from a pretty obvious realization. I understood it in the beginning but seem to need to relearn it. That all my so-called Chinese friends are friends because they all want to leave China. So this week I'm resisting learning Mandarin and feel generally cranky.

I wondered if I could ever bridge the world I come from with the world I'm trying to understand here. I'm so determined to try to understand the Chinese. How they "eat bitterness," control feelings, avoid conflict...then explode and persecute each other. I've been here more than half a year and have little idea about their concept of a friendship, a love relationship, of community. Being in a family or group versus being an individual. But maybe I am absorbing that information in unconscious ways.

Then there is the puritanism. Today, a friend visited a reform school where the young girls were in there for "promiscuity," and the director kept rapping away about hormonal imbalance, and I got very frightened as I listened to this.

Now I know why a Chinese acquaintance told me not to drink this wine. In the space of one page and two glasses, I'm in a stupor. So the question is whether to go to bed or make coffee or keep writing in a stupor. Somehow I need an uninterrupted flow with you. I wanted to show you how I was keeping up with things in the world by referring nonchalantly to the uproar at Cambridge University over structuralism and English literature. I don't know why I have been following it with such zeal. I guess because it's so remote from my concerns and needs here. From the concerns of a billion people. Never thought structuralism would provide escape!

Well, this bloody wine is slurring my typing, so I think I will have to return to this after sleeping it off.

February 28: 12:30 p.m. Letter–continuing

Just got back from my half-day Saturday at the office. Two people were getting haircuts at their desks, most of the others were gossiping in the hallways, so I read the special Time *issue on "American Renewal" aloud to two of my women friends here, the Sri Lankan and French foreign experts at Radio Beijing. We are all bummed out. Is there any unified opposition developing to what's going on over there? Nuclear commitment, defense budget increases, cuts in social programs, aid to El Salvador, increased concentration of Big Business, waiting for the disintegration of Marxism–Leninism in China?*

Meanwhile, I'm impressed by how much some of the Time *stuff sounds similar to the current Chinese direction. They spoke about the need to make higher education a privilege rather than a right. That is exactly the Chinese situation now, as opposed to the initial idea of the Cultural Revolution, which was to make higher education accessible to workers, peasants and soldiers. Now only two percent get to go to university and, as you can predict, they are mostly the sons and daughters of high cadres—few peasants or workers or soldiers. Grading and the degree systems have just returned. People who were trained during the Cultural Revolution are all being reexamined, but they are given several chances over a couple of years to catch up.*

I have been fantasizing about a trip with you. I am weary of traveling alone. We must see Yunnan together, then the old Silk Road route out to Xinjiang. Gobi Desert. Depending on your resources, we could do Inner Mongolia and Hainan Island in the far south. But we have time to work on that. So save your pennies, and I'll have to cook up something outrageous. I have no money. We can go as tramps.

Your devoted friend, Gail

Street food entrepreneur, Xian 1981

Chapter Fourteen

Microphone Dream
麦克风之梦

When it's in a book I don't think it will hurt any more...exist any more. One of the things writing does is wipe things out. Replace them.
Marguerite Duras, *The Lover*

It was the beginning of March, and the bleakness of winter lingered. Smog smothered the city for days, like a gigantic hair shirt only to be ripped away by freezing winds slamming sand and coal dust into our faces. I could not seem to separate the outdoor gloom from the social doom at the office. Combined with the austerity of my love life, loneliness deepened and spread. Like layers of geological strata, these physical and social realities weighed on me, compressing my spirits. I felt as if the lifeblood had been sucked from my veins as I was left to observe the onslaught of age and degeneration. A kind of mummification. Winter, with all its associations with death, kept pushing me further into despondency. My only remedy was to play my blues collection obsessively.

Otis Spann—"Ain't Nobody's' Business If I Do"; Big Mama Thornton belting out something with Muddy Waters; Albert King's "Born Under a Bad Sign." On the first Sunday morning in March, I turned up the volume, louder and louder, as if enough decibel levels and the right song could exorcise the demons, eradicate the dreadful malaise of the colorless, cheerless place that I could not understand. I was relying on this music to pump blood through my veins. Louder and louder, Otis Rush, "Gotta Be Some Changes Made"; Son

House playing bottleneck guitar; Howlin' Wolf's harmonica wailing on "How Many More Years." At full ear-pounding, head-cracking volume, I no longer cared about my neighbors. I needed a fix from my world, however troubled and disreputable that world was. I wanted the culture that spoke to my spirit and my mojo. Then, from guilt or compassion, I turned it down, mellowing the mood. It was as if I had built to an orgasm and then settled into peace.

On this particular Sunday, while these paragons of the blues resurrected my spirit, I was tidying my apartment and heating up canned spaghetti sauce. The big, handsome singer from the Army band, with a voice like Paul Robeson, was coming over with Judy and Yuan so he could listen to American songs that he might like to incorporate into the repertoire of the troupe. I had met Yulian at the pre-New Year's Eve party at the *People's Daily* Institute.

B. B. King was moaning "The Thrill Is Gone" when they arrived at the door. Yulian had a look of dismissive disdain while listening to both King and Sam Cooke singing "A Change Is Gonna Come." Why is it that the Chinese had such difficulty with African-American music? I had witnessed their racism toward Africans. Toward anyone with darker skin. Was it a class thing? Dark skin in China was associated with peasants, country bumpkins and minorities who supposedly lived in the Stone Age until the Han brought them civilization. Wasn't the revolution about overthrowing class advantages and prejudices? All that talk about the Third World. Did all that fail?

For Yulian, the blues were like Peking opera.

"Artists, intellectuals and young people do not like Peking opera," he explained with Yuan translating. "It feels too rough." I had heard a version of this complaint at my bues presentation for Radio Beijing staffers.

Of course, Yulian's negative reaction to the music that had just restored my psyche sent me plummeting again.

I switched and put on Horowitz playing Chopin—a crowd-pleaser—and, predictably, Yulian liked it. Chopin's etudes provided background while I mixed the spaghetti sauce and pasta, all the while delivering an indignant lecture about the significance of the blues and my suspicion about why he didn't like the genre.

Silence. I shook Parmesan from a canister and sprinkled pepper on top.

During the meal, Yulian showed off his mastery at eating slippery spaghetti with chopsticks. I tried for some levity.

"It's been a universal conundrum," I teased, "whether Marco Polo brought noodles to China via spaghetti or whether he took the idea back to Italy. Along the Silk Road."

I don't recall his response, but I do remember that the conversation then took a strange twist.

"Although my work unit is the song troupe," he said, "I am writing a TV script about an American spy lady, and now that I have met you, I understand how to write it."

I scrunched up my face and threw my hands up in the air but let the comment drop since we were working through layers of translation. I wondered if he said it to satisfy the bugs in the wall.

After Chopin and spaghetti, I played a trio of songs by Nina Simone, "O-o-h Child," then "Need a Little Sugar for My Bowl" and, finally, "I Wish I Knew How It Would Feel to Be Free." Judy and Yuan had a lot of fun trying to translate. I wasn't sure that the *double entendre* or the spiritual aspects were being interpreted that well.

"I like," Yulian beamed. He wanted to hear "O-o-h Child" again and began humming along with it.

I could see and feel his seduction by Simone's voice. My mood transformed. Now, despite my earlier crankiness about his reaction to the blues, his vigor and enthusiasm melted my defenses. His physical presence electrified my apartment.

When he left, he took the hallway phone number and invited me to a party the following Saturday afternoon. He could not really believe I was a spy, could he? If he was teasing, I loved the humor. The promise of spring! I had a pulse again!

WITH THE special adrenalin that pulsates from anticipation of a flirtatious gathering, the following Saturday I followed Yulian's markings on my map and bicycled to the end of a *hutong* in the Dianmen district. He was waiting outside. Seeing him again stirred something within me. He was a bit larger than most Beijingers—more compatible to my size.

Inside a rundown traditional courtyard, Yulian guided me to a modest-sized room crammed with beds, dressers, chairs, a desk and a small table. A violin case sat on top of a closet. His friends were rearranging themselves on chairs and beds to make a place for me to sit. I was introduced to two women singers, Li and Liu, as well as Liu's daughter. Two of Judy's students were there to translate.

Li's husband was not present. Zhao, one of Judy's students, was also married, but her husband was absent. Yue, another student translating today, said his wife could not be there. There were two other performers in the troupe whose names I did not catch. They too were married but without spouses that day. When I made a comment that most of the husbands and wives were absent, they giggled and someone piped up, "Yulian's wife, too!"

Yulian explained through an interpreter that he had been separated geographically from his wife for seven years. He saw her once a year for twelve days. They had two children, four and six. He had never lived with them. This was not the context to ask probing questions about their arrangement. At this "party" of married folks without mates in attendance, I stuck to questions about the house.

"Was this the home for one family?" I asked, sweeping my arm toward the courtyard.

"A prince once lived here," somebody said in English.

"No, a rich family—only rich would have so much room," Yue clarified.

"Aren't you afraid to invite a foreigner here?"

"Our neighbors are easy. They do not gossip," Yue translated for one of the singers.

I could not figure out what the gathering was really about. Most of them were in the army song troupe. My cynical self wondered if this had been organized to ask a favor of me. What would it be?

Yulian had described it as a party. Then why were so many mates missing? Had these couples all been separated by the Cultural Revolution? Or perhaps mates were home with children. Why hadn't I queried Judy's students when I had the opportunity to interview them about the effect of separation on married couples? Relationships torn apart by the Cultural Revolution—reeducation farms in the countryside, sent-down youth, labor prisons in remote regions or simple banishment to specks on a map far from Beijing. Some got stuck in the countryside. Some had decided to stay. Some married local folks, then worked hard to get back to Beijing. Did the comrades at this social event have more in common with each other than with their mates in distant regions? Were they more independent? The absent mate might give them cover for a more promiscuous life. Do they have romantic affairs with each other or other married—yet separated—folks? Or maybe I misunderstood the stress of needing to have one person shopping for food, caring for kids and doing errands while the other was involved in some kind of "party"? But some mates apparently lived in other cities.

While those questions pirouetted in my head, the singing began. Except for the translators, each one performed a different song. They all had good voices, but Liu's daughter was the most remarkable. They wanted to know if Americans would like their music. Finally, I knew what my expected role was. I tried diplomacy.

"In the US, people don't generally like high-pitched voices. Just as Chinese don't seem to like rougher, rawer, lower-pitched American voices."

Despite this critical difference, everyone agreed that music was the universal communication.

Like my experience in other local apartments, they had jerry-rigged a table between two beds so we could sit and eat from an array of plates loaded with peanuts, sliced meat, bean sprouts and shrimpies that poof up like popcorn when heated up. There were thin, crêpe-like pancakes and a pickled raw cabbage and carrot dish. Raisins, candies, tea and strong liquor.

Because of the size of the group and the need for everything to be translated, the conversation jumped around between simple comments and questions. Then I raised the issue of restrictions on relationships between Chinese and foreigners. Everyone agreed that they wished it were different.

We talked a bit about children's schooling. They worried that they needed connections to send their kids to good schools. Because journalism students were translating, I asked them about the press.

"The Beijing Evening News has changed since the end of last year. No longer critical," said Zhao.

"Government policy changes as quickly as the weather," added one of the singers, providing a tiny glimpse of Beijing humor.

After dinner, they put on a disco cassette and I was expected to dance. My other role. *Was this my true mission in Beijing? Dance instructor?* Eventually everyone tried. But given the awful disco selection I encouraged a change and a tango cassette was quickly produced. We all watched as Yulian and Zhou articulated a rather formal and stiff tango. I wondered what her absent husband would think of this. Intriguing that this dance about desire, anger, remorse, passion—some say a struggle between a pimp and his prostitute— how this dance was allowed to flourish in puritanical China. I had seen couples practicing under trees in the park, but somehow it felt passionless. Whenever I had asked about the origin of ballroom dancing in China, the response always referred to Zhou Enlai. "He was a good dancer." As if that explained why the tango was OK and rock 'n' roll was not, even though there was much more touching in tango. I was impressed that Yulian could dance reasonably well, however restrained.

As we sat and watched another couple tango, Yulian discreetly handed me a large envelope. Peeking inside I saw his photograph and pre-addressed envelopes. How brilliant. Why didn't Ming figure that out? The photo was signed "student and younger brother," which meant that he knew my age. I thought we looked fairly similar in age. Had I aged so much here? Or was he using "student and younger brother" to be safe in case the package was found by the wrong person. So many unanswered questions.

I wanted to talk to Yulian but could not without an intermediary. Yue, one of Judy's grad students at the *People's Daily* Institute who had been translating all afternoon, finally wanted to talk to me for himself.

"The students miss you," he insisted.

Would I ever be able to change jobs here and work at a university? What a contrast with my radio colleagues.

Calling me "Miss Gail," he wanted to talk about working on an English-language newspaper in the US.

Meanwhile, I stole glances at Yulian, noticing the special energy—remarkably un-Han—that oozed from him. He appeared to be watching me and kept trying to sit next to me. Was he just teasing or was there a hint of a possibility of a romantic affair? There were so many misunderstandings with no shared language, and we could not easily contact each other, despite his stamped, self-addressed envelopes. Besides, he was married. But what kind of marriage was that? Twelve days a year!

It was a cold, misty night, and Zhou and Yue bicycled with me partway home. They shared a joke about the tradition of hosts walking their guests home, then the guests walking their hosts part way back home. We laughed about the endless back and forth, prolonging the social time and obligation. I adored this aspect of the culture and wondered what it would take to discover all the sweetness here. Two lifetimes of Mandarin studies, I suspected.

Continuing on home alone after Zhou and Yue peeled off, bicycling in the frigid and damp air, I reflected upon the mysteries submerged in the "party" with the mate-less song troupe members. Then there was Yulian's desire for physical closeness, his flirtatious facial expressions while studying my reactions.

On the final leg of my cold journey home, I mulled over the gumbo of events of the previous week.

Ron and I, along with a couple of other foreign experts, including Eleanor, from the Italian department at Radio Beijing, were extras in a restaurant scene for a movie about a Kuomintang soldier who returned to the mainland to bury the ashes of his buddies in their native soil. The movie's ideological angle indicated a new softening toward Taiwan and the aging Nationalists residing there.

The movie shoot should have fulfilled a lifelong desire. Ever since I could remember, when teachers or schoolmates asked, "What do you want to be when you grow up?" my response was immediate. Movie Star.

From the age of nine, I hounded my mother about how I could become an actress. My stepfather had a grade-five education and delivered oil to fishing villages, my mother did the books for a restaurant downtown. They knew nothing about acting classes or promoting my participation in school plays. I don't think either of them had ever been to the theater, and our lives were light-years away from Hollywood. But Marilyn Monroe was embedded in my prepubescent mind. In a sultry voice—at age ten—I would sing "Diamonds Are a Girl's Best Friend" from her movie *Gentlemen Prefer Blondes*.

Marilyn's image shaped my desires, fantasies and sense of inadequacies. Her story of being ordinary Jean who then blossomed into this luscious, creamy-lipped, *zaftig*—chunky—bombshell with a siren song offered a transcendence beyond my unglamorous working-class surroundings. It didn't matter that I was a crackerjack in math and science and showed promise in art and playing the piano—I wanted to be Marilyn.

Jump cut to March 1981, Beijing. I acquiesced to an "extra" role because I thought the scene was to be shot in the State Guest House, where Prince Sihanouk of Cambodia lived in exile, but it turned out to be the former Hungarian Legation, south of Wangfujing and down an alley across the street from the Friendship Association headquarters. Too late to cancel. I was already sashaying down the alley in a dress, stockings and high heels for a dinner scene.

The hero was dining with a friend at one table, and various things were going on in the background, including our part—foreigners having dinner. Ken, another foreigner, and I got the walk-off scene that required several takes. The director, Dong Kenan, a mid-fifties woman with a squat, chunky body and the voice of a Marine Corps sergeant, barked orders at everyone.

During dinner with her later in the old wing of the Beijing Hotel, she told us her story. She had joined the People's Liberation Army at fifteen, raised three kids and survived all the ups and downs of the various political upheavals, including reeducation in the countryside during the Cultural Revolution. In 1981, she was one of only six veteran women directors in the country, a fact that she rationalized was due to women's general weakness. While Ron and

I both did a double take, she explained that once she had to direct Chinese Navy ships and airplanes for a scene.

"When it was over, I was exhausted and had to go to sleep! A male director would not have been tired," she claimed.

To our obvious question.

"No, there was no discrimination against women. They just weren't strong enough!"

ANOTHER EVENING I was invited to join Simone from the French consulate, who hosted a group at the famous Minister of Commerce's Restaurant, so-called because it was where the Minister of Commerce used to freeload. He was exposed by a young cook, who then became a national hero and got elected to the District People's Congress. The minister and several other officials, who'd similarly been ripping the place off, paid up. A few of them resigned. Now there were stories that the restaurant was having all kinds of problems getting services, license and supplies.

"Just like Chicago," Ron said.

"The whistleblower cook," Janet added, "is now being ostracized."

"At last, a story I understand!" Ron chuckled.

As foreigners, predictably we were ushered into a private dining room. Siri and Robert were there. I had no recollection of the meal. Ron insisted it was one of the better meals we had that year.

"Not oily. Asparagus, cabbage, celery with almonds, jellyfish, two other fish dishes, green peppers with chicken. Bread rolls, apples dipped in sugar."

I remembered the good French wine.

After dinner, we all progressed to Siri and Robert's luxe apartment in the UN compound and sprawled ourselves over magnificent carpets and cushions—a legacy from Siri's stint in Afghanistan. As we listened to Afghan music, then Mikis Theodorakis and Billie Holiday, our conversation roamed the great cultures of the world and our concern for China's insularity.

Someone suggested we cook up a spring cultural event at the Old Summer Palace. We would call it a "happening" or a "fun festival" and encourage the Chinese to join members of the foreign community to make music, play cassettes, dance, sing. We picked a date.

Spring! Something to get excited about.

A FEW days after the curious party with Yulian's singing troupe, a neighbor banged on my door.

"Telephone for Palita!"

My Chinese name. Professor Li Shutian had taken my last name and tried to make something out of it in Mandarin: Palita, pronounced "paleeta." Extremely beautiful handkerchief.

I never felt comfortable with it. Should I have been insulted by his effort to translate my impossible Anglo name that way? Names were tricky, important, implying character. Handkerchief? Something to wipe yourself with? I wanted to be called "Big Red"—Da Hong. It was so much more dramatic and fun. I had been nicknamed "Big Red" by one of my first American friends when I arrived in San Francisco in 1964. But Professor Li kept squirming in his chair each time I suggested that name. He said it was slang. One of the women comrades whispered in my ear: "Women's monthlies."

What a horrible time to get a phone call. I was in my bathrobe; my hair in rollers, a mudpack on my face. To answer the telephone I had to go into the very public hallway next to the front entry of the building. My neighbor whispered, "Chinese."

"*Ni hao.*"

"I dream you," the deep, resonant voice said haltingly. Yulian.

Just as I was absorbing those magic words, my knees quivering beneath my bathrobe, several serious-looking high cadres from Radio Beijing entered the doorway. They looked at me in disbelief, eyes popping. I turned my back and looked down at my feet that were in logger's socks, drooping down to my ankles. How humiliating!

If I responded to Yulian in my pigeon Chinese, these officials would perk up and take notes. If I responded in English, Yulian would not have a clue what I was saying. So I thanked him in English, then in Mandarin. Quietly. Slowly. Then I carefully suggested he come to my apartment on Sunday afternoon for lunch. I said it in English until the cadres had passed and gone up the stairs, then I tried repeating the invitation in Mandarin. He understood, thank God, so I didn't have to yell it several times—the usual audio approach to Beijing telephones. No such thing as whispering sweet nothings. At least he understood. "Come. Here. Noon. Sunday."

He responded. "I. With. Fish."

I guessed that meant we'd cook fish. My facial mudpack had now cracked.

IT WAS a perfect spring day as I waited at the gate for Yulian to see that he was signed in without being tormented, harassed, arrested or sent away. He was carrying a fish wrapped in newspapers, along with scallions, cilantro, ginger and garlic. Probably blew his weekly budget for groceries.

Kind of Blue was playing on the cassette recorder. Yulian said he wanted to hear more American music.

"I like your blues and jazz." He must have rehearsed that as a way to make up for his reactions last time.

So this would be a seduction scene. Food as enticement, romance on a plate. Miles, Evans, Coltrane and Adderley providing the mood.

Yulian insisted on cooking the fish. There was a lot of nervous energy as we consulted dictionaries and I performed a charade indicating that he could wash the fish in the bathroom sink then prepare it on my coffee table. I cleaned carrots to boil.

He liked *Kind of Blue*, he said. I tried to explain who the players were and their significance to American jazz. To American music, period. But it required too much time and work. I preferred to listen to Yulian's voice. Its pitch seduced me. Resonant, deep, like molasses, perhaps leading me to think we understood more than we did.

While waiting for the fish to cook, Yulian drank a beer and I prepared my desk as a dining table. After much fussing with the final stages, we settled down to eat.

What did we *try* to talk about? *Try*. I so wanted a dialogue of souls, but out of nervousness we focused on food. I have a vague recollection of describing Nanaimo bars from Western Canada—or was it matrimonial cake? Our efforts to express ourselves and understand each other were like being underwater or as if we were talking through dirty screen doors. My metaphors to describe the communication haze changed every month. Talking with our heads wrapped in gauze. Something I had discovered was that people so badly wanted to communicate that we all said we understood when in fact we didn't. With Yulian that afternoon, there was the illusion of understanding.

Did I ask him about where his wife lived? About his children? How it felt to see them only once a year? Or did I avoid bringing them into this magical time? Did we talk about his history? I don't remember.

My memories of the afternoon are all sensory. The sun beaming through the windows on our faces. Al Green singing "Let's Get It On." Yulian's buoyant energy, his animated facial gestures, playful eyes and scent. Was it soap? While nibbling on chocolates, I tried to translate "Let's Get It On." Perhaps that's how we moved from my living room to the bedroom.

He was experienced. Stirring the embers of my deepest libido, he rekindled the fire. I felt like a phoenix resurfacing. A metamorphosis from deepest winter. It was like being in a Japanese movie where nobody talks and passion was everything. Unleashed, raucous abandonment, extended ecstasy. I thought I might explode into flames.

At one point we heard the voices of maintenance workers or guards, outside my ground level windows just as I had when Ming visited. More spying? Voyeurism? Both, most likely.

We shared a cigarette. Our skin flushed, energies spent. Should I have worried that we only knew each other's bodies, nothing of each other's lives? In the end, sex is rooted in the touch of skin and the mind; it is fantasy and anticipation, the spectrum of pleasure and pain, imagination and raw hunger and awkward postures. Maybe all chemical. Or, like all brain activities, it is partly electrical. The need to fuse with the Other. Find deep connection. Overcome death. Fuck history.

Yulian didn't hurry to get up. He took his time. He had confidence. And didn't seem to worry about the guard hut. Yet.

The next day, Monday, going to the cheerless office was like having to leave your warm bed and walk into a cold shower. Leader Zhang pursed her lips, stretched her head up higher and gave me a stony look. I could feel the tension as if it were a physical object in the room—making me feel so taut I could snap. They must have been reading my letters. Or they received a detailed report from the building peepers about what went on in my apartment behind closed curtains. And there was still not one mention of the change in government leadership. So much for information and journalism. Was Radio Beijing Plato's cave? Or was I Alice in Wonderland?

AT A meeting of our study group a few nights after my Yulian Sunday, the group focused on the debate around popular music, movies and literature— subjects that would normally engage me, but that night I became sidetracked by a facial gesture, a bouncing foot, a hand movement or any motion that might remind me of the luxurious pleasures of exploring another body and face. Of Sunday.

Someone reported that the *People's Daily* ran a series of articles about how comrades should assess the new pop music. The newspaper featured a debate about a vocal group called "New Stars," whose concerts at Capital Stadium had been a huge hit with young people. Apparently, one song that was very popular was about a PLA sailor lying on his bunk in a harbor far from home, thinking about how wonderful it was to serve the Motherland.

The debate had to do with the *style* of performance: the clothes, hairdos and the caressing of the microphone, which was thought to be too Taiwan or too Hong Kong. In other words, too influenced by the West.

Apparently, the *People's Daily* took the position that these performance styles were vulgar. That's what early critics had said about Elvis. I free associated. My first class speech in fifth grade was about Elvis Presley, who had just caused a continental sensation by gyrating on the *Ed Sullivan Show*. The cameras were only allowed to shoot him from the waist up. But he was the crack that allowed black performance sensibilities to leak into the white universe. Whites didn't understand that then. And I was only ten, after all. We had just caught the idea of sensual expression. Of rock 'n' roll. Of rhythm. Of playful sexual innuendo and energy.

I was thinking about that extraordinary cultural moment while vaguely hearing Neil Burton defend the phrase "decadent," as used by the Chinese.

"Art that is divorced from or irrelevant to the building of a socialist morality," he explained.

Would he always defend this political culture? What was socialist morality? Torturing and killing people you disagree with? Rejecting the body? Spirit? Expression? Of course, I kept all those thoughts to myself. I was thinking about Yulian's body. Muscular, smooth.

Ron pointed out that the relentless repetitious painting of the Yangtze Gorges, shrimp, goldfish, horses and bamboo should also then be questioned as "decadent." That went absolutely nowhere because we were in a roomful of people who either didn't think outside this box or were too polite to speak up. Or perhaps they were simply not interested.

Janet reported that the controversial film, *Sun and Man*, would be released after all, but with a different ending: they would drop the statement, "I love my country, but my country doesn't love me." And they would cut the image of the question mark in the snow at the end. Viewers would not know whether the hero lives or dies.

Again, Burton emphasized that these artists and filmmakers were not being criticized in the old sense. Not being sent away for reeducation—or jail. Well, that was progress.

I was regretting that I didn't ask Yulian more questions about his past, particularly his experiences during the Cultural Revolution. He seemed reluctant to visit that history. Perhaps it didn't inspire heightened sexual feelings. We knew nothing about each other. Perhaps that didn't matter.

SHI YUNG had stopped coming to my house for calligraphy classes. I suspected he was nervous about the new warnings regarding relationships with foreigners and didn't want any problems that could interfere with getting his passport and permission to go to art school in Chicago.

In 2012, Ai Weiwei, now China's best-known dissident artist, and international cause célèbre, produced a baffling sequence of bronze sculptures that have roamed the world's most prestigious museums—like D.C.'s Hirshhorn and the Tate in London—and public spaces—the Plaza Hotel gardens in New York—with great fanfare. They are called the Zodiac heads. Most Westerners who consider themselves up-to-date on cutting-edge art are clueless as to the layers of meaning embodied in these heads.

Weiwei's sequence of twelve heads representing the Chinese Zodiac—Rat, Ox, Monkey, Goat, etc.—are replicas of those originally designed by an Italian artist to create a water clock in the fabulous gardens of China's greatest palace, Yuan Ming Yuan. The Monkey spouted water between 3 and 5 p.m., the Ox between 1 and 3 a.m. and so on.

Sprawled over dozens of acres on the northwestern outskirts of Beijing, Yuan Ming Yuan, meaning "Gardens of Perfect Brightness," were once Versailles-like imperial gardens, five times the size of the Forbidden City. Hundreds of structures embracing both Chinese and European architectural designs were part of this stunning complex. Built in the late eighteenth century, it was the center of Qing dynasty power. China's Versailles.

But in 1860, during the Second Opium War, British and French troops razed and sacked the complex. It was their way of paying back the Qing emperors who had just arrested and tortured a delegation of British who wanted new concessions on their already-substantial imperialist occupation of China's ports. In retaliation, British and French forces not only destroyed most of the buildings but also looted much of the precious art and antiquities housed there, which then turned up in the Oriental collections of Western museums.

During the Cultural Revolution, these antiquities were denigrated or forgotten. But since the 1980s, the Zodiac heads have become the center of a controversial movement as China embraced its past and set out to retrieve its patrimony. Some of the Zodiac heads have been purchased back at fabulous prices at fancy auction houses in Hong Kong. Ai Weiwei is provoking us on many levels by replicating these heads. Which history gets honored when and how?

ON A hope-filled spring day in 1981, Ron and I decided to bicycle out to the former "Versailles" site, Yuan Ming Yuan, more popularly known as the Old Summer Palace. We didn't understand much about the intricacies of its history back then; rather, it was just one of the wilder places to reach by bike on a perfect day. Ruins were scattered about the vast park.

We met up with Janet and Yaping, who were test-driving their new Suzuki motor scooters. Our agenda for the afternoon was to work up plans for our April "happening," picking out a place at the park for its locus. We had decided on a date: Sunday, April 5.

As we scouted for the perfect ruin on which to center our event, Yaping recognized a friend picnicking with others. He was the famous actor, Shi Weijian, who played the lead in the provocative new movie, *The Legend of Tainyun Mountain*, recently banned. He was there with his wife and some friends. Ron and I had brought some things for a picnic, so we all joined forces. One of the women was a singer with the Peking Film Studio. She sang a lovely Chinese song. The actor's wife, it turned out, was a Peking opera singer whom I remembered photographing in her elaborate makeup backstage, unrecognizable here without the makeup.

There were two brothers—the older, a former army man, and the younger, a law student—who were with a young nurse. Although I did not know it that day, the law student would soon play a significant role on the stage of my Beijing drama.

After a while, Janet and Yaping scooted off while Ron and I were left to wrestle through veils with our few words of Chinese and their limited vocabulary in English, mobilizing lots of sign language. With theater people, charades seemed easier, more imaginative, more fun. Someone had a cassette recorder and disco cassettes. This led to some dancing before a guard showed up and shut our little party down.

Ron and I bicycled out of the park, deliriously happy to have enjoyed some spontaneous moments with locals. Our hopes for the "fun festival happening" were high as they all expressed enthusiasm about coming. Ron headed back to the Friendship Hotel while I bicycled the ten kilometers back to Radio Beijing, thrilled with the fresh spring air on my face, my endorphins blazing. I knew I only wanted to be around people in the arts. They were more relaxed and open, more responsive, eager for foreign contact. They laughed!

As I locked my bike at my apartment building, Xing, the building spy, confronted me. He had a package in his hand.

"This is for you. Someone left it for you. There's a letter inside."

As I took the box, I noticed it was opened.

"Why is this open? Have you no sense of privacy?!"

Xing didn't respond. I headed for my apartment, furious. Plopped in a chair, I studied the gift. A small Chinese porcelain figurine. Kitsch. There was a note inside. That, too, had been opened. Yulian wrote that he had just returned from performing in Tianjin and had come by with a friend. He promised to call this week.

That moment, I sat down at my typewriter and banged out an angry letter to the Foreign Experts Bureau about a whole litany of complaints regarding missing mail, opened mail, especially envelopes that contained photographs, subscriptions that never arrived, gifts from Guangzhou that never arrived, items that were taken from my apartment while I was away over Spring Festival, including my bicycle registration card. I would deliver the letter personally in the morning.

A knock at the door interrupted my fuming.

"Is it possible to love two people at the same time?"

Zheng Su, a fetching twentysomething, brimming with the desires and confusions of youth, had dropped by on this glorious spring evening that had been so ruined for me. I welcomed her intrusion as her presence reordered my emotions. Sitting in my armchair, sipping tea, she was here to practice conversational English, although her English was quite fluent already. I sensed she wanted simply to talk to someone who could not possibly report her comments.

She was a student at the Conservatory of Music next door to Radio Beijing and had come to my blues presentation in December. I was seduced by her radiant demeanor and sensibility immediately. For this first visit to my apartment, she was wearing tight pants and a double-knit acrylic turtleneck sweater over her tall, slender frame.

She had been telling me about her trip to Japan the previous year. "Everybody is rich. Women are more traditional than in China."

"And what did you think about the men?"

"I made a new friend. He has a Chinese parent. A few months ago he visited here. He'll come again." She blushed and giggled. "I like him very much." She wrinkled up her nose and eyes. "But do not tell anyone."

And this, after telling me about her boyfriend from the English department at Radio Beijing, who was now in Iraq. She wrote to him about a recent trip she made to Hangzhou to "play" with an old classmate. "Play" meaning "hanging out with the opposite sex." She also told her mother, who was critical about the plan and insisted she must go with cousins. So five of them "played" in Hangzhou. Her boyfriend wrote back that he would break the relationship if she saw someone else. Worried, he wrote to her mother as well, asking her to intervene.

Zheng Su's mother was the only woman orchestra conductor in China. Su brought tickets for a performance that her mother was conducting that week. She also informed me that my request to photograph her mother and her orchestra in rehearsal had been granted.

"I do not love my boyfriend. But I cannot find another boy who is suitable. He's quiet. He loves me."

"Quiet" was a signifier. We talked about people's caution, self-protection, what happened to folks during the Cultural Revolution when rats, or spies and informants, ruined lives by reporting a comment that might have been slipped in passing.

"I used to be talkative, laughed loud. I spoke out. Then I was criticized. Now I'm quiet and very obedient. When I was in the traditional orchestra, I did what I was told."

I could not figure out which parts of this history were before the end of the Cultural Revolution. But the comments stung me. I was stuck on the word "quiet." She had used it repeatedly. Were these comments meant to caution me?

Su revealed that she visited Wang from our department, the "quiet" bachelor who missed his chance to marry and who played the harmonica beautifully. I had discovered his hidden talent the day I brought a newly purchased harmonica to the office—part of my preparation for the blues presentation. Wang proceeded to play a soulful rendition of "Red River Valley." I wondered what his connection was to Su. Was he a musician? Was he persecuted during the Cultural Revolution? She said he was very smart and very kind.

"He told me you talk a lot!" That was a huge criticism and warning.

She seemed to know others in the English department well. She had been in cadre school—those rural farms providing reeducation through manual labor—with Zhou Hong, Liu Hui, Chen, and Zhao Dong, which meant she was a bit older than I thought. Late twenties?

Referring to one of the comrades, Su claimed in a gossipy tone, "She is competitive, jealous, always wanting to do well politically."

While Su knew some of my colleague well,, she didn't work with them. But her work unit, the Conservatory of Music, was somehow attached to Central Broadcasting.

We looked up "passion" and "communicate" in the dictionary. Then turned our conversation to music.

I told her about the Sheng rehearsal I had attended recently at the Conservatory. After Professor Li had commented that the blues reminded him of music played on the Sheng, someone arranged for me to hear a Sheng band. The Sheng was sometimes called a mouth organ, a woodwind instrument with multiple organ pipe-like tubes sticking up vertically from a mouthpiece looking a bit like a piccolo. The effect of the small Sheng orchestra was like hearing a dozen small pipe organs slightly off-key. Wild cacophony. And I loved it.

"It's music of the countryside," said Su. "Few people are interested in Chinese traditional instruments or music now, because during the Cultural Revolution that was the only music allowed." She wrinkled her nose while grinning impishly. "I would have preferred to study math or science, but during the Cultural Revolution, schools closed. I went to the countryside for a year and then was permitted to stay home and study with my mother. I studied cello secretly. The Cultural Revolution was almost over. Now I have the opportunity to study more in the conservatory."

"How many students to a dorm room?"

"Five or seven—or ten, sometimes! They all go to bed early. I stay up late until midnight. Reading or studying. I go to the studio. My piano is there."

I asked about her schoolmates. Were they friends she could trust?

"Some I only talk to about clothes, some for politics, some for love. Some for music. I have a couple of men friends at school. One who is very young and has suffered from a mean family. He puts his suffering into his music. The other one is the guy I played with in Hangzhou. I like him. But not too much!" She laughed nervously.

While she described her flirtations, I wondered if she was still a virgin. I did not feel free to ask her. There was something so fresh, so candid, so honest about Su that I wanted to embrace her. Sweet, smart and a little mischievous. She told me that young girls now wanted a man who had overseas Chinese relatives. During the Cultural Revolution, people were punished for having them.

"Now some young people are only interested in furniture."

THE NEXT day, I sent a thank-you letter to Yulian using one of his stamped, self-addressed envelopes. I expressed concern that he may have been harassed at the gate. Then I suggested he call me on Thursday night of that week between 6 and 7 p.m. to arrange for an excursion by bike to the Western Hills the following Sunday. Hopefully somebody could translate for him.

The following night, I rushed off to the opera that Su's mum was conducting at the Conservatory, tucked away in the middle of a Blitzkrieg construction project not far from Radio Beijing. There I met up with Ron.

The program began with *Little Red Riding Hood*, a Russian opera fairy tale for children by César Cui; it was composed in 1911 and first performed in Russia in 1921. In Beijing it was coached by a visiting music teacher from New York, Clara Roesch.

Next up was *La Serva Padrona*, translated as *The Servant Turned Mistress*, a short opera by Giovanni Battista Pergolesi from the eighteenth century.

Ron and I looked curiously at each other. Risqué for China, no?

The final selection, and the significant one, was a new Chinese work about Peng Dehuai, who was considered one of China's most important generals from the early Communist period, leading successful military campaigns against the Japanese and during the Civil War against the Kuomintang. Mao made him defense minister in 1954, but Peng became highly critical of Mao's policies during the Great Leap Forward, which resulted in Mao stripping him of all his positions. During the Cultural Revolution, he was persecuted repeatedly, suffering physical and psychological torture, then tried and sent to prison for being anti-Party. He died in jail in 1974. Deng Xiaoping rehabilitated him posthumously in 1978. In this new opera dedicated to his legacy, he was portrayed returning to his native village, celebrating his humble origins despite his great military leadership and accomplishments in creating the People's Republic of China.

This evening's program was a leitmotif for the current cultural moment in China. Very cautious in dealing with Communist history and permissible perspectives on that history, yet a tiny bit daring with foreign cultural product from the distant past. A cultural program still dancing on ideological shards of glass.

At intermission, as I was chatting outdoors with Su and some of her friends, I spotted Ming in the crowd. I hadn't seen him since he had called to say it was too dangerous for us to meet again. I smiled lightly and gently nodded. He was with a pretty young Chinese woman. He looked shocked to see me. His facial reactions were always uncensored, revealing, never discreet. This time was no different. Why so shocked? Because I was at such a "high" cultural event that only the privileged elites got to attend? Or because I was with Chinese acquaintances while he had been warned away from me? I would never know. But he obviously had connections to tickets to the most coveted cultural events for China's upper echelon. Perhaps he had the same curiosity about my access.

I was preoccupied with my concerns for Yulian and what might have happened at the gate when he delivered the gift.

On the designated day and time that I suggested Yulian should call, I waited by the telephone in the hallway near the front door of my building. It was a bit awkward, greeting neighbors as they came and went, but I did not want to miss this call. There was no call. Perhaps he did not receive the letter in time. Worse, perhaps the letter was intercepted. Perhaps he was not interested, but then he had brought a gift and encouraging note and said he would call. I had no way to reach him except by the address he gave me.

I could not go on like this. It felt like prison camp.

The next night, Zheng Su came by at 7 p.m. I offered her tea with peanuts and cookies. She just wanted to talk. Our conversation drifted to her mother's marriages, but all I could think about was wanting to be with Yulian. Why hadn't he called?

"The first was—rough? Is that the right word?" Su began to describe her mother's first husband. "He is uneducated. Has no culture. He is my father. He came to Radio Beijing to see me last year—offering me money. I refused. He is too rough."

If Yulian brought a gift, wouldn't he want to call? What happened at the gate? Was he approached and told to stay away from me?

"The second marriage was to a man twelve years younger. He is a violinist, and they met while they were both studying in Moscow together. It could never happen inside China. It was about passion. I think that's only possible outside the country. Now they hate each other." Su wrinkled her nose.

I thought of the passionate time with Yulian. Is passion forbidden in China? Did I even need to ask this question? Why couldn't I see him?

"Now she is married to a civil engineer."

A match of convenience?

"It's more acceptable for people in the arts to divorce and remarry. But still there is criticism."

Did that mean I could have a relationship with Yulian? Maybe he planned to divorce his wife?

"I have had an exhausting week," I said. "I am very tired. Perhaps we can meet another time soon."

I told her about our festival on Sunday, April 5. She promised to come and bring a friend.

Was that the night I had the microphone dream?

I woke up in the morning and realized I had never noticed a framed painting on the wall before in my room. I went to look closer and touch it. It moved aside to reveal a cubbyhole filled with a Sony cassette recorder and stacks of cassettes. It is the bedroom conversation recordings of thirty years of foreign experts living in this room. I am intensely distressed when I wake up, even though this is patently silly. Yet maybe not!

THE FOLLOWING morning, Saturday, I came home from the office at lunchtime and stayed close to the phone in case Yulian called or a letter arrived. Like high school. Waiting by a phone.

Nothing.

On the Sunday that I had suggested Yulian come by to bicycle to the Western Hills, he did not show up. And there was no telephone call. I lingered around my apartment, moping yet hopeful.

I was going to cancel my invitation to the home of Xiao Bai, a new acquaintance, but decided I needed the distraction after all. Besides, it was a beautiful spring afternoon, and the long bike ride across town and through a maze of *hutong* would be invigorating. My spirits were elevated a bit because Bai was handsome and an intellectual. But I was apprehensive, too, because he was so aggressive in pursuing me. He simply came up to me after a classical music concert where he somehow maneuvered to sit next to me, then bicycled alongside me, determined to follow me to the telegraph office while I sent a telegram to my parents, then proceeded to give me his address and invite me to his house.

Bicycling along Chang'an Boulevard, feeling the pleasant waft of spring breezes spill across my face, the freedom from winter's weight in clothing, liberating my body, drenched in that lightness of being, I came up behind a young kid on one of the new motor scooters. He was dressed very Western: tight designer blue jeans, nylon zippered windbreaker, long hair and sunglasses. He stopped at a red light. As the light changed, I was approaching, so I sailed past him on my bicycle just as he was revving up. I caught out of the corner of my eye that he looked at me, then swerved and suddenly I heard a crash. When I looked around, I was both frightened for him and amused. At first I thought he had hurt himself badly because he seemed to have lunged—forehead first—onto the pavement. But the scene was comical. Young, hip Chinese on trendy new motorbike takes nose dive when foreign devil redhead bicycles by.

I turned back to check the driver's injuries. Reacting quickly, he turned off his engine, stood up slowly, examined his hands and then wiped them on his pant legs. I touched his head and asked if he was OK. I couldn't say much more in Chinese for the occasion, but I noticed he had a number of scabs on his face, so this wasn't the first fall. Clearly he was embarrassed, and I scratched up one more new way to lose face—literally. And then I carried on. *Zaijian, zaijian.* Goodbye.

A few minutes later, as I was enjoying this salubrious ride, I heard his scooter droning behind me. This time, he slowed down at my side and voiced a "hello" in a very familiar—almost intimate—way. His rounded lips almost pursed for a kiss. Surprisingly, I recognized him. He was one of the young waifs who shoveled coal at Radio Beijing! I hadn't seen their faces for months, because all winter they had been enshrouded with padded coats, hoods and face masks against the fog of black dust as they moved all that ebony gravel around.

Here he was, in designer jeans, a windbreaker and a 700 *yuan* bike. Not bad for a kid who probably earned thirty-six to forty-one *yuan* a month. But what did I know about their salaries—and other means to make money? Perhaps, he, too, was a high cadre's kid. Now he motored along at my pace and talked slowly so I would understand.

"Do you want to eat with me?"

He didn't seem to care if other Chinese, like the thousands bicycling around us, saw him talking to me. We crawled along—close enough to converse—for a mile or so. I explained I was going to visit a friend.

"*Mei guanxi.*" No problem. And at that, he turned right at Qianmen.

How bizarre. He must have been twenty years old. I was old enough to be his mother! Hadn't he received the memo on the policy that kept tightening the straightjacket on foreign–Chinese relations? Or, more troubling, was I the subject of gossip and speculation at Central Broadcasting? A single, free-spirited woman from the Other Side who was entertaining Chinese men in her apartment. I passed his group of coal shovelers every day on the way to work. Were they all discussing my private life, which was really public? Deep down, I adored his brazenness.

As I headed through the maze of *hutong* to find Xiao Bai's building, I reviewed the circumstances of our meeting. Su had introduced us at the performance of a child prodigy violinist whom Su's mother was conducting. Xiao Bai had been wearing a Western-style suit and had a Hollywood smile and a well-fed face. Even though he spoke little English, he had insisted on following me to the telegraph office, giving me his address. I was both flattered by and suspicious of his aggressiveness. He told me that his sister lived in Chicago teaching Chinese. His parents were also teachers. He played violin. It took me two hours to figure out later with a dictionary that he was with the Coal-mining Performing Troupe.

After stopping a couple of times to ask directions on my map and turning into yet another *hutong*, Xiao Bai appeared around a corner to meet me as I arrived. He, like all the other local *Beijingren* I had visited, was surprised that I came by bike.

He took me up a dark stairway—always dark stairways—to his room and introduced me—to his wife. Pretty and petite, she put out a candy dish and proceeded to make tea.

Xiao Bai said they had been married for two weeks! If I had earlier thought that he was romantically interested, given his persistence the first night we met, I now realized I was here for something else.

Meanwhile, I scanned the single room of their honeymoon abode. About fifteen-by-eight feet. Double bed, closet, desk, table, two chairs, piano and violin, pretty curtains and bed cover. Not bad for a starter apartment here, given the sad reality for so many young couples still living separately for the lack of a room to share. Either Xiao Bai or his wife had Party connections. That fact depressed me as I thought about the desperation of some of my colleagues in the English department.

I complimented them on their apartment décor. Through our limited vocabularies and dictionaries, Xiao Bai communicated that he made the furniture himself—did I translate that right?—and the light fixtures came from a film company where he worked. Or maybe I completely misunderstood.

He invited another performer to join us, a violinist, who said his English name was Peter. He would interpret. At least, that was what I thought. Except he arrived not only with a dictionary and atlas but also a file of letters. I was going to have to work, I surmised. My mood flattened.

Peter was studying at the Foreign Language Institute. He spoke English well. He wanted to study in the US or Canada and wanted to show me a letter he was sending to schools. He wanted me to edit it. Advise him on what to say.

Is this why I was invited? They needed a letter edited? Did I begrudge their efforts, knowing how difficult it was, the competition, the limited resources? Should I have been ashamed that resentment was rising in my veins? I had grown not only cynical but selfish.

In the letter, he wrote about his family—his grandfather and father—who were esteemed in the medical field. He said more about his family background than about his own accomplishments. How very Chinese. How would I finesse the obvious piece of advice about that? How would I tell him in Canada and the US that higher education was ruled by meritocracy, not by who your parents were. Thirty years of Communist idealism and it was still *who* your family was, who you knew and pulling rank. But then, his age group had missed out on higher education during the Cultural Revolution, so perhaps he needed to prove he came from highly motivated stock.

I helped him edit the letter.

Next, I learned what Xiao Bai wanted. He reported that he starred in movies in addition to playing violin. He would like to have a film of an American city: freeways, buildings, nightclubs for the Xi'an Film Studio. They needed American movies for background scenes. Could I find some movies on VHS cassette for him?

It was not such a bad assignment. Perhaps I could wrangle something out of Don Murray or Robert and Siri, or Joe at the Canadian Embassy. They had TVs and presumably VCR decks and VHS cassettes.

I tried to explain copyright. "I'm not sure I can help you. I'll try."

"*Mei guanxi*," Xiao Bai responded. No problem. Second time today.

Another friend dropped by: Liang, a male dancer. He brought his wife and her seventeen-year-old sister, who was very pretty, tall, slim and had a long pageboy hairdo, wore a red sweater coat and revealed beautiful teeth when she smiled. She wouldn't eat a candy because it would make her fat. This was all new behavior for me to witness.

They wanted to know if I "liked" classical music.

"I'm not so sure it's about 'like,'" I ventured. "It's a huge canon with many periods and genres. I have preferences, of course." That took a long time to translate. "Jazz is America's classical music." I let that sink in for a while, knowing what a shocking concept it was for the Chinese.

When I told them that besides the piano I had also studied dance—ballet, modern and tap—they demanded a demonstration of tap dancing. I had taken it up again in New York and invested in good tap shoes the previous year. Of course, it was impossible without the right shoes. I was wearing sneakers. And there was hardly any floor space. Shuffle, shuffle, step, step. Heel, heel, step, step. Shuffle, hop, step. They right away put on disco music. I discouraged it.

They asked about my work in the States. How refreshing to have questions about my work history. Perhaps I had simply not been meeting the appropriate folks here. I found explaining the nature and significance of community-supported and publicly funded, noncommercial radio very difficult in this milieu where, everything was government funded, supposedly by the people, but in fact under hierarchical Party control and censorship. And how could I explain the eclectic programming of WBAI in New York?

"Women's consciousness-raising groups and live piano lessons on the air, documentaries about nuclear power, about immigrants—legal and not, teach-ins on regions of the world or wars, a story-telling festival."

Peter was struggling with the translation. Their eyes were swimming.

And given the propaganda style of Chinese documentary films, it was also challenging to enthuse them about that part of my history. They looked at me in silence or politely nodded after lengthy interpretations by the earnest Peter.

Peter and I did most of the talking. He was capricious and aggressive. He knew what he wanted. Xiao Bai's wife told him reassuringly, "You'll study in the US or Canada."

That was the confirming clue that the real purpose of my invitation to visit here was for Peter. Editing his letter to the universities. I now understood the obligations. Xiao Bai must have owed Peter a huge favor for something Peter had done for him. Perhaps it was this apartment. That's why Xiao Bai pursued me so aggressively to come over. This realization—although a profound lesson about the culture—made my spirits flag and my body sluggish.

Despite my growing disillusionment, I encouraged them to join us for the Sunday picnic at the Old Summer Palace. Then they offered to get tickets for me to the *Silk Road*, a production for which Liang was rehearsing. Reciprocity. This was the Chinese way, after all. Utilitarian reciprocal relationships of obligations and counter-obligations.

I was gradually absorbing the lessons of *guanxi*: I will scratch your back if you'll scratch mine. Slowly, painfully, I was learning. Perhaps it was not so different in the US. Canadian culture didn't work that way, did it? Perhaps I could have played with this form of reciprocity if I wasn't so emotionally needy. I was desperate for somebody to want to be with me just for who I was! Just for the delight of exchanging histories and ideas, stories and doubts, and all that stuff. It was only at Martha's that I had experienced that. No favors were asked.

They all came downstairs to see me off. My feet felt leaden on my bicycle pedals as I pumped homeward.

The following day I saw Lao Liu (Old Liu) in the foreign experts' office at Radio Beijing. Grumpy and sour, I complained about the situation at the front gate. About my packages and mail being opened. Subscriptions missing. About the lack of response to my letter outlining all that as well as missing items and windows opened. He did not respond to any of it. Only wanted to argue about my vacation time. All this through an interpreter, of course. Meaning everyone knew about the exchange.

I STAYED home for a day with depression. Yulian had not called nor come by nor sent a letter. It was a definite signal that my letter to him had been intercepted.

I felt bitter, unappreciated and increasingly frustrated with every experience and interaction with the Chinese. The comrades only wanted oil from the Friendship Store or letters edited for universities. Su, whom I adored, wanted to warn me to be "quiet." Yung, my calligraphy teacher, had been strangely distant.

My identity was shriveling. Creative work had always occupied a huge place in my sense of self. Along with a deep satisfaction from my work I had sometimes managed a love relationship. Both were absent here. Forget love. There was never any positive feedback for who I was. And I was discouraged that I was unable to report and write about all of this for NPR. I felt envious of everyone around me who was having more contact with the Chinese or making more progress with the language or enjoying the total experience. Then, I could not seem to name those others.

After seven months, my loneliness and emotional rawness had become an eddy gaining thunderous speed in its dizzying pull into a black hole.

The next night, Yulian called. It was brief. And very clear.

"Do not write," he said haltingly. "Not safe. Too dangerous. No can see you. Too difficult. Goodbye. Me sad."

Qing Ming Gathering at the Old Summer Palace, Beijing, April 5, 1981

Plain clothes policemen who shut down our event, Beijing, 1981

Chapter Fifteen

Honoring the Ancestors
敬拜祖先

July 16, 2014, New York, Journal:

Today I am rifling through a stack of small black-and-white photos on my desk. They were taken at the event that Ron and I dubbed the "Spring Fun Festival" on April 5, 1981. We had not originally known this was Qingming Day, an annual ritual that involved honoring the ancestors by sweeping their graves. Nor had we known until just before the event that the date also bore the gravity of April 5, 1976, when, after a huge outpouring of public mourning following the death of Premier Zhou Enlai, police arrested dozens of mourners and removed all the hundreds of thousands of wreaths and poems that had been accumulating in Tiananmen Square. The Gang of Four were behind the police crackdown. But within weeks they, too, would be arrested and what began as the Great Proletarian Cultural Revolution in 1966 was then officially terminated.

Ignorant of these signifying rituals, Ron and I had hoped for a free-form celebration that might have shattered the official barriers between Chinese and foreigners and bring us together to share food and drink, make music and dance. When I study the black-and-white snapshots and another dozen color slides of the event, I think that it looks like we might have succeeded. The photos indicate an impressive number of people showed up—foreign students, diplomats, UN'ers and foreign experts, along with many more Chinese. These images also reveal ruins of some of the remarkable pieces of architecture that once comprised the old Summer Palace when it was China's greatest temple to the riches of its rulers.

But the photos also reveal that Ron and I, when we weren't dancing, seemed to be scouring the crowd. Searching for our acquaintances whom we had invited. A few of them came and stayed. Most checked in and disappeared quickly. Later they explained: "Too many plainclothes police."

Surely enough, one of the photos captures a group of Public Security types. Unmistakable with folded arms and disapproving scowls.

Besides bringing drinks and oranges on our wobbling bikes, I brought a tambourine and maracas that I had found in a music store downtown and lots of music cassettes—from Haitian *compas* to reggae and disco. Someone from the diplomatic community brought a giant boom box. A couple of foreigners brought guitars. Ron brought his gong. Everyone brought food and drink to share.

We turned up the volume on James Brown, Sly and the Family Stone, Bob Marley and Aretha Franklin, and created a rhythm section with our instruments. Everyone was snapping photos, including the out-of-uniform police.

After several hours of fiesta—Ron remembered it as foreigners making music and dancing while Chinese mostly watched—a plainclothes cop strode into the group and ceremoniously slammed the "off" button on the boom box, breaking it in the process. It was a statement. Our effort to hacksaw through the wall that so unnaturally prevented the Chinese and foreigners from simply hanging out together was concluded dramatically. Like a Peking opera.

As we dispersed from our little "Beijing Be-In" to bicycle home, Ron and I came across another gathering in a clearing circled by trees of mostly young Chinese, including the sculptor, Wang Keping. He had joined us for some dancing but then disappeared. Here he was, listening to a series of poets reciting. Helmut, who was photographing, explained these poems commemorated the fifth anniversary of the Tiananmen incident after the death of Zhou Enlai. It made our Be-In effort look frivolous.

Helmut reported that the group of writers and artists clustered in the trees was fearful of the numbers of police around our "foreigners" event. Watching. Making sure West and East were not mixing. Perhaps we had provided a foil for Keping's crowd of dissident memoirists.

Wending our way out of the park, I wondered what it would take to really bring our worlds together. What would it take to effectively sweep the graves? To atone for Western sins committed here on these formerly royal grounds. To overcome the mistrust. Once again, I was compelled to remember the history of the US and the West in China, the US's bullheaded singular support for Chiang Kai-shek and especially the US response to the victory of the Chinese

Communist Party. To having backed the wrong horse. And refusing Mao's overtures. McCarthyism. Smearing the very Americans who were trying to get the US to look more critically at the behavior and ineffectiveness of the Kuomintang and learn more about the actual work of the Communists.

Vicki Graham reported on our celebration for the Associated Press. The *International Herald Tribune* even wrote it up. Hardly worth reporting, Just an attempt at innocent celebration in the open air. Those of our Chinese friends who were brave enough to come told us afterward that they were followed home by Public Security agents. It was a warning.

Back at my apartment that evening, I broke out the Chinese rum and put on Bonnie Raitt. Some of her more melancholy numbers, mostly written by others, but with her unmistakable soul and slide guitar: "Since I Fell For You," "If You Gotta Make a Fool of Somebody," "I Feel the Same"...

I coddled my disappointment at how few Chinese acquaintances came to our event. Their fears about the levels of surveillance and mistrust that the government exercised toward its citizens saddened me.

The experience also reminded me how powerless I felt regarding the very tentative friendships I had explored. I had no choice but to wait for my Chinese acquaintances and friends to call or contact me. I had to wait for Shi Yung, the calligrapher, to call. I could not reach him. He, like most, didn't have a personal telephone. And while he may have had access to an institutional phone, if I called, another person might have answered and would recognize a foreigner's accent. He could get into serious trouble.

Teacher Liang was lectured and cautioned by Shadow Zhang. Ming was frightened off after his bold attempts. Yulian—warned away? "Too dangerous." The few brave souls who had come by from other departments in Radio Beijing or worked in my apartment building never returned. Were they warned? Threatened? Punished in ways I didn't know?

All I knew was that surveillance painted life a dark greenish-grey—the color that accumulates in the sky just before a thunderstorm. Menacing. I wondered if it was accurate to call this a police state. Whatever it was, it created a fearful, anxious state of mind. A self-censoring populace. The simple presence of plainclothes police—always so detectable by Chinese acquaintances—created an atmosphere of distress, even threat for Chinese communing with foreigners, especially journalists.

Sipping my rum and reveling in Raitt's choice of songs, I wondered if my misery was connected to something much more banal. Like the blue room I lived in, which was getting darker and darker as the spring sun changed position so there was less and less light in my ground floor apartment.

Or was my torment about something significant—the shattering of ideals? Was it about the sadness of seeing what Communist Party ideology had done to individuals, to relationships, to trust? Or was I evading something deeper in Chinese cultural history anchored in Confucianism and its prescriptions for relationships? Pearl Buck said understanding China was all about comprehending the rules of friendship. Was I blind to these rules? Was I stupidly abusing them?

In her autobiography, Buck claimed that social relationships were the most complex and most important project of the Chinese. But she was describing the world pre-1949. I had learned that the Communist Party, in its demand for loyalty, broke some of the bonds of fidelity to family. Certainly during the anti-Rightist movements, people were tarnished by their family backgrounds. They were encouraged to rat and report on family members as a way to improve their own lot. Couples divorced to avoid being persecuted by their mates' supposed sins of the past or those of their ancestors. A rigid line branded people "black" and punishable—some to death—based on class, property, associations, choices or expressions of their grandparents and parents.

Rum always made me sentimental and self-involved. I moved onto a review of my relationships with foreigners in Beijing.

Ron—whom I saw more than anyone and whose company I enjoyed more than others because of his intelligence, humor and shared social justice perspective—had never once asked a question about my romantic or sexual history. I likewise found it difficult to explore his. I suspected that he was gay and living deep in the closet in China. I could not imagine how difficult that was. Perhaps I was providing an important cover for him. So honesty—or full disclosure—was not part of the most significant friendship I had in Beijing.

While I saw several foreign women for dinners, our conversations drifted to our needs for affection, our longings. I found these discussions only dredged up unfulfilled desires for a perfect relationship. Was I unwilling to admit that I was not going to find that in Beijing? Perhaps my malaise here had been more about an assessment of my difficulties in life with creating a fulfilling relationship with a man. Perhaps I had traveled this distance with an unconscious fantasy that somehow in an exotic locale I could overcome patterns shaped over the previous two decades.

Then, somehow between the accumulation of fresh air and sun on my skin from dancing outdoors earlier in the day, the warmth of the rum in my veins and Bonnie Raitt's sexy voice, I thought about that incredibly cute law student who showed up at our festival—and stayed! Ron and I had met him and his brother with the film and theater group weeks earlier in the park. In the midst of the dancing, he was actually flirting with me. Spring. Hope.

"IS THAT how Canadians treat lovers? Is that their idea of love? Can they be so cruel?" Tears tumbled down Zhi Mei's cheeks underneath her heavy, dark-rimmed glasses as she stared at the hanky twisted in her fingers. She rearranged herself in my armchair and pushed up her glasses to wipe away tears.

I had met Zhi Mei on several occasions with a group of mutual foreign friends. She worked at *China Reconstructs* with Ron. Over the past month, she had been joining Ron and me at concerts, film screenings and parties. At one of the social gatherings, we began to share a little about our lives. It was as if we were old friends. I was attracted to Zhi Mei's high-octane personality, energy and self-confidence. In her mid-forties, tall and attractive, she spoke English like a native. Her easy smile broke quickly into laughter. Most significantly, she was the first Chinese woman who revealed passions and emotions in my presence. She was also the first Chinese woman to positively acknowledge *my* energy and spirit.

Now she sat in my living room, crying.

"I thought I understood something about Western love relationships, but obviously I understand nothing."

This was the first time we had shared an intimate conversation outside of public venues and social groups. Since she was almost ten years older than I was and living alone, I eagerly pursued her story. I discovered a broken heart.

Through a river of tears, Zhi Mei spun out the tale of her affair with a Canadian teacher she had met when she lived in Harbin in the Northeast.

"While I was teaching," she sniveled, "living a sad and loveless life," more snivels, "married to my second husband, I met Harold, who was there with his wife and kids. His marriage seemed very troubled. His wife and one of the kids returned to Canada. We began having an affair." She blew her nose. "So I believed he loved me. We had a wonderful time together. I love him very much. I applied for a divorce and worked hard to find a new work unit in Beijing. To move back home to be closer to my parents, who are getting very old. And after his contract was up, Harold came to Beijing, too. Our affair became very public because he said he was going to return to Canada, divorce his wife, then return to Beijing and we would get married."

I could see the trouble signs looming.

She continued. "I was exuberant. I experienced love for the first time in my life. Not long after he returned to Canada, I received a letter from him." Her next words came slowly and broken. "I feel so humiliated. I want to die."

Zhi Mei's voice trembled as tears flowed again. I moved to sit next to her, holding her until the sobbing subsided.

"In the letter, he said I should come to Canada and live with him and his wife! How can that be?"

She described Harold as a dreamer. I imagined a guy who, when loosened from family responsibilities of wife and kids, had a torrid affair and made too many promises. His letter revealed a confused and trapped man who wanted the best of both worlds.

"Polygamy!" I teased, in an effort to lighten the mood. "Secretly I think it's what all men want."

Woven through our social times together, Zhi Mei would come to my apartment and share more of her history. It was the most detailed history I had learned yet from a Chinese acquaintance.

"I grew up in Beijing in a traditional house just behind the Beijing Hotel—which was really the privileged center of Beijing. My mother was from a wealthy family, but not my father. He went to Japan in the 1920s, studied economics, then returned to Beijing, married and they had my sister and me. Before Liberation, my father was a banker for the Japanese in Beijing. He was not interested in politics and stayed clear of political movements. I went to Catholic school downtown from kindergarten through high school. That's where I learned English."

I had been in China long enough to recognize that this particular history and family background would have been big trouble for Zhi Mei from the mid-1950s onward. But there was more.

In 1945, when Chiang Kai-shek's Kuomintang arrived, her father quit. He wouldn't work for the Japanese any longer. They lived in a house with a dozen or more rooms, a cook, a rickshaw driver and lots of antiques. Her sister married a Kuomintang officer in 1948, encouraged by her mother because of the instability of the situation. It was seen as protection. But in 1949, when Beijing was liberated by the Communists, he was sent for rehabilitation to the South. Her sister returned after one year, pregnant and divorced.

"When Beijing residents heard that the Communists were going to take over the city, rumors flew: 'You have to share everything, even your women!' Of course, it was ignorant hysteria. After what the Japanese had done in

Nanjing alone and the behavior of many KMT officers, the Communists arrived highly respected for their organizational work in the countryside. And, unlike the KMT, they didn't destroy everything once they reached Beijing. I was innocent and enthusiastic about New China.

"Because I could speak English and type, I got a job with the Foreign Trade Company in 1951, and in the following year, they sent me to East Berlin with a delegation. I studied and worked there for a while and I developed a friendship with an older East German woman."

Zhi Mei explained that when the anti-Rightist movement broke out in the late 1950s and the break with the Soviet Union occurred, she was pulled back to Beijing.

"That's when I had the first experience of how ratting works. People began to accuse individuals of being bourgeois. There was an older man working at the Foreign Trade Company whom I was very fond of. He was hoping I would marry his son. But I got caught up in the process of telling leaders what others said about themselves or about the Communist Party or system. I got swept up with the naïve belief—that the Party promoted—that it's necessary for the good of all. Later—when this man was fired—I realized the pain and suffering I had caused. This was when they first started keeping files. A black mark would stay in your file. The system of ratting was worse in the 1950s than now. People's backgrounds were used to label them as reactionaries, capitalist-roaders, bourgeois, traitors, spies, enemies, devils, poisonous weeds that need to be exterminated."

In 1957–'58, during the Hundred Flowers Movement when intellectuals and professionals were encouraged to speak their minds about policies and methods, many naïvely took the bait. Zhi Mei would soon learn what these intellectuals were about to face. Those who spoke up were attacked and worse. Some lost their jobs, some were sent to reeducation camps in the countryside, some to prison.

At the time, she was in love with a bright young engineering graduate of Xinhua University—the MIT of China.

"He was rising fast, perhaps too fast, for the jealous politicos. He made a fatal verbal slip. He suggested that the Soviets didn't have all the answers and that China didn't need to copy everything from them. He was branded a revisionist and lost everything."

The ironic twist of this story was that, within a few years, Mao would launch his Great Leap Forward movement as a means to counter the influence of the Soviets.

For self-protection, Zhi Mei bowed to social pressures and broke with the engineer. She joined the Communist Youth League. Then, as double armor, she married the League's secretary.

"I didn't love him. But I had learned a lesson. We were married one month when I was sent to the countryside for ten months to do labor. We had sex a few times in that first month, then once more when I returned. I became pregnant and had no more sex for the duration of that marriage. In 1960, I had a baby."

These were the hard years following the disasters of the Great Leap Forward policy, Soviet withdrawal of expertise and aid combined with a severe drought. All Beijing ministries let some of their staff go. Zhi Mei was reassigned because of her family background. She and her husband were sent to Harbin. She left her baby behind in Beijing with her mother.

"In Harbin, I knew I couldn't continue living with my husband. I didn't love him. But he said he loved me. I simply wasn't attracted to him. I had married him for protection and learned the hard consequences of that kind of decision. I asked him for a divorce. He refused. I moved to the singles dorm at the college where I was teaching. He contacted the leaders to try to put pressure on me. I was only more obstinate in the face of him going public with it. It was very messy."

Zhi Mei ended up with nothing from him for her or their daughter. She sent half her paycheck to her mother in Beijing every month.

When the Cultural Revolution broke out in 1966, she heard that her parents' house had been ransacked by Red Guards in Beijing.

"It was a time when Red Guards broke into houses, broke antiques, burned books, except for Mao's writings, destroyed musical instruments, and confiscated clothes and other objects. All of these possessions could mean struggle sessions for the 'bad' family."

Struggle sessions, she explained, meant being confronted by a group of usually hostile interrogators who pressured you to admit to class crimes, which could be profound or trivial, real or imagined, petty or made up. Zhi Mei's parents were not spared.

"While other families were moved in to share the house with them, my parents were made to sweep the alley every day. They were called 'demons and monsters' in the terminology of the time. Two years later, when Yan, my daughter, started school, she was sent home because she was bourgeois."

So Zhi Mei went to Beijing and arranged to send her daughter to Anhui province, where her sister was now living. Meanwhile, the Red Guards in

Harbin labeled Zhi Mei and some others as "spies and traitors." Her file was examined. Her parents' background, foreign books and clothes, letters to and from her East German friend were all grounds for accusation.

"People in the '50s would show the letters they wrote to and received from foreign friends to the Party leaders. I knew the letters were read by censors anyway, so since they were only friendly private letters, I didn't bother showing them to leaders. This was recorded in my file.

"I was called into a room one night for a struggle meeting with a faction of rebels called 'The Red Terror.' I can still see the red light in the room. It reminds me of the pain and horror."

Covering her face with her hands, Zhi Mei continued. "They started slapping me around while accusing me of all kinds of things. I can't remember much because of the beating."

Zhi Mei earlier had explained that she was labeled one of the "bastards" of the Five Black Categories—landlords, rich peasants, counter-revolutionaries, bad elements and Rightists. Since Zhi Mei was a teacher, she was also known as the "stinking ninth category."

"My face was swollen, black and blue. When a friend went to get the doctor at the clinic, the doctor refused. He said, 'We cannot treat bourgeois.' Later, a woman doctor came and said, 'We are doctors, we can't treat only out of political sympathy.'"

Zhi Mei looked at me intensely to make sure I understood this insidious form of punishment. "You know that happened to so many people during the Cultural Revolution. They were forbidden medical care by the radical warring factions. Many victims died as a result."

She paused, inhaling deeply. "My friends were intimidated. They were afraid they would be implicated by their association with me. If you are labeled, everyone you have contact with is contaminated by you. So they stayed away."

Zhi Mei described a factional warfare that kept dividing along different lines, becoming increasingly irrational and frenzied.

"Now, epithets were flying everywhere. We couldn't keep track of who or which group was good and right. All I know is I was expected to 'cast off my old self' and move out of my sunny room, which was reserved for a teacher with revolutionary credentials. A worker, peasant or soldier background."

Zhi Mei's voice dropped to a whisper. "One day, in the toilet, a friend whispered words of support and encouragement because she was afraid I would commit suicide. Many, many people at that time took their own lives as an escape from all the persecution. Because there was no reason in what the accusers were doing, you could not defend yourself. They insisted you confess to things that were irrelevant or which had nothing to do with you or your life. But that day, that friend's comment of support for me was overheard and she was criticized. You know what I mean by criticized? She could be persecuted! Punished! Threatened! Attacked!"

Eventually, in the midst of these accusations and beatings—called "struggle sessions"—Zhi Mei married one of the radicals who had showed some sympathy for her. Another marriage for protection. But one month after their marriage, she was arrested by the rebels and imprisoned—as were thousands of people throughout China—locked in a small room for ten months as punishment for her supposed crimes of being bourgeois and having foreign books and friends.

"With this new husband, it was the same pattern. We had sex a few times in the first month. Then nothing for *ten* years of marriage! I didn't love him. I realize I had married out of fear and self-protection. But he couldn't do anything for me when I was locked up. He couldn't see me. Finally, the radicals admitted they had erred in locking me up, but I still had to make a confession or self-criticism. Thanking them for detaining me and for releasing me. By this time, everyone was accused. Everyone was bad. At least fifty colleagues became serious victims. The people who did the persecuting and attacked victims were rotten. They sometimes were motivated by jealousy or personal revenge. It was all without reason."

"So the Cultural Revolution brutalized relationships?" I asked.

"Yes, but it also drew people closer."

Zhi Mei explained that she lived with her second husband until she got pregnant and had her second baby in 1970. "Lulu is now eleven." She asked for a divorce, and they ended as friends. He was disturbed because he loved her very much and wanted sex with her. She slept in a separate room. "If I had sex with a man I didn't love, I'd be a prostitute."

She had one woman friend in Harbin she could talk to about love and sex. That woman was trying to divorce an impotent husband who refused, so she was locked into her situation.

"I think that situation is common, but most Chinese women will not talk about sex."

Meanwhile, she fell in love with Harold, the Canadian, who taught English in Harbin at the institute where she worked. They made a plan together. She came to Beijing in the summer of 1980 after getting her divorce and found a new work unit.

As Zhi Mei related this saga, I realized how hard she had massaged her connections to secure a position so quickly at *China Reconstructs*, obtain a permit to live in Beijing and score a room. A monumental achievement. Harold joined her when his contract was up.

"I experienced profound love for the first time with Harold. He spent a lot of time with me at my mother's house. Also, he had one of his kids with him.

"Our love affair was very public during the several months we were in Beijing together. Everyone expected him to go back to Canada, finalize his divorce and return to work at the Foreign Language Press...and we were supposed to get married here. Instead, I got that letter."

Zhi Mei's face contorted as if she was ruined. "I am humiliated in front of so many people," she whimpered.

She feared that she would lose face among her colleagues, family and friends—and especially her new Canadian consulate friends once they found out.

"He became part of my family. I have not yet told anyone about this. It is too humiliating for me. Is this what Westerners do?"

I tried to help Zhi Mei analyze the behavior of a cad. Convince her that she had placed far too much trust in a first true love. This was painful anywhere in the world, but especially in China, where the exposure of foreign–Chinese affairs could be disastrous for the Chinese.

There was not much I could say or do to console Zhi Mei. Our only hope for transforming this horrible situation and her humiliation was to distract her by going out together for meals and events to nourish her spirit and bolster her spunk.

SOMETIME IN mid-April, I realized that I had been drinking excessively and needed to confront what alcohol was doing to me. It struck me when I had to take an entire day off to recover from alcohol poisoning after drinking champagne followed by gin and tonics until 3 a.m. Zhi Mei and I had started out at the Great Hall of the People for the Coca-Cola launch party in China. They were opening their first bottling plant in Beijing. Surreal. Getting citizen comrade Zhang Zhi Mei into that sacred place that theoretically belonged to her created a scene at the door while Aretha Franklin was singing "Things Go Better with Coke!" on the loud speaker. All in the Great Hall of the People built by thousands of ordinary Beijing residents back in the early '50s.

Waiters served Cokes on trays, and American executives made their podium toasts with Coke, but all the Chinese *gambus*, decked out in their Sun Yat Sen uniforms, weren't fooled. They were drinking from the trays of Chinese champagne.

Coke was too expensive for locals and required funny money, but the kids wanted it because it was Western and therefore modern. Afterward, Zhi Mei and I walked over to the Beijing Hotel bar and faced the usual ordeal of signing her in.

The next day, while nursing a profound hangover, I admitted that I was failing to discipline myself. I had gained so much weight I could barely fit into any of my clothing. I felt terrible from smoking and drinking. I could wallow in self-loathing or fantasize about another identity or "cast off my old self," in Chinese revolutionary terms. I wondered if I should return to New York before I completely imploded.

But first, Vi and Cy were coming to China.

My incredible roadtrip with my mother, Vi, and her third husband, Cy, began on a high-speed boat from Guangzhou to Hong Kong. Distraught with guilt, I tormented myself for having missed the train that would put me into Hong Kong on time to meet them flying in from Vancouver.

How many times had I been late meeting Vi in critical situations? Once in New York when I overslept. She was waiting, looking distressed, in the grubby and chaotic Amtrak station after a long train ride from Toronto. Then there was the time back in 1962, after she had sold the house in Victoria and bought a round-the-world cruise for $2,000(!). She was returning by by train from Montreal across Canada, and we were to meet at the train station in Saskatoon to journey on west together. I had just ventured to North Battleford, Saskatchewan, to see my biological father for the first time since I was three. But I had miscalculated train schedules and arrived late to the station, where she was perched alone on a bench in an eerily empty waiting room. Worried, disappointed, angry.

We took the next train through the Rocky Mountains together back to Vancouver, each lost in our thoughts about what we had just experienced. She, in her early forties, beautiful, single, having gone ashore in Honolulu, Hong Kong, Bombay, Cairo, Rome and other European ports—a life-expanding journey filled with romantic flings as I read into her tiny colored photos from that trip. After all that flirtatious globe-trotting, she was obliged to wait in a dinky prairie train station, reminding her of all the misery she left behind there seventeen years earlier. Me, processing my visit with my bio-dad.

In fact, that expedition, front loaded with anticipation, curiosity, muddled emotions and hope, made me appreciate just how courageous my mother had been to leave her prairie context—as a heavily judged married woman fleeing a scoundrel husband—and how grateful I was that she had.

After visiting my high school buddy Wendy and her kids for a day in Guangzhou, I was racing to Hong Kong on the hovercraft because the train was sold out. In an era predating cell phones, there was no way to get a message to Vi and Cy at their hotel.

It was not only guilt that prevented me from enjoying the rolling, frenetic boat ride over the Pearl River estuary; it was my angst about the journey ahead. First, two weeks of chaperoning them from Hong Kong to Guangzhou, then flying to Guilin, followed by a train to Shanghai before flying on to Beijing for two more weeks. It was a complex journey to orchestrate. Individual travel by foreigners was not permitted in China in those days. Group travel was the only option. But, as a *foreign* expert, I was permitted to shepherd my parents solo. It required obtaining visas for every city we were to visit, on top of reserving transportation and hotels in a country not set up for independent travel. Mr. Liu from the Foreign Experts Bureau seemed relieved that I finally accepted his help.

Smacking into Hong Kong capitalist culture after nine months in Beijing was a jolt. The cabbie wanted to charge me three times the fare because it was Friday rush hour. My automatic reflexes screamed "Resist!" What a contrast to my reactions in November, when I was eager to leave mainland China and imbibe this lively shopping mecca. Service with a smile, a good cup of coffee, a decent drink, efficiency and all that.

Seeing my mother in the lobby of the hotel was shocking. She looked dreadful. Her eyes were red, as if she had been crying. I knew she had not slept on their fourteen-hour flight from Vancouver. But the real issue was my being late. I was playing out a well-worn script of the unreliable, wild daughter, given to rash decisions and worrisome changes of course. I must be made to feel just how much I have let them—especially her—down.

I tried to distract from the missed train and tardy arrival by explaining what a coup it was to get reservations in the YMCA Hotel in Kowloon. Savvy travelers considered it the best deal. I knew my mother would cheer up hearing that. And besides, it offered great views of Hong Kong. I settled them in and encouraged a nap.

Mum had always been independent, determined. As her only child, I could have turned out no other way. I had my eyes glued to her for nineteen years before I fled her tentacles of control. Control that had to do with judgment about my direction: "What are you doing, leaving university before you are finished? Going to San Francisco alone on a bus? A Negro boyfriend? That will never work."

"Mum, we don't use 'Negro' anymore. It's black."

"A boyfriend from El Salvador? Where's that? What do you mean, the 'Movement'? Why do you think my lawn is bourgeois? A Marxist professor? St. Louis? But San Francisco is so beautiful. I thought you were studying at Berkeley? You are living together? Aren't you afraid of what people will think? What is a consciousness-raising group? Pigs! Do you use that language really? What does a sociology degree mean you can do for a living? I so wanted you to become a nurse. You're going to Boston? But I liked Carl so much. What do you mean a feminist radio collective? You are waitressing...again? After a master's degree?"

Yet I felt the profound need to care for Mum on this journey. Never before had she been dependent upon me. It was a new kind of feeling.

Cy was a different story. Lacking confidence, he reacted timidly to new situations. He carried an enormous shadow—some might call it a monkey—on his shoulder, his being. He grew up in rural Manitoba with an English immigrant father and a Cree Indian mother at a time when "half-breed" was a pejorative expression people spat out or laughed at. He loved to talk about his father. He never mentioned his mother. Despite his sometimes sweet disposition, he tested my patience. And I cringed from his naïveté, his apparent cluelessness about everything.

Cy and Vi had been married for seven years. And it was not a happy fit. They bickered constantly. It was a cycle. She would lose patience with him. He then reacted childishly, which triggered her incorrigible bossiness. It was fatiguing to be around.

I was also becoming aware that there was a secretive background to their bristly relationship. Cy had a drinking problem. When he drank, he became jealous of her. He had been violent. She had threatened him with divorce.

My other stepfather, Harold, had also had a drinking problem. It definitely contributed to killing him in the end, but not before he came after me in shameful ways. And my biological father, Don, had been a drinker, too. My pretty mother. Who married the handsome prince in her small prairie town. The prince who turned into a cruel, cold-hearted, philandering rogue. Not a frog.

My mother kept picking men that infuriated me. I had confronted her already about Cy and the others. I told her that her choice of mates affected me and my difficulties with men because she didn't provide any splendid models of a love relationship.

Why couldn't I have a father figure who was kind and thoughtful and smart and, if not an intellectual, was creative and sensitive and fun to be with and brought out the best in my mother? Somebody who challenged my mother to be something other than a caretaker or boss. And who loved my mother in a way that inspired me. Why?

I hated myself for how intolerant I was with *their* world. The fact that they always had to travel with some cheap vodka in a flask and then bragged about how brilliant it was to mix it with Tang orange soda. They should love the popular Beijing drink, *Zhixue* (pronounced geeshway) that mixed beer with orange soda. Their flask routine defeated the whole pleasure of "going out for a drink" that is only partly about the shot of booze in your glass. It was really more about the ambiance of a bar, a lounge, the other people coming and going, the sparkle and hues of all those liquors in dazzling bottles reflected in the mirror behind the bar and the shiny glasses.

In Hong Kong, "going out for a drink" usually involved a spectacular view looking out over the river at night, illuminated by a theatrical panorama of neon reflecting on the sampans and ferries sliding through the water, their own lights blinking, while glittering high-rises seemed to topple down the hills behind. But, no, Cy and Vi would prefer to sit on the edge of their bed in a miniature hotel room and drink their *gawd awful* concoction from a plastic cup. Other than the economy of it, what was that about? Yet, somehow, if they were friends doing this, I would tolerate it differently. Perhaps laugh. Time to break out the potato chips.

Right away, they recoiled from the food. There we were, in a culinary capital of the world, and they resisted even trying. I could not help wondering what my mother's world cruise taught her about other cultures. She certainly did not learn a thing about world cuisines. She was still a roast-beef-mashed-potato and bacon-and-eggs-with-hashed-browns kind of girl. But at least Hong Kong offered these British menu options. I predicted big trouble ahead.

Another issue. Cy couldn't maintain the walking pace set by Mum and me. He winded easily. Still smoking. It was going to be challenging. So I organized a day ferrying to a couple of the islands. Cruising on water helped ease things.

Looking at the Hong Kong skyline from the boat deck, I had to laugh that, back in the fall, when I was suffering from culture shock in Beijing, I couldn't

wait to get here. Six months later, I was eager to steer Cy and Vi out of there
to see and smell the "Real China." Mainland. Somehow I couldn't reconcile
my litany of grievances about Beijing with my preference for it now. The smells
would be difficult for them. Already their complaints were piling up.

As soon as we changed trains at the border, stepping into the People's
Republic, I heaved a sigh of relief. The attendant in her People's Liberation
Army uniform with a cap perched on her mixing bowl haircut moved like
sludge through the car carrying her big, banged-up kettle of boiling water to
pour into our thermoses. Traditional folk songs blared at high decibels by sweet
soprano voices from crackling speakers. An advertisement-free environment.
No billboards out the windows, no magazines strewn about with their siren-
song ads, no images of the idealized neurotic life of things. And insatiable
desire. None of that.

Arriving in Guangzhou, I was apprehensive about all the visas and
paperwork I had to carry for this trek. We checked into the Baiyun Hotel, one
of the main hotels for foreign guests. Not grand, but at least rooms would have
a bathroom, hot water and toilet paper.

"Luxuries in the People's Republic," I explained to Cy and Vi.

"Gaudy!"

That was the name we christened the restaurant in the hotel lobby.

So un-Beijing, so thoroughly southern. Lights so bright you needed
sunglasses. The color red blasting, decorations for every occasion, all mixed
up. Cy and Vi felt at home, since Chinese restaurants were often like this in
Vancouver. After all, many Canadian Chinese traced their roots to southern
China. To Canton, now called Guangzhou.

My folks were determined to use chopsticks, which they had never really
used at home because the Canadian Chinese restaurateurs long ago conceded
that they would have to provide knives and forks and—sadly—dumb down the
food. Sweet and sour pork became sickeningly sweet, chow mein and chicken
fried rice became staples. These dishes, and others, would be unrecognizable to
anyone from mainland China.

I didn't know whether to discourage Cy and Vi from trying out chopsticks
or swallow my pride at seeing the food fly all over the table. Cy's effort to
cut things first with a knife and fork and then try to pick up the pieces with
chopsticks was charming.

After dinner, I encouraged a walk to the river, taking in the nighttime
street life of Guangzhou. Their nervousness was palpable. Why? No street
lights, no lights from cars, only bicycles passing. Were nighttime Chinatowns

in Canada associated with crime? Drugs? Wickedness? Too many associations from their racist growing up that perhaps I didn't understand? I tried to draw their attention to the dark, tiny rooms off the street with Buddhist altars, the Japanese business outlets, boldly offering big brand names. The Japanese invasion of China, thirty-five years later. What would happen to this one?

Eventually, near the river we found a taxi stand—how different from Beijing— and they arrived back at their hotel without being mauled, mugged, kidnapped or cut to pieces. Witnessing their apprehensiveness about everything, I had to confess to them that I had felt safer in China than I ever had in New York.

The next day was critical for our visas. When I went to fetch the final paperwork, it was all prepared for our journey to Guilin. Then I purchased the plane tickets and negotiated the "foreign expert" price for all three. Cheaper than regular tourists. I was feeling triumphant. Things were falling into place. I was excited, finally, that this trip just might work.

The following day, we were on the tarmac in Guangzhou, relieved to be flying off to Guilin, the historic town on the Lijiang River that was featured in thousands of Chinese paintings with the tall, skinny, jagged mountain peaks towering over a slender, serpentine river valley. My friend Wendy and her daughter Vanessa would meet us there to explore for a couple of days.

Before we took off, steam billowed out of all the overhead luggage compartments. The foreigners on board became agitated. We tried to alert the stewardesses, who were sprawled on the back seats, leafing through Hong Kong movie magazines, giggling. There were no safety instructions from them. Nor were there any seat belts. To keep us further on edge, the trays on the back of the seats kept dropping. It was a prop plane, and while we were bumping down the tarmac, steam flowing out of the overheads, trays clattering down, foreigners all looked frantic. But the attendants were still preoccupied with their magazines.

The flight into the valley was breathtaking. Imposing, craggy, slender mountains, almost close enough to touch out of both sides of the airplane. Our landing was as dramatic as the takeoff, with banging trays, swerving and skidding wheels. A year later, we heard that a plane crashed on this landing. There was a reason that Lao Liu, from the Foreign Experts Bureau who helped with the tickets and visas, said we might not be able to go by plane. There had been troubles there. We were grateful not to know that beforehand.

Wendy and six-year-old Vanny were already waiting at the hotel. Wendy wanted to join us not only to see world-famous Guilin but also because she had always been fond of my mother since high school days when she sometimes unloaded her frustrations and found a sympathetic ear in Vi. Vanny, who had been attending Chinese school, was our translator. Already she revealed signs of exasperation from her linguistic duties. Too polite to be cranky, she simply resisted.

The next morning, we were off to pursue the peak experience. An eight-hour cruise down the Lijiang River. Dreamy drifting. I was exhausted. The task of meeting Cy and Vi in Hong Kong and bringing them this far had been wearing. The complaints about heat, humidity, dirt, bugs and smells had been relentless. Now, on the Lijiang River, the bucolic breezes, cornucopia of greens, gliding waters, all nudged me to let go.

Cy would sit inside the boat cabin all day, drinking beer, smoking and talking if he could find an English-speaking ear. Above deck, Mum attracted all the attention. She made friends—as usual. That nobody spoke her language on the boat was immaterial. I looked over at her, and she was surrounded by young Chinese women. They were interested in her hair (a curly wig), her makeup (turquoise eye shadow and heavy mascara that I was sorry that I introduced her to in 1957), her nail polish (Revlon hot pink to match her lipstick) and her white plastic earrings, bracelet and matching necklace. She was pretty, slender in her dark-blue slacks and tight-fitting t-shirt that revealed her perfect curves. Charming at sign language, compassionate smiles and laughter, she found a way to communicate. I had tried to learn from this aspect of my mother's personality. She could pretty much find a way to connect with somebody in any situation. As long as they were at her class level or a bit below.

If only I could have stayed in the Lijiang River-induced state of contentment. But that night, the real trouble started.

At dinner, Mum went on a hunger strike because the restaurant did not serve Western food.

"I'll throw up if I have one bite," she graciously commented about the profusion of delicacies delivered to our table.

We had ordered some typical Guillin dishes—beer-fried river carp with garlic, tomatoes and soy. Rice noodles in a soup of pork garlic, peanuts, peppers and radishes. Bok choy with water chestnuts. We purposely avoided the locally popular eel, snails and snake. Cy picked, recoiled and made faces.

The next morning, Mum was up at dawn, rushing into my room with the travel guide. She had discovered that there was a restaurant in Guilin that served Western food. In another hotel. She was ravenous, of course, after refusing to eat the night before, ruining the dinner for all of us.

Driven by hunger, she walked briskly in the already-oppressive humidity, her chin thrust up, her lips pursed, to catch the breakfast hour at the other foreign guest hotel. I followed quickly behind in the wake of her resolve only to discover that the "other" hotel now catered to overseas Chinese and there was no bacon and eggs with toast and coffee to be had. She was about to unravel into tears when I told her that perhaps she could get egg fried rice for breakfast. That helped. I knew she wouldn't go for the garlic soup that many Chinese slurped first thing in the mornings.

We spent a grumpy afternoon strolling aimlessly around town. Our train for Shanghai would leave in the evening. We had agreed to separate from Wendy and Vanny, who were shopping. We would just drift. Cy and Vi seemed caught up in a chorus of grievances: the bathrooms, lack of air conditioning, the beds, spitting. Jokes about hamburgers, fries and milkshakes had already become tiresome. In the late afternoon, we met Wendy and Vanny in a shady park to say goodbye, liberating them for more shopping.

Shortly after, I exploded. "It's not going to be like home!" I fumed. "If you don't want to discover other cultures or cuisines, then you should stay at home, where everything is predictable. Your litany of complaints is torturing me. I wish there was something you would find to like!"

They were startled at my anger, but I had to unleash it. The repetition of their grumblings was debilitating and our journey had barely begun. They insisted it wasn't complaining.

"It's only comments," Mum added apologetically.

It cleared the air.

Our train to Shanghai took two nights and a day. Cy slept most of the way, oblivious to the world passing by outside the window—serene, psychedelic green rice fields spreading across the continent. But when we stopped at Changsha, a large city partway, Cy dashed off the train to run along the track to look at the antique locomotive we were riding—gigantic steam engine, enormous wheels, brake linings, the gears. He was fascinated.

That was his field—train maintenance. He'd done it across Canada since he was a teenager. I later learned from a Margaret Laurence novel, *The Diviners*, that one of the only jobs young Manitoba Crees could get was with the Canadian National Railroad. That's how Cy lost his hearing. Putting his ear to a metal device, listening to the ball bearings. "All running so well!" he shouted over the blasts of steam, shaking his head and smiling.

The engineers looked wary watching him, and I explained in my kindergarten Chinese that he worked in Canada on trains. Hearing this, they generously invited him to the engine car to look more carefully. Cy was thrilled. As I was for him.

Meanwhile, Mum was quietly letting go of her hunger strike. I had lost weight already from walking in the heat and drinking less. I was simply melting down to my former size.

In Shanghai, we stayed at the historic Jin Jiang Hotel. Nixon and Mao had signed the Shanghai Communique there in 1972, the first agreement to begin normalizing Sino-American relations. They would not establish diplomatic ties until 1979. But for Cy and Vi in 1981, the Jin Jiang meant finally eating "Western food"—meaning English, Canadian or American, not French, Italian, Portuguese or Greek.

On foot, I led my contingent all the way from the Jin Jiang through the French legation, People's Park and fascinating street markets to the Bund. I remember Mum's horrified expression as I pointed out the live eels being sold from a bucket.

I cannot recall what set of behaviors accumulated the day Vi stopped talking. It had been a pattern between us. She closed down and wouldn't speak. Her face set in the tight grip of anger fused with hurt. Lots of hurt. Sometimes I thought of a wounded bird. I was left to discern what exactly had gone wrong. What did I do? Say? I was seething with frustration at the pent-up feelings that went unarticulated. As I tried to massage some vocal response from her, she was practically sobbing. A lifetime of this pattern enraged me. What did she want? What was I doing wrong?

She began whimpering. "Why do you oppose everything I say, every comment I make?" she sniveled.

I was doubly despondent now. I heard myself criticizing and could not stop. Yes, I confessed, I challenged everything that fell from her lips. I disagreed with her every utterance. I must have been particularly exasperating that day, rationalizing it as part of my vexation with her and Cy. I knew I wouldn't sleep. I was overtired, too. And clearly they were. I had dragged them from one end of Shanghai to the other—on foot.

This journey had provoked yet another examination of my relationship with my mother. My frustrations with her at any given time were never about that moment alone but were packed with all the other incidents in our push-and-pull emotional history. We were intensely close yet competitive and easily jealous of the other. Two bossy controllers bucking heads like rams. I loved her and hated her.

Many of our problems with each other were rooted in her marriages. By osmosis, I had absorbed a general distrust of men after witnessing her broken heart from husband number one, my bio-dad, even though I had been very young. My happiest memory was as a five-year-old, living with her and my grandparents in the Vancouver rooming house. My grandmother would alert me every week night when I could expect to see my mother get off the bus, returning home from work. I would sit on the front stairs at the house on Carolina Street until I spotted her up the road, stepping off of that bus, then shoot like a rocket from those stairs to greet her.

Husband number two, Harold, who entered when I was six, was often mean to me, physically and psychologically, then turned on me sexually. When he died, I was fifteen and relieved. I had tormented myself for years about what Mum and I had been unwilling or unable to reveal to each other. She knew I had wished he would suffer.

I had slept in Mum's bed with her for at least a year after Harold died. My concern was for her feelings of abandonment. I was inhaling her anxieties about financial insecurity. She always worked but as a low-paid bookkeeper. So she took in two college girls to room and board. They usurped my bedroom.

By the second year, Mum must have lost interest in sleeping with her teenage daughter and concluded she could manage without the boarding money. Besides, I was becoming increasingly irritable at being expelled from my room.

At sixteen, I was just beginning to date. She was an attractive fortyish widow who often had dates on Saturday nights while I sat at home waiting for her. This had set up an unconscious competitive dynamic that sometimes burst into the conscious realm with ugly ramifications that had really never stopped. I would condemn her men. She would criticize and make fun of my boyfriends. That and my resistance to her controls had helped to propel me on my long-distance life journey. Yet our heart strings were interwoven. I wrote and telephoned regularly from afield.

In my Shanghai hotel room, feeling worn down by her and Cy's crabbiness with each other as an overlay to the complex patterns of my history with her, I was sick with guilt that she felt wounded from my behavior. Angry that things weren't radically different. The muddle of mother and child.

What would I do to make up? The next day was her birthday. What could I make of the day?

In the morning, I apologized. She did, too. Nothing more was said.

For her birthday, I arranged for gifts and a birthday cake at the famous cake shop where young people ate huge pieces of spongy Western cake with chopsticks. It cheered our spirits. We needed to laugh. Then a birthday dinner at the Red House—Shanghai's most famous restaurant. The name implied happiness for family relationships. It was a total waste of a cultural experience. Shanghai's local cuisine was famous. Fish. Crab. Vi and Cy ordered roast beef and potatoes.

A day visit to Suzhou was filled with the range of our limits: us three; irritating industrial pollution; the angst about rain; Cy's lack of enthusiasm, resistance to walking, fear of unpredictability, absence of adventurous spirit; the model silk factory; my wimpy effort to transcend and endure; my mother's mediator role. We were puzzled by the odd—to us—concept of a garden: pebbles and water in Suzhou versus the flamboyant, obscene display of blossoming plants and shrubs in Victoria and Vancouver. We sat in fatigued silence on the train back, each lost in our own weariness. Then the catharsis.

At the train station in Shanghai, we found a three-wheel tuk-tuk motor taxi to take us back to the hotel. We crammed our three Western bottoms onto the minuscule bench in the back, surrounded by a group of peasants visiting from the countryside, pressing in from all sides, staring at us. Open-mouthed gawking. One of them even had the audacity to open the back flap behind our heads so they could gape even more intently. Some faces exhibited what I imagine were the effects of village inbreeding and lack of dentists. With all those peasant faces peering with astonishment into our faces at very close range, we began laughing hysterically as the *tuk-tuk* took off with its one-cylinder engine. Insane bouts of laughter at our predicament, sitting in this silly vehicle, the fatigue and lunacy of our situation on the road. It was the cathartic laughter we all needed. Tears flowing, the release and acknowledgement at the end of a day of our limitations, our frailties and fears, our exasperation and disappointments and, perhaps, even our pleasures.

In Beijing, I returned to work while the Radio Beijing leaders provided Cy and Vi with an empty apartment in my building for two weeks and arranged tours for them daily. Great Wall. Ming Tombs. Forbidden City. Summer Palace. Even a special visit to the train yards for Cy to see more enormous steam engines. And to meet his equivalent, the head of mechanical systems maintenance for the region. A woman!

My admiration for how my work unit took care of my parents forced a thaw at the office. Perhaps the fact that I was anchored in a family after all made me look more normal.

I was relieved when they finally left. Cy burst into tears at the airport, and

I wondered why. Did he recognize how difficult it had been for me to host and guide them? The stress for me of arranging transportation, tickets, hotels, food, routes and fifteen-hour days with them? Or was he crying for joy at the thought of returning to their comfy home, sports on TV and eating a burger and fries?

There would be days and nights ahead to process this road trip and marinate deep insights into my mother's essence, the nature of her relationship with Cy and my relationship with her. Convoluted. I had fled as far away as possible from her, her world, her men, only to discover that I carried her in my head. She was flowing in my bloodstream.

It was good to be able to do everything for her for the first time in my life. There were so many reasons to be grateful to her. Her tenacity that had worn off on me. Her courage to change her life with a two-year-old in tow. Her determination to make sure I went to good public schools. Paying for piano and dance classes. Was I too selfish and petty in complaining about all the rest? Now I was wiped out but found it a little easier to accept who they were. In Beijing, we laughed more. Had I really come to terms with the fact that I had no choice but to accept my mother's men?

JANET CAME over to tell me there had been a crackdown on young dissidents. While I was on the incredible road trip with Vi and Cy, there had been arrests of editors at some underground journals in Beijing and elsewhere. More arrests were expected. Ron said that while I was away Voice of America reported some of those arrests and press attacks on a particular writer, unnamed.

These events can be traced to Deng Xiaoping's Christmas speech. Some observers interpreted it as his concession to the hard-liners who were opposing his new economic policies. He was throwing them some bones. Bodies. Dissidents. The leftovers from the New Democracy Movement. There were rumors that during the previous month a new Party policy document had been circulating ordering a get tough approach to young democracy enthusiasts—like students and striking factory workers.

Ron decided to leave and made a commitment to helping Chinese get out.

The author with Zhang Zhi Mei at Qing Ming event at the Old Summer Palace, Beijing 1981

Chapter Sixteen

At Last
最终

March 15, 2014, Oaxaca, Mexico, Journal:

Sun-blasted. Magical. More poetic words fail me when I try to describe the house where I lived the past two winters. While the sun rises over the Sierras of San Pablo Etla, a black feral cat with a white bow tie is poised on the sill outside my bedroom window, watching for me to stir. The perky trilling of a horned lark bleeds from the branches of the jacaranda, behind the stove pipe cactus, the bougainvillea and the barren, thorny branches of the acacia tree besotted with epiphytes. It is the end of the dry, brittle season in Oaxaca. An oriole is searching for insects in the deepest crevices of an agave plant. Jurassic-sized bees drone into the purple blossoms of the trumpet vine. The lizard that I never see but that follows me from room to room calls out periodically. Today, like every other day, I answer back. I quite expect a scorpion is watching my every move from his crevice in the "carrizo" ceiling of this "casa rustica" with its adobe-and-brick white walls and red tiled roof. This was the aesthetic that had entered my bone marrow just months before I left for Beijing in August 1980.

As the day courses on, happiness envelops me like an undulating wave to a soundtrack of cicadas droning hypnotically.

The whine of the cicadas transports me back to Beijing during the summer of 1981. Yet none of these seductions by flora and fauna seemed present then. I witnessed so little "nature" in Beijing. I don't remember birds other than tiny canaries kept in little bamboo cages by old men, or those served deep fried, whole, on a plate in better restaurants. No, I never heard a bird sing. People didn't own pets. I cannot remember seeing a cat. And while there were elm trees in my summertime photos, I recall very little in the way of plant life. But Beijing was in northern China. The equivalent of North Dakota. A different botanical story unfurls south of the Yangtze.

Concerns about nature morph into thoughts about erotic love.

Finding someone to love intimately who will return your emotion and embrace cannot be managed, strategized, determined, programmed or predicted. One day, you simply look at a profile, a body contour, a flash of motion and hear a voice, and you wonder just when you first met because something is happening whenever this person enters the frame. A special force passes between you. It was that way with Zhang Fan.

Ron and I had met the Zhang brothers—Fan and Wei—and their friend, Xiao Gong, a nurse, the day we bicycled to the Old Summer Palace and encountered a gaggle of actors and singers and plotted the Qingming Festival event. Later, Fan bravely ventured out to join us for our little multicultural be-in, staying on as we danced and made music. He was there in the photographs. We caught each other's gaze.

Fan was also in the snapshots at the farewell dinner for my parents. We had never met without being surrounded by a group. Yet there was definitely a flirtation going on.

Something roused me in our conversations. Since he spoke minimal English, "conversation" was perhaps a forced concept. His tall, slender physique, exquisitely shaped face, intelligent eyes and hands all disturbed my senses. He was a law student—playful, polite, curious—and twenty-four years old. We had all been told by others that the Zhang brothers were the sons of famous parents—important generals in the People's Liberation Army.

At the dinner for my parents, struggling with dictionaries, Fan wanted to know about drugs in the US and if people really paid a third of their income in taxes. He rattled off some professions and wanted to know which job was tougher: corporate executive, accountant, lawyer, doctor, school teacher, journalist, scientist.

"A job you didn't mention," I responded. "Peasant. Farmer."

He laughed and agreed. "Are women more equal with men in the US than in China?" he asked.

How could I not be hooked?

As far as I could judge through the layers of language uncertainties, Fan was smart, diligent about his studies and, like most local university students, studying English. Significantly, although he was eager to be together, he didn't seem to want help with foreign university applications. Nor had he asked for a favor—yet. He was also one of the first Chinese acquaintances, other than Yuan, to ask me questions about *my* history, where I went to university and what I studied and the nature of my work and professional history.

On a weeknight in early June, Fan called to invite me to the famous Beijing Duck restaurant on the following Sunday. Finally, a flirtatious opportunity to have him all to myself. Being seen with a younger man no longer troubled me. Single men my age in Beijing appeared absent, since divorce was so difficult. Additionally, the fear of consequences was too overwhelming for those in my age group. They had a longer memory of how the smallest slip could ruin your life. Fan's confidence in this daring public act—being seen with a foreigner and older woman—revived my mischievous genie.

When Sunday afternoon arrived, I was trying out different options, since all my clothes fit again. I settled on a dress and heels. My whole body felt moist from the excitement.

While I checked out my profile in the mirror, Fan called to ask if he could bring a friend. My mood deflated. Not so brave after all. At what point, I wondered, did he realize he could not be seen in a fancy restaurant with me alone? With his minimal English, he could never pass as my interpreter.

When Fan and his friend arrived at my apartment, he bashfully introduced her as his classmate from middle school. She was pretty, tall and sweetly shy— the contemporary Chinese version of ultra-femininity. Militant Red Guard unisex images for young women were definitely passé, at least among this urban cohort. The People's Liberation Army baggy suit and cap seemed to be waning. Maybe it was just a summer thing. I noticed a lot more skirts and perky cotton dresses this season. Fan's friend was wearing one of those new bow tie blouses. She had also composed her hair in one of the new styles—pulled back into a ponytail on top while the excess hair hung straight below. And this was the first time I had seen Fan without PLA issue voluminous pants with the cinched and belted waist. He was dressed in what I referred to as conservative Western banker. Grey fine-wool fitted pants. A refined cotton shirt. They both looked beautiful. Despite the classmate, I felt privileged and delighted to be stepping out with them. Perhaps I would be taken for their chaperone.

We took a bus to Wangfujing, then transferred twice, so ultimately it was a three-bus ride to the restaurant. All I could think about was how much this place cost. How could Fan afford it? It was too expensive for my salary, but this is what he wanted to do, and the Chinese did pay lower prices. Generally, the expats thought of this place as catering to tourists, Western businessmen and government officials. The oversized joint was packed.

Fan ordered a half of a duck. A small fortune. When it arrived with the required thin, tortilla-like pancakes to wrap pieces of duck with sauce and shredded scallions, Fan discreetly whispered something to his friend. I think he was telling her not to eat the best part. She ate nothing. It was a little difficult to enjoy this delicacy knowing how expensive the meal was and that Fan's girlfriend wasn't eating. Meanwhile, I was distracted by Fan's fingers on my thighs under the table, as if he was reassuring me that she wasn't a lover.

Perhaps because we were an odd triad, we struggled with talk of romance and friendships, comparing East and West while discreetly fingering our dog-eared dictionaries. Fan had clearly memorized a variety of English sentences on this theme. I had rehearsed some Mandarin vocabulary to discuss relationships, too. If the classmate hadn't joined us, my newly crafted sentences would have been posed in the most teasing manner, but now I took an academic approach.

In my Chinglish, I conveyed the ease of meeting the opposite sex in the West but the difficulty of finding deep, long-term relationships. So much mobility and freedom, available birth control, increasing women's economic independence and fear of commitment. We had to look up all the nouns. They said they understood, but I was doubtful. Yet they both stated clearly their desire to go out with different people. Fan said his friend's father was also a general. He wanted her to have different men friends. How progressive that sounded.

Were these two once boyfriend–girlfriend, and now they were sampling, then comparing notes? Somehow I felt too flustered to ask that because Fan's shoes and knees kept tapping mine, and his left hand was resting on my thigh. Was I dreaming? There was an awkward silence. I decided to back off any questions about virginity, puritanism and double standards. Instead, I told them about my upcoming jazz lecture. I had been invited back to Beijing University to give another presentation.

When the check arrived, I mused about just how Fan convinced his father and mother to fork over the funds to take this older, foreign, North American woman out to the priciest restaurant in Beijing. Maybe he didn't mention the foreigner part.

On the way home, I mulled over some of the more confrontational questions I had prepared in Mandarin but never asked. *Aren't you afraid of contact with foreigners? Terrible things have happened to people in the past for having relations with foreigners, why do you take the risk? Do you want to leave China? Are you applying to American universities? Do you need help with that? Is that why you want to spend time with me?*

My experiences here had turned my normally sanguine disposition with new acquaintances toward cynicism. I would save my lousy questions for next time when we could be alone at my apartment, which was what I was plotting next. In fact, my real desire was to understand Fan's particular history and his reflections about that history as well as the impact on his thinking and psyche of his and his parents' experiences. Given his age, I wanted to know if he was sent to the countryside to labor on a farm or in a factory. But Fan never spoke of it. His fine, long fingers and soft skin revealed nothing but a student's life. Was he so privileged that he could avoid thought reform through manual labor? While many party leaders were persecuted, were PLA generals spared?

If he had been sent to the countryside, I wanted to know how he perceived that period now. For my calligraphy teacher, Yung, those experiences had been transformative. Which was Mao's intent. But the consequences often differed from what Mao might have desired. I couldn't ask Fan how he felt about the choices he had made in life. There were few choices to make in China. Except to study or work hard.

Finally, I wanted to know about his hopes for the future. About the prospects for a fresh definition of socialism. He was part of that two percent of China's youth who could attend university. And for Fan, especially, the privilege of attending a recently opened law school put him into an even more rarefied student elite.

ON A Monday in early June, I gave a second lecture/demo at Beijing University on the history of jazz. There seemed to be more students than there were last time. Did they understand a word I said? What I said was immaterial anyway—the music was the thing.

Again, it was a thrill to study the faces of young people who had only heard negative condemnations of this music, while listening to Charlie Parker's "Yardbird Suite" and "Groovin' High." Like last time, several students rushed to the podium afterwards. *Is there theory and notation for improvisation?* Same question as before. *Yes, yes.* I wished I was a composer or musician so I could help them. I regretted that I wasn't permitted to linger and play more music. But again, like last time, I was whisked away afterward with no chance to chat with a smaller group of students and hear about what they were doing musically. Why? Would I contaminate them? Hear a state secret? Get a phone number? Make critical contact with someone who wanted out? I felt more and more compassionate with people and less and less patient with this mistrustful system.

I also mused for a moment that I should have been on salary at US AID, the government agency, that promoted American culture around the world. But, instead, I avoided contact with the US embassy. I didn't want to endanger my green card. Already the government's knowledge that I was working for the Chinese government had, I was certain, led to the IRS harassing me about my last tax return. Contradictions. Ironies. Here I was, the ambassador for the best of American culture on a Chinese salary!

FAN INVITED a small group of us foreigners, including Ron, to visit his family's traditional *hutong* house with multiple rooms wrapped around a courtyard. Unlike Zhi Mei's family—and so many others—they did not have to share it with multiple families. They seemed to have lived in this house for a long time. Both of those facts indicated just how high a position his parents occupied in the PLA.

Fan proceeded to show us a bunker that took up prime space in the middle of the courtyard in case of a nuclear bomb attack. Fan and his brother, Wei, chuckled as they explained that it was built during the 1950s, when the threat of a nuclear attack from the US seemed imminent, most likely during the Korean War. Ron and I demonstrated the kind of nuclear war training we had as young school children in the early 1950s when we were instructed to crouch underneath our desks with our hands clasped behind our necks, as if that would provide any defense if we were struck with a nuclear weapon. We all laughed at the charade. We told them about the potent images we grew up with—in *Life* magazine—of the humongous orange mushroom clouds billowing in the South Pacific. We drew the shape of those mushroom clouds.

After sharing the common nuclear fears and responses of our radically different cultures, I felt as if a tensile web had enveloped us and pulled us together. We had more in common than we had ever considered. Someone served us tea. We didn't stay long. We never met the generals.

June days were always a surprise. The delicious anticipation of summer with each morning. Even though I needed a sweater to start the day, by afternoon, it was hot. Thunderstorms came and went repeatedly, leaving behind that distinct earthy smell released by a sudden burst of rain. More varieties of vegetables had appeared on the menu at the workers' canteen as well as at my building's dining room. Cabbage was now forgotten.

On a damp Saturday afternoon, after returning from my half-day at Radio Beijing, I read one of the short stories from the new *scar* genre. These were the new post-Mao stories, exposing some of the pain and suffering of the Cultural Revolution. They began appearing in 1977 and '78, paralleling the Beijing Spring movement, and had been quickly translated into English, providing a window for Westerners to glimpse the trauma caused by political purification movements and class struggle. They detailed the effect on children, grandchildren and mates when parents or husbands may have been landlords or were accused of being bourgeois or having had contact with the Kuomintang— defined as being black—with no way to transform that designation. Or someone in the family may have said something critical about the Party. And from Zhi Mei, I had learned that the persecution of individuals could be based on petty personal grudges. Resentment of success, praise or position. A spurned sexual gesture. It had been going on since the mid-'50s and then spiraled into lunacy during the Cultural Revolution.

On this particular June day, I read one of the stories that started the genre, *The Scar*, by Lu Xinhua, that describes a young Red Guard who broke off relations when her mother was denounced as a traitor. The daughter returned home many years later to find her mother dead with a scar on her forehead. Although these stories had begun to describe the sacrifices and betrayals, anguish and loss among intellectuals and Party cadres, there was a sense that much more festered below the surface of these simplistic emotional tales and characters. We had been told the response to these stories in China was immediate and potent. They had opened a vein of moral outrage inspiring newspaper and journal discussions, then movies. For Westerners, their revelations were startling and tragic. The damage to relationships, families, community, trust, morality and psyche was unfathomable. Some referred to this new wave of short story writing as the "Second Hundred Flowers Movement."

In our Wednesday study group, we discussed how the very language of these short stories revealed the corruption of expression after two decades of official communication that had been reduced to repetitive slogans. It was as if these writers were just beginning to relearn how to see, feel and think as well as counteract the destruction that came from politicizing language. Personal, introspective expression was almost absent. This could explain some of my frustrations with sharing or communicating a personal emotional landscape with the Beijing men I had met. Particularly their generation who had known nothing else.

My understanding of the impact of class struggle on people's lives—or, at least, urban educated lives—had evolved since I arrived. Yet despite the revelations of tragedy and trauma experienced by at least two generations of these city professional, intellectual and Party elites, there was a sense portrayed by the storytellers that love and faith in the Party could overcome and heal. Did they really believe that, or did they take that position in order to be published?

Where was truth?

Someone in our study group raised the issue that all of the new scar stories and movies only told the experiences of urban elites. What happened in the countryside during those purification movements from the perspective of peasants would have to wait.

RON CALLED. His Sudanese neighbor, Ahmed, was having a big lamb feast. I was invited, along with the Zhang brothers. Too bad. I was looking forward to seeing Fan alone. Now we were going to be among a large group again. Endless delayed gratification.

I had changed three times by the time Fan and Wei arrived at my apartment. Heavy rain pounded on my windows. We called a taxi.

I was curious about the Zhang brothers' ease of movement around Beijing. How could they come to visit me at my apartment unmolested when every other Chinese had either been too frightened to try or were required to have letters of permission or been harassed at the guard hut? When we arrived at the Friendship Hotel, why weren't we stopped going in? Because we arrived in a taxi? Then, when other Chinese men—one from the foreign ministry—were approached by the guards at the Friendship Hotel about their permission slips, Fan simply shrugged and said, "They asked me, and I said I was a law student."

No more questions? What would the guards assume about law students? That those who get into law school are high cadres' children? Really high cadres? Could the guards simply look at Fan, his height, his delicate features and hands and assume he came from a privileged hierarchy? Did he simply say his parents' names? Just how high in the echelon were they? But my unspoken questions were muffled by the fact that I had such an enormous crush on Fan. And he was offering me an umbrella in the most chivalrous way.

When we arrived, Ahmed, his Sudanese friends, a smattering of other African students and expat neighbors, including Ron, were already drinking heavily. Lamb was imminent.

At the party, Wei regaled us with his stories as Ahmed and another Sudanese translated. Apparently, Wei had been traveling—buying and selling. I was never sure if he was bluffing or testing us. He claimed that he flew to Guangzhou and back in one day after buying wood. Wood from Guangzhou? Really? He reported that he would soon go to Guangxi province for goat skins for the Japanese. He was buying and selling anything that foreign businessmen wanted.

He then told us about his efforts to join the Catholic Church. He said he showed up for his interview to become a Catholic, and it turned out to be the police. He also indicated that he was hanging out in circles close to Zhao Ziyang. We had just begun to hear about this rising star in the Party. A moderate, perhaps a progressive. Wei said Zhao would help him get into church.

"Only in China are there two doors to heaven—one being the back door."

Was Wei testing us to see whether our purpose here was for Christian evangelizing? Was he manic? He was so animated, high energy and scattered compared to other Chinese that I wondered whether he might be bipolar. I felt I must tread carefully around him. Maybe he was giving me too much information. What did Fan think about his brother's adventures? He simply laughed at Wei's stories.

At dinner, I maneuvered to sit next to Fan. He wanted to talk politics at the table with all those foreigners. He wanted to know what we thought of different forms of democracy. He was curious about what we thought about Yugoslavia's system and Tito. Then he wanted to know how we compared Japan's democratic system with the US, Canada, Britain and Germany.

"How does the political system determine the economic system? Or did it work the other way?" he asked."Could you have economic development with a centralized political system the way Deng Xiaoping was trying?"

I was incredulous when I thought about the absence of this discussion with the Radio Beijing comrades. That's where one would expect to pursue these questions. But, then, did they question political and economic systems at Voice of America?

The Mandarin-fluent Sudanese translated our responses, but answers seemed less important. I was impressed by Fan's questions.

At Ahmed's, there were too many men without women. The Sudanese men's eyes betrayed a sadness, a loneliness that I understood only too well. Ahmed served a huge platter of lamb while looking more and more wrecked from alcohol. I suspect it was caused by spending half a lifetime outside of his own country, being unable to effect change in his homeland but rather living those years in a country whose policies and actions destroyed so many souls. The duplicity. The madness. The ruin or demise of so many good people. Perhaps your closest comrades. Was it a betrayal of Communist ideals? Or was that necessary to achieve Mao's version of utopia? It would take years before we understood what happened in sordid detail.

The whiskey was flowing, West African music played on the boom box, and Ron started stripping his clothes off. I laughed and cheered him on, despite my concern for what our Chinese comrades would think. Fortunately, he quit at his underwear and then danced on the coffee table. Given the puritanism of Beijing, I couldn't help thinking Ron was finally acting out against all that repression. Maybe he figured that, given the critical mass of men in the room, this was his chance.

I ached to be alone with Fan. Finally, he asserted himself. We danced. While pulling me closer, his lips kept brushing my cheek. I joked about his coming to sleep at my house during the week, since he shared a dorm room with seven others at school. He went home on weekends. His eyes smoldered and his lips curled into a smile.

"I dream...you."

I had heard this expression before from Yulian, perhaps a cliché of Chinese romantic flirtation. A popular movie. Whatever—I loved it.

In the taxi on the way home, we were pressed together, playing with each other's hands, worn out by the effort to communicate through the boundaries of our illiteracy in the other's language. Yes, playing hands. At thirty-seven with a twenty-four-year-old. Why not? An innocence in the midst of all the withholding and surveillance. When they dropped me off at my apartment, the guard jumped out at the taxi like a jack-in-the box, pointing his rifle. Fan's brother, Wei, hollered something to make the guard retreat while the taxi dropped me at the door. Amazing power. Fan would call.

A few nights later, I left my apartment door open so I could leap out to answer the hallway phone before a neighbor would. Fan was supposed to call between 6 p.m. and 7 p.m. I had been tidying and beautifying my apartment feverishly. Windows open. Incense burning. Finally, the phone rang. He was coming.

Keith Jarrett was working his mercurial fingers around an endless performance piece, riffing on themes—was it classical? Jazz?—that he performed live in Cologne, Germany. This album had been played at all hours during the past ten months.

When Fan arrived, I could feel the drilling of eyes and the perking of ears in the apartment building. There was a nervous awkwardness as he began translating the calligraphy on my walls—a piece by Shi Yung's, then some of my own. Fan flattered my beginner's skill. He also examined my amateurish drawings pinned to the walls, sketches in charcoal, some from photographs, some from memory of figure drawings left behind in New York.

"Who?" he pointed to the quick sketches of female nudes.

"Nobody I know. I simply like the postures." We looked up "posture."

He pointed to my drawing of a scrawny middle-aged man in a factory uniform, squatting on his haunches at the curb with arms resting on knees and head flopped forward. "I like. This is good."

I had sketched it in charcoal from a photograph I took in Tianjin.

"He is tired. Too much work. Life is boring," Fan narrated. "Boring" was a word that young Chinese used a lot as a way to apologize for life in China.

I looked around my living room, trying to see it through Fan's eyes. Should I have been self-conscious about my bohemian sensibility? Was it a mess? Chaos? Several drawings in midstream, calligraphy apparatus crammed onto a small table, reams of paper next to a typewriter, music cassettes stacked in various piles, books scattered and every inch of wall covered in my photographs, drawings and calligraphy. Also tacked to the wall was a Peking opera costume for the scholar's role. Calf-length black satin with long, wide sleeves all covered with gorgeous embroidered flowers now a pale pink. I had found it in a secondhand shop. On the other wall hung a collection of peasants' straw hats and a dragon-head mask lugged back from Guilin. He commented on it all.

He sat at my typewriter and practiced typing in English. He was taking a class in that, he said.

"Would you like something to eat?"

"I eat at school."

He accepted some Chinese rum, and we settled on my couch to look at my Kwakiutl Indian book from Vancouver Island. The totems, masks and dug-out designs and carvings. In our stilted, time-consuming, dictionary-consulting mode of conversation, we talked about motifs, the similarity to some Chinese designs. I talked about the theory of the Chinese crossing over the Bering Strait and down through the Americas, becoming the early American indigenous. The point was not the talk but that we were sitting next to each other, brushing fingers. I was studying his sweet smell.

I dug out a book on Canada, leafing through to an overview map and details of British Columbia to focus in on Vancouver Island and Victoria. I must have sounded schoolmarmish, but establishing where I came from was critical, since in China I felt so uprooted, nonexistent, deracinated.

"Where I went to school." I looked at him to be sure he absorbed that.

He complained that he was getting drunk on rum. More accidental touching.

"I want go...with you...to Inner Mongolia," he burst out, pointing to himself and then to me. Was he serious? Tapping into one of my fantasies?

Was it a metaphor? An expression? I wondered whether it was meant to acknowledge that the minorities were freer to have affairs in their huts, and therefore we could do the same.

I couldn't hold back any longer. I put on Phoebe Snow's "Teach Me Tonight" so I could translate the lyrics and move things forward.

"I am dream about you." Non sequiturs were our major mode of communication. And I loved hearing this one again and again. Although Ming's "You are my chairman" felt more original. I was torn between the romantic and the playful.

"I dream you," Fan repeated.

I don't know why I began explaining Freud's interpretation of dreams instead of kissing him deeply. Fortunately, the phone rang in the hallway, liberating us from the frustrations of looking up *psychoanalysis, wish fulfillment* and *unconscious* in the dictionary.

It was Xiao Gong, Fan's friend, the nurse, who had often joined Fan and Wei in social gatherings.

"I am sick. No come."

I had no idea she was supposed to come. Had Fan called her to meet here as a cover? Or was she a plant? Was I in a Russian novel? It was frustrating as usual that I could not query her with nuance. After I hung up, I wondered how difficult it must be for a woman in her situation. Was she Fan's girlfriend? Wei's? Or did she have hopes? Was she checking up to see if Fan was here? Or, most devious of all thoughts, did Fan know the phone was bugged and he asked her to call to say she couldn't come so the spies and listeners would have a record that this was not to be an illicit romantic visit? She was meant to be here, too. It was too cumbersome to look up the vocabulary for this labyrinthine scenario in the dictionaries. The spell was broken.

I put on the *Talking Heads* since Fan had asked what young people listened to in New York. I had brought their *Remain in Light* album, and then friends sent *Fear of Music* and *My Life in the Bush of Ghosts*. Fascinated, Fan wanted to know what it meant. It would take hours to explain African polyrhythms and the "sampling" of documentary elements, like the preachers' rant, and avantgarde music. Good. More time ahead. Lou Reed would be next. How would I interpret him?

Fan wanted to borrow the music to study it so we could talk about it next time. I suspected he wanted to copy it and share with friends.

"And I want to know...the 1960s and the difference now in the US..."

"When do you want to come and have dinner?" I asked.

"Saturday! Sunday we swim."

"I don't have a swimsuit here."

"*Mei guanxi*. Don't worry. I...find."

Although I was ravenous with desire for Fan, my super ego kept emerging, reminding me he was only twenty-four. Fourteen years younger than I was. It was already a sensation for the spies at my building. Perhaps it must always be forbidden, which only enhanced the anticipation. The excitement.

LATER THAT night, I scribbled down all the possible future conversations with Fan. He had pointed to some books, including Cervantes' *Don Quixote*. I made a note about "tilting at windmills" as a possible topic and "Labors of Sisyphus." Then he had pointed at Thomas Paine's *Common Sense* and Thoreau's *Civil Disobedience*, Walt Whitman's *Leaves of Grass*. He had heard of these authors. He wanted to know more.

I could not believe my ears.

The following evening, Zhi Mei and I ordered food from my dining room and ate in my apartment, where she felt most comfortable to talk. Funny. Ming and Shi Yung both acted as if they assumed that my apartment was bugged.

I shared some of my girlish, giddy crush on Fan.

Zhi Mei turned deadly serious. "You should be very careful."

"You sound like the morals police." I laughed.

"There is always somebody watching," she cautioned, then related her experience of going to the Canadian embassy for a dinner when Harold was in Beijing. "The next day, someone at work approached me and said I should think carefully about what I had done and report it to the leaders. Someone would be talking to me. It was an ominous warning." She looked at me in horror and anguish. "After all I have been through in the past!" she whispered in agony. "There are eyes and ears and rats everywhere."

She took a deep breath and continued. "It is common that people who meet a foreigner are given the opportunity to report on them to save their own skin. They become accomplices of the police who want to know who the foreigner meets. The nature of the conversations. Which Chinese are in attendance."

She warned me to be alert to people who might be working that way. This cautionary advice only depressed me further as I reflected upon all the Chinese who had approached me. Who was "innocent"? Who was working a dual purpose? And if they were reporting about other Chinese, I saw why Zhi Mei would be worried.

It was a sleepless night. Zhi Mei's conversation not only planted seeds of suspicion about Fan and his friend Xiao Gong, but it stirred memories of surveillance in my past.

My most politically active years of the late '60s and early '70s were spent in St. Louis, when I had lived with Carl. I was going to graduate school at Washington University in the famous sociology department, pathbreaking in its radical approach. Despite the prestigious sociologists who had nurtured a nationwide reputation, the administration pushed back at the critical research and activism flowering there and eliminated the department not long after I graduated.

I was a student there from 1969 to 1973, the most animated years of the anti-Vietnam War Movement. I participated fully in the Movement, including opposition to the presence of ROTC (Reserve Officers' Training Corps) on campus. I was also an early activist in the Women's Liberation movement, co-teaching the first classes in women's studies at the university. On any given day, I might have been giving a speech at an anti-war rally, handing out leaflets on campus for the new fledgling environmental movement about our poisoned rivers and skies, traveling to the state capitol to protest Missouri's draconian abortion laws or driving to southern Illinois to distribute issues of the *Outlaw*, the underground newspaper produced by a group of fellow New Leftists. Some weekends, I joined other sociology classmates to scrape lead paint off of apartment walls in poor black neighborhoods. In addition to anti-war movement activity, Carl participated in a study group that analyzed the rising power of corporations and their involvement in the war machine. A St. Louis corporation, McDonnell Douglas, built fighter bombers for Vietnam. Another local corporation, Monsanto, made napalm and Agent Orange. We held demonstrations outside the gates of both companies.

These activities were considered worthy of FBI investigations and infiltrating informants. The context is important to remember. By the end of 1969, we looked back at not only thousands of dead American soldiers in Vietnam (to say nothing of the Vietnamese casualties and their ravaged landscape) but also a string of assassinations—a president and presidential candidate along with civil rights leaders and activists like Medgar Evers; Malcolm X; Martin Luther King, Jr.; Goodman, Chaney and Schwerner; Fred Hampton and more. Blood was flowing on campuses as well. After the National Guard shot and killed four Kent State students and injured many more, some of whom were protesting Nixon's secret bombing of Cambodia, an ROTC building was burned down on the Washington University campus, reflecting not only a fever pitch of escalating anti-war mobilizing but a turn in the Movement—the legitimizing of violence as a means to ending the war mostly promulgated by the Weather Underground.

Carl and I, along with most of our comrades in the Movement, rejected the emerging Weather Underground faction while sympathizing with its frustration. We also made an ethical distinction between targeting symbolic property and endangering lives, although we knew that the destruction of property would alienate people from our cause. It didn't occur to us that we could become targets of FBI informants.

A young man, a transfer student from Kent State, had become very close to both Carl and me. He showed up as a grad student in the political science department, signing up for all of Carl's classes, attaching himself to Carl, hanging out with us for beers and burgers on Friday nights, coming to our parties on Saturdays. He seemed like a passionate student and a little out of control as a party animal. Then, after a grand jury investigation into the burning of the ROTC building on our campus, after the FBI agents showed up on our doorstep, after thugs broke into Carl's office on campus and messed it up, that student disappeared.

During the same period, although we had no reason to be suspicious or link the two together, a young female grad student arrived in the sociology department, and, as I reflected later, aggressively, attached herself to me. She, too, claimed to be a transfer student from Kent State. This student came to every women's meeting I attended or organized and sat in on classes I taught, but, I noticed, she didn't participate. Why I didn't clue into her real work was a mystery. Perhaps I was flattered by the attention. Just before I was getting ready to leave St. Louis in 1973, she, too, suddenly disappeared. Both "students" slipped into oblivion without a trace. Then, only then, did we suspect they might have been plants. By then, we knew about the COINTELPRO campaign of J. Edgar Hoover and the FBI, whereby every movement group was infiltrated and dirty tricks—false mailings, spreading of rumors, etc.—were meant to disgrace leaders, disrupt cooperative relationships between different groups, especially black and white organizations, and provoke conflict between members. The worst of this had been the manipulation of conflict within the Black Panther party leadership.

Years later, when I retrieved my FBI file through the Freedom of Information Act, I discovered that some informant knew every meeting I attended on women's liberation, every class I taught on the subject, every article I wrote, including a review of de Beauvoir's *The Second Sex*, and every demonstration I attended. But the content of the FBI files were hilarious. They included the subjects of my master's thesis papers: one on the family revolution in China. They also mentioned the feminist soap opera I produced and narrated for the local community radio station, KDNA, and the books we were reading by feminists like Robin Morgan's *Sisterhood Is Powerful*. It reported on our consciousness-raising groups where we talked about our lives. That we went off to Jefferson City to protest abortion laws.

To think people earned paychecks to collect this kind of publicly accessible information was dispiriting. Carl and I had been open and trusting. We were enthusiasts for the "politics of experience," a reigning concept at the time. We had nothing to hide. In the end, the consequences of such file reporting and the implications of suspicion had a more serious impact on Carl's career at Washington University than on mine.

I had buried this history in my deep subconscious. After the end of the Vietnam War and Watergate, the culture of surveillance seemed to recede. Now, in 1981 Beijing, I had to acknowledge that I had lived in a country—the US—that had also mistrusted its citizens and used spies, infiltrators and informants to gather information to disrupt and—sometimes—ruin lives. Not only in my era, but previously in the 1950s with the McCarthy hearings.

In Beijing, I was more shocked by the idea that the Chinese surrounding me could all be working for the police. But not Fan, surely.

Saturday, Fan arrived in the late afternoon for an early dinner. He wanted to know about the 1960s in the US. It was questions like this that plucked at my heart strings.

"It may take ten years to explain those years," I started.

"I understand," he smiled. I didn't stop to consider that it might take the next *thirty* years for the Chinese to explain their own "'60s"—the Cultural Revolution.

After dinner, conscious of the amenities at the dormitories, I offered to run a bath for him. He looked shocked. I suggested he might think of the bath as a gift. He was a willing recipient. Without asking or explaining—because I didn't know the words—I walked in and washed his back. He giggled with delight.

It was getting dark outside as he dressed and returned to the living room, where I had closed the curtains against prying eyes. Poised tentatively on the couch, in candlelight, listening to our breath, cautiously touching, fingers, lips, then whiffs of soap and sweat registered our nervousness with each other. When I led him gently to the bedroom, the floors groaned as if to register our plaintive needs. I began undressing him slowly, carefully. He mimicked my actions. The mind emptied out. No more dictionaries and verbal confusions.

Through the fumbling awkwardness, despite inexperience, our bodies knew what they wanted— the desire for deep connection, of meaning, in defiance of this place where erotic love seemed so suppressed. We plunged into a turbulent sea.

When the storm subsided, we lay a long time in the dark recovering our breath and calming our heartbeats.

"What are you thinking about?"

"So good. I did not know slow is so good."

Maxine Hong Kingston thinks erotic love may be more intense, dramatic and romantic in a context where lovers are illiterate in each other's culture.

My limited erotic experiences with Beijing men left me curious as to whether foreplay as an art had yet to be ferreted out of ancient traditions or relearned. What did it tell us about a culture, a society, when the body and Eros were denied? How did the culture become so puritanical? So conservative? Zhi Mei said that it wasn't until she met a Westerner that she understood what sexual pleasure could be.

The next day, a feverishly hot Sunday, Fan and I sat side by side, rowing on a park lake. A photograph taken that day suggests that I was ready to devour him. Other photographs taken later that day in the fading light capture Fan and his friends draped languidly over the edge of rowboats.

I have lingered over these sultry photographs with their aqueous light to stir my memories of that dreamy day. The day when I borrowed a swimsuit and we rowed to the center of the lake with his friends and we all slithered into the water from the boat. I watched water glide off the hairless golden skin of his lanky body. Liking the way a lick of his hair curled over one side of his forehead. Wanting to be elsewhere all year—now finally wanting to be nowhere else but here—floating in the black water, strangely buoyant, and then draped over the boat with Fan staring at the hazy sky, our feet trailing in the lake.

As the sun sank, we drifted through the park our hands and arms touching. I was falling in love with his delight in new things, his quick intelligence and thoughtful manner.

After bicycling home, we made love as if all of the sensual pleasures of the day had concentrated between our legs. After he left, I tingled all over.

ON MONDAY, Leader Zhang announced we should start having classes again for the comrades. Our classes had been canceled since Deng Xiaoping's threatening speech in December. Had I missed a policy shift? Did they awaken to the fact that they were not using my skills enough? Or were the reports of my new affair reaching the office and they wanted to keep me busy with coworkers instead?

On Wednesday night, the comrades arrived *en masse* at my apartment, inquisitively checking out all the new art and calligraphy on the walls, the cassettes, the books. No questions. No comments. Just a lot of looking and whispering to each other in Mandarin. I chuckled to myself about the gossip that must have circulated about my new Chinese friends, since everything was recorded and reported by the building police. Especially by Xing, the Number One Spy.

But I detected a difference in tone as Dam Ping started up. She began complaining about the work and the quality of scripts. She had never been that outspoken. Her frustration and disgust was palpable. Others agreed.

"Shut up!"

I looked to see who said that. It was Xia Xia. Somehow, she had learned that phrase and used it in a way that would probably distress her if she understood how it sounded to a native speaker.

"But you have been rewarded for your work," Dam Ping turned on Xia Xia. "You get recognition. Something. For some of us, we don't really care to work harder because it won't make any difference."

Did this mean Xia Xia was in the Party? How had she been rewarded? By being permitted to accompany a traveling dance troupe or a business delegation around the country? She had also been sent to conduct interviews. Had she also received a raise? We had no time to explore the details. I was left to ponder the fissures in the collective as the conversation changed.

Xia Xia repeated what another comrade had said months before. "All the listeners want is to have their frequency cards verified. They seldom comment about the programming."

"We have no feeling for the audience," Oxbridge Zong piped up.

I had missed hearing his voice. "But I have been trying to educate you a little about your audience and suggest different themes, subjects and a style of reporting on air for the past nine months. Yet nothing has changed..." I let that settle in and then put my hands up and shrugged my shoulders.

Now everyone spoke at once. As if a cork had popped out of a bottle.

"We cannot make changes because we have no information!" someone shouted.

"Whenever we try to research a topic, we cannot get anyone to cooperate at different agencies," the depressed Chen said. "Responsible persons will not be interviewed."

"We cannot develop our own program ideas," Oxbridge Zong added.

"We do not have enough time to develop new stories," Dam Ping muttered.

"How can we spend time reading up on a subject when Leader Zhang always tells us what to do next?" depressive Chen queried.

I recognized I had grown weary of the project at Radio Beijing. My presence there, my editing, my classes and discussion groups had little or no meaning in the overall scheme of things. The scripts remained much the same. We had read a play on the air and interviewed a couple of writers. Otherwise, it continued to be remarkably ineffective as an information medium. The only caveat was that the conversational English of a number of the comrades had greatly improved.

After nine months, I worried more about the lives of individual comrades than about the programming on Radio Beijing. Fan Chaoyang had stopped coming to work to protest the lack of housing for his wife and new baby. His wife had given birth in January. It was June, and they still did not have their own room.

ONE EVENING, Zhi Mei brought her oldest daughter, Xiao Yar (*Little Swallow*) to my apartment. Tall, pretty and in her early twenties, Xiao Yar was trying to move to Beijing from Anhui province, where she grew up with her aunt. Zhi Mei was helping her find a job.

It also meant that Xiao Yar was living in Zhi Mei's ten-by-ten room, which she had just finessed from China Reconstructs.

"I had a room of my own, but just for a moment!" she laughed. Lulu, her youngest daughter, who had been living with her grandparents, had just moved in with Zhi Mei, too.

After Xiao Yar left, Zhi Mei and I decided to walk in the fresh night air. But first we heard my Laotian neighbor answering the phone at the front door as we prepared to leave.

"No, no Palita here!" she yelled into the receiver and hung up.

"That's me!" I called out to her.

She gave me the strangest look. "So you're Palita!" she said in disgust, as if dozens of Chinese men had called.

The scene needled me all night. How many romantic opportunities had evaporated and potential friendships withered at that telephone. I could have wrung my neighbor's neck. Was she punishing me for American atrocities in Laos during the Vietnam War?

To work off my anger at the situation, Zhi Mei and I walked and laughed all the way to Xidan. Her heart was still bleeding profusely over Harold. She also revealed that she had been in touch with her friend at the Canadian embassy about finding a journalism degree program in Canada. He had promised to help her. As she leaped onto her bus to head home, I realized she was desperately trying to get out of the country.

Despite the late hour, I walked back alone along Chang'an Boulevard, relishing my unmolested liberty yet knowing it was a tarnished freedom because of the scrutinizing looks from men and women alike. A woman who dared to walk alone at this hour. A solitary walker. Most likely a prostitute.

Yet I was almost oblivious. Happiness washed over me while remembering the time with Fan on the weekend and marinating in the pleasures of my growing friendship with Zhi Mei.

My dreams were proceeding unrecorded. My letter writing had come to a halt now that I needed all of my energies for these new friends.

Wednesday, June 24, 1981, Journal:
Fan came over. Mutual excavations of ideas and fleshy pleasures continue.

Thoreau tonight. Mixed with kissing fingers and toes and crevices in the elbows and behind knees. Too risky to discuss Chinese political thought. I played some Lou Reed and had fun trying to translate. "Sweet Jane." "Walk on the Wild Side." By then our bodies were dictating.

We also planned a trip the following weekend to Qingdao with Fan's brother, Wei, and Ron.

ON THE train to Qingdao, the coastal town where China's best beer was produced, I was charmed by mischievous thoughts. I was getting away with something so wild and radical...so illegitimate. Traveling for the weekend with my young Chinese lover in the People's Republic!

When Fan and I were sitting together on the bus from the train station to our hotel, I turned around to see that Wei had his arm around Ron and was asleep on Ron's shoulder. Ron rolled his eyes at me and shrugged. Later, we would giggle about the innocent tenderness of it all. How incredibly discreet Ron had been in China about being gay. And this moment must have been excruciatingly bittersweet for him.

In 1981 China, homosexuality was forbidden, denied and punished. But heterosexual men regularly displayed great physical affection for each other in public—they could not make those gestures with a woman.

Fan and I played cat-and-mouse hand games under a sweater on our laps. It provided a glimpse into what Fan's affectional history had probably entailed while we also worked our dictionaries to talk about Qingdao's history during the Century of Humiliation.

Stepping from the train, I could hear the ocean and smell the salt and iodine. On the bus to our hotel, we could see the tiled roofs of this German-designed city meant to replicate a European town. They had built the original breweries here. As we got closer to the sea, we were blinded by the sparkling light, diamonds refracting. I had lived next to the sea most of my life, and I missed its presence in Beijing as if part of my very being were chiseled off. The smells. The moisture in the air. And the sounds when approaching the land's edge. The proximity of the sea in Qingdao was triggering memories from Victoria, Vancouver, San Francisco, Boston, Cape Cod and New York. Foghorns. The clinking of rigging on sailboats parked in marinas. Gulls. Waves. The smell of seaweed mixed with gasoline fumes from outboard and inboard engines. The purr of seaplanes overhead. Memories imprinted with emotions. The tyranny of memory.

Fan, Wei, Ron and I scrambled over rock outcroppings near the sea and in the hills near the town. Fan took a dreamy photo of me where I look satiated, as if from hours of athletic sex, even though that wasn't the reality. I was simply happy. As if time itself was suspended and the weight of the outer world—the world of suspicion, spying and judgment, the threat of punishment—was lifted from us.

The photos nudge me back to that time when I was undergoing a metamorphosis from the miserable, lonely, whining complainer of the winter months into a radiant butterfly with a summer romance. At least a part of my being was affirmed, validated. In Qingdao, I felt liberated.

Of course, the Zhang brothers had to stay in a different hotel. Ron and I could only stay in a foreigners' hotel. Fan came to my room briefly one afternoon. Invigorated by the challenge, we made love fervently, hurriedly and quietly, aware of the eyes and ears of the hotel attendants stationed like spies on every floor. All of this heightened the sense of a profound connection.

For a while, during our train ride back to Beijing, Fan talked about his father describing him as straight-laced and "Chinese thinking." Fan looked at me as if I should know what that meant.

"I look like my father," he giggled. "I like you very, very much," he said, blushing. I was speechless at the sudden change in conversational direction.

We arrived back at the Beijing Railroad station with two enormous cases of Qingdao beer that the Zhang brothers struggled to take home. We found a pedicab driver for them. No doubt their parents had provided the resources for the weekend. And this was the trade-off. Or perhaps the real reason for going. How would we ever know?

The next evening, Fan bicycled to my apartment from his school. More mind and body adventures. He left me a romantic and sexy poem that he had written in English. Typed on translucent rice paper. Perhaps it was copied from somewhere and he "personalized" it for me. It acknowledged our differences, including ages, yet the profound attraction of our hearts and minds. Before he left, he startled me by saying, "You are like Lei Feng."

Lei Feng! I much preferred being called "chairman." After Fan left, I tried to deconstruct the meaning of such a metaphor or model. Lei Feng, the completely bogus model soldier? Laughing to myself, I realized that I knew nothing about how young Chinese connected to their history. Especially jingoistic, propaganda history. But, then, I hardly understood it in the North American context.

As I laid in bed on that deliciously fresh summer evening, staring at the ridiculous blue floral plastic wallpaper, I felt...what?...happiness? Not strong enough. Euphoria! As usual, it came with a rush of energy to make lists, plans. I would apply for a teaching position in Beijing or Shanghai—at least Fan and I could keep a relationship growing through that distance. Meanwhile, I would study Mandarin obsessively. I would nurture, knead and cultivate my relationship with him. Sex would reach new heights of ecstasy. I would disengage from Radio Beijing for my mental health. Do only what was necessary. Eliminate all my expectations.

Along with this list, I acknowledged to myself that my excitement about returning to New York for my August vacation was dimming. Yes, it would feel good to touch base briefly with friends again, and I had to go to renew my green card and for tax issues. But it didn't seem as vital to my soul now that I had found a lover. Was it that basic? Besides, August in New York?

There was something else, ultimately deeper. I was losing interest in returning—even momentarily—to Ronald Reagan's America. During his first six months in office, he had announced a $25 billion increase in military spending, and his Economic Recovery Tax Act was wending through Congress, slashing taxes by twenty-five percent over three years. That would seriously undermine many social programs in the country. His labeling of the Soviet Union as an "evil empire" seemed destined to force confrontation and create a nation distorted by militarism rather than seeking equality and peace through social democracy. He eliminated price controls on oil and gas supplies; consequently, gas was cheap and abundant again post Carter, who had suggested that to deal with high gas prices and scarcity people should bicycle to work and wear sweaters.

No, I was ready to consider a long sabbatical in Asia.

But what could I make of the relationship with Fan? Was there a neo-Freudian analysis that would help me place it in my life? How about the abbreviated affairs I had pursued in Beijing? My propensity for younger men? Certainly, my search for a father figure had died with the end of the JR affair. And letting go of that fantasy felt healthy and smart. But now, was I searching for a son? Were women programmed by their hormones to need to care for a younger, more vulnerable human being? Was it about control, balance of power, safety? Or was it an attraction to risk and danger?

Despite other Chinese men being warned away from me, Fan and I seemed free to pursue our discreet lovemaking without interference. Perhaps he was protected by his parents' status. All I knew was that my heart felt full and my spirit enlivened. My enthusiasm was nurtured by our increasingly versatile language skills that I fancied would promote a richer intellectual relationship. I avoided thinking about what future such a relationship could promise because I was so deliriously happy. I was playing Etta James' "At Last" at least once a day.

OVER COFFEE the next morning, I studied characters to start matching the vocabulary that I was already flexing verbally. Finally, this effort was gratifying!

On the way to work, my step was bouncy as I trilled "*Ni Hao*" to the soldiers at the guard hut and the workers in the alley. When I arrived at the office, I was glowing with warm feelings toward the comrades.

Leader Zhang entered the office and motioned for me to come out into the hall.

"I need to speak with you in private." Her tone was sober.

"What is it?"

She cleared her throat. "The top leaders at Radio Beijing are concerned about the relationship you are having with a local Chinese man. They recommend that you stop seeing him. It is a very serious request." She looked at me gravely.

I was stunned into silence. She turned and left me standing in the hallway. The remainder of the workday became a haze.

That night, Fan bicycled over from school. When he entered my apartment, I knew something was wrong. He was shaking.

"My parents say...senior leaders know about you and me and...I cannot be with you."

Fan looked so forlorn, so serious, so heartbroken, that it made me ache to look at him.

"Sit down. I'll make tea."

I told him what Leader Zhang had said at Radio Beijing. We drank tea in silence. Then we tore into each other as if, with enough intensity, answers would emerge.

After he left, I sat in the dark, thinking about Fan and me and China and the past year, and concluded there was no way I could continue to live and work and love in this atmosphere under those conditions. I had tried. I had given it my all. Fan was at least the fourth or fifth person—that I knew about—who had been warned away from me. There had been the scholar I met at the airport when I arrived, Teacher Liang, Ming, Yulian and now Fan. My only significant Chinese girlfriend, Zhi Mei, was trying desperately to get out. Zheng Su was angling for the same possibility. Shi Yung was going to Chicago.

I felt my work was meaningless, neither reaching nor building an audience with anything they or I would want to know about China.

By 5 a.m., it was clear I wouldn't sleep. I went out to photograph old people exercising in the park. I returned to clean my apartment and iron a skirt and blouse before leaving for the office. Then I typed a letter.

When I arrived at the office, I gave copies of the letter to Leaders Zhang and Ma. It was a resignation letter. I would be cutting out on my two-year contract. I put it in career terms. If I stayed away any longer, I would find it very difficult to reenter my profession. Which was true. But I knew it was more profoundly about my sanity. My soul.

I could not be honest. I couldn't say that I had tried but failed to submit to a system of surveillance, mistrust and authoritarianism. Prudishness. To a political culture that denied life force, desire, lust. A system whereby foreigners could not have meaningful relationships in the open with Chinese citizens. I couldn't say that it was useless to continue on in a propaganda agency that didn't have the heart or motivation to produce great propaganda. So I restrained myself for the first time in China. I couldn't say it was about freedom and self-respect.

Fan and I defied the orders of the Party and continued to remain entwined, fantasizing a future in the US and in China. Both knowing in our heart of hearts that it was pure fantasy. He kept bringing me fresh poems. Each more expressive than the previous one.

During the hot and humid days before leaving, I made my last visits to Eleanor Bidien, Wang Keping and others. Yung had a new girlfriend who was suspicious of Zhi Mei. I didn't know how to analyze that. She also would not talk with Fan. Did she suspect they were informants? Funny, because it was Zhi Mei who constantly warned me to be secretive and cautious. Eyes and ears lurking everywhere.

I had no time to waste on those suspicions. I was too busy selling my refrigerator, typewriter and bicycle to other foreign experts. I wanted to give them to various Chinese friends, but Lao Liu of the Foreign Experts' Bureau had already sent a warning: "That is not allowed." It would make big trouble for my Chinese friends.

One evening, Fan was too frightened to come to my apartment. We met somewhere else in the city and walked in the rain. He talked about trouble. His mother pleaded with him that he must be careful now. He didn't want to jeopardize his privileged access and place at law school.

Fan's resistance was short-lived. By the following evening, he was at my apartment. We both acknowledged that the future was difficult to determine. There was only the present. Escaping through our bodies. Surrendering.

LOOKING AT the last photographs of my Beijing life—those taken at the farewell party organized by a group of friends at Beijing's first private restaurant to open since the Cultural Revolution—I see how my body was lovesick. I had dropped all of my winter weight and then some. Inside that restaurant, the air was unbearably hot and humid. Our faces and bodies were glistening. It was low-key because of the stifling heat.

Ron had already returned to Chicago. But Judy and Yuan were there, along with Zheng Su, Shi Yung, Zhi Mei and the Zhang brothers. My neighbors, Joshi and Punam, Bahdra, Marianne and Nancy. When I look at the photographs of that evening now, I realize that all of the Chinese at the table were trying to leave the country. All except Fan.

Fan had arrived at my apartment earlier to take me to the restaurant. He brought some army clothes for me to take to New York while he was wearing a new shirt. At the dinner, Zhi Mei looked great in one of my dresses. Yuan was interviewing the restaurant owners for a story. Later, he recited a poem he composed about our trip to Mt. Tai. I played Nina Simone's "O-o-h Child," and Zhi Mei cried.

Later, in the relentless humidity, Fan walked me home.

Two days later, Thursday, at 7 a.m., Fan stood at my door. He pushed a ring in my hand. It wasn't particularly valuable in terms of material or design, but it was meaningful. We chatted nervously about my preparations for leaving—avoiding any talk about our future.

Just as he was leaving, Shadow Zhang and my office mate, Yan, also appeared at my door. Had the soldiers at the guard hut alerted the English department that he was at my apartment? Or was it building spymaster Xing? Shadow Zhang, who would never come to my apartment without at least eight other people, was now at my place with only Yan who had never ventured here. This was the final straw. But how could I express "final straw"? The final mistrust. The final intrusion on my privacy. The final act of the morals police.

I was leaving. Let it be.

The day before my departure, Fan appeared again at my door. This time with a handwritten letter. It was a poignant effort at a grand love letter, acknowledging our times together, the meaning of it all for him, his desire to travel, study and live with me anywhere in the world. He acknowledged the wonders of being with someone he loved. It was also charming for its clichés and odd translations. I wondered if some of it was copied from some stock of love letters somewhere, but he had handwritten it in English—more than anything I could do in characters—and tears slowly slipped down my cheeks.

I left China almost a year to the day after I had arrived. Back then, as I was about to land in Beijing, I felt as if I was walking into the ocean on a moonless night. Now, landing in San Francisco, I felt as if I had stepped out of Plato's cave. In the *Republic*, he described how the light would initially be blinding emerging from the cave. Before true enlightenment. Walking out of the airport in San Francisco, my vision was blurred by tears. Was it from the dazzling light bouncing everywhere, the idea of freedom or the admission that I had left behind the promise of love "at last"?

Portrait of Mr. Wang, among a group of peasants, during author's bicycle trip to
Ming Tombs, 20 kilometers north of Beijing, 1980

Epilogue
后序

Arriving back in the United States, I was penniless and homeless. But not friendless. Generous friends from San Francisco to New York offered me refuge.

I had returned with a broken heart wrapped in a blanket of depression, smothered under the emotional weight of a year where my very being had been challenged to the core. And then there was the shock of quitting midway. Cutting out on a two-year contract. Coming back after only one year. Finally, impulsively, saying "Enough." But my proud refusal to carry on in the Kafkaesque madness of Beijing soon shriveled into "What have I done?" My confidence was shattered.

Given the nature of my work at Radio Beijing, I worried that my reportorial and production skills had languished. Despite those concerns, I was convinced that I had acquired valuable knowledge to exploit. If I could find a position with a TV network, then return and report on China, I might be able to make sense of my experiences there while being reimbursed in American dollars for the frustrations and surveillance. Perhaps I could continue to see Fan. Secretly. Besides, liberated from the stress of necessity, I was dreaming and chattering to myself in Mandarin. I didn't want to lose that momentum, either.

Acutely aware of the difficulties that the networks were encountering in their efforts to report from Beijing, I visited the offices of ABC and NBC, where I had contacts. The news directors of both networks looked at me across their desks as if I had a gigantic red star stuck to the middle of my forehead. No matter what I said about story ideas, my knowledge after working inside a Chinese institution, potential connections or addressing some of the difficulties of operating in China, they were aghast that I had worked for the Chinese. I was back in the land of "You're either with us or against us." Back to the old post-WWII McCarthy-era mentality of "Who lost China?" I was treated like a CIA journalist-spy in Beijing and as a Communist agent in midtown Manhattan.

Next, I headed to Washington, D.C. to meet with the director of NPR News and Public Affairs. I presented a proposal for a series of in-depth stories on China, the kind that nobody was telling in the US media. Since I had a four-year track record as a freelance producer for *All Things Considered*, I felt certain that she would treat my proposal seriously.

Frowning, she said, "Well, if *you* can raise the money, we *might* consider it." Might? I should raise the money?

That's how little China, or my experience there, mattered in those days. Perhaps she, too, saw a red star emblazoned on my forehead.

Whether it was true or not, I felt blacklisted. Although I was fragile from the emotional marathon in Beijing and the loss of Fan's affectionate presence, I had to find work quickly. I was broke. I scurried to make radio documentaries for NPR and the CBC—one from my interviews with the graduate students from the *People's Daily* Institute on romance and marriage in China. I wrote an article for the *Quill*—a periodical for journalists and journalism students—about my year at Radio Beijing. I kept the piece close to the bone of the programming, my coworkers and the building.

When I met with James Aronson, by then professor emeritus at Hunter College in New York, who had been the conduit to my invitation from Radio Beijing, he was interested neither in my critique of surveillance and mistrust nor the history of class struggle abuses then being revealed nor even Deng Xiaoping's crushing of the New Democracy movement. It saddened me. I knew from his resistance that truths about China weren't going to be easy for some Leftists.

I started to write this book but realized that these simple stories and anecdotes could make so much trouble for people, even if I changed names. The web of surveillance of everyone around me, all those paper chits and records, would lead to the real people. These acquaintances and friends could have lost everything for being too close to a foreigner. Some were trying to leave the country. I didn't want to jeopardize their efforts. So my journals, letters and notes were stuffed into a big box and shoved under my desk.

I made inquiries to attorney friends and law schools on Fan's behalf to find him a place to study in New York. Our letters about that effort grew more muddled. We both knew he would need to master English before being accepted by a university in the US. I nurtured a shattered heart as the time between our love letters stretched like evaporating ripples on a glassy sea.

China was finished. I began the tough, penurious project of resurrecting my career while doing freelance radio and video projects. Long hours for meager pay. It took two years to land a position as a producer at the newly expanded *MacNeil–Lehrer NewsHour*.

One day, while passing their reception desk, a young assistant called out to me and said, "Gail, somebody just called to ask if we realized that we had a Communist on staff: Gail Pellett?"

"Did you get their name?" I asked.

"No, they hung up immediately."

We both laughed. I was too busy producing pieces about a Grandma Moses exhibit, the closing of a blues bar in Chicago, a Mardi Gras Indian's costume making and a photographer who documented children at play on the Lower East Side of New York City—the culture beat. The Communist culture beat.

Eventually, I found a home for my journalist's soul. In the late '80s, I was hired by Bill Moyers' company and for the next two decades produced documentaries and public affairs programs, first with Moyers and then with my own company for PBS, a rewarding career into my sixties.

Beginning and end are just points on a road. It's the journey that matters. The path itself changes you.

I made this note in a journal but cannot find a source. For my generation, it has become common wisdom influenced, no doubt, by Buddhism. Rainer Maria Rilke wrote something similar: "The only journey is the one within." These thoughts prod me to question how I understand my China journey these many years later. What did I learn? How was I changed?

First, my comprehension of the historical moment that I witnessed in Beijing would ebb and flow in undulating waves, not just during the year after leaving but also for the next thirty years.

Gradually, like a slow drip seeping into my consciousness, I began to visualize my colleagues at Radio Beijing as the living ghosts of the Cultural Revolution and those earlier movements. They were survivors, sleepwalking while breathing through an airhole during a moment of liberalization in 1978 and 1979. Then, during my year there, the oxygen was thinning again. Like a mask tightening. I didn't have the perspective to see this in the moment.

The rise of Deng Xiaoping had ushered in a period of "Reform and Opening," whereby windows were thrown open for a moment, but during my sojourn, they were also being slammed shut. If Party authority and respectability had been undermined during the Cultural Revolution, the new leadership under Deng was reasserting control. There were still at least two opposing lines or camps within the Party, and if Deng was going to open up to market forces from the West, there were other leaders demanding a countervailing force to prevent Western contamination. During the year I worked at Radio Beijing, I was experiencing the push-pull of these two camps.

Not long after I left, Party leaders initiated the Campaign against Bourgeois Liberalization, and then the Campaign against Spiritual Pollution. Both were reactions to Western influences that were creeping into China as a result of the new economic reforms. Although it took time to report, more than a million folks were arrested during the Campaign against Spiritual Pollution and some 24,000 executed.

My reflections have forced me to reexamine an extraordinary life-shaping period of my own history—my own politicization and radical activism in the late 1960s and early '70s. By the time I landed in Beijing, I too was sleepwalking after my own Cultural Revolution, recovering from euphoria and disillusionment. Adjusting to the collapse of ideological movements and the changed political terrain in the United States.

Wrestling with what I had learned in China about class struggle, and the Cultural Revolution in particular, was not simply disturbing—it was devastating. We New Leftists in the West had been influenced profoundly by the ideas and slogans of that revolution and its egalitarian, anti-authoritarian, anti-bureaucratic thrust, its effort to overthrow elites and elevate the power and wisdom of the underclasses. Yes, and some of us mouthed slogans calling for the militant confrontation of the powerful.

We understood the power that resided in educational institutions and consequently challenged our professors about the curriculum, perspective and analysis. Like our Chinese counterparts in the late '60s, we confronted our professors about the very purpose of education itself, emphasizing Marx's dictum, that it's not simply enough to understand the world—the point is to change it. But—and it's a big "but"—we didn't beat our professors to death. We didn't torture administrators and bureaucrats, deny them medical care and humiliate people for vengeful purposes and call it "class struggle."

In March 2014, I read a story on the "Sinosphere" in the *New York Times* about a former Red Guard leader who, after several decades, visited her Beijing high school, where the Red Guards had beaten an assistant principal to death. This Red Guard, Song Binbin, the daughter of a very powerful and well-known general, had meanwhile immigrated to the United States, received a degree from MIT, worked in the States for years and now returned to her former Beijing school to apologize.

Apparently, there was immediate and overwhelming reaction across China's blogosphere. Some congratulated her for her contrition, but others condemned her for not taking personal responsibility for the murder of her school administrator. Reading this story, I felt compelled to write an article in which I argued for a Truth and Reconciliation Commission in China, much like the one that occurred in South Africa.

I had produced a documentary with Bill Moyers in 1998 called *Facing the Truth* about that extraordinary effort at restorative justice in South Africa following the end of apartheid. It was a process that required truth telling. It might begin in China with an acknowledgement of scholars' estimates that, during the Cultural Revolution, at least 1.5 million lost their lives in the countryside and that approximately 100 million throughout the country were persecuted in some way.

As I tried to make sense of my tiny grain of experience in the great dunes of Chinese history and modernization, I have watched from afar news reporting about China's economy as it has transformed landscapes and lives, igniting desires and disappointments as mobility for workers loosened. And, after the military atrocities against students and workers in Tiananmen Square in 1989, I observed the Party's commitment to ratchet up the material lives of the urban classes and allow artists to flourish in a brand-new art market, both efforts to stifle dissent.

Sometimes I think the China that I witnessed has been completely drowned out by this unprecedented economic wave. Yet almost daily there are news stories about political repression that feel so familiar. As if nothing really changed. Contemporary China watchers and human rights activists argue that there is more oppression today than in the 1979–'81 moment of "Reform and Opening" or "Socialism with Chinese Characteristics." The new human rights attorneys are being jailed or kept under house arrest as they try to defend citizen activists.

But I keep side-stepping the burning question: what to make of my story? If it was a journey within, what had I learned about myself? I would like to think I have worked out something about my new self-knowledge in these pages. Besides, while contemplation or reflection is essential to derive meaning from the events and characters swirling around us, life only gains complete meaning by being engaged with the world beyond the self.

I have always been more interested in the world outside myself than the one inside—in communities and characters beyond my comfort zone more than those in my immediate radius.

In China, I bit into Mao's Pear, a metaphor he used for how engagement and experience change us. Yes, I bit into Mao's pear, and yes, I gained knowledge—sometimes bitter, sometimes sour, and occasionally sweet. The most painful discovery for me was learning that the products of Mao's ideas, the comrades, Chinese citizens, were the forbidden fruits of his legacy. The social world around me in Beijing was comprised of the forbidden fruits of his philosophy, strategies and actions. I was not to touch them nor taste them. Certainly, I was not to have an open, honest, trusting and meaningful relationship with any of them.

While living and working in 1980 Beijing, I wrestled with a troubling question that many anthropologists have posed for more than eighty years— can we ever really understand another culture? This may be the deepest lesson for observers, witnesses, documentarians and scholars. We are too rooted in our own cultures. It was the journalists' hubris as well—the belief that we can be completely objective. That we don't already come to another culture deeply saddled with our own concepts of good and evil, right and wrong, strength and weakness, masculinity and femininity. Perhaps it is only our relationship to or interaction with another culture that we can meaningfully describe. And it's a delicate balance between intuition and discovery. That's how I read this book of memories, reporting and reflection.

Biting into Mao's pear, I learned about my ignorance, so that engaging with things Chinese was a regular exercise in humility.

If we are going to take the risk, the plunge, of trying to comprehend another culture, the first prerequisite is language. I had the hubris to go to China without speaking and reading Mandarin. I couldn't read the signs and slogans on the walls or a newspaper or a menu. Hubris writ large. It was a slow learning process—about myself and the culture of privileged global gadabouts from which I beckoned. Unlike the few Western journalists, who had been posted to Beijing, whose institutions had paid for their Mandarin lessons, I was the lone ranger, the solitary walker—as usual—making it up all on my own. Plunging into the abyss.

I am still grappling with the question of how China changed me. I have come to believe that the most painful lesson for me was about failure. The failure to lose my own ego in the encounter with or embrace of the forbidden Other: the comrades, acquaintances, potential friends, lovers.

Another thing—I knew from the start that China would be a confrontation of values, beliefs and commitments. But my experiences in Beijing forced me to examine those values and, along with my political consciousness, to understand where they had been forged. And nothing was disturbed more than my old belief in social, political and cultural utopia.

After China, I understood that utopia—for me, it is that egalitarian, just, fair, peaceful, nurturing, generous, environmentally sane, social democracy where Eros, art, music and celebration are vital—yes, *that* utopia—was about the *process*, the *means*, not the end. Perhaps that's where failure morphed into success. In Beijing, I was compelled to excavate deeply into my past, my soul, my heart, my character, my yearnings for the future. Through the pain of that undertaking, I was strengthened, transformed. It didn't happen that year, nor in the few years following, but in the reflection of that experience for the next several decades.

Some anthropologists of the first half of the twentieth century believed that each culture possesses dominant strains that define it, which are usually taboo subjects for conversation. Like capitalism, racism and war in my own culture. In the China I witnessed, I grew to believe it was the issue of mistrust of a populace who might think and act independently, of surveillance and the threat of punishment for transgressions. It might explain the tendency for reticence and restraint in Chinese behavior. I remember the warnings about "talking too much."

In Beijing, dozens of folks were mobilized to report on my every move. And as long as I spent my time with foreigners, I was of little concern. Well, maybe not all foreigners. Foreign journalists were off-limits. Anyone who lived with the Stasi in East Germany might recognize this as a system of espionage and control designed to involve almost everyone. Daily life privileges might be meted out to those who provided a little information that they knew, overheard, saw. So many could be complicit, however innocent some of their information might be. The consequences of not participating could be punishing, or at least diminishing. Perhaps I am overstating things and this system was collapsing during my time there. Perhaps I am wrong about mistrust explaining restraint. I really know nothing, after all. How could I appreciate what my colleagues had experienced? Why would they trust me? Why shouldn't the Party know everything? After all, they provided for everything as well.

As I look back at my concerns about surveillance in 1980, the methods seem quaint compared to the invasive surveillance that characterizes the digital age of Big Data, in the United States as well as in China, along with the depth and extent of hacking pursued by both countries.

In Beijing, my concerns about surveillance became so muddled with my desire for genuine friendship and love with a few Chinese comrades that the quest took on Jurassic-sized emotional proportions mixed with frustrations, suspicion and doubt. That search for friends ignited a deep examination of relationships in my life.

Understanding friendship is a lifetime project. Friendships provide a critical reason for living. Our friendships shape who we are, leaving traces in our bloodstream or hidden auras that may stay with us for the rest of our lives. Given my peripatetic history, the constructed kinships in my life are always changing, ebbing and flowing, gathering strength or dissolving. Few long-term friendships have remained constant in a predictable level of intensity or engagement.

Some friends sail in and out of life. Others change course, tacking this way and that, or perhaps drift off to sea or are lost in the fog of life or become challenged by changes in nature and age by one or the other in the relationship—boredom, crankiness, betrayals, disappointments, assumed slights, jealousies, changing values or priorities. A few friendships stay in harbor for a long time and endure the storms and tribulations.

Now that I have reached the age when friends are dying, I appreciate the remarkable and mysterious nature of those bonds even more. It is that harbor of friends who have kept my spirit afloat, kept me engaged, growing and confident that I could write this book.

I spent considerable time tortured by the obstacles to friendship in Beijing. Before then, I had never paused to notice that most of my friendships back home were forged through shared values, work, politics, engagement with the world. Shared meanings, history, goals, experiences. A revolutionary or moral kinship forged in community radio, the Anti-War Movement, the Women's Movement, the New Left, a commitment to social justice. Without language, with a punitive government policy policing us, there was no way to experience that kind of deep connection in Beijing. Yet a few seeds of friendship were planted. Some blossomed. Others faded.

If life is a constant search for love, recognition, affirmation, affection, the tactile and emotional warmth of another, in Beijing I had found it for a sparkling instant.

Nothing, however, was more important when I returned to New York from Beijing than meeting somebody with whom I've shared a life and home, dreams and fears, successes and failures, tears and laughter ever since. The love of my life. A man sixteen years younger. Perhaps my Chinese romantic adventures had left traces in my bloodstream after all.

Stephan has been a patient listener to stories about Beijing for more than thirty years. We understand that life is a search not only for love but for truth and beauty, justice, fairness and a great dance floor, and that we tell stories to live. And Stephan is my best friend.

End

Acknowledgements

There are many to thank for the journey of this book. It was my old high school friend from Victoria, Canada, Wendy Allen, who first planted the idea of my going to China. The late James Aronson provided the connection with Radio Beijing. Glen Shive, who ran the Fulbright program in Hong Kong for many years, visited New York shortly before I left for Beijing and said, "You'll write a book, either in the first two weeks, or it will take ten years because you'll never trust that you have it right." How about thirty-five years?!

Along the way many friends encouraged my writing about China. When I landed in San Francisco from Beijing, Deidre English plunked me down and said "Write!" I tried, but the project was too huge, painful, chaotic and overwhelming. A couple of months later, Ron Dorfman convinced me to write about Radio Beijing for The Quill. Dean George Gerbner, from the Annenburg School of Communications at University of Pennsylvania and Susan Rosenblum at Washington University in St. Louis brought me to those institutions to present a slide show and lecture about my experiences in Beijing which helped to organize some thoughts for the book early on. Ellen Willis, an editor at the Village Voice, encouraged me to write about Chinese dissident artists who were arriving in New York City in the mid-eighties. Twenty-five years later, Susan Meiselas recommended that the editors at Trans-Asia Photography Review should assign me the task of reviewing Ai Weiwei's "New York 1983-1993" photography exhibit. Then, Bill Moyers' website published my essay suggesting a Truth and Reconciliation Commission for China. Alan Adelson encouraged me to think more carefully about that.

Over the years, my dear friend Karen Brown, a path-breaking feminist scholar of religion and anthropology, stimulated so many thoughts about our relationships with other cultures and how we write about them, that although her mental capacities were deteriorating as I began to write this book, her insights have flowed through my veins.

Once I decided to tackle the project, my old friends, Marnie Mueller and Alix Kates Shulman, supported and encouraged my push to the finish line. My friend and Beijing calligraphy teacher, Shi Yung, couldn't understand why I would write about 1980 Beijing so many years later when so much had changed. Colleen Leung and Zheng Su both offered to be helpful with the book, but since I was writing about them, I had to turn down their offers. Cecelia Cancellero, a seasoned editor, confronted me—however gently—with some tough questions. Tom Shachtman and Lawrence Goldstone both read segments and offered rigorous critical comments. Jenna Rohrbacher labored intensely on the copy-editing but I am solely responsible for the violations of verb tenses.

I am profoundly grateful to many, many friends who have kept me buoyant and prevented me from sinking under the weight of this project. My deepest gratitude goes to Stephan who lived with my self-obsession while listening patiently to these stories for almost thirty-five years.

Bibliography

BOOKS—referred to or as source:

Apter, David, (2005) *Bearing Witness: Maoism as Religion*, Copenhagen Journal of Asian Studies

Bacon, Edmund (1974) *The Design of Cities*, Cambridge, MIT Press

Banner, Lois W. (2004) *Intertwined Lives: Margaret Mead, Ruth Benedict and their Circle*, New York, Vintage Books

Bernstein, Richard and Ross H. Munro (1997) *The Coming Conflict with China*, New York, Alfred A. Knopf

Bronte, Charlotte (1847) *Jane Eyre*, London, Smith, Elder & Co.

Buck, Pearl S. (1936) *The Fighting Angel-Portrait of a Soul*, Norwalk, CT, Charles W Hayford

Burton, Neil and Charles Bettelheim (1978) *China Since Mao*, Monthly Review, July-August

Camus, Albert (1965) *Notebooks, 1935-51*, New York, Alfred A. Knopf

Cao Xueqin (1978) *A Dream of Red Mansions*, translators: Yang Xianyi and Gladys Yang Beijing, Foreign Languages Press

Carroll, Lewis (1865) *Alice's Adventures in Wonderland*, London, Macmillan

Cervantes, Miguel de Saavedra (1605 & 1615) *Don Quixote*, Madrid, Francisco de Robles,

Crook, David and Isabel (1959) *Revolution in a Chinese Village, Ten Mile Inn*, London, Routledge & Paul

de Beauvoir, Simone (1949) *The Second Sex*, New York, Alfred A. Knopf

Dickens, Charles (1854) *Hard Times*, London, Bradbury & Evans

Ding Ling (about) ed. Merle Goldman (1977) *Modern Chinese Literature in the May Fourth Era*, Cambridge, Harvard University Press

Dimnet, Ernest (1929) *The Art of Thinking*, New York, Simon & Schuster

Du Fu (1952) *Tu Fu, China's Greatest Poet*, translator: William Hung, Cambridge, Harvard University Press

Duras, Marguerite (1985) *The Lover*, New York, Random House

Fairbanks, John K., (1953) *Trade and Diplomacy on the China Coast: The Opening of Treaty Ports 1842-54,* Cambridge, Harvard University Press

—ed, (1974) *The Missionary Enterprise in China and America*, Cambridge, Harvard University Press

—and Denis Twitchett, eds, (1978) *The Cambridge History of China*, Cambridge University Press

Foner, Eric, (1977) *Tom Paine and Revolutionary America*, Oxford University Press

French, Paul (2009) *Through the Looking Glass: China's Foreign Journalists from Opium Wars to Mao*, Hong Kong University Press

Freud, Sigmund (1913) *The Interpretation of Dreams,* London, Macmillan

Guilbaut, Serge (1985) *How New York Stole the Idea of Modern Art*, Univ. of Chicago Press

Gogol, Nikolai (1960) *The Diary of a Madman & Other Stories,* translator: Andrew MacAndrew, New York, New American Library

Goldman, Merle (1977) Editor, *Modern Chinese Literature in the May Fourth Era*, Cambridge, Harvard Univ. Press

Gramsci, Antonio (1973) *Selections from The Prison Notebooks,* London, Laurence & Wishart

Hampl, Patricia (1981) *A Romantic Education*, Boston, Houghton Mifflin

Hinton, William (1966) *Fanshen, A Documentary of Revolution in a Chinese Village*, University of California Press

Kafka, Franz (1971) *The Complete Stories*, New York, Schocken Press

King, Lily (2015) *Euphoria,* New York, Atlantic Monthly Press

LaFeber, Walter (1963) *The New Empire: An Interpretation of American Expansion 1860-1899*, Cornell University Press

Lao She (Shu Qingchun), (1979) *The Rickshaw Driver*, translator: Jean James, Honolulu, University Press of Hawaii

Laurence, Margaret (1974) *The Diviners*, Toronto, McLelland & Stewart

Leys, Simon (1977) *Chinese Shadows*, New York, Viking Press

Link, Perry (2000) *The Uses of Literature: Life in the Socialist Chinese Literary System*, Princeton University Press

Lu Xun (1972) *Selected Stories*, translators: Yang Hsien-yi and Gladys Yang, Beijing Foreign Languages Press

— (1973) *History of Chinese Literature*, translators: Yang Hien-yi & Gladys Yang, Westport, CT, Hyperion Press

MacFarquhar, Roderick and Michael Schoenhals (2008) *Mao's Last Revolution*, Cambridge, Belknap Press

Mao Zedong (1964) *Quotations from Chairman Mao Tse-tung (The Little Red Book)*

—(1942) *Talks at the Ya'nan Forum on Literature and Art*

—(1927) *A Report on an Investigation of the Peasant Movement in Hunan*, Beijing, Foreign Language Press

Morgan, Robin, ed (1970) *Sisterhood is Powerful*, New York, Vintage Books

Navasky, Victor (1980) *Naming Names*, New York, Viking Press

Oliver, Paul (1969) *The Story of the Blues*, London, Barrie & Jenkins

Plato (1970) *The Symposium*, New York, Penguin Classics

Price, Ruth (2005) *The Lives of Agnes Smedley*, Oxford University Press

Ruykeser, Muriel (1978) *The Collected Poems*, New York, McGraw Hill

Rousseau, Jean-Jacques (1977) *Reveries of the Solitary Walker, New York,* Penguin Classics

Schell, Orville (1977) *In the People's Republic: An American's First Hand View of Living and Working in China,* New York, Random House

Schurmann, Franz (1969) *Ideology and Organization in Communist China*, 2nd edition (Center for Chinese Studies, UC Berkeley) University of California Press

Smedley, Agnes (1943) *The Battle Hymn of China*, New York, Alfred A. Knopf

— (1976) *Portraits of Chinese Women in Revolution*, Feminist Press

Snow, Edgar (1968) *Red Star Over China*, New York, Grove Press

Solomon, Richard H. (1971) *Mao's Revolution and the Chinese Political Culture*, University of California Press

Sontag, Susan (1977) *On Photography*, New York, Farrar, Straus & Giroux

Spence, Jonathan (1980) *To Change China: Western Advisors in China*, New York, Penguin

Strong, Anna Louise (1963,64,65) *Letters from China*, Beijing, New World Press

Thoreau, Henry David (1975) *Civil Disobedience and Other Essays,* New York, Dover Publications

White, Theodore H. and Annalee Jacoby (1946, 61) *Thunder Out of China*, New York, William Sloan & Co

Whitman, Walt, (1983) *Leaves of Grass*, New York, Bantam

MUSIC—referred to:

Ray Barretto, *Cocinando*, written by Ray Barretto, *Que Viva La Musica* album, Fania, 1972

Bee Gees, *Stayin' Alive*, written by Barry, Robin and Maurice Gibbs, RSO, 1977

Chuck Berry, *Maybelline*, written by Chuck Berry, Chess, 1955

James Brown, *I Feel Good*, written by James Brown, King, 1965;

Cold Sweat, written by James Brown and Alfred "Pee Wee" Ellis, King, 1967;

I Feel like Being a Sex Machine, written by James Brown, Bobby Byrd, Ronald R. Lenhoff, King 1970

Van Cliburn, *My Favorite Debussy*, RCA Victor Red Seal 1961

Sam Cooke, *A Change is Gonna Come*, written by Sam Cooke, RCA Victor, 1964

Miles Davis, *Round Midnight*, written/composed by Thelonius Monk, Bernie Hanighen, Cootie Williams,

—*Ah Leu-Cha*, written/composed by Charlie Parker,

—*All of You*, written by Cole Porter,

—*Bye Bye Blackbird*, written by Mort Dixon, Roy Henderson, all on *Round About Midnight* album, Columbia 1957

Kind of Blue album, compositions by Miles Davis and Bill Evans, John Coltrane and Cannonball Adderley on saxophones; Bill Evans, pianist; Paul Chambers, bassist; Jimmy Cobb, drummer, Columbia 1959

Eric Dolphy, *Out to Lunch* album, Blue Note 1964

Duke Ellington, *Take the "A" Train*, written by Billy Strayhorn, Ellington's first instrumental recording: *Never No Lament: The Blanton-Webster Band*, Bluebird 1941

Brian Eno and David Byrne of Talking Heads, *My Life in the Bush of Ghosts* album, Sire/Warner Bros. 1980/81

—*Remain in Light*, Sire 1980

—*Fear of Music*, Sire 1979

Ella Fitzgerald, *Cry Me a River*, written by Arthur Hamilton (pub. 1953) Columbia 1961

Aretha Franklin, from *I Never Loved a Man the Way I Loved You* album, Atlantic 1967:

—*Respect*, written by Ottis Redding

—*Dr. Feel Good*, written by Aretha Franklin and Ted White

—*Let the Good Times Roll*, written by Sam Cooke

Erroll Garner, *I'll Remember April*, written by Gene DePaul, Patricia Johnston, Don Raye, and *They Can't Take That Away from Me*, written by George and Ira Gershwin, from *Concert by the Sea* album, Columbia 1955

Marvin Gaye, *Let's Get It On,* written by Marvin Gaye and Ed Townsend, Tamia 1973,   *What's Goin' On?,* written by Obie Benson, Al Cleveland and Marvin Gaye, Motown, 1971

Gloria Gaynor, *I Will Survive,* written by Freddie Peren and Dino Fekaris, Polydor, 1978

Al Green, *Let's Stay Together*, written by Al Green, Willie Mitchell, Al Jackson, Jr., *Al Green's Greatest Hits* album, Hi/Right Stuff/EMI 1975

Billie Holiday, *Strange Fruit*, written by Abel Meeropol, first recorded by Commodore in 1939

Vladimir Horowitz, *The Great Horowitz Plays Favorite Chopin*, RCA Victor Red Seal, 1957

Son House, *Downhearted Blues*, written by Alberta Hunter & Lovie Austin, first recorded by Hunter in 1922; Son House recording, Columbia, 1970

Ahmad Jamal, *Poinciana* album, Argo, 1963

Elmore James, *Dust My Broom*, derived from earlier song by Robert Johnson, James' version recorded on Trumpet in 1951

Etta James, *At Last*, written by Mack Gordon, & Harry Warren, *At Last!* album, Argo Records, 1960

Keith Jarrett, *The Cologne Concert*, composer, Keith Jarrett, ECM Records 1975

Robert Johnson, *I Believe I'll Dust My Broom,* written by Robert Johnson, Vocalion 1937

Albert King, *Born Under a Bad Sign*, written by William Bell and Booker T. Jones, from *Born Under a Bad Sign* album, Stax 1967

B.B. King, *The Thrill is Gone,* written by Roy Hawkins and Rick Darnell, recorded by King, Bluesway/ABC Records, 1969

Gladys Knight and the Pips, *I Heard it Through the Grapevine,* written by Norman Whitfield and Barrett Strong, Motown, 1966

George McCrae, *Rock Your Baby*, written and produced by Harry Wayne Casey and Richard Finch, TK Records, 1974

Thelonius Monk, *Monk's Mood, Round Midnight,* on *Thelonius Himself* album, Riverside Records 1957;

— *Epistrophy, Thelonius Monk: Genius of Modern Music* album, Bluenote, 1951

Charlie Parker, *Yardbird Suite*, by Charlie Parker, Dial, 1946

—*Groovin' High* , written by Dizzy Gillespie, Bluenote, 1947

Esther Phillips, *Such a Night*, written by Dr John, Sony Music 1974

Bonnie Raitt, *Everybody's Cryin' Mercy*, written by Mose Allison, and *Guilty*, by Randy Newman, *I Feel the Same*, by Chris Smither, *Takin' My Time* album, Warner Bros 1973,

—*Women Be Wise*, written by Sippie Wallace, and *Since I Fell For you*, by Buddy Johnson, *Bonnie Raitt* album, Warner Bros '71

—*If you Gotta Make a Fool of Somebody*, by Rudy Clarke, *Give It Up* album '72

Lou Reed and Velvet Underground, *Sweet Jane*, written by Lou Reed, from *Loaded* album, Cotillion/Atlantic 1970

—*Walk on the Wild Side*, written by Lou Reed, *Transformer* album, RCA 1972

Otis Rush, *Gotta Be Some Changes Made*, Alligator 1971

Leon Russell, *A Song For You*, written by Leon Russell, Shelter Records 1970

Shirley & Co., *Shame, Shame, Shame*, (lead singers: Shirley Goodman and Jesus Alvarez), written by Sylvia Robinson, Philips 1974

Nina Simone, *Oooh Child*, written by Stan Vincent, *Here Comes the Sun* album, RCA Victor 1971

—*I Want a Little Sugar for My Bowl*, written by Clarence Williams, J. Tim Brymn, Dolly Small, Nina Simone, *Nina Simone Sings the Blues* album, RCA Victor 1967

—*I Wish I Knew How It Would Feel to be Free*, written by Billy Taylor and Dick Dallas, *Silk and Soul* album, RCA Victor, 1967

Bessie Smith, *I Need a Little Sugar for my Bowl*, written by Clarence Williams, J. Tim Brymn, Dolly Small, Columbia, 1933

Phoebe Snow, *Teach Me Tonight*, written by Gene de Paul and Sammy Cahn, *It Looks Like Snow* album, Sony BMG Music Entertainment, 1976

Otis Span, *Dust My Broom*, written by Robert Johnson, Prestige 1965

—*Must Have Been the Devil*, composed by Otis Span, Chess Records, 1954

—*T'Ain't Nobody's Business If I Do*, written by Porter Grainger and Everett Robbins, *Blues Is Where It's At* album, Bluesway 1967

Supremes, *Stop in the Name of Love*, written by Holland/Dozier/Holland, Motown 1965

Art Tatum, *Night and Day*, by Cole Porter, *The Tatum Group Masterpieces, Vol. 8*, Pablo 1975

Big Mama Thornton, *I Have a Heartache*, With the Muddy Waters Blues Band, Arhoolie 1966

Chavela Vargas, *En Un Rincon de Mi Alma*, written by Alberto Cortez, Rama Lama 2002

Jr. Walker and the All Stars, *Shotgun*, written by Walker and Autry DeWalt, Motown 1965

Muddy Waters, *Rollin' Stone*, derived from Delta blues song in 1920s, Chess, 1950

— *You Can't Lose What You Ain't Never Had*, written by McKinley Morganfield aka Muddy Waters, Chess 1964

Sonny Boy Williamson I (John Lee Curtis), *Sugar Mama Blues*, Bluebird, 1937?

Howlin' Wolf, *How Many More Years*, written by Howlin' Wolf, Chess 1951

Central Broadcasting Beijing Symphony Orchestra, *Little Red Riding Hood*, Russian opera fairytale written by Cesar Cui, performed Beijing 1981

— *La Serva Padrona*, Giovanni Battista Pergolesi, performed Beijing 1981

Gail Pellett has produced documentaries and written articles about the world "out there" for more than forty years. This is her first work that turns a lens and microphone on her own life, thought, and feeling. Every film, every radio program, every article was challenging, but this work of memoir was the most difficult of all. She lives in New York City and Oaxaca, Mexico.